THE
HINGE
FACTOR

THE
HINGE
FACTOR

HOW CHANCE AND STUPIDITY
HAVE CHANGED HISTORY

ERIK DURSCHMIED

ARCADE PUBLISHING · NEW YORK

FIRST U.S. EDITION 2000

Copyright material from *Pursuit* by Ludovic Kennedy reprinted by permission of The Peter Fraser and Dunlop Group Limited.

Library of Congress Cataloging-in-Publication Data

Durschmied, Erik.
    The hinge factor : how chance and stupidity have changed history / Erik Durschmied. — 1st American ed.
        p. cm.
    Includes bibliographical references and index.
    Contents: A wooden horse : Troy, 1184 BC—The loss of the True Cross: the Horns of Hattin, 4 July 1187—A rabble with bare feet : Agincourt, 25 October 1415—A barrel of schnapps : Karansebes, 20 September 1788—A fistful of nails : Waterloo, 18 June 1815—The fourth order : Balaclava, 25 October 1854—Three cigars : Antietam, 17 September 1862—Two counts and one prince : Königgrätz, 3 July 1866—A fair fight : Spioen Kop, 24 January 1900—A slap on the face : Tannenberg, 28 August 1914—The sting of a bee : Tanga, 5 November 1914—Der Halte Befehl : France, 21 May 1940—A shark on the loose : North Atlantic, 27 May 1941—The Sorge enigma : Moscow, 6 December 1941—One man's death : Vietnam, 31 January 1968—And the Wall came tumbling down : Berlin, 9 November 1989—The zero factor : the Gulf, 17 January 1991.
    ISBN 1-55970-515-9 (hc)
    ISBN 1-55970-572-8 (pb)
    1. History—Miscellanea. 2. Chance. I. Title.
D24 .D87 2000
900—dc21   99-89506

Published in the United States by Arcade Publishing, Inc., New York
Distributed by Time Warner Trade Publishing

Visit our Web site at www.arcadepub.com

10   9   8   7   6   5   4   3   2   1

PRINTED IN THE UNITED STATES OF AMERICA

For William and Alexander

Acknowledgements

I owe a great deal to many who pointed me in the right direction, who opened the right page in the right book for me: historians, librarians, journalists, geo-strategists, scientists, and generals. In particular, I wish to mention Colonel Kenneth Hamburger, U.S. Army (ret.), professor of history, U.S. Military Academy at West Point, N.Y., for his advice on the American Civil War, and General Pierre Gallois, father of the French nuclear strike force, for his help on modern weaponry and the results of the Gulf War; also The Peters Fraser & Dunlop Group Ltd. for allowing me to use material from *Pursuit* by Ludovic Kennedy. But most of all, I dedicate this book to those who lived through it, and my colleagues and friends who were there with me. My special thoughts go to those who stayed there forever. E.D.

Acknowledgements

Contents

Illustrations

Prologue

The Hinge Factor: sunny and clear . . .

'Chance and uncertainty are two of the most common and most important elements in warfare.'
Carl von Clausewitz, *On War*, 1832

A silver-grey Superfortress of the 509th Composite Group, 20th US Air Fleet, rumbled down the runway of Tinian Atoll. It carried neither bombs nor other means of destruction. Only twelve pairs of eyes. And yet, this plane was to be responsible for the sudden death of over a hundred thousand civilians.

Thirty minutes later, another plane, bearing the number 82, and a circled 'R' on the tailfin, lumbered off the same runway. Painted beneath the Plexiglas cockpit were the first names of the pilot's mother, *Enola Gay*. The pilot was US Air Force Colonel Paul W. Tibbets, and this aircraft carried a bomb, a big bomb.

When Tibbets and his crew of twelve took to the sky, he was provided with four possible targets. Which one, he had to decide for himself. His orders from US Airforce General Thomas T. Handy were quite specific: '. . . to deliver the special bomb to a target *depending on good weather conditions* and to be dropped onto one of the following targets: Kokura, Niigata, Hiroshima, Nagasaki . . .'

At 07.42 hours on the morning of 6 August 1945, while cruising at 26,000 feet above the Pacific, Tibbets received a coded message from the meteorological observer in the scout plane, the one which had preceded the *Enola Gay* by thirty minutes.

One target was obscured by clouds. Another had only limited visibility. But one mark was in clear sunshine. The big bomber turned onto its final heading because of a message which read:

'CLOUD COVER LESS THAN THREE-TENTHS. ADVICE: *bomb primary.*'

By caprice of nature a town was chosen for doom.
BOMB PRIMARY was a city called Hiroshima.

One sunny day in September – I was eight at the time – my father came home and said to me: 'Hitler has declared war.'

I knew all about Hitler. I had seen him on the Ringstrasse when he made his triumphant entry into my native Vienna. But war? So I asked: 'Father, what is war?'

Since that autumn day of 1939 I have learned what war is all about. First, while I sat, shivering with fright, in a coal cellar as Allied planes unloaded their bombs onto my city, my house and my family and, afterwards, when my whole life became inextricably connected with war. For thirty years I was dispatched from conflict to conflict, and thus able to observe from close-up the folly of men like Hitler. There may be just wars, but never have I witnessed one that hasn't ended in terrible suffering.

War is about battle, and the clash of arms. No matter how purposeless it seems, battle is the heart of war. It's an obsession where everyone can, and does, participate. Some die, some cry. Others remember and celebrate. And then there are those who plan. I have met men whose minds were obsessed by a desire for military glory, men who moved tin soldiers around a sand box and conquered cardboard cities. Then they went into the field and used real soldiers. Somehow, it never turned out the way it did in the sand box.

History bears witness. Great armed hosts have been defeated through the stupidity and the incompetence of their leaders. War is not about trumpets and military glory, war is about death. Or, to paraphrase Georges Clemenceau, the man who led France out of the horrors of the First World War: '*War is much too important to be left to generals.*'

Some chroniclers wish us to believe that battles are won by valour and the brilliance of war lords, on whom they bestow the accolade of 'genius' when they are triumphant. They record the victor as being brilliant and the loser as not. And yet, there is no secret formula to the victorious outcome of a battle – except that much depends on who commits the bigger blunder. Or, to put no finger point on it, many battles have been decided by the caprice of weather, bad (or good) intelligence, unexpected heroism or individual incompetence – in other words, the unpredictable. In military terms, this phenomenon is known as: *The Hinge Factor.*

In many cases, the scenario leading up to disaster has been assembled well before the play was ever written. The annals of war are loaded with examples which prove that incompetence is (most of the time) not due to a failure of intelligence, but of character. Wooden-headedness, while assessing a rapidly developing situation in terms of preconceived fixed ideas, is invariably a good reason for downfall. Time and time again, brave men have been thrown away in reckless attacks. Orders given not from a clear perception of the situation, but from ignorance, spite or simply to achieve personal glory. Before setting off into the desert to confront the Saracen host of Sultan Saladin, the heroic Raymond de Tripoli asked his Frankish king, Guy de Lusignan: 'Sire, ask yourself the question: "Why do I want to give battle? Is it for my country's glory – or for my own?"'

When an industrialist picks on a bad design he risks closing down the factory and putting his workers out of a job; when a financier speculates foolishly on the stock market he may lose the money of a many investors. These things are painful – but not lethal. But if a military leader commits a blunder such an error is disastrous, paid for in blood and human suffering by thousands, and sometimes by many more.

Then there is always the unexpected brought on by divine design, the cloud which hides one target and so condemns another to obliteration. The fluke, a secret battle map found by the enemy. Or, perhaps the most unpredictable of all, the way that people behave under stress and fire. The personal initiative and the heroism, not necessarily by some sabre-raising general whose memory will be perpetuated with a bronze statue, but by the unknown, unheralded soldier buried in an unmarked grave.

Recorded history tells us what happened. But there is invariably a 'Reason why' it had to happen. (In this, I make no claim to present a coherent or definitive explanation why the outcome of any particular battle suddenly took a turn.) At the end of every conflict, it has become standard practice that politicians and generals justify their action in print, explain their moves across the chessboard of battle, or discuss in dry statistics the mega-deaths they've caused. The simple foot soldier writes home about the way he has lived through it. It is from both of these records that my *hinge factors* have been selected.

Reading about a particular combat many years after the event, sometimes turns into the complex problem of separating a reliable source from poetic licence. At the abyss of disaster prevailing conditions of unbiased reporting can be, at best, chaotic and records incomplete or perhaps they have disappeared altogether. Others may have been falsified by contemporary chroniclers and poets for reasons of their own. That goes for yesterday as it does for today.[1] The medieval narratives by Juvénal des Ursins about the massacre of the French nobility during the battle at Agincourt project his French perspective. When the Duke of Wellington spoke about 'a close run thing' at Waterloo, he never mentioned Ney's blunder, nor Blücher's part in *l'affaire*. *The Times* man-on-the-spot, William Howard Russel, reported on the bungled Charge of the Light Brigade and was accused of betraying sensitive military information.[2] The same senseless sacrifice was glorified in a poem by Lord Tennyson. Where then lies the truth?

War has always been the province of confusion. I cannot tell if war is really indispensable to the advance of humanity, I only know it is man's favourite preoccupation, and that it has dominated all other human activities.

E.D.
Domaine de Valensole
Winter 1998

*   *   *

[1] This is particularly true for the numbers game about strength of fighting forces and losses. To give an example: at Agincourt (1415), the loosing French side is quoted with 8–10,000 dead knights, while the English suffered only 400 casualties. Considering the hand-to-hand slaughter, this is hard to believe. We don't even have precise figures of the atomic victims at Nagasaki and Hiroshima, and that was only a few years ago and duly recorded.

[2] It reminds people in my trade, so frequently considered by the military as 'professional voyeurs', that our accounts distil the chaos of combat into indelible icons, and that the impact of the events we report outlasts the next day's edition.

THE
HINGE
FACTOR

1

A Wooden Horse

Troy, 1184 BC

'Do not believe this horse. Whatever it may be,
I fear the Greeks, even when bringing gifts.'
Virgil's *Aeneid*, 20 BC

The year is 1184 BC.

A god descends from heaven; disguised as a swan he lies with Leda. Their love results in a daughter, Helen, a maiden so fair that every prince desires her for his wife. She chooses Menelaus, King of Sparta. One day a handsome young prince comes to visit them. He is Paris, son of King Priam of Troy, a fortified city on the eastern coast of the Mediterranean. Paris is royally received but does not reveal the purpose of his visit.

Before Paris left his native Troy, King Priam had been warned that his son would bring ruin to his country. And so it came to be. The high drama began the day Paris was visited by three goddesses, Aphrodite, Hera and Athena. They handed him a golden apple and asked him to choose the fairest among them. Hera promised to make him Lord over Asia and Europe, Athena said that she would lead him to great victory over the Greeks, and Aphrodite offered him the loveliest maiden on Earth. The Judgement of Paris went to Aphrodite, goddess of love. She told him about Helen of Sparta.

While Menelaus leaves for Crete to do war, Paris takes Helen to Troy. It is not certain if she follows for love or by force. On his return from Crete, King Menelaus calls upon all the Greek heroes to help him punish the wicked deed and lay Troy in ashes. Under the leadership of Agamemnon,[1] the Greek Army is strong. But so is Troy. King Priam has brave sons, the bravest is Hector,[2] who has only one equal, the champion of the Greeks, Achilles. For years on end they fight it out, and for many years victory wavers. Once again, a fierce battle rages, when Helen appears on the ramparts. Her face is so lovely that all fighting stops, only Achilles and Hector continue in single combat. Athena hands her spear to Achilles who drives it into Hector's throat. 'Return my body to my father,' begs the dying Trojan hero.

'I would that I could make myself devour your raw flesh for the evil you have brought upon me,' replies Achilles. The Greek warrior then drags the slain Hector behind his chariot around the walls of Troy.[3] Aphrodite gives Paris a poisoned arrow. Paris takes aim and shoots it into the Greek's only vulnerable spot, his heel. Achilles dies. Then another arrow strikes Paris, and he dies.

But Troy holds out. After a siege which has lasted ten years the war has reached a stalemate. Unless the Greeks can break down the walls they will never conquer the city fortress and must accept defeat. Odysseus, the cleverest of the Greeks, devises a cunning plan: to build a wooden horse, slightly

---

[1] The remains of his castle can still be seen near Corinth.
[2] Hector, in ancient history, is on a par with Julius Caesar and Charlemagne
[3] With the death of his hero, Hector, Homer ends his *Iliad*, the rest comes from Virgil's *Aeneid*, written a thousand years after the fall of Troy

taller than the Scaean Gate. Then hide Greek warriors inside the horse, and leave it standing outside the walls of Troy. That done, the Greeks set sail, but hide their fleet behind the nearest island. To make sure the Trojans fall for his ruse, Odysseus leaves Sinon the Greek behind who convinces the Trojans that they must pull the horse into the city as a votive offering to Athena.

King Priam falls for the Greek trickery and orders the horse to be brought in. For this, the Trojans will have to break a hole into their walls. Troy's chief priest Laocoön warns his king: '*I fear the Greeks, even when bringing gifts.*'

Priam, a ruthless potentate, is infuriated that a mere priest dares to question the will of his king. Yet Laocoön is not the only one who fears deceit. The king's beautiful daughter, Cassandra, stands up to her father and echoes the priest's warning. '*Oh miserable people, poor fools, you do not understand at all your evil fate.*'

The judicious counsel by the philosopher-priest nearly convinces the Trojans, when destiny takes a hand. Two serpents rush from the sea to crush Laocoön and his two sons. Fate comes to pass, a doom destined for so many prudent sages over the next three millenniums. People never listen to their prophets, rather they watch them being silenced and stride blindly forth to disaster. The Trojans remove the lintel stone from the Scaean Gate, which brings their walls tumbling down. They drag the horse to Athena's temple and celebrate a great feast. '*With song and great rejoicing, they brought death in, treachery and destruction.*'

In the middle of the night Sinon unlocks a secret door beneath the Wooden Horse. Odysseus and his warriors steal out while the rest of the Greek host rushes in through the breach and sets the city on fire. By the time the Trojans rise from their drunken stupor, blood flows in rivulets. This is not fighting, it is butchery. Desperate men bear down on each other, killing before they are killed. Trojans take off their own armour and put on that of the dead Greeks. Greeks, believing they are being joined by their own units, pay for that error with their lives. From the rooftops, Trojan women hurl burning beams on their attackers, a palace tower crushes a great number of Greeks. But the contest is unequal, too many Trojans have already died and the Greeks smash their way into the palace. King Priam is brutally struck down in front of his wives and children. With his death the Trojans lose heart and the Greeks rape, pillage and plunder. They kill the men, hurl the children from the battlements, and carry the women into slavery. Troy dies.

Only Aeneas,[4] Aphrodite's son, escapes the bloodshed. He crosses the sea and the winds push his vessel onto a distant shore, at the mouth of the River Tiber. There he founds a town which is to become Rome, the city state that will eventually defeat the conquerors of Troy.

Ultimate justice shrouded in the veil of mythology.

What really took place that night, three thousand years ago, we can only guess. '*To the gods I owe this woeful war*', proclaimed a downcast Priam.[5]

We may forget about an active participation by the gods, and turn towards more strategic, military and economic aspects. In the late nineteenth century, a German amateur archaeologist, Heinrich Schliemann, discovered ruins of what may have been Priam's Troy, a fortified city founded by the warrior tribe of Phrygians on the Mound of Hissarlik.[6] From

---

[4] Hero of *Aeneid*, written by Virgil to glorify the power of Rome.
[5] Homer, who wrote around 850 BC, ends his *Iliad* with the death of Hector. The best source of the Fall of Troy comes from Virgil's *Aeneid*, written a thousand years after the Trojan War, and embellished with vivid tales which had been passed down orally over the ages. Perhaps a Queen of Sparta was really abducted by the Trojans in a previous raid, which led to the punitive action by the Greeks. In the fifth century BC, Herodotus, the Father of History, tells us that the Trojans assured the Greek envoys that Queen Helen was not in Troy, but that the gods wished for war.
[6] Located on the Asian side of the Dardanelles.

its geographic location, we can assume that Greek and Trojan maritime ambitions clashed. Vital control over the Hellespont (today's Dardanelles), the Aegean Sea, and with it, the trade routes along the Mediterranean, was at stake.

As for the ten-year siege, no siege could have possibly lasted ten continuous years; without harvesting seasonal grain, armies on both sides would have starved. Therefore, the war must have been a series of raids, and possibly actions fought by sea.

A vital factor which should not to be overlooked is the warning by the philosopher Laocoön, which, assuming that Troy was run by a despot, shows opposition to tyrannical rule, a trend carried to new summits by the greatest of Greek philosophers, Socrates, and his disciples.

Ten years passed and nothing happened. Suddenly, everything was resolved in a single instant. The Wooden Horse is certainly not a figment of fiction;[7] ruse has always been employed during the siege of fortified places, the simplest way to put the vigilance of the defenders to sleep and breech the walls. Thus, the story of Odysseus' Horse is something tangible, a *conquest by stratagem.*

Strange are the circular paths of history. The Greeks learned from the Trojans, Trojan refugees founded Rome, and the Romans conquered Greece, only to adopt its culture.

The Hinge Factor at Troy was victory by stratagem.

---

[7] Pausanias (second century AD) in *Descriptions of Greece* states that the horse was a war machine or siege catapult.

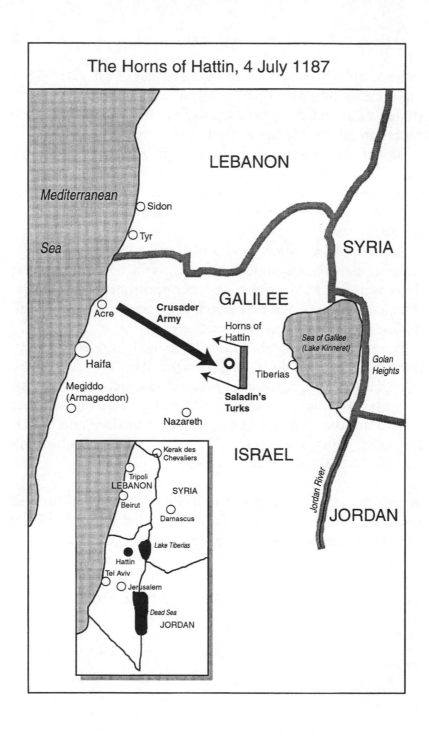

The Horns of Hattin, 4 July 1187

2

The Loss of the True Cross

The Horns of Hattin, 4 July 1187

'I shall not lay down my arms
until there is no more infidel on earth.'
Sultan Saladin, recorded by Beha ed-Din
Ibn Shedad, 1187[1]

Spread out before the Frankish host lay a desert, hot and dry, the Plain of Baruf. To venture into it during the heat of the day would mean courting certain death for a great army of iron-clad and chain-mailed knights. Yet Guy de Lusignan, King of Jerusalem, ordered them to do just that. A tall man approached the king. He was dressed in chain mail covered by a white cloak with the embroidered crimson Cross of the Holy Quest. Around his waist, dangling from a leather belt, was his long, straight sword. The baron's head was protected by the type of bullet shaped helmet with nasal guard worn by Crusader knights. He was a heroic figure of medieval history: Raymond III, Count of Tripoli. 'My liege, why are you ordering your host to move into these barren lands?'

'To succour your lady in distress.' The king referred to a

---

[1] A contemporary and friend of the Saracen Sultan Saladin, or Salah ed-din.

message received from the Lady Eschiva, Countess of Tripoli, besieged by the Saracens inside the walls of Raymond's fortress of Tiberias, situated on the Lake of Galilee.

Raymond, who knew that the leader of the Turks, the Sultan Saladin, would always conform to Saracen honour and never hurt a woman of rank, also understood that the same Saladin was as smart as a desert fox. He wished for nothing more than to lure the Frankish army onto a hasty rescue mission that could only then lead to disaster. That's why Saladin had allowed the messenger, dispatched by Lady Eschiva, to pass without hindrance. 'Sire,' replied Raymond, 'if you wish to do combat with Saladin so, let this be near our fortress of Acre. If matters go ill we can count on the town to march to our rescue. On the other hand, if God is with us, we can blunt the Saracens.'

'Blunt them?' shouted one of the noble barons, Reynald de Chatillon, the Lord of Kerak. 'Blunt them? What perfidy do I hear?'

'Aye, blunt them,' replied the Count of Tripoli, 'and blood them as well, and Saladin will be so crushed that he must flee the Holy Land, never to return. My liege,' he turned towards the king, 'out in the desert, Saladin has the advantage of mobility, his strength will ride over us. Then who is there to defend Jerusalem?'

The king tended to agree with Raymond's wise counsel.

That night, after a repast which King Guy had shared with his barons, the loom of intrigue, vanity and ambition began to weave. The cunning Gérard de Ridefort, Master of the Templars, came into the king's tent. 'Sire, the Count of Tripoli wishes us to cringe like cowards.'

The king, fearful of the Templar, a man of great power who had been instrumental in helping him usurp the crown from the rightful heir, wavered. He pulled back the flaps of his tent to look at the night sky, at the same stars his adversary would be looking at on the other side of the desert. His mind was engaged with the problem to seek certainty which might justify his act. As it has happened so many times to other men of ultimate power, having staked their whole future on one decision, he too became uncertain, he feared that his travel order might lead to tragic consequences. But Ridefort was not about to let pass an opportunity to prove himself invaluable to his king. 'My King, you know the Count of Tripoli doesn't like you. He speaks treason and only cares to uphold his truce with the Turk. We are of superior mettle to the pagan. I counsel you to go from hence and march on to glorious victory.'

That same night, it is said that a servant of the king spotted an eagle with seven darts in its claws pass overhead. He heard it scream: 'Beware, Jerusalem!'

Yes, there was treachery in the air, and foolishness, but it did not come from the Count of Tripoli, a knight who had studied Saladin's generalship. He knew that the Sultan would lay wait for them in ambush. One last time, before sunrise, the count tried to change the king's mind. '*Roi Guy*, I warn you, do not stir from this place or Saladin will assuredly set upon us in the desert.'

Confronted by the only baron who had failed to support his claim for the throne of Jerusalem, the king now turned on the knight, and spoke furiously: 'It is not for you to tell your king what to do. I want my knights to mount up and prepare to move for Tiberias.'[2]

And so, the Frankish King of Jerusalem headed for a disaster of his own making.

The beginning of the Crusades can be set with the defeat of the armies of the Eastern Empire, at Manzikert in 1071,[3] by the

---

[2] *Estoire d'Eracles*, a French text from the thirteenth century, possibly after *Guillaume de Tyr*.
[3] On the edge of defeat, the Turkish Sultan bought Byzantine's mercenaries, and their treachery led to a crushing victory by the Turks.

Seldjuk Turks' rider hordes which spilled from the steppes of Asia and adopted Islam. Constantinople, despite its ongoing quarrel with the Church of Rome, asked the Pope for his help to recover Asia Minor. In 1095, Pope Urban II launched the First Crusade, an adventure which, even by today's standards, can be considered unique. Godfrey de Bouillon led a host of French nobility, knights from the military orders on their 'Way to the Cross'. His followers were promised forgiveness for their sins and salvation for eternity. By 1099, the Crusaders had captured the City of God – a victory stained by the massacre of Jerusalem's entire Muslim population.[4] This led directly to a holy *Jihad* which lasted the next two centuries, and, in retrospect, has never ended. The first Frankish Crusaders founded the Kingdom of Jerusalem. For nearly a hundred years, all went well, the Christians held the walled towns and strong places, such as the Acre, Jaffa, Tyre or the *Kerak des Chevaliers*, while the countryside was beset by roving bands of Saracens. It was not until the disastrous defeat of the Eastern Emperor Manuel at Myriocephalum in 1176, that events began to move towards their final climax. Without Byzantine support the Frankish knights had no longer sufficient men to hold out against the forces of Islam brought against them in Palestine. Christians and Muslims moved rapidly towards a confrontation.

To make matters worse, the age of chivalry in a quest for the Holy Cross had passed to a ragamuffin band of barons, eager to fill their pockets. Reynald de Chatillon was one of the adventurers who had come to the Holy Land to seek fortune. Instead of proving his valour as a defender of the True Faith, he seduced the widow of the Prince of Antioch, who became so besotted by his charms that she gave him the key to her provinces. Quickly tired of her ageing charms

---

[4] *Guillaume de Tyre*: 'One saw with horror the mass of dead ...'

he rejected her to marry another noble maiden, the Lady of Kerak, and then continued with his business, which was to rob caravans. Another knave was Gérard de Ridefort, who had applied a ruse to get himself elected Master of the Templars. He then used his noble warriors to terrorise and plunder helpless citizens. The most vicious of all was the Patriarch of Jerusalem, Heraclius, a 'chaste monk' whose mistress was a notorious prostitute, known to all in the Holy City as 'The Patriarchess'. This unholy threesome was to lead the Kingdom of the Franks to its downfall.

Confronting this villainy was the noble Raymond III, Count of Tripoli,[5] the appointed Regent of Jerusalem and one who upheld his oath to his child-king, Baldwin V. But the feeble infant died, and Guy de Lusignan, another adventurer who had married the king's aunt, usurped the crown. Raymond fell out with the new ruler over this. It was a grave blow to the cause of Christianity, since Raymond was the only baron who enjoyed the trust of Saladin. In 1185, the Frankish prince and the Saracen sultan had established a truce, based on mutual trust and the word chivalry. It was only after the incident at the Springs of Cresson, when the Saracens were about to invade Galilee, that his fidelity to the Christian cause forced Raymond to rejoin his liege.

At the end of the twelveth century, the Frankish Kingdom of Jerusalem was faced by the greatest of all warrior sultans, the fabled Salah ed-Din, or Saladin. He was a Turk[6] whose ancestors had migrated from the foot of the Altai Mountains of Central Asia. In the tenth century, that warrior tribe came into contact with Islam. It can be said that the conversion of the Turks to Islam had a similar impact on the Orient as Teutonic Christianism had for the Occident. Saladin, born as the son of a lieutenant to Sultan Nur ed-Din, Emir of Aleppo

[5] The county of Tripoli was founded by his grandfather, Raymond de Toulouse.
[6] Meaning strength, or power.

and Damascus, had proven his valour in a series of battles against the Franks as well as dissident Moslem rulers. By 1169 he became Vizier to the Caliph,[7] and in 1171 he deposed the last of the decadent Fatimids. As new Caliph of Egypt and Vizier of Syria he now held the Crusader Kingdom in a vice, leaving open only the sea lanes to Cyprus and Europe. For thirteen years the Christians could hold Saladin at bay, until two events upset this delicate balance. The first was set in motion by Reynald de Chatillon.

One night a spy arrived at Lord Reynald's castle to inform him about the passage of a pilgrim caravan on its way to Mecca, bearing great riches. The Lord of Kerak and his followers went on a raid and seized the camel train. This caravan not only carried gold and spices, but an even greater treasure: the sister of Saladin, 'a maiden so fair that the nightingale praised her beauty'. The Sultan dispatched a messenger to King Guy's court to demand that his noble sister be set free immediately. Reynald de Chatillon, who expected a sizeable ransom for the royal lady, refused to obey the order by his king, claiming that, contrary to Raymond de Tripoli, he had never concluded a truce with the Saracens.

About the same time (30 April 1187), the son of Saladin, Malik al-Afdal, asked Raymond of Tripoli for passage through the count's provinces, which Raymond granted on condition that the Muslim host passed through his lands between sunrise and sunset without bothering his towns. To make sure that all knew about this promise, the count sent a covering letter to Gérard de Ridefort. Instead of adhering to the truce, this overbearing knight in search of personal glory led his ninety Templars and ten Hospitallers to confront the Saracens. They found the Turks peacefully in camp around the Springs of Cresson.[8] A Templar, Jacques de Mailly, warned

[7] Caliph means 'successor to the Prophet'. In Christian terms this would be the Pope.
[8] Today Saffuria.

his hotheaded leader, who snarled: 'Is it that you wish to keep that pretty blond head of yours? Then run.'

'I will die a brave man, but you, Master, you will run!' retaliated the insulted knight. His prediction was to come true. The insolent Ridefort, with an unfounded contempt for the fighting spirit of the Saracens, attacked the 7,000 Muslim warriors with his handful of knights. The inevitable happened, the Saracens surrounded the knights. Ridefort plus three of his knights abandoned the fight and escaped, the rest were captured and their heads cut off. The Turks paraded the heads on the tips of their lances under the walls of Tiberias before they retired into their own lands, as promised, before sunset.

Without trying to find out about the cause for this slaughter, King Guy foolishly ordered all Christian knights to join his banner, and told the Patriarch of Jerusalem, Heraclius, to fetch the True Cross so that it might lead the Christian Army into battle. The Patriarch took the cross from the Church of the Holy Sepulchre, and never again would it return to Jerusalem.

Following the unpardonable affront brought onto his sister, Saladin swore a sacred oath that he would personally behead the villain Reynald. He raised 'an army without number, like the ocean',[9] and units joined him from Egypt, Mosul and Maridin. Following the skirmish at Cresson (1 May 1187), Saladin was joined by his son near Astara[10] and together they set off on 27 May to establish their camp at Dabeira. On 2 July he attacked Tiberias, where, due to careless manipulation with a torch, one of his Turks set the storage houses on fire. Soon the whole town was in flames, only the citadel survived.

[9] 80,000 men.
[10] Today Bursa.

*   *   *

It was on the following day, 3 July 1187, a Friday, that the Frankish host set off into the waterless desert which separates Saffuriya from Tiberias. Fifteen thousand knights and foot soldiers began their march towards the distant Sea of Galilee.[11] The vanguard was led by Raymond of Tripoli, the rear was brought up by Balian of Ibelin. In the centre rode King Guy de Lusignan protecting the Bishops Ruffin of Acre and Bernard of Lydda, bearers of the True Cross. Seen from the distance, the Crusader Army presented an impressive sight, the lines of white-robed riders and the companies of crossbow men in dun-coloured kilts and leather jerkins. Since the distance to travel was relatively short[12] the king hoped to cross the barren lands in less than one day, and he didn't wish for his army to be slowed down by water carts pulled by oxen,[13] and had decided against dragging these along. A disastrous miscalculation. What a mounted knight could accomplish in hours of brisk canter took several days for a foot soldier. And, travelling as a combined army, the mounted *chevaliers* could move no faster than their foot soldiers and crossbow men.

The vanguard under Raymond of Tripoli had deployed well; the count had put a phalanx of his best fighting men in front. Platoons of crossbow men guarded the sides of the advancing columns, and screens were well out to the flanks to warn of attempts of an attack on the True Cross. The centre was not quite so orderly, foot soldiers mingled with mounted knights and servants carrying tents. Soon the army began to stretch out, with foot units lagging behind on the mountainous path. The king called for a brief halt

[11] Just before setting off, the army had been swelled by 1,200 knights and 7,000 foot soldiers, paid for by the ransom money Henry II of England had to pay for the murder of the Archbishop of Canterbury.
[12] About twenty miles by modern roads
[13] Water carts were the normal means employed for crossing a desert; however, these were drawn by oxen, a very slow method of travelling.

to give the trailing elements a chance to catch up, but the groups became even more disorganised as they piled onto one another.

When Saladin was informed about the move by the Christian king, he was delighted: 'This accords well with my wishes. Once we have destroyed this Infidel host, we shall have Tiberias, and with it, the coast line.' He ordered his army to take up a position at Lûbiya, and dispatched his riders on their light ponies to harass the slowly advancing Christians. They taunted the Crusaders with arrows without launching into a concerted attack, aware of the accurate missiles fired by the Christian crossbow men. King Guy wasn't overly worried; skirmishing archers couldn't take on his heavily armoured knights; that is, unless he was foolish enough to provide Saladin with a suitable killing ground.[14] Though the foot soldiers protected the knights from these pinprick attacks, they couldn't shield the mail-shirted knights – nor themselves – from the relentless desert sun. The limestone reflected the heat from the cliffs and turned the valley into a cauldron of intense heat. Soon their water bottles were empty and they began to complain of thirst. King Guy de Lusignan missed a chance to provide water for his troops when he ignored a small detour towards the Springs of Turan. By late morning, everyone was well aware that they couldn't count on more water before they reached the Sea of Galilee. It didn't take long before the column began to look more like a mob than a disciplined army. They slugged on listlessly. King Guy soon began to realise his mistake; but for him, retreat meant losing face, and that was out of the question. The long column had reached the scorched plateau when suddenly figures popped up from holes in the ground and

[14] The type of bow used by the Saracens was the short bow, which did not have the penetrating power of the English longbow as used at Crécy and Agincourt.

put torches to the dry brush that had been cut and left in piles, forming a semicircle of fire around the path. The heat and dense smoke added greatly to the discomfort of the knights. A strong wind fanned the flames so that the uncut brush, covering the desert floor, also caught fire. Flames barred the track ahead and the long column stumbled around in smoke and flame, galled by a shower of arrows from ever-increasing numbers of circling Saracens. This was the final straw; withdrawal became finally impossible and their thirst unbearable.

More than any attack by Saracens, the thirst was starting to take its heavy toll on man and beast alike.[15] While the animals became lethargic and simply collapsed, the men were maddened by a craving for water and quarrels broke out. The knights who tried to escape through the dense smoke were cut down by Saracen blades. Others, wounded by arrows or made dizzy by thirst, fell off their horses and were left to roast in the burning brushwood. Some foot soldiers broke away from the formation and surrendered to the Saracens. In exchange for water they accepted Islam as their new faith. Even some of the knights relinquished their arms,[16] and when they were brought before Saladin, they said: 'Sire, why dost thou wait? Fall upon them because they're all dead.'

From their position on the heights the Crusaders could see in the distance the sparkling clear water of the Sea of Galilee; this added greatly to their torture. But the Frankish host couldn't reach it, their road was barred by a huge body of men: the Army of the Sultan.

Raymond knew of a well in the mountainous region to the

[15] Morrison, in his *The Recovery of Jerusalem* (1871) describes it: 'The road from Sefariah to Tiberias passes up a long open valley till it reaches Lubieh where it commences to descend to the lake. Up this road, where there is no water, no shade, and where the glare of the limestone adds to the intense heat of the sun, the Christians advanced harassed on all sides by the light horse of the Saracens.'
[16] They are given by name in *l'estoire*: Bald de Fortuna, Raymundus Buccus, Laodicius de Thabaria – they betrayed the king's plan to Saladin.

north. This would redirect their route away from Tiberias and the Sea of Galilee; however, as water was now vital, this was their only chance for salvation. Thus he rode up to his king and suggested to move the Frankish host into the hills, towards the springs at the Horns of Hattin.[17] This watering place was on the count's lands, and the king ordered Raymond to attack the enemy and breach the way.

When the Frankish host turned north, Saladin, who had already been appraised of Raymond's plan by one of the captured knights, realised that he had to block the Crusaders' passage towards the well. He launched a full rider attack under his newphew, Taqui ed-Din, who put up a barrier on the slopes leading to the Horns of Hattin. At the very spot where, according to legend, Christ delivered his Sermon on the Mount, Raymond charged and the ensuing fight was terrible in its slaughter. The din of battle was everywhere. Piles of bodies covered the stone-strewn plain leading up the mountain.

Saladin watched the battle from a nearby copse. He saw Taqui's waves break against the mail-clad knights, who fought with the fury of men maddened by thirst. The Muslims' numerical superiority could not develop as they attacked on a narrow front. The Turkish line began to weaken and the Christian knights charged into them like an irresistible battering ram. Their long swords cut a swath through the Saracen army, catching Taqui's foot guards on the flank. The Saracen line wavered and broke.

The furious charge by the Count of Tripoli had achieved the breakthrough, and he turned in his saddle to wave to the main body around the king. They wouldn't move! Raymond had worked a miracle in breaking through the Turkish line at great costs to his knights; however, as if he was afraid to

---

[17] The mountainous crest of the Horns of Hattin is located NE of Tabor and SE of the village of Hattin (or Hittin). It is about three miles from Tiberias, roughly three and a half hours by foot.

expose their holy relic, the king didn't move! A messenger of King Guy reached Raymond to deliver a fatal order. Instead of pursuing the fleeing Turks, the count was ordered to halt and establish a camp on the rocky ground. In desperation, Raymond rode to see the king: 'My liege, we must move or this is the end, the war is over, we are betrayed and our lands are lost. If we cannot reach water by tonight, our host is finished.'

The king wouldn't change his mind and ordered his tent to be pitched on a nearby hill.[18] That night, the full might of Saladin's army moved up and surrounded the camp so tightly that 'not even a cat could have escaped.[19] Four hundred camel loads of arrows were brought up and distributed to the Sultan's warriors, after which they all kneeled and offered a prayer. The sound from thousands of throats of 'Allah akhbar – Allah is great' echoed from the hillsides, followed by the Sermon of the Fighters of the True Faith.[20]

The night vigil of the knights was made unbearable by scorpions and spiders which crept under their armour. Throughout the night, Saracens taunted them, holding up precious water in their cupped hands which they then let trickle into the sand.

At sunrise on Saturday, 4 July 1187, the king, surrounded by his barons, sank to his knees to implore the Almighty. 'God, look down on your children carrying in your holy name the cross of the true faith,' he silently prayed, 'if we must give final battle then let it be my God, not his.' But God would not consider any kingdom but His own.

---

[18] After the battle, by order of Saladin a mosque was built on the same hill.
[19] *Estoire d'Eracles.*
[20] Mohammed, *Koran IV*, 72 ff: '*Es moegen fuer die Sachen Gottes jene kaempfen, welche dem irdischen Leben die andere Welt vorziehen; denn, wer fuer die sache Gottes kaempft und getoetet wird, dem werden wir grossen Lohn geben. Was ist's denn mit Euch dass Ihr nicht kaempfet fuer die Sache Gottes?*' (from old-German manuscript)

A sound of galloping hooves broke the silence. A young man in a splendid tunic, a gold-sheathed Saracen blade on his side, jumped from his horse. 'Sire,' he spoke in a clear voice so everyone could hear his message, 'I come in peace from my liege, the Sultan. He wishes you to know that you must abandon your quest, return from whence you came beyond the sea, never to return.'

'By the Holy Cross, never', yelled Reynald de Chatillon.

'Never, you tell your infidel potentate', voiced the Templar. The king looked around for counsel, but was met by hostile stares of his knights in chain mail. The wise one, the only one who could have averted certain tragedy, Raymond of Tripoli, wasn't nearby. Slowly, Guy de Lusignan turned to the messenger. His face was pale when he spoke. 'Tell your sovereign, I, King of Jerusalem, summon him to the Tribunal of Heaven.'

When Count Raymond was informed of the king's reply to the Turk, he advanced towards King Guy, knelt on his right knee, and said: 'My liege, if you mean to die here today, I will stand by your side. It will be no victory no matter how many we destroy, for we will have given this Holy Land to Saladin.'

To which the king replied: 'I'd rather die with my knights here on this field than see Jerusalem the Holy fall to the Infidel.'

This said, he ordered his Frankish host to break camp and climb the long slope towards the Springs of Hattin. Instead of advancing in orderly columns, which might have provided some protection, many of the foot soldiers broke ranks and rushed for the hills, hoping to reach the well. They found themselves blocked by heavy formations of Saracens who felled them with a cloud of arrows. Those who managed to escape were cut down by Saracen blades. Then Saladin's cavalry struck at the wings of the Crusader knights. Raymond's vanguard took the initial shock. His remaining foot soldiers grounded the butts of their lances and angled them for the eyes of the attacking horses. The Saracen mounts couldn't stand it. The Saracens dismounted and attacked with arrow and sword. The wall of iron-clad knights stood their ground, their heavy mail invulnerable to the arrows fired from the short bow. A young mameluk hurled himself against an exposed portion of the Frankish line and brought down a number of crossbow men before he was cleaved in half by the blade of a knight. This so infuriated the Turks that they charged on pell-mell. They were driven back by a furious counter-charge of the knights as a new wave of Turks charged into their midst, turning the fray into a tangle of shouting men and clanging steel. They cut each other down in gruesome slaughter. Saladin watched the outcome with growing anxiety. Despite their feeble number the knights pushed back the Turks, who proved no match for the heavier weapons wielded by the knights. The battle went to and fro; the Templars and Hospitallers rushed at the Saracens until a new wave of Turks would charge into the Christians whose numbers dwindled with every consecutive assault. It couldn't last, the few hundred Crusader knights could not hold out much longer against the successive waves of thousands which rolled down on them from all sides.

Count Raymond of Tripoli raised his sword and led the small circle of his kinsmen in a furious charge against Taqui ed-Din's centre of the line. Perhaps by order of Sultan Saladin, who more than anyone respected the valour of this Christian opponent, the Saracens put up almost no resistance to Raymond's charge before they opened ranks and allowed the count and his suite to get away into the hills. Then their line snapped back into place and the fate of the king and his last remaining faithful was sealed.

Saladin observed the battle with his son Afdal.

'And Afdal sat on his stallion beside his father, the noble Sultan, when they saw the King of the Franks retreat to the top of a hill. The Infidels were brave men, and they fell one after another. Saladin was of great sadness and tugged at his beard: "Give the devil the lie!" he shouted, and our men surged forward. "They flee", shouted Afdal, but his father, the Sword of Allah, cut him off: "Be silent! they will not be defeated until the king's tent falls." '[21]

The remaining Christian foot soldiers fled up a hill and left the knights to their fate. No arguing and begging by King Guy made them move back to join in the fight. So King Guy rallied his dwindling forces around his royal banner to defend Bishop Ruffin of Acre and the True Cross. Now Saladin pushed in his last reserves, who formed a strangling noose around the dismounted knights. What finally broke Frankish resistance was not the fall of the king's tent, but a spirited attack by the Sultan's nephew who slashed his way through to the Bishop of Acre, who was killed. The Turk picked up the True Cross and galloped across the battlefield, holding it high for all to see. The Turks broke out in jubilation. But with the loss of the most holy relic of Christianity the morale of the Frankish knights broke. They lay down their arms and waited to be captured. The Saracen hordes stormed forward and slaughtered most of them. Only 200 knights and 1,000 foot soldiers survived the massacre.[22] On the spot where the Frankish host had made its final stand around the cross Saladin got off his horse, put his carpet on the blood-splattered sand and gave praise to Allah, the Almighty.

'The Christians were lions at the beginning of the fight and at the end they were only scattered sheep. Of so many thousands only a small number were saved. I looked in horror at those smashed faces glued to the sand, their bodies covered with the dust of the desert, and gave thanks for our deliverance to Allah, the One.'[23]

[21] Account by Ibn al-Athir, an Arab chronicler.
[22] Among them: Raymond de Tripoli and his four sons, Hugo, Guillaume, Raoul and Otto, and Balian de Ibelin.
[23] Imad ed-Din, a contemporary, in his *Chronicle of Hattin.*

The captured Frankish barons were led before Saladin. There was King Guy de Lusignan, his brother Geoffrey, Gérard de Ridefort, the Bishop Bernard of Lydda, Honfred de Turon, son of the Lord of Kerak, and Reynald de Chatillon. Saladin treated his prisoners with great courtesy, as he was a man who appreciated bravery wherever it was found. When he saw their sorry state and the king's thirst, he had a chalice filled with delicate sherbet of fruit and snow and handed it to King Guy. But when the Frankish king passed on his cup to Reynald de Chatillon, Saladin became angry: 'It displeases me that you give him drink from my cup. This accursed will not drink with my permission in my tent, and if he so does his life will not be spared.' However, he did let Reynald finish his drink, but promised that he would never drink again. He then demanded of Reynald why he had broken the promised vow of knighthood, to which the Lord of Kerak replied: *'C'est la coutume entre les princes et j'ai suivi le sentier battu* – Such is the custom among the princes and I followed only the designed path. '. . . *upon which, Saladin threw him a hateful glance, but still offered to spare his life if Reynald would denounce his church and adhere to the true faith, which Reynald refused contemptuously. For no riches that anyone might be able to give him would Saladin let Reynald live any longer.*[24] When the Lord of Kerak had put down the cup, Saladin had him led outside his tent. There, the Sultan took a sharp blade, and with a mighty stroke, cut off his head. Upon his order, the head was put on a lance and *'paraded throughout the land as a sign of Allah's victory over the infidels'*.

That day, Jerusalem was lost forever.

*   *   *

[24] *Estoire d'Eracles* and *Passio Reginaldi*, by Saladin's contemporary, Pierre de Blois.

What if . . .

What if – Reynald de Chatillon had not attacked Saladin's
          caravan?
          The delicate truce, established between Saladin and
          Raymond of Tripoli, might have continued and
          ensured the survival – at least for some time – of
          the Frankish Kingdom of Jerusalem.
          It is doubtful if Saladin, a devout Muslim, would
          have tolerated much longer a Christian presence in
          the holy places.

What if – Gérard de Ridefort had been killed at the Springs of
          Cresson a few months before the disaster at Hattin?
          Guy de Lusignan would not have had to listen to
          bad counsel.

The facts

In the years after the first Christian conquest of Jerusalem
in 1099, much was made of keeping the delicate balance
between two warring doctrines, Islam and Christianity. Both
religions claimed to be the sole defenders of the True Faith.
This distinction became confused as secular power began to
extend into divine papal doctrine and temporal forces used the
Crusades for their own enrichment. The Frankish armies did
battle against each other, but, at the same time, the Sultanate
descended into corruption. Then came Saladin. The Christian
barons, forced by Saladin's meteoric rise, reunited, and only a
wafer-thin truce kept the Islamic and Christian armies from
slaughtering each other.

   As it turned out, Saracen honour eventually transcended
Christian treachery. Saladin, unquestionably the greatest and
most noble warrior of the time of the Crusades[25], took up

---

[25] He once sent a stallion to Richard Coeur de Lion when his opponent became
unsaddled in battle.

the sword. The loss of the True Cross at the Battle of Hattin shattered the Franks' faith, and victory went to Allah, not to Jesus. Hattin was the end of Christian supremacy in the Middle East, and brought the whole Crusader movement tumbling down.

The rest can be called 'Saladin's Blitzkrieg'. Three days after Hattin, on 7 July, Tiberias surrendered, and on the 10th, Acre opened its doors to the victorious Sultan. Then fell Jaffa and Nazareth, followed by Saffuriya, Caesaria and Haifa. Nablus was next, Sidon fell on 29 July, and Beirut on 6 August. Raymond de Tripoli, who had escaped to his fortress of Tripoli, died of pleurisy at the beginning of September. Only Tyre held out due to the timely arrival by sea of Count Conrad de Montferrat and his knights. Saladin raised the siege and moved on Askelon which surrendered on 5 September. From there Saladin headed north, towards the heart of the conflict, Jerusalem, a city defended by Balian de Ibelin. The Sultan arrived before its gates on 19 September and soon his engineers had breached the wall. Still the defenders held out, but by 2 October it was all over. The town was sacked, the Christian symbols destroyed, and its Catholic population ransomed or killed.

Out of the confusion, following Saladin's triumphant entry into Jerusalem, was born new calls for Crusades and history moved with great speed. Guy de Lusignan, pardoned by Saladin, went to Cyprus. King Philip Auguste of France, Henry II of England, and the Holy Roman Emperor Frederick I, called Barbarossa, took the cross. Henry II died, Barbarossa drowned, and Philip Auguste returned to France. Richard Coeur-de-Lion took their place, only to leave the Holy Land before he had recaptured Jerusalem. Pope Innocent III launched the Fourth Crusade, yet those who followed his call went not in a sacred quest, but to plunder the riches of the Orient. Hordes of knights ventured into these foreign lands, sacked Constantinople, plundered churches and raped

Christian women. The values of this world quickly began to replace the values of the Hereafter. An age of heresy began,[26] which brought the church into conflict with temporal power. In 1229, Frederick II, the excommunicated German Emperor, used a fratricidal quarrel between the Muslim rulers of Syria and Egypt to force them into signing the Treaty of Jaffa, which, for a brief time, returned Jerusalem to Christianity (1229–44), but didn't end the controversy in the Christian camp, since the Emperor used the Teutonic knights of Hermann von Salza to kick out the French Templars.

The Kingdom of Jerusalem, which ever since the Battle of Hattin had been reduced to a string of coastal fortifications, came to its bloody end with the fall of Acre and the massacre of its defenders, on 18 May 1291.

Jerusalem, the cradle of Christianity, never again became a Christian town.

The Hinge Factor at Hattin was a merciless desert.

'. . . because it is written, he who ventures forth into the barren lands without offering homage to Allah is doomed to perish . . .'

---

[26] Such as the Valaisans and Albigeois in Southern France.

Agincourt, October 25 1415

3

A Rabble with Bare Feet

Agincourt, 25 October 1415

'Follow your spirit; and upon this charge
Cry "God for Harry! England and St George!"'
Shakespeare, *Henry V*

The night before St Crispin's Day, the Constable of France, Charles d'Albret, Count of Dreux, rode from his camp to inspect the plain on which he had chosen to give battle. He was accompanied by the Duke of Alençon. From the dark forest of Tramecourt to the woods of Agincourt, hundreds of camp fires lit up the moonless night. Servants and foot-men hurried between conical tents. Every one displayed the proportionate wealth of its owner. Archers in leather jerkins, embroidered with the crest of their liege, held torches. In their pool of light could clearly be seen the noble standards planted in front of each tent. Hail Burgundy, hail to you, Armagnac, Orleans, Bourbon, Alençon, and hail Brabant. The flower of chivalry about to ride into their final joust.

From the tent city of nobility, a mud track, jammed with mule carts, led to a camp of another kind. There, crossbow men mingled with cooks, prostitutes and scavengers, all profiteers of slaughter. Some distance from the rowdiness, the male cursing and female squealing, a monk was on his knees, murmuring a prayer.

The two noble knights ignored the noise, their eyes were fixed on the dark contours of a field. Three times during this day, the Constable had changed his choice of battle ground. Finally he decided on a half-mile wide plain of rich, agricultural soil. Vassal farmers of the *sieur* of Agincourt had recently ploughed the earth to prepare the ground for the winter seed.

The Constable pointed in the direction of the English camp fires.

'We shall attack in two columns. You will take one wing of six hundred knights and *gens d'armes* down the left side. Beware of the English longbow men; make at them in great haste and ride them into the ground.'

'And who will take the right wing?' asked the duke.

'I will. Now, let us return to camp to prepare for the joust.'

A joust, he called it, not a battle. His 8,000 knights and 10,000 men-at-arms and foot soldiers faced a meagre thousand men-at-arms and 5,000 starving archers and foot soldiers, not much of a contest.[1] Tomorrow, God willing, that English plague would forever vanish from the hollow ground that was France.

Across the field, so near they could hear the shouts from the French camp, lay the English army of King Harry. It was a hunted rabble, suffering from dysentery and malnutrition. They had been chased all the way from Normandy. Now their backs were to the wall; the French host had cut off their retreat towards the fortress of Calais. King Henry was aware that he

[1] The number of actual combatants at Agincourt differs from one contemporary account to another; perhaps there were as many as 25,000 French facing 5,000 English. The numbers do not change the sequence of events.

must stand and he must fight, he was left with no other choice. He also knew that the overwhelming might of French chivalry would thrash his foot soldiers into the ground.

'The French march with 8,000 lances', he thought, 'I have but one thousand.'

He had done it before, but never had he felt so isolated. He was only twenty-eight and keenly felt his youth. It says much for his charisma that his men obeyed him at all. His camp was silent, none of that boisterous noise that drifted across the field from the drunk, brawling French soldiery and the impertinence of their camp women revelling already in their assured victory. Henry felt cold and perhaps intimidated. He walked up to a fire where his archers rested, that rugged bunch of cutthroats, dressed in leather jerkins and kilts.[2] One of them, a gnarly chap, his face tanned to leather, recognised Henry.

'Up men, don't you see he's coming,' he yelled; 'do homage to your king.'

They rose as one man. With a 'Ho, Harry!' they displayed their loyalty.

Those longbow men were England's strength, and had been ever since Henry's great-grandfather, Edward III, defeated the French at Crécy in 1346. Henry could trust them. Yet he felt pangs of guilt.

'I've led you on to be killed in a strange land.'

The tan-faced leader replied, 'My king, will that be worse than to starve in England?'

Starve in England? How little he knew about the plight of the simple man, he who had caroused in the brothels of London with his obese friend Falstaff.

'What's your name, archer?' he demanded of the soldier, taking his measure.

---

[2] 'The wearing of armour and the use of weapons was reserved by God and nature to persons of quality' (Colonel Lloyd, *History of Infantry*)

'Fluellen, sir, Fluellen from Wales.'

For an instant the glance of a king and that of a lowly archer interlocked. 'Well, Fluellen from Wales, may the Lord grant us victory and 'tis my solid promise, after tomorrow you and your men shall hunger no more.'

'For Harry and England', shouted Fluellen. Like a wave, the roar was picked up by others. Soon the whole camp shouted, 'Harry, Harry, Harry . . .'

Henry of Lancaster, by the grace of God, King of England, forced himself to remain impassive. But he could not help thinking about death. By next morning's light, on a freshly ploughed field far from home. While the king knelt for evening prayers, a light drizzle began to fall. Soon this drizzle turned into a downpour, dousing camp fires and soaking deep into the fields of freshly turned earth.

It kept on raining all night.

We are in the year 1415. It is the end of the Middle Ages. Nations don't exist, only fiefdoms of kings, princes and feudal overlords, with their inherited right to conduct private wars and coin money. The cathedral builders have lost their faith, plague has invaded the Continent, and the countryside is sick of war – a devastating war which has lasted for seventy-five years.

The Hundred Years War was not started in the reign of Edward III as history records. It was not a war of only one century. It began three hundred years before, or, more precisely, in the Year of Our Lord 1152, when Eleanor of Aquitaine married Henry Plantagenet, Earl of Anjou, Duke of Normandy. Her wedding gift was the south-west of France, the rich province of Aquitaine. Two years later, Henry laid his hands on England's crown and became Henry II. The rest is three hundred years of history steeped in blood. A time which some recall as 'when knighthood was in flower', while others refer to it as 'the dark Middle Ages'.

France, with its 14 million is the most populous country in Europe, while England boasts a mere 4 million. Each belligerent has a feudal army – men serving a limited time in return for land tenure. Both countries use the unit of a lance: a knight, his squire, several archers and common pike men. Victory, or defeat of the mounted knights, usually decides the fate of their auxiliaries. In the past the quality of the English Army has made up for their numerical inferiority, especially its use of the longbow, a primitive weapon taken over from the savage Welsh and Scots. It out-ranges the French crossbow, and has four times its rate of fire. With it, the English kings have won a string of battles, at Crécy and Poitiers, and their armies have gone from strength to strength, as will Napoleon's armies 450 years later, or the Allied forces after Stalingrad and El Alamein. But here, on this field of 1415, for Henry V the foe's numerical superiority is too vast to hope for anything but a noble death.

Henry of Lancaster comes to the throne on the death of his father, Henry IV, in 1413. He is a young man of unlimited ambition, keen for military glory and victory. He assembles an army of 6,000 men-at-arms to re-establish his claim to the French throne. On 13 August 1415, he lands near Harfleur, in Normandy. When he hears of a great French host being levied against him, he decides to retreat to his fortress at Calais. But fever and starvation slow up his army, a French vanguard blocks the only passable ford across the Somme, and the main body of French knights catches up with him on 24 October, only one day's march from the walls of Calais.

25 October 1415. St Crispin's Day. Dawn broke, the rain had stopped. King Henry assembled his meagre forces. He asked his followers to stiffen their sinews, summon up the blood and imitate the action of the tiger. His mail-gloved hand reached out for the royal banner.

'Once more unto the breach, dear friends, once more;
Or close the wall up with our English dead . . .'

The archers of Fluellen from Wales cheered: 'Henry! Henry!'

'They have the lances, but we have our arrows. Let them taste the flight of English shafts.'

The archers cut down small trees and sharpened their ends over the fire for the purpose of planting a pike barrier against the expected charge by mounted knights. The king lined up his forces into a single rank of battle. His noble knights were near him: Warwick, Oxford, York, Talbot, Gloucester, Exeter, Bedford. Once again, the king knelt.

'*Memento Nostri Domine!* Our enemy is assembled and their hearts are filled with conceit. Lord, steal their courage and make them flee so that they know that nobody fights for us but you, Our Lord.'

Then he leaned on the royal banner, and waited.

The sky was grey and overcast. An impartial herald, the Earl of Montjoie, stood by to observe that battle would be conducted by the rules of chivalry. Accompanied by two cavaliers who carried his white herald's standard, he rode into the English camp.

'My lord,' he asked of the king, 'is it battle that you wish?'

'No,' replied Henry. 'Tell my cousins I am willing to speak in peace. But, if stand we must, stand we will.'

The herald took the message across the field to the French side. The distance was roughly a thousand yards.

'*Connétable*, your adversary speaks in peace. Will you come to terms?'

Charles d'Albert looked at the assembled dukes and counts. 'Well, messires, *Le roi Henry* makes us an offer. What say you?'

The Duke of Alençon replied for all: '*Sans pardon*. Honour

demands we fight. Up and at them, I say.' The Constable nodded in agreement.

'You've heard the verdict, herald. Go and tell King Henry he must stand and he must fight.'

The herald left to carry the challenge into the camp of the enemy. Nothing could stop the inevitable.

On the French side, the noble knights confessed themselves to their priests. For the first time in many years, the invisible threads of power and intrigue, the mistrust, vanity and ambition had been put aside. A spirit of some national unity prevailed, even the rival Counts of Armagnac and Bourbon shook hands.[3] The princely heralds sounded their clarions. The knights, in their polished chain mail and riveted steel armour, were helped by their yeomen onto their steeds. The horses seemed to resent their heavy burden. The knights and their retinue of men-at-arms were handed their lances. These had been shortened because of the wet ground. The crossbow men lined up in divisions in front of the mounted knights. The Constable had ordered the French to form three lines: two lines of foot soldiers and crossbow men in the vanguard, followed by the mounted knights.

From the wet earth rose a mist which made the pennants droop limply from the shafts of lances. Before mounting up, the Constable checked the ground. He had taken everything into account, everything except the weather. The rain had turned the freshly turned fields into a brown, slippery quagmire. This would present a serious obstacle for horses, heavily weighed down by the armour of iron-clad knights. The earth was so heavy that the servants had to place wooden logs on the ground to take the weight of the horses while they helped their knights into the saddle.

[3] On 24 November 1407 the Duke of Orleans was assassinated. A bloody civil war broke out between the Burgundians and the Armagnacs (Orleanists).

Charles d'Albret, the experienced warrior, knew that the chargers of his chevaliers would not find a firm footing. Contrary to many of the nobler princes, the prudent d'Albret had the warrior's wisdom, earned in many harsh battles, not to boast of triumph before it was achieved. Certainly, he had a crushing superiority under his command, but it was the wet ground that worried him. Rather than stake everything on a premature attack the *Connétable* tried to reason.

'*Messires*, we must wait, for the ground's too wet.'

'And I say, let's hit them now', growled Antoine, Duke of Brabant.

'Our horses will get mired in mud', cautioned Philippe de Nevers.

'Are you afraid of that *canaille aux pieds nus*,[4] my noble count?' challenged haughtily the Duke of Brabant. The vengeful feud between French nobility was once again coming out into the open. The passion of the two rivalling French camps, momentarily suppressed in the cause to face a common enemy, was called into question.

The *Connétable* realised that it was useless to continue his argument; whenever a French knight's courage was called into question common sense was tossed to the wind. It took all of d'Albret's diplomatic persuasion to stop a brawl among the princely pros-and-contras for immediate attack. What they failed to realise was that this decision had already been removed from their hands.

It can be said, Henry of Lancaster was an excellent judge of men. The reply brought to him by the impartial herald had made it clear that the French were aching for a fight. Henry understood that it called for a bold stroke; no one in his right mind would send in the heavy cavalry across ground so wet that their horses couldn't accelerate for 'the moment

---

[4] *Canaille aux pieds nus*, or ragamuffin rabble, refers to a socially inferior class.

of impact'. Therefore, his only chance to survive the day was to goad the French into an attack while the fields were still soggy, their horses vulnerable, and his archers and pike men could benefit from a certain advantage. The French were heavy, the English were light. The terrain was in his favour, the French had chosen badly. Despite their vast superiority of mounted knights they had picked a plain too restricted and narrow to bring their mass of cavalry into formation. The forest on both sides would cause their mounts bunch up to and limit their choice of manoeuvre. He must gall them in order to provide a massed target for his longbow men. That was his only chance.

He ordered his wagon train to the rear. It contained the royal treasure, his crown and the personal baggage of his noblemen, as well as the 'booty-wagons' carrying the spoils from his *chevauché* across Northern France. Owing to the feeble number of troops at his disposal, Henry was forced to leave the wagon park only lightly guarded, a factor which was to add a tragic twist to the battle. Next, he took a calculated risk when he ordered his archers to advance to a distance where their arrows might do some damage. The line of English longbow men advanced carefully. The right of the English line, led by the Duke of York, was anchored by the forest; the centre, under Henry, only slightly behind; while the left, guided by the Lord Camoys, was again ahead of the centre. In this way, the English line formed a half moon which placed each flank's longbow men in an oblique position to the expected attack's front and centre. Eight hundred yards from the French, the English archers planted their hedge of pikes.

Here occurred an incident which history has never explained. Either upon an order by the king, or just for a bit of derring-do, a small group of English longbow men advanced stealthily along the treeline. When they reached bow range, they loosened their arrows. Three or four struck a target, although without doing much harm. But it was enough to provoke a furore among the French knights. This pin-prick challenge precipitated events and upset the *Connétable* d'Albret's advice to wait until the ground had dried. Pennants were raised, trumpets blared, steel clanked on steel. There was great jostling for position, the knights were spoiling for a fight, the price was glory and its reward was immense: titles, castles, land. In vain, d'Albert tried to establish some semblance of battle formation. Clusters of groups gathered, each liege called his own *gens d'armes*[5] to his banner. The crossbow men and foot soldiers were hastily pushed into line by their captains and began a slow advance. The field was heavy, their step was slow. Behind them, impatiently waiting for their signal to advance, sat the French chivalry on their massive war horses.

Henry took in the developing scene. As soon as the French vanguard of crossbow men had reached five hundred paces, some of his longbow men, specially selected for their mastery of distance and accuracy, strummed their bows. They loosened their arrows. A half-dozen reached their target, bringing down a few crossbow men. Part of the French line hesitated and wavered.

This taunt was too much for the agitated mounted knights. Their pride, combined with impetuosity and the contempt they held for their enemy, made them disobedient and reckless. Constable d'Albret's last attempt to reason, his plan to send out a screen of crossbow men to eliminate the English archers, was rejected with arrogance: 'You're trying to deprive us of our glory.'

Some hot-heads clamped their steel spurs into the flanks of their chargers. Led on by undisciplined feudal lords, uncoordinated groups fell into a trot, soon followed by others who had no intention of missing the fun. The rest chased after

[5] *Gens d'armes*, men of arms, is today's gendarme.

them, yelling and screaming. On their advance they pushed aside their foot soldiers and brought the line of crossbow men into complete disarray. It rendered their steel missiles ineffective as they could not fire into the backs of their own masters. Two distinct columns of some six hundred armed riders each under Guillaume de Saveuse and Clignet de Brébant advanced on the English line. As the *Connétable* had predicted, the horses sank into the morass. What had been planned as a furious high-speed charge turned into a timid forward movement so dreadful was the ground, so heavily laden were their mounts. Horses slid and stumbled, riders bumped into each other on the narrow approach. The knights tried to force their horses forward at full speed to close up with the English archers. It could not be done, the soggy ground gripped their horses' hooves like thick molasses.[6]

The English archers in front of their protective stakes, faced the charging cavalry in grim silence. In their leather jerkins they were rather drab, nothing like the approaching splendour of polished armour-plate. A trumpet sounded. The riders spread out, two hundred abreast, a ripple went down the advancing line as their mighty lances fell into place.

Henry watched anxiously as the great mass of chivalry bore down on his men. The experienced jouster in him recognised that their charge was much too slow and made for an ideal target for his archers. Patiently he awaited the right moment. When they were a mere three hundred paces from his pikes he lifted his sword: '*For England and St George!*' he cried.

And all along the line his archers and men-at-arms echoed the call: '*For Henry, England and St George!*'

A thousand longbow men pulled back their strings until

---

[6] '*Les Français étaient pesamment armés et étaient en terre molle jusqu'au gros des jambes, ce qui leur était moult grand travail: car à grand peine pouvaient ils ravoir leur jambes et se tirer de la terre*' (Juvénal des Ursins).

the nocked arrows reached their cheeks.[7] A zinging sound like that of a million harps was heard and the sky darkened with a swarm of arrows. The advancing French were hit by a storm of feathered darts, the most concentrated missile weapons until the arrival, four hundred years later, of the massed firepower of Napoleonic infantry. The impact clatter of the cloud of chisel-pointed arrowheads on steel was deafening. The *bascine*[8] helped to deflect the arrows from the head and shoulders of the knights, but many of the less-protected horses were struck. Even as the first flight struck home a second was already on its way. As many as 40,000 arrows came down on the French cavalry every minute, its result immediate and devastating. On the orders of King Henry, the archers fired obliquely, their targets not the steel-clad riders, but the unprotected hindquarters of their steeds. Horses reared up and threw off their riders, who then lay helplessly on their backs, like giant silver beetles, held prisoner by their heavy armour. More *chevaliers* were thrown to the ground while the English longbow men poured flight after deadly arrow flight into the mêlée.[9]

The arrows flew. There were shouts from the still mounted French knights. Safety was ahead, through the hail of gull-winged death. Three more times the arrow cloud descended upon the advancing French chivalry. The archers did not try to stand their ground, but slipped between the planted pikes to seek shelter from the imminent crash of horse against man. Those of the attacking French that made it through the hail of arrows now found themselves suddenly confronted by a new, even more deadly obstacle, the pointed stakes. The ones

[7] It is interesting to note that the obscene expression of 'two-fingers' is not in fact obscene at all, but derives from the English bowmen taunting the French by showing them their bow-fingers. If caught by the French, a bowman would have these two fingers cut off, so that he could no longer pull his string.
[8] A wide-brimmed helmet.
[9] '*Les archers d'Angleterre, légèrement armés, frappaient et abattaient les Français à tas . . .*' (Juvénal des Ursins).

in front impaled their mounts on the needle-points of the planted tree trunks, while others who did manage to stop their horses in time were unsaddled by the collision of the rear ranks crashing into them. Some horses shied away from the obstacle they couldn't jump and came to such sudden halt that their knights were catapulted over their mounts' necks into the array of pointed stakes. The first to die on the pikes was their leader, Guillaume de Saveuse. The arrows came no longer in massive flights. The archers picked single targets, and, at this close range, the deadly arrow points pierced the steel-plated armour of the knights.

Henry sat on his great war horse and observed the slaughter, his mouth set in a hard line. He raised his banner to signal his right wing. The mounted knights of the Earl of Oxford wheeled around their pikes to crash into the enemy. The French in front of Henry's position were caught by a battering ram of pointed steel from Oxford's lances. Swords came down on armour plate, helmets split, lances pierced under armpits. Still, the French wouldn't run. *L'honneur de la chevalrie* was at stake. They had forgotten that more than one battle had been lost because of a misplaced dictate of honour.

The *élan* of the next wave of French cavalry was not heightened by the spectacle they found before them. It became even more disorganised as their unchecked advance made their chargers stumble over dead horses and fallen knights. Riderless steeds raced off in great panic, crashing into the oncoming waves of French infantry and dismounted men-at-arms. Retreating knights and riderless horses collided with their advancing foot soldiers and knocked them over like bowling pins. Though mangled and disorganised by this reverse charge, the French foot soldiers were headed in three dense columns for the English battle flags. Because of this three-pronged concentration on a relatively narrow front, the French bunched up and were not able to deploy their overwhelming numerical superiority. In a final rush across the soggy ground they reached, out of breath, the point of contact. Both lines thrust their spears at each other. The first line of French men-at-arms was pushed into the lances of the English by the terrible press from behind. There were as many as twenty rear ranks who tried to get in on the fight, but could not see the confusion that went on in front. This created an undulating line and robbed the French of any hope of a decisive breakthrough. The lances broke, the distance between the combatants suddenly narrowed, and now began hand-to-hand combat, terrible in its furore, with battle-axe, mace and sword. The fight developed quickly into single combat between men-at-arms in the confronting first rows. Knights fell, others took their place, slipped on the armour of the fallen and stumbled, quickly to be dispatched by thrusts through the visors or into the vulnerable parts under their armpits. The mounds of bodies began to build up. The line following could no longer move into battle other than by climbing with their heavy steel-plated armour over the slippery obstacles on the ground. The din of battle was at its fiercest. There was desperate fighting all along the line. Still the throng of French columns pushed relentlessly from the back; their front line was forced forward and toppled over those fallen before them. This was the worst moment for a fresh attack. Yet, instead of readjusting their battle line, the French second line of foot piled pell-mell into action. They fared no better than those who had preceded them. The hand-to-hand butchery was so ferocious it resulted in a tremendous pile-up of the dead, which chroniclers referred to as *the building of a wall of dead knights*. Soon the shapeless sprawling hummocks were so high that they prevented the following waves of French men-at-arms from advancing. In these initial fifteen minutes of carnage the outcome of Agincourt was decided.

Henry raised his sword, clamped down the visor on his helmet, and cried: '*St George!*'

He led his lances from between the stakes to charge into the retreating French. The *chevaliers* of Charles d'Albret were broken up into scattered groups, no longer the solid wave of polished armour but a disorganized horde of fugitives. Their escape lanes were choked with dead knights and horses. The Duke of Alençon, who had led the charge of his kinsmen against the banner of the Duke of Gloucester, had become surrounded by English men-at-arms. Over the din of battle, Alençon yelled his submission to King Henry, but before the king could stop his men, the noble duke was cut down.

The English archers had almost run out of arrows. On the slippery ground in front of their pikes lay, supine, the flower of French knighthood, trapped by the weight of sixty pounds of armour. There they flopped on their backs like helpless beetles, their steel-enclosed arms and legs pumping the air. That was the problem with armour-plate; the protection it provided came at a high price. When the archers perceived the disorder in the French ranks, they rushed forward and began to attack isolated knights. Going at them, three and four to one, the *canaille aux pieds nus* bashed in the heads of the nobility with the mallets that had served to drive in the stakes. It was butchery at its worst. This unexpected flank attack from a socially inferior enemy, which they held beyond contempt, completed the French debacle. The archers quickly stripped the wounded and dying of their precious jewels. They slashed throats and cut off fingers to get at the precious rings of the noble. These boys, from the slums of London or the vassal farms of Wales, Kent and Sussex, no longer thought of battle, only of the immense riches they stuffed into their arrow pouches.

Some English knights raced up to the scene of horror to stop their men from slaughtering their prized hostages. For that reason alone, the lives of many a French knight was saved. Stripped of gloves and helmets, the hapless survivors were herded to the rear and guarded by a considerable number of their captors. Every knight protected his prize for ransom.

At this time, when King Henry thought the battle won, he spied two new dangers. The first came from the rear. Looters had attacked the thinly guarded wagon train, killed the sentinels, and were trying to make off with the king's treasure. Henry, thinking of it as a new attack against his vulnerable flank, ordered a large troop to take care of the matter, which they did with great brutality, although they soon found out that the looters did not represent a concerted attack by French knights, but were merely local peasantry out for a quick gain. Bereft of part of his men-at-arms, a new danger arose in front of Henry's line. His left flank was being severely tried by a sizeable formation of French, Bretons, Gascons and Poitvins. Heedless of losses they spurred on their horses and cut through the line of archers. The French knights fought bravely, and got among the pike men, where they struck down the thin line of English yeomen. In the ensuing struggle more French riders pushed into the cleared lanes. Henry rode ahead to put his weight into the fight. Suddenly he found himself isolated from his men. A young French knight, the Chevalier de Rohan, saw his chance to make a name for himself. He charged straight for the king. Before Henry could duck aside, he received a blow on his helmet.[10] Then he delivered on the young Rohan a stroke so mighty that it split his head in half. But the danger persisted. The French pressure was simply too great, the English pike men and archers fell back, soon they would pile up against the royal banner. If the French could breach the flank they would roll up his centre. The critical moment of battle had come. The English pike men, without the support of the armed knights, were lost. The French charged wildly into the mass and quickly speared them. There was nothing Henry could do

[10] Still today on his tomb at Westminster Abbey.

to help out, since his own column was heavily engaged in the centre. He called for more lances, but there were none readily available. Part of his reserves were taking care of the looters around the baggage train, while some of his best lances, the ones he so desperately needed to repulse the French charge, were guarding their French prizes. If he could not put a stop to the French attack, they would overrun his line and liberate the prisoners. Then, these would pick up the swords of the fallen and crash into his men from the rear.

With a feeling of grave anxiety, King Henry V now took a step completely contrary to the knightly behaviour of the period, something which history was to remember him for. With great despondency he issued one of the most controversial commands of chivalric warfare: '*Let everyone of my lances kill his French prisoner.*'

His knights reproached their king: 'This is expressly against the law of arms.'

They refused to obey his order, perhaps not only from humanitarian reasons but also because every captive represented his weight in ransom gold. Upon their refusal, the king called on his archer sergeant-at-armes, Fluellen from Wales. While knights risked dishonour over such dastardly deeds, archers were not included in the chivalric system and could participate in wholesale assassination, especially as many of them were actually convicted criminals, thieves and murderers who had joined Henry's lot to escape the gallows. Upon their sergeants' bidding, two-hundred archers force-marched a long line of captives from the field of battle, perhaps as many as two to three thousand. Most of the prisoners were in pitiful shape, too exhausted to resist their guards. They could not imagine what fate awaited them and stumbled stoically to their end. Near a cottage, they were herded like cattle into packets. When Fluellen brought down his mallet on the first knight, a great moan of despair went through the attacking French line. More prisoner heads were bashed in.

Only those who held a promise for great ransom were spared. In cold blood, Henry's executioners butchered a great many of the nobility of France. Blood flowed, throats were cut, the screams of the dying carried over the din of battle. Furious but impotent to stop the outrage, the attacking French observed the frightful spectacle – a noise and sight so painful that it blunted the French charge.[11] Henry called on his few lances and led them forward to stiffen his retreating line of pike men and archers. The French wave broke, they turned and rode off, hotly pursued by the Duke of York cavalry. Only those on horses could save themselves, all others perished. Almost at the end of battle, which had lasted four hours, the Duke of York was cut down by a lance.

For a moment Henry lifted his visor to observe the masses of dead prisoners. Those knights had fought well and did not deserve such an end. He had ordered it because he needed to, but he knew that history would mark him down as a cold-hearted, ruthless man.

King Henry V, with victory at hand, raised his banner. A cheer went down the line. The king knelt to give thanks to the Lord. He then sent for Montjoie, the French herald whose duty it was to observe the fight and act as impartial umpire. The knight, dressed in impeccable white, appeared. He clamped his mailed fist to his armour.

'*Sire*, you have sent for me.'

'Herald, how call you the battle?'

'*Une victoire anglaise* – an English victory.'

The herald was greatly upset by the ignominious act of butchery perpetrated by the Lancastrian, but his face remained impassive. It wasn't his role to judge, only to

---

[11] '*Henri V ordonna que chacun tuât son prisonnier. Mais ceux qui les avaient pris ne voulurent pas les tuer, car ils en attendaient grande finance. Les archers se chargent de la besogne: moult pitoyable chose. Car, de sang-froid, toute cette noblesse française fut là tuée et decoupés têtes et visages*' (*Chronique de Jean Lefèvre*).

report. Let this vile knave be tried by his peers. Or by history.

'Tell me, herald, what is the name of yonder castle.'

'Agincourt, *sire*.'

'Then let it be known that stout and brave Englishmen achieved victory at the Battle of Agincourt.'

Come nightfall, the ground was covered with the slain. Heaps upon heaps of French nobility, 1,500 knights, including the Dukes of Brabant, Alençon, and Bar, the Count of Nevers, Jacques de Chatillon, Sieur Guichard, and the Constable, Charles d'Albert. The herald's men counted well on 10,000 slaughtered French foot soldiers.[12] There were some French who considered Agincourt a profitable day – the looters who followed an army to benefit from the windfall of battle. During the height of it they had even managed to steal Henry's royal crown.

Among the few English casualties were the Duke of York and the Earl of Oxford and a few hundred commoners. Henry's army, gorged with victory and wearied by slaughter, lay down to rest.

On the following morning, Henry V of England threw a final glance at the field where he had come so near disaster. A pitiful sight spread out before his eyes, a field covered by the great noblesse of France who had died for their sovereign seigneur, *le roi de France*, Charles VI, a mentally retarded cripple who hid his infirmity behind the walls of a distant castle. The bodies of the fallen knights had been stripped of their armour by scavengers and lay naked before the victor. They had paid dearly for their pride and vanity.

King Henry climbed on his horse and headed for Calais.

*   *   *

[12] *Ouvre de Dieu qui leur était adversaire*' (Charles d'Orléans in captivity).

What if . . .

What if – it hadn't rained that night before the battle?
> Henry V's archers would have been trampled into the ground under the impact of lances, and the Hundred Years War would have ended half a century earlier.

The facts

At Agincourt the flower of medieval knighthood on horseback was cut down by the socially inferior foot soldiers of Henry V. The French had not learned their lesson from the Battle of Crécy in 1346, and their out-dated values of honour and courage coupled with the superior firepower of the time – long-distance archery – led them again to disaster.

For the Plantagenet king, the stigma of the massacre of the prisoners lingered on and shocked medieval chivalry.[13] More than their battlefield defeat, it instilled in the French a hatred for anything English, which was to continue for centuries to come. This hate gave rise to a wave of French revanchism the English never again overcame.[14]

1429, Orleans. Jeanne d'Arc's enthusiasm delivered the French from their obsession of inevitable defeat. The tide changed. Her death on the stake elevated her into a martyr, her spirit lived on and turned France into one single nation. The Hundred Years War came to its bloody conclusion on 17 July 1453, at Castillon, when the last English captain, the elderly Talbot, rode with his cavalry headlong into artillery, a weapon which was destined to become the decisive influence of a new era.

The Age of Feudalism was over. The Age of Gunpowder had begun.

[13] *Troisieme defaite, et cette fois le massacre sauvage de toute la haute noblesse de France . . .'* (Histoire de France).
[14] Even in today's colloquial French, everything evil is *anglaise*.

The Hinge Factor at Agincourt was the weather, a field of battle made heavy by rain, and the fatal disregard by nobility of a socially inferior enemy.

Karansebes, 20 September 1788

Donau

Budapest

HUNGARY

ROMANIA

Theiss

Temesvar
(Timisoara)

Siebenbuergen

1359m △ Turkish
Army

Timisul
(Temes)
Austrians
(Josef II)

Karansebes

Eisernes △ Tor Pass
2511m

Transsilvanian Alps

SERBIA

Belgrad

Walachei

4

A Barrel of Schnapps

Karansebes, 20 September 1788

'I shall rid the world of this barbarous race.'
Joseph II, Emperor of Austria,
campaign of 1788

Another loud crack followed the crashing and screaming nearby. Caught in that brief instant between sleep and consciousness, the soldier's mind struggled to filter through the confusion. It was all noise, darkness and shock. And that strange metallic smell of blood. There were no stars to give him light. He hugged the wet ground, his fingers scraped the earth. Where are my boots? Why is everybody shooting? He could hear the sound of battle clearly. The noise and the dying. 'Not me, oh God, not me . . .' His mouth opened in a silent scream. Paralysed by fear, he couldn't move. He said his prayer over and over again. 'Not me . . .' Cold sweat ran down his face, his chest heaved, he gulped for air. Panic held him in its iron grip. That ugly tangled knot banging on his brain, 'Now I'm going to die'. There was no hope for dawn, it would be lonely to be dead . . . Was it all a bad dream? No, this was no dream, the flashes lighting up the night, the

roll of cannon's thunder, the screams of the wounded and
the moans of the dying: 'Save yourselves. *Turci! Turci!* All is
lost, the Turk is upon us.'[1]

Joseph II, by the grace of God Emperor of Austria, had a
weakness, and not a small one. He wished to be remembered
through history as a military genius, as big as, if not bigger
than his shining model, the great Frederick of Prussia. The
main problem with the benign Austrian Emperor was that he
simply didn't have what it took. Neither with his diplomatic
skill nor with a marshal's baton. At an already advanced age
he suddenly decided to deliver the Balkans from the Turks.
The King of Prussia, Frederick Wilhelm, offered his gracious
office to help settle the dispute between the Sublime Porte
and the House of Hapsburg in a diplomatic manner. Instead
of accepting the gracious offer, Emperor Joseph managed to
insult the Prussian king by writing him a note: 'The House
of Hohenzollern came to power by the same fickle means as
the evil Turk.' This affront was enough to make the King
of Prussia sign a military treaty with the King of Sweden.
Together they marched against the only ally the Austrians
had, the Empress Catherine of Russia. In the meantime,
Joseph had begun to knock on the gates of the Balkans.
But he'd forgotten to inform the Turkish envoy that Austria
was actually at war, and had been for the six months since
his army had entered Turkish territory.[2] To correct this
oversight, he sent a brief note to his State Chancellor, the
Fürst of Kaunitz: 'I am sad to say that the Sublime Porte has
entered into a war with my ally, the Czarina. According to
the treaties between Russia and us I am obliged to go to the

[1] Most of the direct quotes come from the notes of a contemporary in the camp
of the Emperor, A. J. Gross-Hoffinger. For obvious reasons, his account was
never published in Austria, but appeared in Germany in 1847 under the title
The History of Joseph II.
[2] On 2 December 1787, the Austrians attacked the Turkish fortress of Belgrade;
however, the war was only declared on 2 February 1788.

help of the Empress. I order you to instruct the Sublime Porte that a state of war exists between Austria and Turkey.'[3]

In March 1788, Joseph set forth on his long and tiresome journey from Vienna to Walachia,[4] the disputed border of confrontation between Islam and Christianity. He undertook it to obtain fame and enter history. He did indeed enter history, but not in the way he intended.

The initial objective of the Austrians was to liberate the Save, a strategic waterway, by subduing the Turkish strongholds of Schabaz, Belgrade and Vidin. And finally, following the conquest of the key fortress of Nis, to incorporate all of Serbia into the Austrian Empire. In order to achieve this the Emperor had gathered the military might necessary for the task. Six army corps, totalling 245,062 men with 36,725 horses. Under his direct command stood a main force of 125,000 soldiers and 22,000 horses. His artillery boasted 898 field guns with 176,700 cannon balls and 1,000 tons of black powder. To feed this army on the march took a daily ration of 800 tons of flour and 200 beef cattle.[5]

This force was led by men remarkable in the annals of Austrian military history for their stupidity and incompetence. Coburg, Fabius, Wartersleben, Mitrovsky, Devins, Liechtenstein. The only competent leader, the ageing Marshal Laudon, who served so well his Empress Maria Theresia, was left behind. The Emperor had considered him too old for such an exhaustive exercise. It seems, the only talent the Austrian Emperor possessed was to pick always the wrong man for the job. This time he hit upon the dumbest of them all, Marshal Laczy, whose singular achievement throughout his career had been to agree with his superior. In other words, a yes-man

---

[3] *Briefe von Joseph II an Fuerst Kaunitz, 1788.* The orginal text was in French.
[4] Transylvania, today part of Romania.
[5] Instead of taking along efficient officers, the Austrians prefered bureaucrats, who left these statistics.

who had little to add to the limited military experience of his Emperor.

'The Austrians beheld with great apprehension the presence of their Emperor in a military campaign. He was well known for his humanitarian views, and nobody could see what his presence would add to win the war. But, because of his attraction towards the glory which comes with victory, Joseph could not be otherwise convinced. Therefore, many predicted already at the beginning of the campaign a bad ending, and future events were to prove them right.'[6]

Joseph's original plan of campaign, if ever he had one, was to employ his overwhelming forces not, as may be expected, in a major aggressive action, but to settle for a kind of defensive impasse. Thus, the Emperor of all Austrians began his campaign with a whimper, not with a bang.

The attack on the Turkish fort of Belgrade was scheduled for 16 May. The guns were in place, the infantry stood ready. On the evening of the 15th, the Emperor suddenly changed his mind, and, rather than attack the weakly defended garrison, he ordered a retreat. He based his decision on the fact that the Russians had not come to his support.[7] Joseph's courage was certainly nothing like that of the model he so desperately tried to imitate, Frederick the Great, a leader of men whose grasp of war and harsh decisions he never understood.[8] To make matters worse, the Emperor's health deteriorated, and with it his indecision mounted. His hesitation sacrificed a sizeable portion of his army to epidemic swamp fever when he ordered his generals to pitch camp in the mosquito infested

---

[6] A. J. Gross-Hoffinger.

[7] Due to his diplomatic blunder, the Russians were now fighting a Prusso-Swedish army. Kaunitz writes: 'We cannot count on the Russians. They have put us to sleep with promises.'

[8] 'The *coup d'oeil* of a general is the talent which great men have of conceiving in a moment the advantages of the terrain and the use they can make of it with their army' (Frederick the Great).

bogs along the Danube. Soon the situation in the Austrian camp became desperate. Yet the Emperor refused to break camp. The deadly disease decimated the regiments, and the common graves began to overflow. In no time at all, 172,000 soldiers were afflicted by bouts of malaria and dysentery, and 33,000 of his best troops died. Joseph could have taken Belgrade or defeated a great army of Turks alone with the number of troops he had so carelessly sacrificed to the lethal fever. Those who weren't affected by the fever suffered from military inactivity. While the poisonous climate continued to take its toll of their comrades, the men sat around and played cards. Fights broke out among this patchwork of ethnic auxiliaries: the Hungarians fought with the Croatians, the Lombardians hated the Slovenes, and none of them liked their Austrian officers. Still the Emperor held back, awaiting the arrival of the promised Russian reinforcements, which never materialised.[9] Soon the camp ran out of bread: its flour rations had been used up and new supplies had to be shipped down the Danube from distant Austria. When these arrived they were found to be crawling with maggots. To add to this problem the war chest for the soldiers' salary was empty.

In the meantime, the Turks had managed to reinforce the fortress of Belgrade with 9,000 fresh troops, and the Turkish governor of the city offered a bounty of 10 gold ducats for every Austrian's head cut off and presented. This became known to the Austrian troops; whenever a soldier disappeared (probably drowned in the river or simply wandered off to go back to his family), rumours of Turkish atrocities spread throughout the camp. Troops lost faith in their officers and officers grumbled about their Emperor. Finally, Joseph was forced to beg the old Laudon to take over as head of the forces. '*I do not order you, my dear Field Marshal Laudon,*

---

[9] It was said that Prince Potemkin intrigued with Catherine against helping Joseph.

to take command of my troop, but I ask you humbly to do it for the best of state and the love for your Emperor.'

Laudon accepted, not for love of his Emperor but to save his beloved Austrian army. On 18 July he reached Imperial headquarters and on the 19th he conquered the fortress of Dubicza. At last, the army was on the move. Unfortunately, his generals were not as efficient as '*der Alte*', and suffered a number of setbacks. There were a few notable feats of heroism. In the castle of Rama, the young Lieutenant Lopreski and 23 men held out against 4,000 Turks, until, true to the legend of Leonidas and his forty Spartans, all were dead.[10] On the Boza Pass, a division of 4,000 Austrians bloodied the noses of 10,000 Turks. But such exploits were the exception and made no real difference to the overall conduct of the war.

As the Emperor had no better idea, he issued a plea to the church to offer prayers throughout the monarchy: 'Oh Lord, the Almighty, you who smites the enemies of your Goodness, grant us your mighty protection. Spare your fighters from the dangers brought upon them by the Infidels.'

It seems that the prayers by the Infidels had more impact: 'Allah, You who holds the sun, the stars and the whole universe in Your hand, You who has sent us Your Prophet to teach Your children the true faith, why do You let it happen that the enemy destroys our land? Rise, Almighty, and give Your people the power to proclaim Your Gloria in the temple of Mecca.'

Laudon worked miracles and conquered a number of minor places, but his arm wasn't long enough. A division under General Papilla faced up to 13,000 Turks and was decimated, and on 18 August, Major von Stein had to relinquish the strategic position at Dubowa. After his withdrawal, the Austrians had to give up the Danube Valley all the way to Belgrade. Next

---

[10] This so impressed the Turks, that by order of the Pasha, the body of the heroic Lieutenant Lopreski was wrapped in silk and returned to the Emperor.

came the message that a Turkish force of 70,000 under the Grand Vizier Jussuf Pasha marched on Vidin, while another army of 30,000 led by the Seraskier of Rumelia,[11] was on its way to Nis. For the Austrians it became high time to deliver battle. Which meant that their main force of some 100,000 had to take up a position along the River Timisul around a small town by the name of Karansebes.[12]

'Here we have to win,' the Emperor joyfully exclaimed; 'history has planned it this way. It was here that Prince Eugene achieved a brilliant victory over the Turks, and this is the best place to beat them again.'

Yes, there would be a Second Battle of Karansebes. But what was to take place there is probably unique in the history of warfare. An incident which, more than anything else, demonstrates the moral decline from which the Austrian army suffered, *'whose worst portion was made up of people from barbaric tribes, and whose better part mistrusted their leaders'*.[13]

It was a moonless night, this 19 September 1788, when a vanguard of Imperial Hussars crossed the Timis Bridge at Karansebes. Having reached the opposite shore of the river, they did not find hostile Turks. Instead, they discovered a wagon camp of wandering Walachians[14] who joyfully welcomed the riders and offered them schnapps and girls. After a brief bargaining session, a price was agreed upon and the hussars swung off their horses to indulge in a bout of revelry. Some hours passed when the first companies of foot soldiers crossed the same bridge, their throats equally dry. However, by now the hussars had bought up all the schnapps. To defend against these undesirable newcomers,

[11] A local potentate known for his cruelty.
[12] Karansebes, or today, Caransebecs, is near the Romanian Timosvaro. The name Karansebes comes probably from a Roman ode by Ovid: *Cara mihi sedes*. The poet is buried there.
[13] A. J. Gross-Hoffinger.
[14] Trades people of mainly gipsy background.

the hussars quickly established a fortified position around their barrel of schnapps and chased away the foot soldiery. That greatly upset the thirsty men.

A shot rang out, followed by a scream, and a body tumbled forward. The hussars pulled out their sabres and attacked the infantry, driving the soldiers back. It was the noise of the shot that had frightened the men on foot, but once they had recovered from their initial shock, they too began to shoot. Soon a regular little battle was going on. More shots were fired and people began to die. Next, the soldiers tried for a frontal rout but the hussars wouldn't yield. To chase the riders from their fortified position, the foot soldiers attempted a ruse. They yelled, '*Turci! Turci!*' The mere idea of facing a Turkish host so frightened the inebriated hussars that they galloped in flight across the bridge. But the foot soldiers also drifted back, frightened by their own shouting. Their colonel tried to stop the rush by barring their way: '*Halt Stehen bleiben! Halt!*' It was of no use, these men were Hungarians, Lombardians or Slovaks with hardly a word of German between them. There was no such order in their limited vocabulary. They had been taught the word '*Vorwärts!*' but never '*Halt!*' Perhaps they simply misunderstood, perhaps they just wanted to move to the rear instead of going into battle.

'*Halt! Halt!*' the Austrian officer kept yelling. Some young soldiers mistook this command for: '*Allah! Allah!*' and now the shooting began in earnest.

Meanwhile, on the other side of the river the whole of the Austrian army had gone to sleep only to be suddenly awakened by firing on the distant shore. *The vanguard had encountered the Turks!* They couldn't imagine what else could have started the shooting and screaming, since everything took place in total, frightening darkness. The noise of battle, the moans of the wounded and the death cries helped to intensify their terror. What they heard but couldn't see confirmed a feeling deep inside them – the big fear of dying.

Fenced off in the midst of the camp was a herd of cart-horses. These animals became so frightened by the increasing bedlam that they knocked down the fence and thundered off, making a sound like advancing cavalry. A corps commander misinterpreted it for an attack and ordered his cannons to open fire. The night was lit up by blue flashes and thunder claps, and more soldiers began to fall. A roar went up: 'The Turk! The Turk! Save yourself! All is lost!'

Quickly the panic took hold of the entire army, and it became pointless to try telling that polyglot force what had happened at the other end of the bridge. The first regiment drifted to the rear, quickly followed by another and another. Soon a mass of soldiers fled back in a human tidal wave. Owing to their varied ethnic backgrounds, most regiments couldn't converse with each other, which made them imagine that the shadows rushing at them were the enemy. Terrified by the thought that they were about to be overrun by scimitar-wielding hordes of Turks, they fired into their own decamping ranks.

The Emperor, still weak from his illness, had taken a nap in his carriage. Drugged by sleep and medicine, he stumbled from his coach staring at the bedlam. He could hear the cries of the frenzied mob coming towards him. An aide helped him onto his horse. No sooner up, he was swept aside by the fleeing mob. One of his aides stood firmly in front of him, striking out at the fear-crazed soldiers; he felled a few with his sabre before he was trampled to the ground and his breath crushed from his body. The Emperor was thrown from his horse, ending up in the river. Wet, and beset by the fear that he would soon fall into the hands of the Turks, he crawled into a house in Karansebes from where his personal guards finally delivered him. (An almost similar fate happened to his brother, the Archduke Franz, who was eventually rescued by a *carré* of his regiment.)

The drivers of the munitions wagons used their horses to

make good their escape, swiftly followed by the gunners, who cut the harnesses between horse and cannon before they dashed bareback to the rear, abandoning their field pieces. This mad cavalcade hacked down anyone who dared to put himself into their path. Many officers were killed that way, and the panic took on incredible proportions. Everyone ran, cursed, prayed, fired or died. Houses were plundered, women raped, and villages went up in flames. The path of panic was strewn with discarded muskets, saddles, tents, dead horses, and all the jetsam of a defeated army. It was only much later that the generals managed to put a halt to the mad flight. The Austrian army was in shambles, the shock which followed the devastation was stunning.

Two days later, the Grand Vizier and his army finally showed up before Karansebes. They didn't find an Austrian army. They did, however, find some 10,000 dead and wounded Austrians whose heads were speedily lopped off by the Turks.

What if . . .

What if – Austrian officers could have conversed with their units in their ethnic language?
            Perhaps the panic would never have occurred.

The facts

Following the debacle at Karansebes, the Emperor sent a note to his brother: 'I know not how to continue. I have lost my sleep and spend the night with dark thoughts.'

In a dispatch to his chancellor Kaunitz, the Emperor wrote: 'This disaster which our army suffered due to the cowardice of some units is incalculable for the moment. The panic was everywhere, among the army, among the people of Karansebes, and all the way back to Temesvar, a good ten leagues from there. I cannot describe in words the terrible rape and killing that went on.'

Only the bravery of Count Kinsky and his cavalry regiment stopped the rider hordes of the Turkish Pasha from annihilating the Austrian army after Karansebes. Later that fall, the old Laudon re-established order in the army and led Austria to a series of victories. Then came winter. The Emperor was near death. This ended the campaign of 1788.

In the spring of 1789, the young Selim III ascended to the throne of the Sultanate and led his army into war. But this time the Turks bit into a stone in the person of Marshal Laudon, who made short shrift of their attempt and pushed them out of the Banat. The Danube became once again an Austrian river. While this combat was still raging, Emperor Joseph II died with these final words: 'All I wish for is a durable peace over all of Europe.'

On 14 July 1789, the citizens of Paris stormed the Bastille, and a new age began. Europe was not to find peace for the next twenty-five years.

The Hinge Factor at Karansebes was a barrel of schnapps.

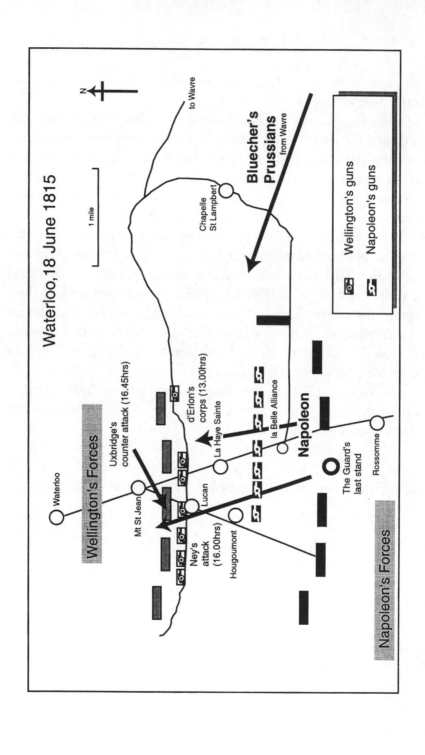

Waterloo, 18 June 1815

N

1 mile

to Wavre

Bluecher's Prussians
from Wavre

Chapelle St Lampbert

Wellington's guns

Napoleon's guns

Wellington's Forces

Uxbridge's counter attack (16.45hrs)

d'Erlon's corps (13.00hrs)

la Belle Alliance

La Haye Sainte

Napoleon

Waterloo

Mt St Jean

Lucan

Ney's attack (16.00hrs)

Hougoumont

The Guard's last stand

Rossomme

Napoleon's Forces

5

A Fistful of Nails

Waterloo, 18 June 1815

'A plan which succeeds is bold, one which fails is reckless.'
General Karl von Clausewitz. *On War*, 1832

Thirty paces in front of the corps rode the general, solidly anchored to his saddle. The eyes in his tanned face seemed bluer than usual. He observed his horsemen calmly. These were the élite of the élite, *les Cuirassiers de l'Empereur*, tough men wearing proudly their shiny breastplates and the long horsehair plumes on their Grecian helmets. A thin smile of satisfaction crossed his face. Yes, with these men he could ride into hell and back. The general knew only too well how victory often depended on their speed and ability to jump the enemy's defences.

The air was heavy with the sweat of animals, the rancid odour of gunpowder, the human electricity of fury – a fury funnelled towards an enemy lined up ahead on the distant ridge. Everyone was preoccupied with their own thoughts, whatever else was happening was no longer of concern. Fear had no hold on them. All were veterans, trained to obey in silence. Five thousand men who had charged across the fertile soil of Austria, Prussia, Italy, Russia, in places with immortal names – Austerlitz, Wagram, Jena, Friedland, Borodino. They had covered themselves with eternal glory.

The general let his eyes wander along the row of faces who bore cruel witness to the many battles fought for their Emperor, hymns of glory and of death. There were also many young faces, recruits to fill the depleted line, adolescents who had grown up too fast. Boys who had not yet heard the noise of battle, tasted the moment of victory. Only, battle wasn't about noise and glory, battle was about death.

It was now mid-afternoon. Along the line, the dismounted riders maintained their silent attention as they had done ever since the first thunder of the cannons around noon. Pascal le Meunier, thirty-two, from Maubeuge, a lance-corporal in Milhaud's *4me Corps de Cavalerie*, suffered from a nasty cut across his forehead. He had received it two days ago, during the skirmish with Lord Uxbridge's cavalry near the strategic road junction of Quatre Bras. Flies had settled on the wound, but le Meunier didn't raise a hand to chase them from the festering sore. Self-control was the first, and perhaps most, barbaric lesson a *cuirassier* had to learn. To suffer in silence.

A group of plume-hatted officers galloped towards the troop. In front rode a short, stocky man in the resplendent uniform of a *Maréchal de France*. His name was a legend. Michel Ney, Prince of the Moskowa, *le Brave des Braves*. A mounted officer left the ranks and came to a stop in front of the marshal. General Delort, commander of *la division des cuirassiers*.

Ney smiled. 'Glad to have you with us again, General.'

'*Toujours heureux de servir aux ordres de mon Maréchal.*'

Delort held a privileged spot in the marshal's heart. That day, at Jena in '05, the Prussians had directed their artillery on the attacking waves of *cuirassiers* and Ney found himself separated from his cavalry. Delort, then only a simple *cuirassier*, dashed onto the open plain to provide a human shield for the general. Napoleon himself had promoted him to the rank of lieutenant. Delort's combat experience, his life in the various campaigns, but most of all, his devotion towards his Emperor had advanced his career in leaps and bounds. He carried his scars like a badge of courage. In the next hour, only the iron discipline of the seasoned commander would help younger ones to overcome the pitfalls of the coming battle. Delort also knew that many must die, but those who'd survive would be proud to proclaim they had done battle for their Emperor, and for France.

Ney turned to the Corps Commander, General Milhaud.

'*General, prenez le commandement du corps.*'

'*A vos ordres, mon Maréchal.*'

Milhaud nodded to Delort.

'*Division des Cuirassiers*, mount up.'

Five thousand horsemen, which included also detachments of Dormon's and Dubervie's *Brigades légères*, lined up in the face of an enemy protected by his artillery. It wouldn't be easy. The squadron commanders placed themselves twenty paces ahead of their squadrons, sixty men in first line, sixty in second.

'*Première division?*'

'Ready.'

'*Deuxième division?*'

'Ready . . .' from along the long line. Milhaud advanced his horse several paces, raised his sabre and saluted the man with the white-plumed hat.

'*Mon Maréchal*, the *4me Corps de Cavalerie* awaits your command.'

For a brief moment, Ney lifted his eyes towards a heaven that knew neither pardon nor pity. Then he stared at the squadrons: *cuirassiers, lanciers rouges, chasseur à cheval de la Garde*. The sun reflected off 5,000 polished cuirasses and the steel tips of their lances.

'*Pour le salut de la France! En avant!*'

Five thousand sabres slapped against the steel of their *cuirasses*.

'*Vive l'Empereur!*'

A bugle blared. The Prince of Moskowa raised his sabre. As far as the eye could see, a mass of 5,000 riders, welded into a solid unit by the *esprit de corps*, began to trot slowly up the slope.

The time was three minutes past four in the afternoon.

The date was 18 June 1815.

The place was Waterloo.

The day Emperor Napoleon I fled from Elba, 27 February 1815, signalled the start of the One Hundred Days, a time when nobody slept well in the capitals of Europe. Once Napoleon reached Paris he organised an army that was now headed to confront two hostile forces in Flanders. Napoleon knew speed and surprise were of the essence since, facing him, were two redoubtable adversaries. Arthur Wellesley, Duke of Wellington, hero of the Peninsula War, and his old nemesis, Marshal Gebhard von Blücher, the 'Iron Prussian'.

Blücher he knew well, but the Emperor had never before seen a Wellingtonian army in action. He had always attributed the series of French defeats during the Peninsula War to the incompetence of his subordinates and not to the tactical superiority of Wellington's formations. And so it happened that one of the greatest military geniuses committed the cardinal sin of underestimating his enemy. With his unique grasp for any given situation, Napoleon had discovered the inherent flaw in the Allies' deployment: their forces were divided. He seized the initiative to enter Belgium and beat separately the English and Prussians before they had a chance to unite. On 12 June, he was joined by Ney, who, one more time, had changed allegiance, only three months after having promised King Louis XVIII to deliver 'Napoleon in an iron cage'.

Napoleon of 1815 was no longer the feared Napoleon of

Austerlitz or Jena. The stress of command had taken its toll. The Napoleon of Waterloo was unwell, both mentally and physically, suffering from chronic diarrhoea and prolapsed piles which made it difficult for him to mount a horse. He began to commit errors of command and left too much responsibility to others. Napoleon's initial mistake during the Waterloo Campaign was in the distribution of the principal roles. Most of his great marshals, capable of independent command, were dead or had switched allegiance. Devaix, killed at Marengo, Lannes at Aspern, Junot, who shot himself. Or those no longer available: Masséna, Murat, Macdonald, Suchet, St Cyr, Augereau. His biggest loss was Berthier, the supremely capable chief of staff, who Napoleon had to replace with Soult, never a strategist. To protect his back against a royalist revolt, the Emperor left Davout as governor in Paris and gave his left wing to Ney, a cavalry leader capable of incredible feats of boldness, but otherwise a rash hot-head. The right wing went to Grouchy, an ossified general brought out of retirement and sadly lacking in ardour. The same could not be said about *l'esprit de la troupe*. A report which reached Wellington compared Napoleon's Army of 1815 to the enthusiastic revolutionaries of the Battle of Valmy in 1792, capable of heroic efforts. Or, as General Foy wrote in his diary: 'Our line troops show not only patriotism and enthusiasm, but a true rage for *l'Empereur* and against his enemies.'

Napoleon's Army of the North was made up of five infantry corps, plus the Imperial Guard and the Corps of Cavalry. The infantry corps commanders were d'Erlon, Reille, Vandamme, Gérard and Lobau. The Guard was under the command of Friant, Morand and Duhesme, the cavalry under Milhaud, Kellermann, Guyot and Lefebvre. The reserves were under Grouchy.

Facing this formidable array was a composite force of Wellington's 93,000 British, Hannoverians, Dutch, Belgians,

Brunswickers, Nassauers, and Blücher's 117,000 Prussians. The 210,000 Austrians under Fürst Schwarzenberg, and the 150,000 Russians of Barclay de Tolly were still too far away to come into immediate play. Even more important than their numbers were their leaders. The military ability of Wellington and the tenacity of Blücher.

While Napoleon moved his army north, what was Wellington up to? Apparently nothing, if one can believe the Reverend Spencer Madan who wrote from Brussels on 13 June: 'Today the noble Duke took Lady Jane Lennox to a cricket match for no other object than to amuse her . . .'

During the night of 14–15 June 1815, the French suddenly advanced on Charleroi and surprised the Prussians in camp. Blücher was forced to withdraw on Ligny. It was at this moment that a French General, Chouan Bourmont, defected to the Prussians and revealed Napoleon's strategy. As soon as the Emperor learned about the betrayal, he dispatched Ney to occupy the strategic road junction at *Les Quatre-Bras* (i.e. Cross Roads) to prevent Wellington and Blücher from uniting. Faced by only a token force from the British contingent, Ney failed to take the hamlet. Napoleon, who had taken strong drugs to fight a bout of dysentery, had gone to bed and didn't hear about Ney's check until the following morning, while Blücher had used the night to build his defence around Ligny. The old fox knew he'd be the first to be hit. Soult dispatched a note to Ney at Quatre Bras. 'It is the intention of His Majesty that you attack whatever is before you and after vigorously throwing them back, join us to envelop the Prussians.'

On the morning of the 16th, Ney attacked again at Quatre-Bras. By this time, Wellington had recognised the strategic importance of this road junction, and dispatched additional units, who put up a stiff defence. While Ney fed in his ground troops piece-meal, Napoleon ordered d'Erlon's corps to bolster Ney. However, a confusion arose over a scribbled order from the Emperor which Ney misread. The marshal diverted d'Erlon's corps away from Quatre Bras. D'Erlon's troops began a useless wandering between two battle fronts. This manoeuvre deprived the Emperor of a third of his army's strength since d'Erlon's corps was now neither involved at Quatre-Bras nor at Ligny where Napoleon had struck at Blücher's centre. 'The Prussian army is lost if you act with utmost vigour. *Soldats de l'Empire, la France* is in your hands', the Emperor exhorted his troops prior to the attack. The force of French *élan* crumbled Blücher's line. Near a windmill from where the Emperor observed the attack and expected Ney to catch Blücher in the flank, he mentioned to Gérard, 'It is possible that in three hours the war may be decided. If Ney carries out his orders, not a single gun of the Prussian army will get away.' But Ney did not follow up. Had he done so, Prussia would have ceased to be a military power and the future of Europe may well have been altered.

Things were not going well for the Prussians. Blücher's horse was shot from under him and rolled over the ageing field marshal. He was left for dead on the field and only a quick action by his aide-de-camps, Nostitz, who flung his cloak over the body to hide him from the passing French cavalry, saved the Prussian general's life. The battle ended with 16,000 Prussians dead to Napoleon's 11,000. In the absence of Blücher, who by now everyone considered to be dead, his chief of staff, Count August von Gneisenau, took charge. In a series of brilliantly executed manoeuvres he managed to disengage his mangled divisions. Gneisenau, always at loggerheads with his English ally, considered himself betrayed by Wellington. The duke had promised to rush to their side. Influenced by this, Gneisenau ordered his Prussians to withdraw on Liège, away from the British. But the 'Iron' Blücher wasn't dead. They found him in a farm yard, rubbing garlic on his bruises and swilling beer. When he became informed of Gneisenau's plans, he countermanded them and ordered the three corps of von Bülow, Pirch and Ziethen to head for Wellington's last known position. A place called Waterloo.

Napoleon, not certain of the victory over Blücher, dispatched Grouchy with 33,000 men to chase the Prussians across the Rhine. The wily Blücher sent several badly mauled divisions in that direction. Grouchy fell for the ruse and his corps began to chase stragglers towards the east. As soon as Wellington heard about Blücher's defeat, his own position at Quatre Bras became untenable. The French plan became obvious. Napoleon would cut off his retreat and hit him in the flank. He ordered an immediate withdrawal to the next high position, which happened to be a gentle slope leading up to the plateau of Mont St Jean before the village of Waterloo. There he intended to offer battle – that was, if the Prussian field marshal could support him with at least one corps.

Ney had lost his former boldness; instead of vigorously pursuing the retreating English, he held his men in bivouacs. Furious over this missed opportunity, Napoleon took matters in his own hands and began a relentless drive. Then God intervened in the form of a thunderstorm which bogged down the French advance just as it had caught up with the fleeing English. This saved Wellington's army from destruction. Before retiring to bed, the Emperor dictated a message to Grouchy: 'His Majesty is going to attack the English Army which has taken up its position at Waterloo. His Majesty desires that you will head for Wavre in order to draw near us, and place yourself in touch with our operation, pushing before you those portions of the Prussian Army which have taken this direction.'

At two in the morning, a reply came back from Grouchy that the Prussians had divided into two columns: Small parts of the Prussian forces might join up with Wellington, while the centre under Blücher, retires on Liège. Unfortunately, it was just the opposite that took place. While the Emperor slept, the main force of Prussians was marching to the aid of Wellington.

18 June 1815. The rain squalls had passed and given way to a glorious morning. At 09.00 hours Napoleon had breakfast with his generals at Rossomme Farm, the Emperor's HQ. Marshal Soult worried about Wellington's strong position on Mont St Jean.

'Just because he once beat you, you now consider him a great general?' scoffed the Emperor. 'We have ninety chances in our favour.'

And that he had, with his 72,000 men and 246 guns, to Wellington's 67,000 men with 156 artillery pieces. Napoleon, the artillery genius, understood that it wasn't the shock force of men and bayonets that counted, but the placement of guns. He had pushed this art to a true mastery. The improvement of modern artillery had been as decisive to warfare as the bayonet charge developed half a century earlier by the Great Frederick of Prussia. The Emperor's tactics led to a dominance of cannon over the infantry's musket. The man instrumental to this development was a Frenchman, the Inspector General of Artillery under Louis XVI, Gribeauval. With his introduction of uniform limber boxes and gun carriages he allowed the rapid deployment of the attack gun. The muzzle-loading bronze cannons, used both by French and Allied artillery, were mostly 12- and 16-pounders, devastating pieces when used against massed columns of infantry. Their projectiles, round ball or grape shot, were fired by holding a glowing fuse, or mêche, to a narrow firing, or touch hole, drilled through the solid bronze.

Napoleon was dressed in a grey topcoat, a mauve silk vest and white trousers over which he wore a pair of hussar's boots. He rode a smallish grey horse. His troops had been put in battle formation before he passed them on review.[1] *Chasseurs, fanatassins, hussars, dragoons, lanciers, cuirassiers, La Garde Imperiale*. A single cry went up: '*Vive l'Empereur!*'

The Emperor turned to Ney. 'If my orders are well executed we shall sleep tonight in Brussels.' And it would succeed – if executed at once!

'*Sire*,' interjected General Drouot, a capable artillery man, 'the ground is too wet for our horse artillery to deploy. It will be better to delay for an hour.' Unfortunately for France, Napoleon listened to Drouot. The Emperor, suffering from a *malaise*, retired to the *Ferme du Caillou* where he slept for two hours. In any case, he wanted to await the arrival of Grouchy's reserves from Wavre. A fatal error, as it wasn't Grouchy who advanced on Napoleon, but Blücher's best corps under General von Bülow.

Physically shaken from his fall, but mentally quite solid, Blücher dictated a letter to Quartermarshal Müffling *to be dispatched with great haste* to the Duke of Wellington:

Wavre, 18. Juni 1815, 1/2 10 Uhr.
'*Your Excellency.*

I, as ill as I may be, will march at the head of my army in order to engage the right wing of the enemy the moment that Napoleon should launch a hostile action against the army of the Duke of Wellington. Should this day pass without an attack by the enemy, it is then my strong belief that by tomorrow, combined, we shall attack the French army.'[2]

---

[1] This was not only a parade, but a show of strength to intimidate the enemy.
[2] *Ew. Hochwohlgeboren ersuche ich namens meiner dem Herzog Wellington zu sagen, dass, so krank ich auch bin, ich mich dennoch an die Spitze meiner Truppe stellen werde, um den rechten Flügel des Feindes sofort anzugreifen, sobald Napoleon etwas gegen den Herzog unternimmt; sollte der heutige Tag aber ohne feindlichen Angriff hingehen, so ist es meine Meinung dass wir morgen vereint die franzosische Armee angreifen* (Bluecher, Dokumente der Befreiung, 1815).

Looking down from his vantage point on the Brussels Road onto Napoleon's lined-up army was a worried and undecided Duke of Wellington. Bonaparte, that wily fox, had cleverly split his army. Grouchy would certainly strike at his Allied forces from the flank. Should he withdraw? The decision to stand or to withdraw was about to be solved for him. While Napoleon went back to sleep, a Prussian dispatch rider arrived on a foam-covered horse to deliver the marshal's letter, and added:

'Your Lordship, Field Marshal Blücher wishes to inform you that General von Bülow's corps has been on the move since daybreak, followed by Pirch's Corps. He further wishes you to know that Ziethen's Cavalry as well as the Ist and IIIrd Prussian Corps will hold themselves in reserve ready to move at any time.'

The message contained another piece of information and Wellington couldn't believe his good luck. That fool Grouchy, he had taken Bonaparte's reserves and was running off with them to the east! The threat to his flank was suddenly removed. This made Wellington decide to stand and fight. All depended now on his precious 156 pieces of artillery to hold off a massed infantry attack until the Prussians could come to his aid.

Marshal Blücher climbed on his horse and addressed his army:

'My children, we must advance. You may think it isn't possible, but it has to be. I have promised it to my brother Wellington, and you don't want me to break my parole?'[3]

The Prussian Army picked up their muskets, and began to march.

*   *   *

[3] '*Kinder, wir müssen vorwärts. Es heisst wohl es geht nicht, aber es muss gehen, ich habe es meinem Bruder Wellington versprochen. Hört ihr wohl? Ihr wollt doch nicht dass ich wortbrüchig werden soll?*'

Waterloo Campaign, 16-18 June 1815

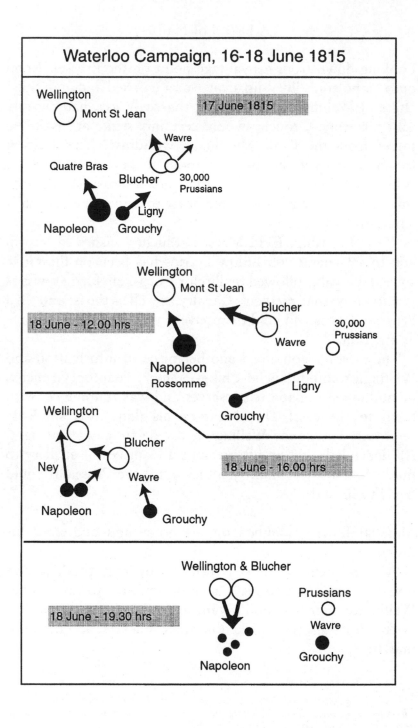

It was 11 a.m. Surrounded by his generals, the Emperor slouched in his saddle, a whiteness on his face. He wasn't well, but shrugged it off with, 'Momentary indisposition'. After which he turned towards his assembled generals, pointed at the windmill of Mont St Jean, and said: '*Messieurs*, there is your enemy. Our first objective is to eliminate his strong points at Hougoumont and La Haye-Sainte. We cannot engage in any major action before these two flanking bastions are carried.' His mind wandered off to other great battles, of conquerors long buried.

'*Sire*, the cavalry is ready.'

'Hold them in reserve. Reille's Corps is to engage first. With Jerome in support.'

Napoleon studied his top lieutenant. Ney, a superb cavalry corps commander, perhaps volatile but certainly aggressive, was today in charge of a whole wing, infantry and cavalry. Would he be able to handle it?

'*Messieurs*, join your units.'

At 11.30 a.m. Napoleon gave the signal to do battle, and *La Grande Batterie* of 120 cannons roared as Reille's 2nd Corps attacked the Château of Hougoumont, defended by the 2nd Brigade of Coldstream Guards under Colonel Macdonnell. Instead of using his mobile artillery to smash the buildings with concentrated fire, Jerome and Reille attacked with successive waves of infantry. The operation drew in French battalions, at great loss, and nothing was decided. Hougoumont held out, though at one point a troop of French infantry managed to crash through the gate of the château. A large formation of fusiliers rushed into the court-yard, but was repulsed by a hearty bayonet charge led by a Captain Wyndham and a Sergeant James Graham. With the help of three others, they managed to bolt the door. Then Sergeant Graham rushed into a burning outbuilding to fetch his wounded brother, after which effort he continued to fire through loopholes at the French.

Wellington, who had established his observation post beneath a gnarled elm tree along the ridge of Mont St Jean, could see the French waves breaking against the stone walls of the château. Meanwhile, shells rained on the slope of Mont St Jean. But Wellington had learned never to place troops in a position vulnerable to artillery bombardment. He held the bulk of his troops in reserve behind the rise, where the flat French trajectory could not reach them. Only a token force of Dutch-Belgians under General Bylandt was deployed forward, where they were subjected to a terrible beating.

While this action was well under way, Grouchy's 33,000 reserves sat idle while their commander and General Gérard were having a late breakfast at Hollert House. They could hear the deep rumble of distant gunfire.

'The *bataille* has opened', mused Grouchy with a sour face.

'*Mon Maréchal*, we must immediately march on the cannons', insisted Gérard. Grouchy wouldn't listen. He must obey his Emperor's orders which, with his limited intelligence, he had utterly failed to understand all along.

Reille's and Jerome's Corps had been stopped by Macdonell's Coldstream Guards before Hougoumont. The Emperor now ordered Ney to take the buildings of La Haye-Sainte. After a furious hand-to-hand combat along a stone fence, Ney's infantry penetrated into the vegetable gardens but failed to storm the buildings, held gallantly by Major Baring and a company of the King's German Legion. That too turned into nothing, and both fortified bastions remained serious threats to an attack up the centre.

Around one o'clock, a vital factor entered into the battle. An aide of the Emperor spotted a cloud of dust on the horizon. Napoleon stared through his spyglass to see a mass of troops advancing on Wellington's left. He gave a sigh of relief – Grouchy was moving into the Duke's open flank. His exaltation lasted only a short time, until a German-speaking prisoner was brought before him. Then the news fell like a hammer. It wasn't Grouchy, but von Bülow's Prussians on their way to link up with Wellington! The Emperor was convinced that Grouchy's 33,000 would soon block the Prussians, however, to insure against surprises, he dispatched a message to Grouchy: 'Bülow about to attack our right flank. Therefore do not lose a minute to draw nearer us and join us to crush Bülow whom you will catch in the very act.[4] To secure against surprises, he ordered Dubervie's and Dormon's Light Cavalry to screen his right flank against the slowly advancing Prussian formation, and sent Lobau's 6th Corps to follow with his infantry. The Emperor knew that he had the means to ruin Wellington long before sufficient Prussians could arrive to make the difference. Napoleon checked his situation. Both Hougoumont and La Haye-Sainte were still in the hands of the enemy, and a steady stream of Prussians endangered his flank. It was time to attack the centre of Wellington's line.

'Soult, send out the order to d'Erlon's 1st Corps, and tell Ney to support him with Milhaud's Cavalry.'

'But, *sire*, the Prussians . . .'

'Damn be the Prussians, we'll have Wellington before they can get here . . .'

He knew that he was right, the Prussians were advancing too cautiously to make any difference. His immediate task was to break the English centre.

Wellington hadn't strayed from his elm. Shells were screaming overhead and landing harmlessly in the fields behind him. The sun was quite strong, but he had no feeling for temperature, his mind was focused on the slope in front of

---

[4] Incredible as it may seem, even when Grouchy finally saw for himself the Prussian main force cross his line of advance and move towards Mont St Jean, he still did nothing to screen them.

him. There was new movement. Massed infantry emerged
from the dense smoke put up by their artillery; d'Erlon's
corps of four divisions of infantry, supported by light artillery. Soon they overran the Sandpit and Papelotte farm,
but La Haye-Sainte held out. Wellington was worried, the
juncture between his regiments began to show serious gaps.
He called on Bylandt's Dutch-Belgians. 'General, you cannot
withdraw. If you do, our line becomes flanked.' Bylandt
understood. But how could his decimated force stop four
fresh divisions?

D'Erlon checked his line of men moving to the roll of
drums, a heart-stopping sight, thousands of bayonets glis-
tening in the sun. His corps slowly ascended towards the
plateau of Mont St Jean. A slow march forward, four divisions advancing in battalion formation, a clumsy way to
attack. The Emperor, watching through his spyglass from
Rossomme, was furious. He saw squares of twenty-four
ranks move uphill, through fields of wheat flattened by
artillery. Attacking in such formation made the dense column
vulnerable to grape shot from Wellington's cannons. It was
too late to dispatch an order extending d'Erlon's corps into
the wide-attack formation along divisional lines only three
ranks deep. The Emperor could only hope and pray. For the
first time the greatest general of his time was faced by an
equally astute adversary, one who had already discovered
D'Erlon's blunder and now gave an order which was to alter
the next stage in this desperate struggle.

Sergeant Jacques Gourmelin had been at Austerlitz, Wagram
and Borodino, but never had he seen such a perfect order of
attack. Sweat covered his face from the climb; up ahead of
their line of advance he saw the gaping mouths of British
artillery. Why were their guns silent? he asked himself. He had
a sudden, numbing thought: there was something between
them and the British guns. Yet he felt no sensation other

than the certainty of impending combat. The drums rolled, the columns advanced.

General d'Erlon was furious. He didn't know what lay ahead of his troops. 'Where is that goddamn supporting cavalry?' he shouted. Infantry without cavalry was about as bad as cavalry without infantry. The cavalry were his eyes, and he had to advance blindly.

At his observation post at Rossomme, Napoleon bent over a map. 'Send in Ney to help out D'Erlon.'

'*Sire*, Ney is engaged at La Haye-Sainte.'

'Then get Kellermann.'

'I will send out the order immediately', replied Soult. A dispatch rider dashed across a field which was under constant artillery barrage. The Emperor's order to his cavalry unit was never delivered. Kellermann and his 3,678 riders sat in reserve and waited while D'Erlon's formation climbed towards Mont St Jean. His columns reached the first line of defence. Bylandt's depleted Dutch-Belgian regiments were routed and ran. To Napoleon, observing through his spyglass, it seemed the day was won when he saw the line break.

On top of the ridge, looking like a statuesque houseman, was the British General Picton. He surveyed the field in front of him and observed coolly the first column of French infantry climbing over a rise. He ordered his regimental aide, 'Tell our men to hold their fire until I raise my hat.'

Marching in the front rank of his battalion, *Fusilier* Sergeant Gourmelin had almost reached the sunken Wavre Road when he noticed a man on a horse waving his hat, before pointing it straight at him. Suddenly, like phantoms rising from the grave, a double line of red-clad soldiers popped up. At forty paces their muskets went off and the first line of French crumbled. The *fusiliers* were staggered. Some wanted to advance, some stopped to fire, others turned around. Gourmelin's heart rolled. Blessed be the Lord, he was alive.

Another volley, and still he was standing. Dizzied by noise and smoke, he began to lose track of the events, saw only death and a line giving way. '*Vive l'Empereur*,' he howled with fury. His cry was answered from a thousand throats – all those who had survived the deadly musket fire. It didn't need a general's call for attack – groups and individuals raced uphill, bayonets at fix. A British redcoat threw away his musket and tried to run, but Gourmelin was already upon him. Another line rose from the wheat, but this time the French were prepared and fired first. With sheer *élan* they drove back the British. Owing to their exuberance, they now lost the coherence of a solid line. Small groups of soldiers advanced to engage in man-to-man combat. Some bounded over the dead, the dying, the wounded. They were all locked in deadly combat, roaring like mad-gone animals. Some turned and ran. Total confusion, until . . .

The English generals Pack and Kempt held their regiments hidden behind the row of hedges that skimmed the Wavre Road. The order was passed down the line: 'Fix bayonets!' The French were almost upon them when one of the colonels raised his sword, and with the greatest sound he would make all his life, yelled: '*Charge!*' The two regiments rose as one man, poured over the edge of the road and pounded downhill. John McGrath, a raw recruit from the slums of Glasgow, didn't hear the bullets go by, he saw only those devil French ahead of him, confused, terrified – open mouths without a sound. Around him others roared and screamed in thrust and parry. He stumbled, fell into a shell hole, got up to fall again. It was a wildly leaping bayonet charge that smashed into the disjointed French line. Everyone fired and slashed, stabbed and trampled. Death was spreading like a river overflowing. Sergeant Gourmelin found himself in the centre of the fight. Two men went down, side by side, leaving a big gaping hole in the line. Gourmelin, his face blackened by smoke, noticed the hole, jumped into it to block it with his body. He saw redcoats coming down on him, firing as they ran. Muskets began to fall. Gourmelin saw his line waver and break. He was struck in the chest and sank to his knees. He licked blood from his mouth. 'Am I going to die?' With a final effort he pushed a ball down his musket. 'A target, please, give me a target.' His prayer was heard, an officer on a horse rose over the ridge . . . a badly wounded French sergeant took aim and slowly squeezed the trigger.

A riderless horse stood on the ridge. General Picton was dead. So were most around Gourmelin, stabbed while the remainder of D'Erlon's columns fled.[5] There were dead bodies and wounded men strewn all along the plateau, their blood seeping into the rich soil and covering in dark patches the trampled wheat. Here was an English boy dying, there was a Frenchman with a terrible bayonet wound who uttered a final word. A lieutenant sat on the ground, trying to stem the blood from a stump that once had been his arm but was sliced off by a shrapnel ball.

'Chase them!' the chief of English cavalry ordered calmly. Lord Uxbridge pushed the riders of the Somerset and Ponsonby brigades into the fray. They managed to cut across the French stragglers, rode over the French outposts and then exposed themselves hopelessly. Uxbridge realised the danger and desperately sounded retreat, but nothing would stop the mad rush by the British horsemen.

Until this moment, Colonel Martigue and his *lanciers* had seen no action. '*Vive l'Empereur*', he yelled and crashed into the side of Ponsonby's Scots Grays. Ponsonby was cut off and chased across a field by half a dozen *lanciers*. Three lances pierced his body.[6] The French riders did not know who they'd just killed. Soon, the English cavalry was in full flight. 'If we could have formed a hundred men we could

[5] Gourmelin survived and wrote about it ten years later.
[6] Ironically, he was killed because he had left his best horse behind. He had thought it too valuable for battle.

have made a respectable retreat and saved many. But we were as helpless against their attack as their infantry had been against ours.' Uxbridge's charge had wasted a good portion of Wellington's cavalry. Of the 2,407 riders of Somerset and Ponsonby's brigades, 1,058 were killed.[7]

For Napoleon time began to press. More Prussians were coming up by the minute and still no news from Grouchy. La Haye-Sainte held out to Ney, but the marshal's thoughts had begun to stray to bigger objectives – Wellington's intact centre. Pushed by his conceit Ney would not allow another man to reap the final glory. His inflated ego told him that he and he alone could and would win the decision. With this in mind he rode up to General Milhaud's *4me Corps de Cavalerie*. A mass of French horsemen stood ready, forty squadrons enface. With the crushing impact of his cavalry he'd wipe the cursed English from the plateau.

Ney was to change history, but not in the way he intended. He now committed the error so common for a cavalry man, by attacking infantry squares without support infantry. His strength had always been in lightning strikes by his élite corps of cavalry. Let others worry about infantry backup. He overlooked the fact that he was no longer a cavalry corps commander but the leader of a whole army wing, and that the infantry wouldn't move without his specific order. But cavalry man that he was, he forgot about the infantry he could not see. Reille's twelve battalions, on standby at some distance from Milhaud's corps and readily available to back up the cavalry attack, were never ordered up. Destiny took a side.

'*Mon Maréchal*, the 4th Corps of Cavalry is ready.'

For a brief moment, Ney raised his eyes towards a sky that knew neither pardon nor pity. Then he looked at his squadrons. The sun reflected off 5,000 polished cuirasses and the

[7] Häussler.

tips of lances. Pennants fluttered in the wind. For a last time, the marshal reviewed the situation. One bold sweep, push the enemy back from their guns, then cut down their *carrées*. Yes, it would work. It had to! He knew from past experience that the moral effect of a well-executed cavalry attack was more devastating than the actual losses sustained by the enemy. The British would run when faced by his *chevauché*! For this, he would not divide his divisions, but attack on a single, broad front. Maréchal Ney stood up in his stirrups. *'En avant, pour le salut de la France!'* Five-thousand riders, welded into a solid unit by the *esprit de corps*, advanced slowly up the slope. The time was three minutes past four in the afternoon.

The French cavalry advanced in echelons, supported by their artillery. But soon the French batteries ceased firing. A momentary hush fell over the battlefield as the divisions opened into line formation, stretched out as far as the eye could see. Delort's division was in the centre of the attack, his riders headed directly for the British batteries, when the British guns opened up with double-shotted canister, thousands of round pellets fired from giant shotguns. Ney pointed his sabre forward to signal *la charge*. Five thousand horses broke into full gallop, the ground trembled from the pounding of hooves. *'Vive l'Empereur!'*

Colonel Cornelius Frazer, a battalion commander in Maitland's brigade, looked down along the Brussels-Charleroi road. Before him was an unbelievable sight. Stretching from Hougoumont to La Haye-Sainte, a steel tide advanced on his position behind the Wavre Road. 'They'll roll over us', he thought, but his face showed no fear. He hadn't time for that. 'Form squares!' Soon they'd be within grapeshot range. How many rounds could his gunners loosen off? Two, three rounds? Certainly not more before the horsemen would roll over his cannons.

They came on, riding knee to knee, two ranks deep, headed straight for the deadly balls of fire. Canister tore into limbs, horses stumbled, riders went down, but nothing stopped the charge. At the sound of a bugle – *Charge with lance!* – 5,000 spear tips came down. Held out in front of their horses, they formed a battering ram of pointed steel. Another blast from the enemy's guns tore into the line of riders . . .

'Load! . . . Fire! . . . Load! . . . Fire! . . .'
    'We can't do it faster . . .'
    'Save your breath, boy, load and fire . . . you, there, steady, boy . . .'
    John Cutler, the sour-faced artillery sergeant in the battery of Captain de Cleeves, felt a hundred years old. He had experienced it all before, in the Peninsula, but never anything like this suicidal charge straight into his belching cannons. Every gun, every battery on the hill was blasting away. Nothing stopped the heroic charge of the 5,000.
    General Delort took it all in at once. His riders were up to full speed, too fast for the enemy up ahead to reload their cannons. His men raced ahead, not wanting to miss their part in cutting down the English.
    Cutler's gunners managed to loosen off one more round of double-shotted canister at seventy paces. Riders and horses piled up on each other like cards, those killed in the saddle carried by their horses right across his battery. Cutler yelled, 'Gunners, into the squares!' before he threw himself under one of the cannons.
    Ney was out in front. One final discharge of canister ripped into his riders, more horses stumbled and more riders were unsaddled. The British infantry had formed into defensive squares. He saw the gunners drop their sponge-staves and abandon their cannons to seek refuge inside the infantry squares. Then his riders reached the line of enemy artillery, placed twenty metres in front of the square. His charger carried him right over the gun position and he hacked away as he turned for the square. His horse was hit by a musket ball.

The marshal sailed over its head, but was unhurt. He grabbed the reins of a riderless horse and swung himself back into the saddle. The whole thing had been so fast, only five minutes since they had climbed into their saddles. Now they were up on top, amidst English squares and abandoned guns.

As the leading wave of riders raced towards his square, Colonel Cornelius Frazer dropped his sword: 'Fire!' The muskets spoke, musket balls ricocheted off the pigeon-breasted cuirasses like hail on a shingled roof. 'Aim for the horses,' yelled a sergeant. A few riders went down, but others pushed forward, their lances tearing into flesh, their horses jumping over wagons and dead bodies, wheeling around the cut-off square. 'Second rank – fire!' Another volley. While one rank pointed their bayonets at the driving horses, the one behind rammed lead balls down their muskets.

For the first time since he'd led his 5,000 riders up the hill, Ney sat still, watching the situation develop. During the dash he had lost his plumed hat, and his tunic over his cuirass showed holes. But what counted was that his divisions had overrun the British line. They had driven back General Alten's division, and Maitland's men were in total disarray. Stragglers, who tried to make it to the rear, were cut down by his *cuirassiers*, hacking, slashing, stabbing at the hapless foot soldiers. The day was carried, and he, Michel Ney, Prince of the Empire, had done it on his own. For as long as men would talk about glorious military achievements, his name would stand alongside all the other great military leaders. *Ney of Waterloo*. Disregarded among the debris of battle stood all of Wellington's abandoned pieces of artillery.

Something slapped into the old elm, cut a neat round hole into its bark. The Iron Duke hardly noticed. Ney's attack had captured all his attention. With great anxiety he observed as his English, Hannoverians, Brunswickers and Germans formed into twenty isolated squares. For the time being, the

line held, but if one of the squares retreated everything
was lost. Yet the loss of his guns was what worried him
the most. Without them he couldn't face another infantry
charge which he knew had to follow soon. His only option
was to withdraw, or stand and face annihilation. He watched
as more riders breasted the plateau. Where was the French
infantry to solidify Bonaparte's victory? When would French
grenadiers turn English cannons on English squares?

The Iron Duke gave a sigh: 'I wish it were night, or the
Prussians came . . .'

But the Prussians had been stopped at Plancenoit.

The Emperor had been distracted by persistent gunfire from
the right flank. Von Bülow's artillery had joined in the action.
That's why he didn't notice Ney's impulsive charge right
away. When he discovered it, he cried out: 'Too soon, Ney's
acted too hastily. It will lead us to disaster.'

'This man is still the same,' stated Soult; 'like at Jena he
will compromise Your Majesty's victory.'

'Where is his support infantry?' demanded the Emperor.
'Throw it in, Soult, throw it in. God let it be that it is not
too late.'

The entire plateau of Mont St Jean was flooded with Ney's
horsemen wheeling madly around the British squares. The
squares held, three ranks of bayonets stuck out like an
evil porcupine. Only artillery, or a charge by musket-firing
infantry, could make them disintegrate. French artillery could
not fire without striking their own riders. But other guns were
in place – the entire captured English artillery park.[8]

Colonel Frazer's square stood. Though he had full confidence in his troops he doubted the Duke's wisdom of making

---

[8] It has been said that a cavalryman will not climb from his horse before he is
dead. That is perhaps the explanation why the French riders did not use the
English cannons.

a stand exposed like this, along the ridge line. The moment he saw the *cuirassiers* leap over his guns he was certain that the battle had been lost. The only question was, when would the French finally turn his own artillery pieces on the square? Strangely, they didn't. Instead, they wasted their time chasing isolated stragglers. In defiance of the attackers his soldiers stood by their three flags, the Union Jack, the King's Flag and the battalion's colour pennant. Frazer knew that should one of these banners fall, half of his unit would try to save themselves anyway they could. The square was in constant movement, stretching, bulging, reforming. As soon as a rank fired, it retreated behind the next rank to reload. The extended French lances were taking a great toll on the foot soldiers. Frazer felt a shock and a searing pain in his leg. A bone stuck through his tunic. He grabbed for the musket of a fallen soldier and used it as a crutch. Another shot had struck down a flag-bearer. With immense effort he picked up the pennant and held it up for all to see. The British soldiers did not waver. As Frazer would have to report afterwards, 'Never did cavalry behave so nobly, nor was received by infantry so firmly.'

It is always at the moment of greatest peril that the qualities of a great commander are brought forth. Wellington turned to his cavalry general, Lord Uxbridge. 'What have you got?'

'My Lord, the mounted men of Doernberg, Arenschild, Brunswick, van Merlen and Ghingy.'

'How many are still up?'

'Four, five thousand.'

'Put them in at once. Make haste before Bonaparte dispatches his infantry. We must get our cannons back, or all shall be lost.' The British cavalry mounted up to attack. In the van were the bright uniforms of the Inniskillings and the Scots Grays.

Colonel Heymès, Ney's aide, could hear the sound of an approaching tidal wave – Uxbridge's cavalry. Heymès turned his head and suddenly stared at the silent mouths of the British cannons, still lined up where his *cuirassiers* had overrun them. In the excitement following their initial success, they had completely forgotten about the abandoned guns and had made no effort to pull them off or render them useless. If Wellington's horsemen succeeded in pushing his cavalry back . . . ? Heymès looked for his superior, but Ney was busy ordering his units into line to face the onrushing British cavalry. Heymès had to act, and act quickly. '*Les clous!*' he yelled. 'Get nails and spike the guns!'

It was common practice to render the enemy's artillery pieces useless by hammering headless nails into their touch holes, and every cavalry unit had a certain number of men who carried hammers and nails in their saddle bags. 'The nails – the nails – dammit, doesn't anyone have nails?' The call went from troop to troop. More and more desperate, Heymès raced along his line of riders. '*Les clous!*'

None of his surviving riders had nails. Those who had were all dead. Only a handful of nails to put these guns out-of-action, and nothing, not even the Prussians, could have saved Wellington that day.

What took place next was the most savage and heroic clash in the annals of cavalry battle. Never before, and never thereafter, would history witness a clash of such extreme brutality by two giants: Napoleon's *Cuirassiers Imperiales* against Wellington's Heavy Brigades. Before the French cavalry were able to build up a momentum the Scots Grays and Inniskillings were upon them. During the Peninsula War these units had deservedly earned for themselves a reputation for leading the most cutting cavalry charge. The British charged headlong into the French and the sides impacted with a resounding crash of steel on steel. It opened a terrible mêlée of the *Hussars* of Arenschild, *cuirassiers* of Delort, *Black Lancers* of Brunswick, *lanciers rouges* of de Stuers, and

Dragoons of Doernberg. The storm wailed around them as if the whole land had risen up and was screaming at them, screaming with a rage that went right down to the centre of the earth. Soon the field was littered with the corpses of men and horses as the battle lost all coherence of formation and dissolved into individual combats.

Lieutenant Hamilton of the Scots Grays had such an encounter. 'One of the *lanciers rouge* put his lance to my horse's head, I made a cut at his arm as I rode past him. On inspecting my sword I saw that I had succeeded in wounding the lancer and possibly thus saved my life. My fears were, when I saw him, that he would shoot me with his pistol, having heard of the *lanciers rouge sometimes doing that.*'[9]

Cuirassier Pascal le Meunier drew his pistol and shot a passing rider in the face. Another redcoat stabbed at him with his lance and Pascal parried with his sword, hacking the enemy from the saddle. Then his helmet was struck by a terrible blow; he wavered and slowly dropped from the saddle and, rolled on the ground, his attention distracted by searing pain. He looked up just in time to watch a huge charger roaring up on its hind legs, before its steel talons came down on him.

The cavalry battle was short, but conducted with extreme violence. The French riders and their horses soon tired from their earlier uphill charge, and the freshness of the British cavalry began to tell. Ney raced up and down trying to rally his wavering men, horses were shot from under him, but he survived. All his efforts were to no avail; *les cuirassiers* had met their equals, the once invincible French cavalry was breaking up. The British infantry squares began to cheer and move forward at bayonet point, forcing the remaining *cuirassiers* from the plateau. Ney experienced the agony of responsibility. Instead of having led cavalry in support of

[9] Lieutenant Hamilton of the Scots Grays (H. T. Siborne).

infantry, he had thrown away the Emperor's most valuable *troupe* – and all that without silencing Wellington's artillery!

As so frequently happens after a moment of utter frenzy, there followed a lull while the British cavalry regrouped. Rather than engaging in another reckless charge after the fleeing French riders, and thus opening themselves to the deadly fire of massed French artillery, a bugle called the British horsemen behind their line of batteries while the gunners rushed from the squares to recover their cannons.

Then happened what had to happen. A sharp crack, a whistle, and the first cannon ball struck the retreating French cavalry. All along the line the picture was the same. One by one, like a sputtering fuse, the British guns belched yellow flame and death as they poured grapeshot and solid ball into the fleeing *cuirassiers*. With fists clenched behind his greatcoat, Napoleon had to look on as his cavalry was cut down by a torrent of cannon balls.[10]

The Iron Duke and Lord Uxbridge observed with relief the successful charge by the British cavalry. Once again, the French guns fired to cover Ney's retreat. Here occurred an incident which gave rise to one of the most famous anecdotes in military history. When a cannonball shattered Lord Uxbridge's leg, he is reported to have called out: 'By God, sir. I've lost my leg.'

To which Wellington replied: 'By God, sir. I believe you have.'

Napoleon watched Ney's debacle. 'Send in D'Erlon's infantry immediately.'

---

[10] 'The cuirassiers might have charged through the Battery as often as six or seven times, driving us into the squares, under our guns. A squadron or two came up the slope on our immediate front, and on their moving off at the appearance of our cavalry charging, we took advantage to send destruction after them ...' (Rudyard, an officer in Lloyd's battery of 9-pounders)

'*Sire*, they are still reforming.'

'Flahaut, ride to Kellermann, he is to support Ney with all he's got.'

While issuing the order he must have realised that it was already too late. But he could not afford to let Ney down and risk a general panic among his front-line troops. While Kellermann mounted up, Ney raced over to where D'Erlon was reassembling his corps. 'D'Erlon, hold fast, my friend, because if we don't die here, we only have to die by the balls of the émigrés . . .' Prophetic words these were.[11]

The confusion spread and cavalry generals took it upon themselves to repeat Ney's blunder and throw their riders into the fray. First was L'Heritier's 1st Division to charge off, then Roussel's 2nd, soon followed by Guyot and Levebvre, all with neither plan nor orders. Ten thousand horsemen, jammed together on a front-line of less than 500 metres, a field so crowded with horses that any coherent manoeuvring became impossible to execute. Instead, they presented an ideal target for massed artillery, because, by now, all of Wellington's pieces were back in action, spitting fire and death! The second cavalry attack suffered a similar fate as the one before. Only this time, they charged in bunched-up formations into the 156 guns on the ridge line. It was slaughter at its greatest.

Blücher's 2nd Cavalry Corps under Ziethen, the general with the grey pony tail and the handlebar moustache, had joined up with von Bülow's corps. The Field Marshal's infantry attacked Napoleon's Young Guard and quickly took the village of Plancenoit. The Emperor threw in a single battalion of the Old Guard. They walked through the advancing Prussians like a hundred-gun warship through a group of fishing boats. The Prussians were brought to a halt.

With the Prussians stopped, the battle took yet another

---

[11] Ney was executed in December 1815.

turn. Ney's foot troops finally carried the buildings at La Haye-Sainte. This made the British centre cave in. Ney, who had recovered from his disastrous cavalry charge, pushed his infantry columns along the Brussels road. There had never been a better moment to roll up the entire enemy line; a few extra battalions could achieve victory. If Napoleon now dispatched but a token force of *la Garde Imperiale* to support him, Ney would turn his breakthrough into a rout of the enemy. He recalled Napoleon's own dictum: '*The fate of battle is all in a single moment, a single thought . . . the single moment arrives, and the smallest reserve settles the matter.*' To this purpose, Ney dispatched his aide, Colonel Heymès, to the Emperor's HQ.

'*Votre Majesté*, the Marshal asks for infantry.'

'Infantry,' yelled the Emperor, still infuriated by Ney's earlier cavalry action, 'where do you expect me to get these? Do you think I make infantry?' He was by now heavily engaged on two fronts and had thrown most of his reserves against Blücher's black-coated Prussians. And yet, he still had on hand his fourteen élite battalions, eight of the Old Guard, and six of the Middle Guard. Had Berthier acted as his chief of staff, the man would have immediately seen the opportunity to strike, and convinced his Emperor. But Soult was no Berthier. Perhaps Napoleon was angry or tired or ill; in any case, he did nothing, and allowed his final chance to slip away.

This was the moment 'Der Alte' Blücher showed up with the bulk of his army. '*Vorwärts, meine Kinder!*' Consecutive waves of black-clad soldiers overran Plancenoit and began to push towards Napoleon's open flank at La Belle Alliance. Ziethen ordered his chief of staff, Colonel von Reiche, to join with his Corps of Cavalry at the centre of the British line.

By now Napoleon had recognised his mistake of having refused extra infantry support to Ney. But he thought he could still crush the British centre, who had suffered as severely as his own troops. Therefore, he decided to stake everything onto one card, his venerated and pampered Old Guard. 'Drouot, I want Friant to take five battalions of *grenadiers* up there.' He pointed to the shot-up windmill on Mont St Jean. Led by 150 bandsmen, playing *la marche du Carousel*, Friant brought his 6,000 *grenadiers* to La Belle Alliance where he presented them to the Emperor. Napoleon, wincing with pain, climbed on his horse and led them personally to Marshal Ney at La Haye-Sainte. 'Your infantry, *maréchal*. Take that cursed hill.'

Too little too late. General Friant formed his *Grenadiers de la Garde* into attack formation. They presented a splendid sight in their long blue greatcoats, huge epaulettes with red plumes waving from on high, and hairy bearskins. In their haversacks they carried the ceremonial uniform for a victory parade in Brussels.

'*En avant en bataille!*' And five battalions of the Garde marched alone against the English Army.

That was the moment a French officer defected to Wellington and divulged to him the Emperor's plan of attack. Wellington hadn't much left. Most of his battalions were so decimated that they had stopped being useful units. Hastily he formed new battalions from wounded and stragglers and used his last reserves to establish yet another defence line on Mont St Jean.

19.30. The French artillery fired more furiously than ever. Their thunder shook the earth. This time they did not aim too high. Wellington could see the first cannon balls strike his centre, where he had put Maitland's Guards and Adam's Light Brigade. Soon his lines were obscured by the dense black-powder smoke from his own guns.

Down the line, Captain Powell of the 1st Foot Guards watched his men being smitten down by the hail of iron pouring down on them. Shells shattered the ground, ripped limbs, blew huge gaps into his rifle formation. Horse artillery moved around aimlessly, riderless horses raced across the fields, bodies lay scattered like broken toys. The scream of the wounded was drowned by the howl of shells and the sharp crack from their own cannons. Some units had found refuge behind the shallow wall of a country road, but the majority crouched behind clumps of earth thrown up by shell impacts, or simply cowered behind the bodies of their fallen comrades. The bursting thunder was so great that it lulled Powell's men into the false security of eternal sleep. Their fingers clutched the ground, waiting for the inevitable end. How could these shell-shocked men ever repel an attack if they could not even stand up to reload their muskets? Powell had no choice. He could not pull them back. The order had come from the Duke himself: 'Die to the last man if you must, but give the Prussians time to get here.' As suddenly as it began, the bombardment ceased, the smoke cleared, and the thin English line looked upon a heart-stopping sight. The slow, methodical advance of the grenadier battalions of the Imperial Guard.

All their commanders were out front. Friant, Porret de Morvan, Harlet, Michel, Mallet, Henrion. Leading them was Ney. The knees of his horse buckled, the marshal thrown to the ground. Two *chasseurs* pulled him up. He continued his advance on foot, sword raised. The *Grenadiers de la Garde* moved with slow but deliberate steps, a stubborn, unstoppable look on their faces. Ahead of them, the mouths of the English artillery blossomed with deadly red flowers. Smoke rolled across the hillside. From the guns which Ney's cavalry had failed to spike belched canister shot, thousands of metal balls, every one a deadly missile. Gaps were beginning to show, but *la Garde's* measured step, dictated by the beat of drums, never broke. 'Close it up,' shouted their commanders, 'close it up.' They closed up and advanced. 'Double-time!' The drumbeat increased, *la Garde* accelerated its step. Then they were almost on top, in front of the English guns spitting fire.

The Belgian General Chassé raced forward with half a dozen cannons from van der Smissen's Dutch contingent, and unlimbered these at the edge of the Wavre road. There they stood, their ugly snouts silent and waiting.

The 33rd Regiment of General Colin Halkett was falling back. The general grabbed the regimental colours, trying to rally his men to the flag. Moments later he was cut down. Obscured by dense black cannon smoke waited Colonel Sir John Colborne, a tall aristocrat trained on the playing fields of Eton, whose men had given him the name 'The Fire Eater'. He wheeled his 52nd Light Infantry into parallel formation to the French columns.[12]

The 1st and 2nd Battalions of the *3me Chasseurs* had reached the crest of the plateau when, suddenly, to their flank rose a wall of red uniforms. Their muskets thundered. Three hundred *chasseurs* threw up their arms and went down.

Captain Powell of the 1st Foot Guards was almost directly in the path of the advancing French column. He saw what happened. 'They ascended the rise *au pas de charge*, shouting '*Vive l'Empereur*'. They continued to advance within fifty paces of our front when the Brigade was ordered to stand up. Whether it was the sudden and unexpected appearance of a corps so near them, which must have seemed as starting out of the ground, or the tremendously heavy fire we threw into them, *La Garde* who had never before failed in an attack suddenly stopped.[13]

Colborne's men of the 52nd rose, stormed into the smoke and, for a brief moment, were lost from view. Suddenly they found themselves a mere fifty paces from the French flank. Lieutenant Gawler was in charge of the lead company. He

---

[12] The 52nd fronted 250 men, with three more rows behind them. Which means that a total shock of 1,000 musket balls fired at a distance of 50 yards. They were supported by the 95th.

[13] From an account by Captain Powell to Major General Siborne.

could see the *Garde* stop, before he heard the crisp order by their commander.

'*Demi Bataillon de la gauche ... joue! ... feu! ...*'. *La Garde* turned as one man and fired. Their salvoes tore into Gawler's first rank. One of his old soldiers mumbled while he bit off his cartouche to reload: 'Cum'on, boys, it's now up to those who kill the most ...'

Colonel Colborne knew he could not survive another devastating salvo. He put his hat on top of his sword. 'Up, men! Up and at them!' He raced in front of his troops, straight for the middle of the enemy battalion nearest him, heard the clang of ramrods as the *grenadiers* finished their reloading. Another blast of musket fire exploded at his ear. His line faltered, his men went down rubbery and loose.

Lieutenant Gawler stumbled, his tunic stained with the blood of the boy next to him, who lay now with half of his face blown away. For a brief moment, the lieutenant hesitated, thought about the boy who had taken the ball intended for him ... there must be a special niche in heaven for a young recruit ... another volley tore into his ranks.

Now something took place which saved the 52nd from certain annihilation. Because of the 52nd's attack on their open flank, and their half-turn to the left to face the British charge, the French battalion was placed obliquely to the Dutch cannons of General Chassé. From up on the hill came a roar like the ground opening. At 200 paces General Chassé's six-cannon round of well-aimed grapeshot ripped into the closed ranks of the *grenadiers* and knocked them over like bowling pins. But they remained faithful to their motto: *La Garde* never gives in!

'52nd, with me!' shouted Colborne and picked up the colours. Lieutenant Gawler was still alive, although his hat had been blown off by a musket ball. He moved the last paces like a sleep walker, drawn on by an inner calling: *For King and Country!* Everything in front of him happened in slow motion. White smoke filled his eyes, men fell, others took their places . . . A flurry of fire broke out on his left . . . ours? theirs? . . . more and more men coming out of the smoke . . . grunts, wails, a terrible, final scream. A bayonet was thrust at his face. He parried the thrust with his sword but the bayonet glanced off and tore through his tunic. Gawler crouched down numbed. He felt something warm running down his chest before he got up and moved forward again . . . *For King and Country!* . . . Three steps in front of him a tall, bearded Imperial Guardsman, in clothes shredded by shrapnel, took a ball which doubled him over . . .

'52nd, forward!' yelled Colonel Colborne.

'We're the 71st, Sir!'

'Charge seventy-first, they will not stand . . .' The English guardsmen pounded ahead to hack at their enemy. 'No quarter! No quarter!'

The French were severely shaken. Their commanders were all dead, their columns crippled and broken . . . Ney, back on yet another horse, saw them falter and one last time he tried to rally them. He raised himself in the stirrups:

'*Mes amis, avec moi*, or watch a Marshal of France die in honour!'

He didn't die that day. Five horses had been shot from underneath him.

The opportune arrival of Ziethen's Second Prussian Cavalry Corps, which moved on La Haye-Sainte, ended it for good. Ney could no longer stop the inevitable and the incredible happened: *La Garde Imperiale* retreated!

The moan swept like a wave through the French Army: 'We are betrayed. *Sauve qui peut!*' Napoleon watched the battle dissolve into a nightmare. His proud army was coming apart, turning into limping clots of men in tattered clothes and blackened faces with a few Imperial Eagles, not carried proudly but used as crutches by the wounded. While up on the distant crest, near a gnarled elm tree, he saw a solitary figure before he heard enemy troops raise their muskets to cheer that man . . .

For the first time since the beginning of battle, Wellington spurred his horse to the edge of the plateau. There, in view of all, he raised his hat and slowly moved it forward, towards the French. *The signal!* His whole line rose. Forty-thousand men, that multi-national force Napoleon had derided as 'a polyglot rabble', led by Vivian's hussars and Vandeleur's dragoons, advanced down a pock-marked and blood-covered slope.

Napoleon ordered that his last six battalions make a final stand, but his fate was sealed. The *1er Grenadiers* of the Imperial Guard, *l'élite de l'élite*, formed up in three squares around their Emperor. Wellington ordered that the cannons be brought up which, unbelievably as it might have seemed to Napoleon at this point, had been in French hands for almost an hour. The guns were placed at sixty yards from the French squares.

A moment of bleak silence . . . Heavenly Father . . . *Mon Dieu* . . . *Lieber Gott* . . . British and Hannoverians, Belgians and Dutch, joined by Blücher's Prussians, surrounded the remnants of Napoleon's Empire. *Le Bataillon Sacré* of the Imperial Old Guard would not yield. Until the very end they remained faithful to the oath given to their Emperor.

La Garde meurt mais ne se rend pas – The Guard dies but does not surrender. General Cambronne, the commander of *La Garde Imperiale*, astride his horse inside the square of the *1er Chasseurs Imperiales*, was asked by Wellington to surrender. Cambronne replied with heroic brutality: '*Merde!*'[14] His grenadiers stared with final defiance at the gaping mouths of the British cannons. They knew what to expect when

---

[14] In French colloquial use this expression is known as 'the word of Cambronne'.

Wellington dropped his hat. Their squares dissolved in smoke and thunder . . .

The Battle of Waterloo was over. In darkness, while the British band played 'God Save the King', and the Prussians sang '*Lieber Gott Wir Loben Dich*', an ageing field marshal met an Iron Duke. Blücher leaned from his horse to embrace Wellington.

'*Mein lieber Kamerad,*' he said quietly, '*quelle affaire!*'[15]

7,000 Prussians, 15,000 English, and 25,000 Frenchmen lay dead on the ground. Perhaps the drama was best expressed in a dispatch by Wellington after surveying the battle field.

'*Nothing but a battle lost can be so melancholy as a battle won.*'

What if . . .

What if – Blücher had been killed when he fell from his horse at Ligny, and Gneisenau had gone through with his plan to withdraw the Prussian Army towards Liège?

Without the Prussians, Wellington would have been smashed.

What if – Grouchy had acted on reports by his scouts instead

[15] After the battle, the old Marshal Blücher sent two letters. The first went to his wife:

Genappes, 19 Junius 1815. Schlachtfeld by Belle Alliance.
Was ich versprochen habe ich gehalten, den 16. Junius wurde ich gezwungen der Gewalt zu weichen; de 18. habe ich in Verbindung meines Freundes Wellington Napoleon den Garaus gemacht. Wo er hingekommen weiss kein Mensch.

The second was Blücher's political testament. It went to his king.

Wavre, 24 Junius 1815.
'*Ich bitte alleruntänigst Ew. Majestät, die Diplomaten dahin anzuweisen, dass sie nicht wieder das verlieren, was der Soldat mit seinem Blut errungen hat.*' 'I ask most humbly Your Majesty to instruct the diplomats not to lose this time what the soldier has won with his blood.'

of chasing two decoy divisions, or had listened to
Gérard, to head for the noise of guns?
It would have stopped the Prussians from coming
to Wellington's aid.[16]

What if – Delort's riders could have produced a fistful of nails
and successfully spiked Wellington's guns?
The English artillery would have been out of action,
and nothing – not even the Prussians – could have
saved Wellington that day.

What if – Napoleon had been victorious at Waterloo?
He would have lost another day.

The facts

Waterloo, though certainly the single most decisive battle of
the Napoleonic Wars, changed little.

In 1805, Britain had already established its maritime supremacy
with the decisive victory at Trafalgar, and from then on
England became the bankers of the world. For the next
hundred years, their *Pax Britannica* ruled supreme.

In 1806, the 800-year-old Holy Roman Empire collapsed
with the abdication of Emperor Francis II of Austria. It was
replaced by a loose German Confederation of forty sovereign
states, all under the tutelage of an emerging military power,
Prussia.

At Jena and Auerstaedt, Napoleon destroyed the last ves-
tiges of European feudalism. From it emerged the present-day

---

[16] In his memoires, Napoleon states: 'Marshal Grouchy, with 34,000 men and 108
guns, had discovered a secret which seemed impossible, of being neither on the
battlefield at Mont St Jean nor at Wavre.'
    What was Grouchy's defence to the accusations? 'Inspiration in war is
appropriate only to the commander-in-chief, and his lieutenants must confine
themselves to executing orders.'

European nationalism, which, seven years later, in 1813, during the Battle of Nations at Leipzig, destroyed him.

Waterloo merely put the seal to Napoleon's fall.

The French Revolution destroyed the Old World. Napoleon rebuilt a New One. Whether we like it or not, our Present Age dates from him. When a brilliant deed lasts that long, and bears so much fruit, it carries its justification in itself . . .

The Hinge Factor at Waterloo is almost too ironical. A handful of headless nails and a few hammers could have made the difference.

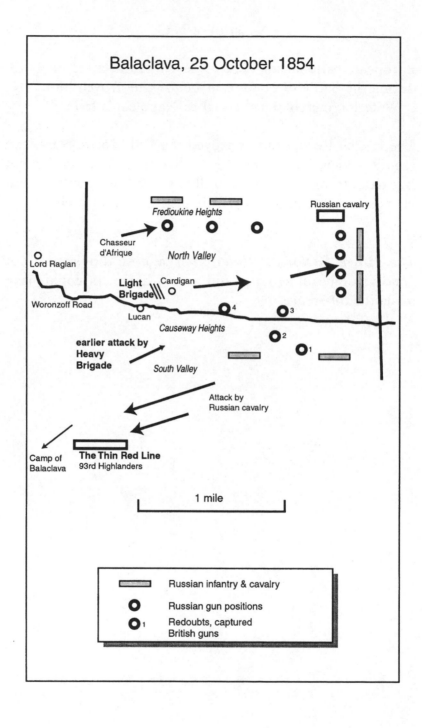

Balaclava, 25 October 1854

Fredioukine Heights

Russian cavalry

Chasseur
d'Afrique

North Valley

Lord Raglan

**Light
Brigade**

Cardigan

Woronzoff Road

Lucan

4

3

Causeway Heights

**earlier attack by
Heavy
Brigade**

2

1

South Valley

Attack by
Russian cavalry

Camp of
Balaclava

The Thin Red Line
93rd Highlanders

1 mile

Russian infantry & cavalry

Russian gun positions

Redoubts, captured
British guns

6

The Fourth Order

Balaclava, 25 October 1854

'Theirs not to reason why,
Theirs but to do and die,
Into the Valley of Death rode the six hun-
dred.'

Alfred, Lord Tennyson, 1809–1892

It was a splendid autumn day, that 25th of October. Spread out in front of the observers on top of the mountain was the South Valley, bathed in sunshine. Two cavalry formations faced each other. One was huge and grey, the Russians. The other was red and tiny, the British Heavy Brigade of General Scarlett. The clash was imminent. The small red unit suddenly did the unexpected, they wheeled uphill – and attacked!

Only 500 metres from the open flank of the Russian cavalry sat another body of horsemen, the Light Brigade, inactive and cursing. A few days before, Lord Lucan had dispatched a circular:

'The chief duties of the Light Brigade are to ensure the safety of the Army from all surprises. It is not their duty needlessly, without authority, to engage the enemy and on no account should any party attack or pursue, unless specially instructed to do so.'

That's why the commander of the Light Brigade, Lord Cardigan, remained idle and did nothing. To act on his own initiative never even occurred to him. And so, his Six Hundred sat at bay, and watched idly the white-moustached General Scarlett draw his sword to lead his 300 Heavies in a suicidal attack against a packed mass of 5,000 Russian cavalry.

It was eleven o'clock in the morning.

In retrospect it can be truly stated about the Crimean War of 1854, that the sheer stupidity of the commanders increased in direct proportion to their rank. To lead élite units of the British cavalry it took only two qualifications, title and money. The cavalry was commanded by Lord Lucan, who possessed neither the intelligence nor the experience. To put his brother-in-law, Lord Cardigan, under his direct orders was the summit of stupidity. Their dislike towards each other was only matched by their arrogance towards their troops, and an obsession for glittering uniforms, medals and glory.

The only positive thing which can be said about the Commander-in-Chief, Lord Raglan,[1] is that he never got involved in directing any part of the action. He preferred to observe each battle as a distant spectator. Although at war with Russia, he kept referring to his allies, the French, as *the enemy*. These three key players were to lead the Light Brigade to its total destruction. Afterwards, Victorian poets found it necessary to put the emphasis on heroism, and fudge the incompetence of military leadership.

[1] Lord Raglan served as a subaltern under Wellington at Waterloo. He still lived in an age of bayonet charges *á la Napoléon*. Science and mechanisation, sweeping Europe, was absent from his mind. His only reading was the *The Count of Monte Cristo* (C. Hibbert).

It took a hundred years before the *Encyclopaedia Britannica* stated: '*The Crimean War must be considered as the worst conducted military campaign in British history.*'

The key to Balaclava was control over the Causeway Heights and the strategic Woronzoff road which led directly to the Allied encampment. The defences on this series of hills had been strengthened against Russian surprise attacks by six redoubts, armed with 12-pounder cannons. These redoubts were spaced along the spine of the Causeway Heights which separated two distinct depressions, the South Valley and the North Valley.

Earlier in the morning of October 25th, 11,000 Russian infantry with thirty-eight guns had advanced on the redoubts. Lord Lucan, the cavalry commander, drafted an urgent note to Lord Raglan. Other than reading the note, the Commander-in-Chief did little else, and his only observation was: 'Very well, pray inform Lord Lucan if there's anything new to report back to me.'

Lord Raglan suffered from a fixed idea that this attack was only a feint, that the main force Russian infantry was still inside Sebastopol, and that Prince Menschikoff's[2] real intent was to attack only those of the Allied troops that besieged his fortress. Thus, Raglan remained a passive spectator to the upcoming battle. From the platform on his *Feldherrnhügel*, surrounded by his aides and the wives of some of the British officers who had joined their husbands for the campaign on their personal yachts, and one journalist, William Howard Russell[3] of *The Times*, Lord Raglan looked down on both

[2] Prince Menschikoff, Russian Commander-in-Chief. For him, Sebastopol was the climax to a disastrous diplomatic and military career.
[3] William Howard Russel's dispatches to the London *Times* is the best source of information for the events at Balaclava. Even today, he is still considered the greatest war correspondent of all times. It reminds people of my trade (I was a war correspondent) – so often considered by the military as 'professional voyeurs' – that we are not invisible, and that the impact of the events we report outlasts the next day's edition.

valleys, sharply divided by the shadows of the morning sun. Creeping along the valley floor like an army of ants, enemy regiments approached Raglan's six gun positions on the Causeway Heights.

The 1,000 Turks of the Allied Force, holding these redoubts, suddenly faced a huge mass of Russian infantry advancing on them, without the slightest move by the British cavalry to come to their rescue. Soon the Russians were flooding across the last ditch into four of the redoubts, killing a few Turks while the rest ran away, yelling, 'Ship, ship!' With great dismay Lord Raglan had to watch as the Russians took possession of seven British 12 pounders, a fact which was to play a substantial role in the ensuing calamity.

George Paget, another lord, who commanded the Light Brigade in the absence of Lord Cardigan, withdrew his unit and took up a tactical position at the end of the Causeway Heights. He expected to see action as soon as this mass of Russians started its predictable move on Balaclava. The situation was grave, serious enough for Lord Cardigan to interrupt breakfast on his yacht in Balaclava harbour and ride up to join his unit.

With the fall of four of his redoubts, the Allied Commander-in-Chief finally had incontrovertible evidence that the target of the enemy was indeed his encampment at Balaclava. Lord Raglan issued the *first* of four orders: '*Cavalry to take ground to left of second line of redoubts occupied by Turks.*'

Lord Lucan didn't know what to make of the order. There was no second line of redoubts other than the two gun positions still held by the Turks. Removing his cavalry from their covering position on the high ground of the Causeway opened the entrance into the Balaclava gorge, as well as cancelling out all protection for the soldiers of the 93rd Argyle & Sutherland Highlanders, the only force in place to stop 11,000 Russians from rolling down on the Allied camp. Lucan was so angry that he ordered Raglan's dispatch rider to stay on and watch while he executed the order, so he wouldn't be blamed for the obvious debacle afterwards. He withdrew his brigade and left the door open. Between the Russian Army and disaster stood 550 Highlanders, plus 100 invalids dragged from their beds, propped up against rocks and handed a weapon, and a few Turks who had fled from the redoubts and were highly unreliable. Slowly, the huge mass of Russians began to march down on them. 'Highlanders,' ordered their colonel, Sir Colin Campbell, 'you cannot retreat, you must die where you stand.'

Four cavalry squadrons bore down on Campbell's small force. This cavalry attack so frightened the already shell-shocked Turks that they threw down their rifles and ran for their lives. To the Russian cavalry, cresting the last ridge, the entrance into the Balaclava Gorge seemed wide open, when, all of a sudden, out of the ground popped a double line of red-coated Highlanders and made history as *the thin red streak topped with a line of steel*.[4] The Scots were determined to sell their lives dearly. The Russians were puzzled, reigned in their horses, and stopped. A deadly volley of musket fire brought down heaps of Russian cavalry, followed immediately by a second volley. More horses and riders came down. The Russians were confused, the Highlanders agitated, panting as they stormed uphill with fixed bayonets. Their colonel had to restrain them: 'Hold on, Ninety-third. Damn all that eagerness.'

A third, well-aimed volley broke the Russian cavalry which fled in disorder, chased by the triumphant shouts of the Highlanders.[5] The thin Red Line held and their brief action became immortal. However, it was only a side action to the one to follow. Balaclava was still endangered by the

[4] W. H. Russell, *The Times Dispatches*.
[5] In 1858, Sir Colin Campbell by then Lord Clyde, led on the same troops at the relief of Lucknow in India, with a 'Remember Balaclava'.

main force of Russian cavalry. Since the leaders of both armies were equally incompetent, neither side had sent out scout patrols and their main forces were about to bump into each other as in some accidental road crash.

Lord Raglan had positioned himself so far from the action that it took his dispatch riders about half an hour to convey his orders. Also, by placing himself on the heights above the valleys, on a kind of balcony, it robbed him of any perspective of the terrain; what looked to him flat and dry was, in fact, hillocky and soggy. He now issued his *second* order: '*Eight squadrons of Heavy Dragoons to be detached towards Balaclava to support the Turks who are wavering.*'

By the time this message reached the commander of the Heavies, the 'wavering Turks' he was ordered to support had fled the battlefield and were trying to climb aboard any available vessel in the harbour. General Scarlett, a man with a red face and a monumental white moustache, whose good-natured behaviour was in contrast to that of the arrogant earls, obeyed Raglan's order. But this move took his troops straight across the path of the advancing main force of Russian cavalry. Scarlett was left with no option but to perform one of the great feats of cavalry against cavalry, just as Lord Uxbridge before him had achieved in his crushing charge against Ney's *cuirassiers* at Waterloo.

The Russian horsemen outnumbered him by at least ten to one. Four thousand Russians versus 300 Brits. Scarlett drew his sabre and ordered his riders to charge in line – uphill! The Russians were so surprised by the sheer audacity of this unorthodox manoeuvre that their bugler sounded a halt. It put the Russians into the most unfavourable position any cavalry could find itself in: to sustain a charging impact while stopped. It is the very principle of any mobile-force, such as cavalry, that it is only effective while on the move. The Scots Grays and the Inniskillings,[6] led by a furiously sword-waving General Scarlett, crashed into the Russian line and found themselves immediately swamped by the mass of Russian horsemen. For the observers on the high ground an incredible spectacle began to unfold. The red coats of the British were everywhere, small islets of hacking, slashing fury. And yet, they never fell nor wavered, their battle cries could be clearly heard, everyone gone berserk with pistol and sabre. Scarlett's second line, the 5th Heavy Dragoons, crashed into the mêlée, chopping their way into the confused mass of grey Russian uniforms. The Russian cavalry began to break up. The opportune moment had been reached for a decisive final charge. The Heavy Brigade had no more reserves, every single one was engaged in hand-to-hand combat. Meanwhile, the 600 riders of the Light Brigade stood idly by and watched the battle from a mere 500 yards, a minute on a galloping horse. Their charge never materialised. They were sitting in their saddles, watching the action, furious and impotent while their commander, Lord Cardigan, couldn't be persuaded to act without higher orders.

Later he was to defend his inactivity with the earlier orders from his superior. 'The Lieutenant-General the Earl of Lucan has ordered me that on no account am I to leave my position, and only to defend it against attack by the Russians. The Russians did not attack.'

This showed that the man was not only incapable, but dangerously stupid as well. Part of his Brigade were the 17th Lancers who had a commander of great talent and courage, Captain Morris, a graduate from the Royal Military College.[7] Because of his squat figure his men had bestowed upon him the honorary title of 'Pocket Hercules'.

---

[6] By pure coincidence, again side by side as at Waterloo.
[7] Morris wrote in his diary: 'The more I see of Lord Lucan, and Lord Cardigan, the more I find them despicable. What ignorance, but what arrogance!'

He was immensely popular with his troop, as was his closest friend, Captain Edward Nolan. Both had already participated in four cavalry charges, and both held their arrogant commanders in utter contempt. A cavalry officer's talent lay in assessing a rapidly developing situation and striking at the opportune moment. From the Middle Ages through to Napoleon, every great leader had passed on that principle. Neither Lucan nor Cardigan possessed such talents. As the Russians began to flee Captain Morris rode up to Cardigan: 'My lord, is the Brigade not going to charge the fleeing enemy?'

'No. My orders are to remain in position.'

'But, sir, it is our positive duty to follow up on this advantage.'

'No, sir. I will not break my orders', repeated the Third Earl of Cardigan.

'Then allow me, my lord, to take my 17th Lancers and charge the enemy. You can see they are in disorder.'

'No, sir! You will do no such thing!' replied the lord in a haughty tone, obviously upset by his subordinate's insistence. Morris, in great rage, turned to some of the staff officers present. 'Gentlemen, you are witness to my request', he managed to spit out through clenched teeth. A private of the 17th, standing nearby, said out loud what all of them felt: 'My God, what a chance we're losing! We're goin' to pay for it!'

The mangled Russians made their escape across the Causeway. They finally stopped to unlimber their horse artillery at the end of the North Valley. At the close of the victorious action, Lord Lucan sent a rebuke to Lord Cardigan for not having come to the support of the Heavy Brigade, an argument which was hotly fought out over the years to come in the columns of *The Times*. Scarlett's amazing feat had changed the outlook of the battle. Lord Raglan now saw the opportunity to recover the redoubts, and, with it, his prized cannons. He sent Lord Lucan the *third* order: '*Cavalry to advance and take advantage of any opportunity to recover the Heights. They will be supported by infantry, which has been ordered to advance on two fronts.*'

There was a major problem with the wording of that order. When it reached Lord Lucan, the text was spelled differently. After the word 'ordered' followed a full stop. The next word, 'advance' was written with a capital 'A', thus, it actually told Lucan that *his cavalry was to advance on two fronts* with both Heavy and Light Brigades. Furthermore, Lord Lucan understood that he was to recover the redoubts *with support infantry which has been ordered*. He waited for half an hour, but no infantry showed up. To charge without infantry would amount to recklessness. His men of the Heavy Brigade, still under the impulse of their earlier victory, were getting restless, they wanted to move but Lucan held them back. That moment a new element was added to the drama. One of Raglan's aides spotted movement in the lost redoubts.

'By Jove, they're going to take away my guns', exclaimed Lord Raglan. Losing guns would be valid proof for a Russian victory. (Actually, the Russians were only shifting the captured artillery pieces to place them in position for the expected attack.) Therefore, Raglan dictated a quick order to his aide, General Airey. The general scribbled a pencilled note.[8]

It was to become the fateful *fourth* order: '*Lord Raglan wishes the cavalry to advance rapidly to the front – follow the enemy and try to prevent the enemy carrying away the guns. Troop Horse Artillery may accompany. French Cavalry is on your left. Immediate. (signed) R. Airey.*'

Airey handed this scribbled order to his aide, Captain

[8] This order still exists today.

Leslie, the designated dispatch rider. Fate intervened in the person of Captain Edward Nolan. The same Captain Nolan who, with his friend 'Pocket Hercules' Morris, held utter contempt for the 'conceited earls'. He grabbed for the note, and, before anyone could stop him, drove his charger towards the path leading into the North Valley. As he was about to race down the steep descent, Lord Raglan called after him: 'Captain, inform Lord Lucan the cavalry *is to attack immediately.*'

Any other man would have given thought and changed the events to come. Not so Captain Nolan, a man obsessed by ambition and raging over the shameless inactivity of the Light Brigade during the heroic charge by the Heavy Brigade. Nolan was a headstrong man with reckless courage. He rode up to the earl he so deeply despised – 'that plumed peacock incapable of independent decision' – sitting stiffly in his dress uniform in front of the two brigades. 'Lord Raglan's orders, sir.' He handed the pencilled note to Lord Lucan. The earl read the order and it left him completely perplexed. Since he was placed on the bottom of the valley, and did not benefit from the bird's-eye view as did Raglan, he couldn't see the redoubts, nor a single Russian soldier along the North Valley. He certainly did not see any cannons to be recovered as specified by Raglan's order. While he read it, and twirled his handlebar moustache, Nolan sat beside him, boiling with impatience and fury. Finally the captain could no longer contain his anger. His face twitched and his words shivered with hate: 'My lord, the Lord Raglan's final orders were that the cavalry *is to attack immediately.*'

With a look of unmitigated arrogance the lord looked at his subordinate: 'Attack, sir? Attack what guns, sir?'

Fate is not something that is chosen, it just happens and affects man's life and death. Fate is the event whose occurrence depends entirely on the will of other people.

Such as a stupid order, and such as men stupid enough to carry it out. Or, as was the case at this instant, a haughtiness of words arousing a spiteful reply. All the elements necessary for a military disaster were present: an arrogant earl, a garbled order, and a hot-headed captain. Edward Nolan, the brilliant cavalry man, who had been the impotent bystander to a lost opportunity – and that due to the inactivity of his idiotic commander, another puffed-up earl – allowed fury to overtake reason. The highly decorated officer of an élite cavalry regiment brought up his arm and pointed straight ahead, not towards the lost British guns inside the four Causeway redoubts, but towards the end of the valley, into the mouth of Prince Menschikoff's massed artillery.

'There is your enemy. There are your guns.'

With a single sentence, an excited officer sealed the doom of the Light Brigade. Nolan wheeled his horse away from Lord Lucan and joined his friend, Captain Morris of the 17th Lancers. They started an animated conversation, but Morris never revealed what their talk was about. Until the end of his life he defended his belief that Edward Nolan had passed on to Lord Lucan the instructions in the same way as they had been called out to him by Lord Raglan.

Lord Lucan faced a dilemma, one he wasn't prepared to solve by his own initiative. He stuck to Queen's Regulations, and these were quite explicit: '... orders sent by aides-de-camp are to be obeyed with the same readiness as if delivered personally by the general officer who issued these ...'

Lucan, straightened his tunic, shrugged his shoulders and trotted off to see Lord Cardigan, sitting in front of his Light Brigade. It was the first time since the beginning of the Crimean Campaign that the Third Earl of Lucan directly addressed the man he so despised, the Seventh Earl of Cardigan.

'Lord Cardigan, the Light Brigade is to advance up the North Valley. The Heavy Brigade will follow your brigade.'

Both Lucan and Cardigan must have realised that this order was tantamount to sacrificing the English Cavalry. Had it not been for the consummate hatred between the two earls, had they discussed the order instead of staring each other down, perhaps the Light Brigade could have been saved. Eventually Cardigan said: 'Sir, allow me to point out to you that the Russians have a battery in the valley to our front, and batteries and riflemen on both sides.'

'I know it,' answered Lucan with a shrug of his shoulder, 'but Lord Raglan will have it.'

Lord George Paget, Cardigan's second-in-command, couldn't believe his ears. This was sheer insanity, sending cavalry, unsupported by infantry, into a horseshoe of massed artillery. He had just lit a precious cigar, should he put it out? 'The hell,' he said to himself, 'I might as well enjoy my last smoke.'

Cardigan came riding towards him. 'Lord George, we are ordered to attack to the front. You will take the second line, and I expect your best support.'

'You shall have it, my lord.' With which he clamped his teeth on his precious cigar and wheeled to form up his line, the 4th Light Dragoons and the 8th Hussars.

At the same time, Cardigan formed his first line of attack. The 11th Hussars, the 13th Light Dragoons and the 17th Lancers. At the last moment, the 11th Hussars were pulled back to form a third line. Lord Cardigan placed himself in the van, drew his sword and ordered in a clear voice: 'The Brigade will advance – walk – march – trot.'

In perfect order of parade, the Light Brigade began their ride into the Valley of Death.

*   *   *

A hush descended over the battlefield. There were no shots and there were no hurrahs. Just silence. To the British soldiers lined up on the ridge to watch the spectacle of a precision advance of the three lines, this presented an incredible sight. As it did for the Russian officers – perhaps, just for a moment, they wondered what must go on in the mind of commander who led his unit to certain destruction.[9]

Along the Fedioukine Heights, on the left flank of the Light Brigade, the Russians had placed eight battalions of infantry, four cavalry squadrons, and fourteen cannons. Flanking the Brigade's right were the redoubts, manned by eleven Russian battalions and thirty guns, plus an additional battery of field artillery. At the end of the valley waited the concentrated mass of Russian cavalry, backed up by twelve pieces of heavy artillery. Against such massive array rode a force of 673 lightly armed men. In front rode Lord Cardigan. This was to be the greatest day of his fifty-seven years on earth. He may not have been possessed of great intelligence, but he certainly made up for it in courage. Stiff as a board he sat in his saddle, a resplendent figure in his cherry-colour and royal blue uniform with fur-trimmed collar and great ostrich plume on his cocked hat.

The silence was shattered by the crack from a Russian gun. Soon shells began to fall in ever-increasing number, cutting riders to pieces. Captain Morris felt naked and exposed, 'like some beetle creeping along the valley floor'. He threw furtive glances at the hills. All around them, behind rocks and shrubs, were the Russians. At that moment, an incident occurred which was never explained. Captain Nolan, riding alongside Captain Morris, suddenly spurred on his charger. Morris called out: 'That won't do Nolan!' But Nolan dashed

---

[9] The disaster was brought about by a lack of communication between five key players: Raglan, Airey, Lucan, Cardigan, and the impetuous Nolan.

ahead, then wheeled his charger across the first line of the Brigade and, in an unprecedented breach of military etiquette, crossed in front of Lord Cardigan. The earl was livid, while Nolan waved his sabre and screamed like a madman. His words were drowned out by the explosions. What really went on in Nolan's head we shall never know. The most likely explanation is that he became suddenly beset by guilt and, realising the terrible blunder he had committed by directing his comrades to certain death, tried to turn the Brigade around. Shrapnel of a shell tore into his chest. With a wide gash in his uniform which exposed his heart, he kept on screaming and clung to the reins of his horse. It bore him clear through the line of the advancing riders before the horse came to a halt and Edward Nolan slid dead from the saddle.

The Brigade had reached the halfway mark of the valley. Russian guns opened up from both sides. Their salvoes struck down the targets offered to them by the measured step of the perfect lines. Captain Morris felt the hairs on the back of his neck standing on end. Never before had he experienced anything so terrifying – shells bursting in front, at the back, in their midst; musket balls zinging through the air, striking men and beast. He looked over his shoulder. His men were right behind him, moving forward through thick clouds of smoke, erupting soil, clumps of earth and riders flung high into the air. He felt quite helpless, his instinct telling him to dash ahead as fast as his horse would carry him. To get out of the murderous crossfire and ride into the frontal guns represented the lesser of two evils. But Cardigan wouldn't give the order to charge. Morris rode up to his commander. 'My lord, we must charge or suffer the heaviest of casualties.'

'Yes, sir, I think you are right. But those are Lord Lucan's commands. Steady as they go, tell your men to close ranks and ride to your front.' Perhaps it was this slow, deliberate, parade ground advance that led to the immortality of the *Charge of the Light Brigade.*

Lord Raglan, from his observation post high on the hill, watched this madness in horror. He couldn't understand what was going on in the minds of these men before him. He thought his orders had been quite specific: recapture the guns on the redoubts! And now this insane charge into three-sided artillery! He could see the flash and twinkle of sabres amidst the bursting shells. Officers around him burst into tears. The final word must go to French General Bosquet, who observed: 'C'est magnifique – mais ce n'est pas la guerre.'

More shells fell and more gaps appeared in the lines. More men fell. Lord Lucan, who had followed the Light Brigade with his Heavy Brigade, finally ordered a halt to the Heavies' advance.

'They've already sacrificed the Light Brigade, they shall not have the Heavy Brigade too. The only thing we can do is to protect the Light Brigade on their return.' And so, the Heavies looked on in horror as their friends disappeared into the smoke at the end of the valley.

The French General Morris couldn't watch the massacre any longer. Acting on his own, he led his *Chasseurs d'Afrique* in an attack against the Russian guns on the Fediouskine Heights. His wild Atlas Mountain warriors succeeded brilliantly and the cannon and musket fire into the left flank of Cardigan's men ceased. The first line of the Brigade had almost reached the end of the valley and the line of the Russian artillery. There was only a second or so to take in the scene, but one detail registered clearly: the mouths of the cannons were gaping black holes . . . There was no time to be frightened and there was no choice but to continue forward. Without orders, the surviving riders broke into full charge, bent low over the necks of their horses. They wielded their sabres and screamed their defiance. More fell, riderless horses dashed across the line of advance, were pushed aside. Then there was a tremendous, earsplitting roar as all the guns fired at once. Horses stumbled and men died. The second line, with Lord Paget furiously clamping his cigar between his teeth, rode over the dead and those not quite dead, giving Lord Cardigan 'his best support'. Paget's horse was hit, blood gushed from its side, but it stumbled forward. The young lord was surrounded by riderless horses. Bullets zinged through the air, guns belched yellow flame, and still the men of the Light Brigade went on. Still the crash of shells and yells of 'Close in! Close in! Head for the centre!' Canister shot took down whole lines of riders; the boom of guns drowned out the thunder of galloping hooves. Lord Cardigan was ahead of everybody. They were now less than a hundred yards from the mouths of the guns. Eighty yards . . . seventy . . . sixty . . . perhaps they could make it after all. A blast of heat and a roar rolled over them as all twelve cannons fired again. The first line of riders dissolved, blasted out of their saddles or buried beneath their horses. The second line drove into the smoke and stench. They fought like wild cats, but never had a chance in the face of the overwhelming mass of Russian cavalry and infantry advancing on them.

Surprisingly, Captain Morris was still in the saddle. His eyes smarted from the dense powder smoke, he couldn't see Cardigan or any of the rest of the Brigade. His mind was transfixed by the wild lunge over the row of smoking guns. With blood singing in his ears and his sabre held high, he began to ride around aimlessly. He tried to think of what had happened, why he, of all his men, was still alive, and what would now happen on their way back. There was but one thing to do for an honourable gentleman whom fate had placed in such a cruel position. Round up what was left of his decimated 17th Lancers and lead them from the inferno.

That's when he noticed a large body of Russian cavalry moving in on them. 'Seventeenth, with me!' Twenty riders, that's all there was left of his Seventeenth! With these twenty he charged straight into the advancing Russians. He gave off a howl like a wolf, hacking and cursing with every blow. Colonel Mayow had collected a few more survivors of the 13th Light Dragoons and came to his assistance. Together they pushed the Russians back from the gun battery. Next came Lord Paget and crashed with what was left of his 11th Hussars into the mêlée. They hit the Russians in the flank and drove them from the field. The 4th Light Dragoons fell on the Russian gunners and cut them down. This finally silenced the guns. While these isolated actions took place, a huge Russian force was advancing on the 11th Hussars and the British had to beat a hasty retreat. Lord George Paget stopped the flight. 'Halt front, my boys! If you don't halt front we're done for.' They obeyed as one man. The remainder of the 11th and the 4th joined together, a mere seventy. A trooper shouted: 'They're attacking from the back, my lord.' Lord George asked: 'What the devil shall we do? Has anybody seen the Lord Cardigan?'

Cardigan had led the attack, survived, and then ridden back. In his splendid uniform he crossed at twenty paces in front of 500 Russian horsemen. Their commander, Prince Radziwil, recognised the lord and prevented his Cossacks from cutting him down. Cardigan managed to dash away from them. He had no idea what fate had befallen the remainder of his Light Brigade. He felt no responsibility for the disaster, he had done his duty and 'led the Brigade with due impetus'.

What men there were still able to ride, walk or stumble were now completely cut off, with the Russian masses at front and back. The length of the valley floor was covered with British dead and dying, the guns from the redoubts on the Causeway continued to harass the staggering survivors.

Captain Morris ran the gauntlet and led his remaining handful to the back where they were met by the Heavy Brigade.

Meanwhile, Cardigan rode up to General Scarlett and launched into a series of accusations, not against the order by Lord Raglan, but against the affront he had suffered from Captain Nolan. 'The gall of that man, what insubordination, riding out in front of me, screaming like a mad woman.' At which point Scarlett held up his hand and stopped him. 'My lord, you've just ridden over Captain Nolan's body.'

The retreat was even more terrible than the advance. Horses leaked blood like sieves, men with terrible wounds staggered across the valley floor, being picked off by sharpshooters. Then came the Russian cavalry. Fortunately, in the confusing situation they came under fire from their own guns and retired. Only seventy of Lord Paget's 11th Hussars and 4th Light Dragoons managed to escape encirclement, by charging their exhausted horses into the Russian Lancers. Fifteen of the decimated 17th Lancers joined a handful of 13th Light Dragoons and dashed hell-bent through the midst of Russian infantry.[10] When the Russians saw them coming they panicked and yelled: 'Ghosts.' Thus the last of the Brigade benefited from the surprise of their breakthrough.

'What a scene of havoc was this last mile,' Lord Paget was to write later that evening, 'strewn with the dead and wounded – all of them my friends.'

Then a much reported encounter took place. Lord George Paget, on his way back from the cannons and the slaughter, met up with the Earl of Cardigan, riding up from the opposite direction. Paget was furious, and for good reason. After having been ordered by Cardigan

[10] At the end of the retreat, the 17th Lancers of Captain Morris were down to thirty-seven, while the 13th Light Dragoons counted eight survivors.

to give his 'best support', he now saw his commander approaching him from the rear.

'Hallooh, Lord Cardigan. I say, were you not there?'

'Oh, wasn't I though!'

This brief exchange, overheard by troopers and passed on to a journalist covering the war, gave rise to a persistent rumour that Cardigan had not been in on the charge. This was unjust. He had been there, but once he saw that his brigade was lost, he simply rode off without a backward glance.

Of the 673 riders who had gone down the valley, 195 returned, and many more died of their wounds owing to lack of proper medical care.[11]

From the moment Lord Cardigan had ordered *'The Brigade will advance!'*, the action had lasted a mere twenty minutes, but twenty minutes which were to go down in history as *The Charge of the Light Brigade'*.

. . . Or, in an immortal poem honouring their bravery:

> *'Someone had blundered:*
> *Theirs not to make reply,*
> *Theirs not to reason why,*
> *Theirs but to do and die,*
> *Into the Valley of Death rode the six hun-*
> *dred.'*

What if . . .

What if – the *fourth order* had been more specific?

> Lord Lucan would have probably understood its true intent and not engaged in a cavalry action without infantry support.

---

[11] Portrayed by Errol Flynn and David Niven in Michael Curtiz' film, *'The Charge of the Light Brigade'*.

What if – Lord Lucan's behaviour had been less arrogant
     towards the impetuous Captain Nolan?
     TheLightBrigadewouldhaveattackedtheredoubts,
     recovered the British cannons, and Victorian poets
     would have been robbed of the material for a
     drama.

The facts

The rest of the Crimean Campaign bears witness to the
blatant incompetence of its leaders. From October 1854
to April 1855 no more major action occurred. And yet,
in this period, the Allies suffered 18,000 casualties. They
died not from Russian bullets, but from starvation, cholera
and the cold.[12] Although 9,000 greatcoats were in storage at
Balaclava, these were never issued to the men. As specified
in Queen's Rules, a soldier was only allowed one greatcoat
every three years . . . thus they died – like forty years before
them Napoleon's *Grande Armée*, or ninety years thereafter
the armies of Hitler – all victims of the Russian winter.[13]
     Upon their return to London, Lord Lucan and Lord
Cardigan were severely attacked by the press, a storm
which led to a military inquiry. In July 1856, a panel of
generals, which many called 'The White Washing Board',
exonerated the two lords. Lord Raglan managed to put all
blame on his aide's badly worded fourth order. And General
Airey, the man who scribbled the fourth order, spoke the
epitaph on the fateful charge: 'These sort of things will
happen in war.'

---

[12] Florence Nightingale drew the scandal of the squalid conditions to the attention
of the public, and the Crimea Campaign led to the creation of the International
Red Cross.
     '. . . for the thousand and more who suffer from diarrhoea and dysentery there
are only twenty chamber pots . . . amputated limbs float in the water of Balaclava
harbour . . .'
[13] See under chapter: 'Moscow: The Sorge Enigma', pp. 291.

The Hinge Factor at Balaclava was stupidity and obstinacy. A badly worded pencilled order and the unguarded words of a hothead officer.

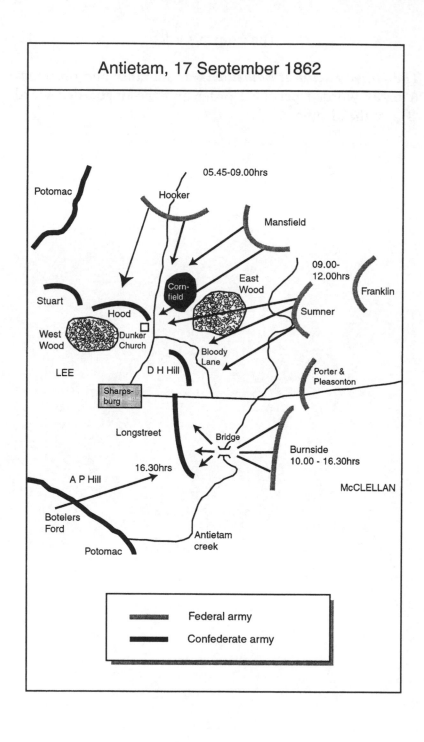

Antietam, 17 September 1862

Potomac

Hooker

05.45-09.00hrs

Mansfield

Stuart

Corn-field

East Wood

09.00-12.00hrs

Franklin

Hood

West Wood

Dunker Church

Sumner

LEE

Bloody Lane

D H Hill

Porter & Pleasonton

Sharps-burg

Longstreet

Bridge

Burnside 10.00 - 16.30hrs

A P Hill

16.30hrs

McCLELLAN

Botelers Ford

Antietam creek

Potomac

Federal army

Confederate army

7

Three Cigars

Antietam, 17 September 1862

'Put a man in a hole, a good battery on a hill behind him, and he will beat off three times his number, even if he isn't a good soldier.'
Colonel Theodore Lyman, *Union Army Headquarters*.

Sergeant John Bloss shivers in the pre-dawn darkness as he peers into the mist that obscures the creek in front of the bivouac area of the Union's 27th Indiana north of Sharpsburg. On that chilly morning, there are none of the bonfires that soldiers like to warm up around. The commanding general has forbidden them. The men of 'Old Fighting Joe' Hooker are chewing coffee grounds to try to get a lift.

'There's gonna be a fight here today, yessiree. Our whole army of the Potomac has moved here; mark my word, today's gonna mix it up,' he said with the conviction of a soldier who has seen battle before.

A few hundred yards across a small creek, on Nicodemus Hill, Confederate Lieutenant A. W. Garber strains his eyes to penetrate the same mist from where he has emplaced a battery of guns from General Jeb Stuart's horse artillery. The evening before, he had observed the Union Army as they moved into position to block Bobbie Lee's march on Washington.

Suddenly the mist lifts and he can make out the faint shadows of the enemy's encampments. He orders his battery to open fire on them.

It is 5.45 a.m. The bloodiest day of the American Civil War has begun.

Robert E. Lee realised only too well that with the meagre forces at the South's disposal he couldn't hope to continue for long against the industrial might of the North. He had to finish the war, and soon. For this it took a daring move and Robert E. Lee was just the man for it. A strike at the heart of the enemy: Washington, the nation's capital! Following his victory at the Second Battle of Bull Run in August, he needed to keep the Union Army off balance and, at the same time, re-supply his own forces from his enemies' bountiful stores. With this in mind, he dispatched 'Stonewall' Jackson with six divisions to raid Harper's Ferry, and General James Longstreet to Hagerstown to pick up stragglers. Ten days later, having his army once again reunited, he intended to move on Philadelphia, Baltimore and Washington. The war would be over in weeks, if not days. To that purpose, on 10 September 1862, General Robert E. Lee sent out two hand-written copies of his detailed plan of attack in *Special Orders, No 191*.

On 13 September, while sections of the Union Army's XII Corps were trailing the Confederates near Hagerstown, a scout patrol led by First Sergeant John Bloss and Corporal Barton Mitchell stopped off at the same spot where a Confederate unit had bivouacked earlier that day. The cinders of their campfire were still aglow. Bloss noticed a bulky envelope. When he opened it, a parcel, wrapped in white paper, fell to the ground and Sergeant Bloss had found himself a treasure. He picked it up with glee: 'Hey ya, guys; look at them ceegars! Barton, gimme a light, will ya!'

But Barton didn't have a light, so while the corporal scurried off to find matches, Bloss took a second glimpse at the paper. Though he couldn't read, the stamp and signature looked official enough to bring it to the attention of his company commander. The young lieutenant took one glance before he began to shake. Cigars were an unexpected luxury for these men from the North. Even more unexpected was the note in which they were wrapped: *General Lee's order of battle*![1] The lieutenant immediately dispatched it to the supreme commander of the Army of the Potomac, General George McClellan. Seldom had a commander been given such an advantage. Because of three mislaid cigars, fate moved two armies towards a confrontation.

General George Brinton McClellan, thirty-five, Commander-in-Chief, Union Army, called by his troops 'the young Napoleon', turned to General Ambrose Burnside and smiled: 'If I cannot whip Bobbie Lee now, you may call me whatever you please.'

Here was his incredible opportunity. The order told him that Lee had split his forces. McClellan recognised the once-in-a-lifetime advantage fate had provided him; he could drive a wedge between his adversary's wings, his namesake Napoleon's favourite manoeuvre; divide the enemy, then destroy him at leisure. And yet, incredible as it may seem, he hesitated and did nothing. He performed no reconnaissance and issued no orders, and not a single one of his commanders dared to tell him to do so. It goes to prove that the Union forces were led by a number of not overly competent

[1] It was the copy sent to General A. P. Hill.

men. There was Major General Ambrose Burnside, a nice
man pushed beyond his ability. Brigadier General Joseph
'Fighting Joe' Hooker, ambitious, hard driving, but lacking
the character of a top leader. Brigadier Edwin V. Sumner,
an ossified cavalryman, impetuous. Brigadier General Joseph
Mansfield, almost sixty, in and out of retirement.

These Northern commanders were faced by an army of
unruly but highly motivated, rebel soldiers. They were armed
with the rifled .577 calibre Enfield muskets, which, contrary
to the 50-yard efficiency of a Napoleonic flintlock, could hit
a bulls-eye at 500 yards. It was ideally suited for the character of the Confederate soldier, who employed it with the
accuracy of a squirrel hunter. But, the South's real strength
lay in their high command, men whose fame would continue
for centuries: Robert E. Lee, 'Stonewall' Jackson, James 'Old
Pete' Longstreet, Jeb Stuart, Ambrose Powell Hill – all better
and more courageous leaders than their counterparts. This
was the true strength of the Confederacy.

A spy had informed Lee that his battle plans had fallen
into Union hands and that the entire Northern Army had
been moved into a position astride the road to Washington
But the Southern general had a well-founded contempt for
his opponent, General McClellan. With the Confederates'
possible retreat cut off by a river, and an enemy three times
his strength,[2] Robert E. Lee took the audacious decision
to stand along a small, yet unknown river in Maryland,
the Antietam Creek. It was D-minus forty-eight hours. The
pieces moved into place, the stage was set.

17 September 1862. The bit-players of all great battles, those
who will die for a cause, or whatever, were in bivouac. Men
such as Sergeant Billy Boy Coons from the cotton fields of

[2] 87,000 Union soldiers versus 30,000 Confederates.

Alabama. On 14 September he had celebrated his nineteenth birthday. He and many of his comrades woke up to the last day of their young lives. The bivouac stirred. Some men were brewing coffee, others stared into holes in the dense mist. Some others again ... well, the rebel army had suffered from a serious problem which sapped the men's strength: diarrhoea. But now that the shooting was about to start in earnest, their thoughts were no longer preoccupied with looking for a tree, if not for personal protection. Billy Boy Coons looked forward to the shoot-out, he hated 'them fancy Yankees'. 'What do I want? Kill me a few o' them bluecoats,' he said with a grin that split his face, 'then chase girls, sit in the hay and drink whisky. I guess it'll have to wait until after tonight.'

In the North Woods, Union Sergeant Bloss – the one who found the cigars – was in a bivouac a few hundred yards across the creek. Like everyone in his company, he knew that they couldn't avoid battle. His lieutenant, that pimply faced squirt from West Point, had said so. Bloss wasn't quite as enthusiastic to do battle as the boy facing him. Not that he was scared. But it was the cold and the hardtack biscuits which made him suffer from the same gastric problem as the soldiers on the other side of the line.

'I can't wait until I get home and get me some decent grub.'

At Union headquarters, located in the stately Pry House, General McClellan paced the floor nervously. The men were ready, the guns were in place, now all it needed was his executive order. But he couldn't make up his mind. Surrounded by his top lieutenants, he studied the map with its many-coloured flags and pencilled arrows. Lee's Army of Northern Virginia was positioned in a line which was anchored by Jeb Stuart's cavalry in the north, then bulged out around the town of Sharpsburg and followed the Antietam Creek until it met the Potomac River in the south. At 5.30 a.m. McClellan finally issued an order, as confused as it was open for misinterpretations:

'Make attack on enemy's left, create a diversion in favour of the main attack, with hope of achieving something more, and as soon as one or both flank movements are fully successful, attack the centre with any reserves I might then have in hand.'

A group of Federal skirmishers advance through the morning mist along the Hagerstown Turnpike. On a hill they can see a white washed country church, and, in front of it, the unlimbered cannons of a battalion of Southern horse artillery. Napoleons mean mothers. And those boys in grey know how to use them. Suddenly all hell breaks loose.

Both artilleries begin firing as soon as the gunners can see their targets. And targets there are a plenty. General 'Fighting Joe' Hooker lives up to his nickname when he pushes his corps in a wide formation towards the Confederate line. His bluecoats are met by a hail of grapeshot from the high ground, around Dunker Church, where 'Stonewall' Jackson has massed his artillery. A detail of Jeb Stuart's artillery is on Nicodemus Hill. This way the Confederate gunners can bring crossfire against the Federals attacking up through this area.

Hooker's initial attack is stopped cold. He orders his own artillery brought forward. Gunners on horse-drawn carriages race across the field and get into position on a shallow rise overlooking the Hagerstown Turnpike. Beyond the road is a large patch of gold – a field of corn, about thirty acres, near Dunker's Church.

That's how General Hooker sees it: 'From the sun's rays falling on the soldiers' bayonets, projecting above the corn, we could see that the field was filled with the enemy. My instructions were for the assemblage of all my spare artillery to spring into action and open with canister shot at once.'

Now canister is something nasty – gun ammunition, composed of hundreds of lead balls, and put into a tin can for easy loading. When the cannon is fired, the tin can bursts apart and the artillery piece acts like a giant shotgun – a deadly weapon against massed infantry such as those hapless rebels lying in the cornfield.

One may well imagine what must go on in the minds of those boys, crouching beneath the stalks, their heads down, not seeing what takes place around them, until the corn and they themselves, are suddenly mowed down. What now takes place is perhaps the singly most horrible butchery of the entire Civil War. Massed artillery against a massed static troop formation. The first Union soldiers who rush into the cornfield slide on the blood-soaked ground, so frightful is the carnage. Hooker's violent attack carries his forces through the cornfield and up to the church before 'Stonewall's' Texas Brigade counter-attacks and retakes the ground. Throughout the next hour, attacks and counter-attacks seesaw. Canister shot rains down in floods, from the Confederate guns at Dunker Church and the Union guns beyond the corn field. They cut bloody swaths through attackers and defenders. Lines stall, move on, retreat, get mowed down.

Cries of '27th Indiana with me!' answered by 'Virginians, with me!'

Sergeant Bloss is in the midst of the slaughter. He sees men break and flee, chased by grey-clad soldiers screaming their spine-chilling rebel yell. The blue wave falls to grey bayonets. The West Point lieutenant, his arm tied up with a bloody scarf to stem the blood pouring from the stump, rallies the company. Then again it is the blues who chase the greys up the hill, towards that little white church. Like wheat in a storm, waves of men move back and forth. They walk on the backs of the dead, blue and grey – except that those lying on the ground are now of one universal colour, red as in blood.

One of the casualties is the soldier who, by his find of three cigars is in a sense responsible for this fratricidal carnage. Sergeant Bloss has led a platoon of skirmishers around the Confederate right flank when they stumble into a company of Jeb Stuart's cavalry. The riders hack down most of his men, Bloss manages to escape by playing dead.

The Union's overwhelming force in men and fire power is beginning to prevail on the Confederate's left wing. The blue wave has almost reached the rebel artillery position at Dunker's Church. A quirk of fate plays into Lee's hands. With victory assured, General 'Fighting Joe' Hooker mounts his impressive white stallion which makes him stand out like a beacon in a wild sea.

Seventeen-year-old Ossie Davis, a musketeer of the 19th Mississippi lies in an ambush position behind a log fence. He's just rammed a Minié ball down his long musket barrel when out of the dense powder smoke comes a rider on a white charger rising over the crest. Ossie doesn't know who the man is, only that he must be an officer. The boy, who had learned to fire a musket from his father when he was eight, puts spittle on his finger to wipe the halo from his gunsight, an old trick he had learned hunting opossums. Then he takes careful aim and slowly squeezes the trigger. The white stallion roars up and 'Fighting Joe' Hooker falls from the saddle. The shot isn't fatal, but it smashes Hooker's leg. As his orderlies carry him from the battlefield, the general is convinced that the attack by his Union Corps has carried the day.

A military dictum has it that *the climax of a successful assault is the moment of greatest peril*. It is at this point that a secondary line must be at hand to make good the victory of the initial attack. It calls for reinforcements to

widen the breach and hold the ground. The great Napoleon miscalculated at Waterloo, and 'the young Napoleon'
now copies him. McClellan hesitates too long, and loses
the opportunity to achieve victory. Without their dynamic
leader, Hooker's Union Corps breaks on the Confederate
line. By the time Brigadier General Mansfield's Union Corps
is ordered into action the grey line has stabilised. Still, the old
general manages to push through the cornfield and almost
reaches Dunker Church where his men are stopped, bruised
and spent. So much time has been wasted since Hooker's
successful breakthrough that Lee has managed to move part of
Longstreet's reserves to cement the breach. The field in front of
the little white church is heaped with bodies. Brigadier General
Mansfield is mortally wounded and his Union Corps retreats.
The Union Army has taken tremendous losses: one after the
other its divisions have been chewed up and everything is in
total confusion. Now, McClellan has no senior commander
in charge of his right flank, yet he does nothing to remedy
the situation. Officers issue conflicting orders, countermanded
by others.

There follows a lull in the fighting, since both the Union
Corps who have led the attack are wrecked, and the Confederates haven't got enough soldiers to mount a counter-
attack. For the next hour, artillery on both sides makes the
ground shudder. One thing becomes clear, the Union attack
in the north has fizzled out.

The second act opens around 9 a.m. in the West Woods.
General Edwin Summer, the sixty-five-year-old cavalryman
commanding the Union's XII Corps, expects to be ordered
into line as soon as the first shot is fired. For two hours
he has heard the cannon-fire on his right flank, yet he
still has no order to attack. He dispatches Captain John
Hastings, his aide, to McClellan's headquarters. His envoy
never reaches McClellan. Instead, Hastings is taken aside and
told by the general's aide: 'Inform General Summer, that's

just skirmishing. We shall send you orders when General McClellan is ready to commit XII Corps.'

Even before this message is passed on, and without insight into what is going on or where 'that accursed Bobbie Lee' is making his stand, Sumner, the impetuous cavalryman, determines to throw his weight into the centre of the line. But his problem is that he doesn't know where the centre of the line is, nor what lies in front of him. Worse still, through a set of confusing orders it so happens that, instead of using his whole corps in one crushing blow, he will confront the rebel line one formation at a time. He marches his lead division in massed brigade front into the teeth of the Confederate line. On his flank, in the West Woods, hides a formidable Confederate reserve, commanded by none other than sourpuss 'Stonewall' himself. Two entire rebel divisions hit Sumner's attack in the side and completely rout the Yankees. For his rash action Sumner has nothing to show but several thousand casualties. He is suddenly beset by panic and dashes back to stop the rest of his divisions from entering the slaughter. But he is too late, the trailing divisions of XII Corps are already in motion. They reach the East Wood, expecting to follow the lead division. Their commanders are not aware of the massacre that has befallen Sumner's lead division. When they see a few bluecoats to their left the divisional officers assume that's where the action is and veer their columns in that direction, towards a narrow country road. Without realising it, two Union divisions march towards the weakest point in the Confederate line, held by a few companies of Alabamans.

General Lee spots the imminent danger. Unlike the Union commander, who sees only a small sliver of fighting through a telescope from his isolation at Pry House, Lee is at the flashpoint of the battle.[3] He has galloped to the 6th Alabama,

---

[3] Lee will be wounded five times that day before he is carried to the rear.

holding a sunken country lane where their battalion commander assures Lee, 'General, your Alabamans are going to
stay here until the sun goes down or victory is won.'

Some of the most vicious fighting will take place where
this road sinks a yard below the field. That's why farmers
have called it *the Sunken Road*. It is about to change
names. This marks the moment of glory for a small group
of Southerners under the command of Sergeant Billy Boy
Coons, the Alabaman who loves whisky and to chase girls.
With pieces of wooden fencing torn from a farm enclosure,
they have erected a breastwork on the ledge of the road.
From there they can fire without offering much of a target for
the attacking Federals. Through the wooden poles Billy Boy
Coons watches as Sumner's divisions draw up as if preparing
for an inspection. There is no hurry in their movement. They
commence their march, four ranks deep, advancing like on
Easter parade. He remembers something his daddy had told
him when they went duck hunting. 'Always shoot the last in
line, then the others won't notice and you bag the lot.' Billy
Boy crawls along the line to tell each of his sharpshooters
the same thing: 'Don't shoot at the first rank. When they
kneel to fire keep your heads down. Let them shoot and
waste their balls, then aim well, but at the second line who
hasn't fired as yet. That'll give us time to reload; we just have
to be faster than them Yankees, and then we'll hit them.'

There is nothing more he can add. He closes his eyes
and silently calls out to the Lord. It's out of his hands.
Long moments of silence, nobody speaks; only the distant
thunder of guns and the measured step of approaching
columns. Billy Boy is startled when one of his Alabamans
tells a joke. Coon hisses: 'Shuddup, boy.' The 'boy' is at
least thirty, and he is only nineteen – too young to die. He
looks over the ledge. Still too far away; let's give them cursed
Yankees time to get close, and then send them to hell. An
officer stands erect behind the men crouching in the sunken

road and waits until the Northerners are within a hundred yards and their first line kneels down to take aim. A sharp crack and a volley sails across their road. The officer goes down, wood splinters but none of the soldiers is hurt. Billy Boy takes command of his sector.

'Alabamans,' very softly spoken; then, a shouted command: 'Fire.' The Southerners fire as one man. Their aim is deadly. A whole line of attackers staggers, falls, the rest stop in confusion. It takes half a minute to reload a musket, long enough to pour two more rounds into the bluecoats before they turn and run, leaving piles of bodies in front of the breastwork.

Here is the situation: the Union attack on the northern flank has come to a standstill. Hooker's corps is used up, as are Mansfield's soldiers. Hooker is wounded, Mansfield is dead. Sumner's initial attack has failed disastrously, the Confederate centre holds, and McClellan still hasn't committed his reserves.

Sumner's divisions try, then try again, to force a passage across the sunken road. Men rush forward, screaming their fury at the men crouching behind the barricade. They stop to fire, they stop to die. Dead and wounded pile up in prodigious numbers in front of what will become known to history as 'Bloody Lane'. More of Sumner's men arrive, but to no avail. The rebels have also suffered great losses, but nothing will get them to move. They've promised their Bobbie Lee to hold the line, and hold they will, or die doing so.

A New York regiment has managed to infiltrate on the Alabamans' flank from where they can look down into the lane. They take aim at the crumpled grey uniforms, and pour a hail of fire into the backs of the valiant defenders. One by one, the rebels die. Billy Boy Coons and the last of his men are still holding off the frontal charge. It is slaughter at its most frightful and heroism at its greatest. Coons' Alabamans are down to sixty, then thirty . . .

For the South it is the moment of truth. Should Sumner's charge succeed, the Southern army will be broken into two ineffective factions. McClellan must now display energy and send his fresh reserves into the centre and push the army of Northern Virginia into the Potomac. Lee recognises the great danger to his centre. He patches his line with whatever is at his disposal – cooks and clerks take up the muskets of the fallen, die in the road. Bloody Lane is heaped with bodies. Then suddenly a miracle takes place! The blue wave grinds to a halt. Lee wonders what McClellan is up to. Nothing, if we can believe written accounts.

Summer has had enough and McClellan still cannot make up his mind to release his reserves. The reason for it has never been fully explained. Probably because McClellan does nothing to assess the real situation for himself and bases his decision on the gloomy reports of Sumner's abortive attack, and the fact that the Union has lost most of their top commanders: Hooker, Mansfield, Richardson. McClellan thus concludes that his entire right wing is on the verge of disaster and that his centre is failing. And yet, he has a full army corps in position, 30,000 men under General Franklin. Instead of ordering them to attack, and cave in Lee's threadbare centre, he puts the corps on the defensive! McClellan's battle plan is out of control: the fighting spreads like a bush fire from the north to the centre, and is about to flare up in the south.

Major General Ambrose Burnside, the commander of McClellan's left flank, who has expected since early morning to be called into action, receives no orders until 9 a.m., by which time the Union attacks conducted from their right wing and into the centre have failed. Eventually, a message arrives at Burnside's HQ: 'General McClellan desires you to open your attack, for all is going well!'

Burnside, led to believe that Lee's centre has been broken, launches an attack against Antietam Creek. It is too late and too unco-ordinated. His only intelligence about possible crossing points of the creek comes from querying two farmers who happen to be hostile to the Union cause. Burnside's fixation centres on a very particular bridge which will forever carry his name. He orders his Pennsylvanian and New York regiments to take that bridge, but runs into a problem, and not one of rebel resistance. For days he has refused to allot the whisky ration to his troops and now they demand their dues before they will launch into their attack. Even after a considerable alcohol intake, the troops do not press home their attack with much enthusiasm, and it takes them two full hours to storm across the bridge, although in face of four fresh divisions Lee has only one regiment in place.

Burnside's delay proves to be costly. There is an irony to this concentrated effort by an entire corps to carry an eight-foot-wide stone span. In late summer the water level of the Antietam Creek is only knee-deep and Burnside's 30,000 could have waded across the narrow river. What is more, the mile-long river bank is undefended – there isn't a single Southerner along the entire bank, because by now Lee's troops are so thin on the ground that he simply doesn't have any more with which to protect the length of the line. He relies on the fact that no soldier would ever walk blindly into brush as dense as that which covers the river bank, and he is absolutely right. That day, no Northerner gets his feet wet.

In the north the battle has reached a stalemate; in the centre, the sacrifice by the Alabamans has brought Sumner's corps to a halt, and now Ambrose Burnside bungles his attempt to cave in Lee's southern flank. For Robert E. Lee the situation is still critical. However, a new element is about to come into play in the form of a wild bunch of rebels, dressed this time in blue. These are the men of Confederate Major General Ambrose Powell Hill who wear brand-new uniforms and shoes liberated from the Union Army's stores at Harper's Ferry. General A. P. Hill has been pushing his divisions the seventeen miles from Harper's Ferry to Boteler's Ford in what will prove to become the most pivotal forced march of the entire Civil War.

Scouts have informed McClellan about A. P. Hill's drive to join up with Lee's bulk of the army. McClellan still has Franklin's entire corps at his disposal, plus his cavalry reserves. Lee has been correct to count on his rival's in-activity. The 'Young Napoleon' writes finish to his military career when, plagued by self-doubt, he fails to order the 11,000-strong cavalry reserves to block A. P. Hill's advance. Also, he commits a cardinal error when he omits to advise his southern flank commander, General Ambrose Burnside, of the imminent arrival of several enemy divisions.

Act three, early afternoon. Despite 'the whisky problem' and the holding action put up by the Southern regiment on the bridge, Burnside's weakly conducted attack has finally carried the bridge. His four divisions flood across the stone span and advance in the absence of further resistance. Soon Lee's army will be cleaved in two. Fortunately for the South, 'Whiskers' Burnside doesn't push his divisions to great haste since he has received no orders to do so, nor has he got the slightest idea about the overall situation.

The battle takes a dramatic turn. From the moment the armies have confronted each other, Lee's last piece slips into place when it is most needed. General A. P. Hill meets General Robert E. Lee on a copse. His appearance highlights one of the strange features of this battle. The two friends embrace each other. 'You've come in time', says a greatly relieved Lee. 'Put your men in on the right.'

Just as Napoleon did at Waterloo with Blücher's Prussians, General Ambrose Burnside makes the same mistake when he suddenly notices a dark cloud of soldiers approaching his flank from the distance. He checks through his spy-glass and waves his hand to calm his staff. All is well – they wear blue uniforms. Those are McClellan's promised reserves; at worst, those are Union stragglers. His orders are to hold fire on the newcomers in blue. The first indication that all is not well comes when an officer's horse, with blood pumping from bubbly holes, wanders across the battlefield. Burnside recognises it as the mount of one of his divisional commanders. In the time it takes him to send out orders and to reorganise his divisions, the howling and yelling rebels of A. P. Hill's Corps are upon him.

It now turns into the Battle of the two Ambroses: Hill and Burnside. The Southern Ambrose proves much more efficient – his men's fierce drive, pushed with extreme ferocity, stops the Federals in their tracks. The air is rendered with the savage rebel yell. Even the whiplash of Union artillery fire cannot drown that blood-curling howl. The combat has gone completely out of control, there are skirmishes everywhere, commanders are killed, headquarters no longer control the situation as they don't know where their units are, or who is still in fighting trim. Tactical details lose their meaning, wounded cover the field, their screams are drowned out by the roar of the cannons, some pounding each other from as close as 100 yards. Then the guns cease firing. Lee and Hill are worried. There are no more cartridges for the muskets of their men. Should McClellan launch a counter-attack, their corps will be wiped out. But there is no sign of a counter-attack, the enemy has had the same hard time. Burnside's corps has been pushed back across the creek. The rebels halt at the edge of the water.

It is just after five o'clock. The Battle of Antietam is over.

Thus one of the bloodiest battles of the Civil War ended. Both armies held much the same ground they had held twelve hours before – except that on the battlefield lay 14,000 Southerners and 12,000 Union casualties.

Sergeant Bloss from Indiana was badly wounded but survived to fight in yet another battle. He was killed at Gettysburg.

Sergeant Coons, the boy who wanted to chase girls, sit on the farm and drink whisky, Billy Boy Coons,[4] died in Bloody Lane.

After the battle, a boy from Wisconsin wrote home to tell his mother that he had experienced 'a great tumbling together of heaven and earth'.

A Southern surgeon, covering his face behind his blood-stained hands to hide his tears, burst out: 'I hate cannons.'

David Strother, the enterprising war reporter of *Harper's Weekly*, found bodies hideously swollen and blackened. He wrote in his dispatch: 'Many were so covered with dust, torn, crushed, and trampled that they resembled clods of earth, and I was obliged to look twice before recognising them as human beings.'

A Confederate in the cornfield had the final word. When a Union officer paused to tell the dying rebel, 'You fought well and you stood well,' the rebel replied, 'Yes, and here we lie!'

*   *   *

[4] One of his descendents, Harry Josef Coons, led the charge on Hill 943 in Vietnam.

What if . . .

What if – Sergeant Bloss hadn't had such a craving for
            cigars?
            Robert E. Lee would have found an open road to
            take Washington.

What if – McClellan had acted more decisively when he was
            handed Lee's battle plans?
            He could have driven a wedge between Lee's
            Confederate Army and annihilated it piecemeal.
            In both cases the war would have been over.

The facts

On the battlefield nothing was decided. Ambrose Burnside
was no Stonewall Jackson, and George McClellan no Robert
E. Lee.

Antietam, or as some call it, Sharpsburg, was a moral
victory for Lee and a political one for the Union. The
overshadowing factor of Antietam is that Abraham Lincoln
now took the initiative, and the face of war changed
forever.

Antietam prevented Britain and France from recognising
the Confederate States of America. Had the two major
European countries done so, it would have split the United
States into two separate republics, 22 Union states and 13
Confederate states.

And Antietam did provide President Lincoln with a favourable opportunity to issue his Emancipation Proclamation.[5]
Within two generations, the United States of America became
the greatest industrial power in the world.

A historic afterthought: by studying closely the tactics of

[5] The Anti-Slavery Law.

Antietam, the European Powers could have avoided the enormous blunders perpetrated during the European wars of 1866 and 1871, and most certainly, at the beginning of the First World War. The horror of concentrated artillery fire against massed infantry was an example clearly to be seen, but nobody had learned the lesson.

The Hinge Factor at Antietam was a parcel with three cigars. Because of it, the American Civil War was to continue for another four bloody years.

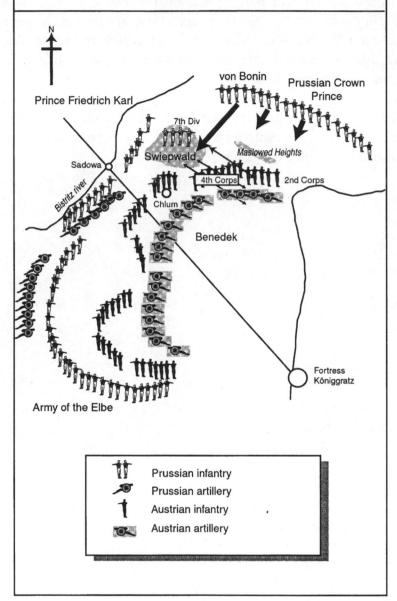

Königgratz, 3 July 1866, situation at 14.00hrs

N

von Bonin

Prussian Crown Prince

Prince Friedrich Karl

7th Div

Sadowa

Swiepwald

Maslowed Heights

4th Corps

2nd Corps

Bistritz river

Chlum

Benedek

Fortress Königgratz

Army of the Elbe

Prussian infantry

Prussian artillery

Austrian infantry

Austrian artillery

8

Two Counts and One Prince
Königgrätz, 3 July 1866

Ihr glaubt Ihr habt ein Reich gegründet.
Und habt doch nur ein Volk zerstört.
Franz Grillparzer, 1866

'You think you have founded an Empire.
Instead you have destroyed a nation.'

The commander of the Austrian fortress of Königgrätz ordered the opening of the sluice gates. The water-belt in front of the battlement walls rose steadily. A single-lane dam which led across the flooded *glacis* was hopelessly jammed with an army *en deroute*. The ramparts of the fortress were lined with officers who shouted orders in German, Hungarian, Polish, Serbo-Croat and Italian, trying to disentangle the chaos before them. As far as the eye could see, a line of soldiers in white, muddy uniforms, flecked by gunpowder and stained with blood, straggled from the river towards the fortress gates. Carts, piled high with wounded, were pushed out of the way and into the rising waters. Drowning men screamed for help. Artillery pieces were shoved over the edge; riders forced their horses down the steep embankment, only to break the necks of their mounts, or their own necks. Run, army, run, 'cause everything is lost. Slowly an evening fog rose from the flooded fields and laid its covering blanket over the tragedy.

The head of the defeated army saw nothing of this. He had remained on the field of battle until the end, then passed across another bridge further south before he reached the very inn from where he had set out that same morning. Only twelve hours ago – but twelve hours which were to influence the future of Europe. Around a table he found the vanquished generals. Finally the thin man with the big moustache raised his glass: 'Let us remember all those brave men who died today in vain.' Twelve hours before, he had led 215,000 enthusiastic young soldiers into battle. Now he led them back, the remnants of a once proud army. Fate had been most cruel. Slowly the Field Marshal got up and walked out of the door. He climbed on his horse and rode off.

By nightfall, the commander of the fortress cabled his emperor: 'All Army Corps *en débandade* in and around Königgrätz. Any further defensive action out of the question. Please cable orders.'

No orders came.

The Austro-Prussian War of 1866 has always been overshadowed by the Franco-Prussian War of 1871. But it was this conflict that set the stage for Prussian military expansionism, which ended with the creation of the German Empire of the Hohenzollern in the mirror hall of Versailles. Had Austria been victorious at the Battle of Königgrätz, Otto von Bismarck's role in history would be but a footnote describing someone whose vision had exceeded his capacity, and his grandiose scheme for a German unification would have been pushed back, or even never have taken place. There would have been no Kaiser Wilhelm I and II, and probably no World War One and Two. German marching orders would never have become the model of military effectiveness throughout the world.

Bismarck's strategy was simple: to keep the armies of that vainglorious French emperor, Napoleon III, long enough away from the battlefield to defeat the Austrians and gain Prussian control over Germany. This called for a fast and decisive victory. But one that would not humiliate Austria. He needed Vienna to remain neutral in case of a war against France, and furthermore, as his future ally against Russia along its Eastern border.[1] It took speed and daring. For this, Bismarck had wisely picked his military instrument to impose his political will, General Count Helmuth von Moltke.

Austria was a huge empire made up of many ethnic tribes, races, languages and religions. There had been uprisings in Poland, Hungary and Italy against the iron rule imposed by Vienna. All these revolts were brutally put down by the armies of Emperor Franz Josef. By the mid-nineteenth century, the Austrian Army had become the central institution of a 600-year-old Hapsburg monarchy tottering towards dissolution. The army alone bears responsibility for losing wars against two relatively inferior enemies, Italy (1859) and Prussia (1866).

The overriding factor in these defeats was the incompetence of the Austrian officer corps who had wasted the long years of Metternichian peace on ceremonial drill instead of teaching their men how to use a rifle, and paid little attention to morale, except to authorise double wine rations before going into battle. Money was lavished on superfluous officers and a stifling bureaucracy. Administration of the army was as ineffective as it was corrupt, available funds being used up on salaries instead of purchasing modern weapons. The technical factors, which revolutionised the conduct of warfare in this

[1] Bismarck's whole politic depended on avoiding a two-front war. When Bismarck's politics were ignored at the beginning of W.W. 1, it led to the downfall of Germany.

booming industrial age, were ignored. This was to result in astronomical casualty figures and eventually served to laud the effect of the Prussians' rapid-fire Needle Gun beyond its real merits.

The Austrian divisional commanders of the mid-century still clung to the Napoleonic *charge à l'outrance*. Thus huge armies were wasted in senseless attacks. And yet, the Austrian infantry, competently handled, did quite well. At Magenta (1859), their centre held off the *furia francese* and repulsed the French decisively.[2] At Solferino, Count Stadion threw back Napoleon III's Imperial Guard before he had to withdraw. But he left behind an enemy so badly mauled that the French couldn't take advantage of the Austrians' ordered withdrawal.[3] That day, the multi-lingual force showed its mettle, especially under the brilliant leadership of an Austro-Hungarian corps commander. He was General Ludwig Ritter von Benedek, a man beloved of his troops and held in high esteem by his superiors as well as his enemies, who named him 'The Austrian Bayard'.[4]

Benedek was a Magyar, which was a decided disadvantage in the Austrian Army hierarchy. However his leadership qualities were soon discovered by the old Field Marshal Radetzky.[5] At the outbreak of the war against Prussia, Benedek, now sixty-two, became the obvious choice to take overall command of the Austrian forces. Pushed by his emperor, Benedek accepted with great reluctance. First, as he explained, he knew nothing about the Bohemian theatre of war, where his battles would have to be fought; secondly, he

[2] The Austrians under Count Gyulai would have carried the day had their commander not panicked.
[3] Though Napoleon III dispatched a cable to Paris: '*Grande bataille, grande victoire.*'
[4] Bayard was a sixteenth-century Frenchman, known as '*Bayard, sans peur sans reproche*'.
[5] More than for his military achievement, Radetzky is remembered for a march composed in his honour by Johann Strauss, which ends every year's New Year's Concert in Vienna.

had only done battle against the Italians and French and had never faced the Prussians. Most important of all, he was aware of his own limitations. Though a daring corps commander, he could not see himself leading an army of a quarter million men. To make matters worse, the Emperor forced him to accept as his chiefs of staff two men totally unsuited for this task. Krismanic was clever but lazy and Henikstein was aggressive but dumb. When Benedek learned about their appointment by Imperial Decree, he declared: 'Both are about as fit to fill this position as I am to compose an opera.' Benedek was a field commander, not a paper man. He became bowed down by the task at hand. From the moment he took command, defeat was in the air.

Facing him was Count Helmuth von Moltke, straight, ruthless, Prussian. He had studied the Austro-Italian War of 1859 and found that the infantry's fire-power was the battle winner of the future. To achieve tactical success he had armed his units with the revolutionary, breech-loading Dreyse needle gun.[6] He tried it out against the Danes in 1864. His infantry battalions' vastly superior rate of fire, and the vital fact that they could reload lying down, produced devastating results. To him it had become obvious that this rifle would lead the Prussian Army to victory over the muzzle-loading Austrians.[7] On attack, the enemy, even firing from behind a protective cover, could not load fast enough to stop Moltke's infantry from getting close and pouring their murderous high-speed fire into their enemies' ranks, while in defence they could lie down and let the enemy run into their wall of fire.

[6] So called owing to its long needle which had to penetrate a cardboard cartridge The English Army hesitated. Lord Wavell put it: 'There is no room in war for delicate machinery.' Studying the decisive effects of Königgrätz, the French adopted the Chassepot rifle, developed by A. M. Chassepot in 1863, which was superior to the Prussian Dreyse gun.
[7] The Dreyse gun had a shortcoming. After a few discharges, the bolt action would no longer seal the breech and gases escaped which burnt the riflemen. Thus, they no longer put their cheek to the rifle to take careful aim. Instead, they fired from the hip.

If the Needle Gun became king, artillery was still 'the queen of the battlefield'. The Austrian Army's strong point lay in its superb gunnery. Following their defeat at Solferino, they rearmed with rifled, muzzle-loading 8-pounder guns made of bronze.

When the British Royal Navy realised that its supremacy of the seas would soon depend on steam-driven, ironclad ships, they began to experiment with wrought-iron guns bound with steel coils. This was followed by an epoch-making invention. Alfred Krupp, a Rhineland steel mill owner, devised a revolutionary process to allow steel to cool into flawless tubes. The breech-loading cannon was born. Moltke equipped some of his field batteries with this new gun. But guns alone could not decide the outcome of a battle. Only leaders could. And on the battlefield at Königgrätz, half a million stood face to face, awaiting their orders.

Austrian HQ at Königgrätz. A message was received from the Austrian General Gablentz that his corps had achieved a victory at Trautenau. That was good news. Not so welcome were the casualty figures – three-times that of the Prussians. That was the problem, thought Benedek, the Austrian Army had not been trained to fire rifles and depended entirely on bayonet charges, even when on defence. Meanwhile, Benedek was being bombarded with telegrams from his emperor. He replied: '*Bitte Eure Majestaet dringend, Frieden zu schliessen. Katastrophe fuer Armee unvermeidlich.*' ('I request urgently of Your Majesty to come to a peaceful settlement. A disaster for the army is unavoidable.') The Emperor's reply was sharp and brief: 'To make peace impossible. I order, if no other option, to retreat in good order. Has a battle taken place?'

Benedek was given no choice. He elected to make his stand at Königgrätz. It was a good, defensible position, from where his gunners could enjoy a free field of fire over some 2,000 yards. His centre was based on the forward slopes of high ground with the Elbe River at his back. His right flank was anchored on the river, his left in heavily wooded ground which prohibited advance by large formations. The left flank was intended for a holding action and could fall back on dug-in artillery positions.

'*Getrennt marschieren, gemeinsam schlagen!*' Moltke's principle: 'March separated, do battle together.'

The Prussian general had taken a calculated gamble and split his army into two major prongs of attack. Success depended on the precision movement of two separate army wings. The 1st Army was led by the Crown Prince, the 2nd Army was commanded by Prinz Friedrich Karl. Had Benedek been blessed with Napoleon's genius, had he attacked each of the Prussian armies in detail, he would have achieved certain victory. Good fortune comes with daring, and daring was on the Prussians' side. The cavalry scout patrols of the Austrians were unadventurous and Benedek was left with no clear idea as to the whereabouts of Prince Friedrich Karl. In fact, the Prussian 2nd Army had joined up with the Elbe Army of von Herwarth during the encounter at Gitschin, while the main Prussian forces were strengthened by von Bonin's and von Steinmetz's corps. All that took some delicate manoeuvring. By 1 July both Prussian armies had closed up sufficiently to catch the Austrians between two fronts. From reports provided by his scouts, Moltke studied carefully the Austrian positions and realised that the key was Chlum, a sleepy hamlet of farm houses around a church and a main street, protected by a forest known as the Swiepwald.

At midnight on 2 July, General Moltke presented his final plan to the King of Prussia. The Elbe Army was ordered to attack the Austrian left flank, Friedrich Karl's 2nd Army strengthened by von Bonin's corps was to head for the Austrian centre while, at the same moment, the main thrust, led by the Prussian Crown Prince, would force the enemy's right flank. The weather got worse, it rained all night. Through a muddle in communications, the 2nd Army of Prince Friedrich Karl set off at 03.00 hours, while the main forces under the Crown Prince remained in camp until morning.

Ritter von Benedek had spent the night at the inn 'Zur Stadt Prag'. He looked out of his window. The morning was wet and humid, with steam rising from the trampled wheatfields. He sat down to write a note to his wife. '*Wenn mein altes Glueck mich nicht ganz verlaesst, kann es zum guten Ende fuehren, kommt es jedoch anders, dann sage ich in Demut: wie Gott will. Du, mein Kaiser, und Oesterreich werdet meiner allerletzten Gedanken und Gefuehle beherrschen. Bin ruhig und gefasst, und wenn erst die Kanonen in rechter Naehe donnern werden, wird mir wohl werden.*' ('If my old luck should hold this can take a happy ending. Should it be otherwise, let me declare humbly: You, my Emperor, and Austria will be my final thoughts. My mind is set at rest, and I will be happy when I hear the roar of cannons.')

Before he finished the letter, he heard a rolling thunder.

Neither side knew much about the other. Benedek was in a good tactical position, although with his back to the Elbe River. By 07.00 hours, the first columns of Prince Friedrich Karl's 2nd Prussian Army reached the Bistritz Valley. Thinking that the Austrians were across the river – the logical military strategy – and without awaiting the arrival of the Army of the Prussian Crown Prince, Prince Friedrich Karl dispatched a regiment of cavalry to force the bridge across the Bistritz at Sadowa. They blundered into an Austrian *Jaeger* battalion[8] who had been posted there to fight a delay action. Though taken by surprise, the Austrian batteries placed further back quickly responded and put down a violent barrage on the Prussians, who were forced to pull back with great loss. Next, the Prussian prince sent forward several battalions of infantry assisted by a heavy bombardment from their artillery which flattened the villages on the opposite shore of the river.

While this initial action took place, Benedek was still on his way to his command post. He reached his headquarters near the village of Lipa where he met Krismanic, who just at this moment was being informed that he had been sacked by the Emperor. Benedek's second ADC, Henikstein, seemed quite delighted over the misfortune of his colleague.

Benedek studied the situation: his centre was held by 44,000 men and 134 guns; on the left flank were 51,000 men and 140 cannons; while the right wing was composed of 55,000 men and 176 guns. In reserve were 47,000 soldiers, 11,500 cavalry and 320 guns. Benedek had built an impregnable position – that is, if all his corps commanders obeyed their orders and did not move from their assigned positions. He decided to move up part of his reserve artillery to strengthen the centre. For that, he made a personal inspection tour of his reserve units. The 'Bayard of Austria' was as popular as ever, and the troops cheered him with a hearty '*Hurra!*' or '*Zivio!*' or '*Eljen!*' while the regimental bands played the Radetzky March. After which he rode up a hill to view the battle panorama. As instructed, his three advance corps had withdrawn in good order to the forest area near Sadowa. The wonder-rifle of the Prussians was of little use in the dense woods. When the Prussians tried to advance, they came under the withering fire of Benedek's batteries. In the

---

[8] Jaegers, or hunters, were soldiers that had great experience as game wardens and were known for their accurate fire and use of the terrain.

Swiepwald forest Prussian battalions were decimated by the Austrian guns.

While the first shots thundered down the Bistritz Valley, the Crown Prince was still at breakfast and then took the parade of his own regiment.[9] A dispatch rider raced up: 'Your Highness, the battle has opened.' It was the same situation as fifty years before, at Waterloo. Prince Friedrich Karl (Napoleon) attacked and the Crown Prince (Grouchy) heard the sound of distant cannons. Only, in contrast to Grouchy's error, the army of the Crown Prince began to march towards the cannons' thunder.

To the Austrians, one thing became clear. Moltke had blundered. To attack with only one army was a grave error. There was definitely the opportunity for victory as there was still no sign of the Prussian Crown Prince and the main army. Benedek's hope that his superior artillery would demoralise the Prussians and hand him victory was not a whim. But for an event about to occur, he might have pulled it off.

The Counts von Thun and von Festetics were two Austrian corps commanders, both far too wealthy and well connected to obey orders from a mere 'Ritter' to hold their flank position against the expected attack by the Crown Prince's army, which was nowhere in sight. The counts, sitting on the commanding heights without having to engage an enemy, found their inactivity boring and dishonourable. They now committed the error of advancing their Corps a thousand yards ahead of the main Austrian defence line, until that moment, solidly anchored along a series of heights. Their move was exactly the situation which Benedek's disposition had been designed to avoid. The two counts advanced against the Prussian 7th Division of General von Fransecky who suddenly found himself attacked by waves of massed Austrian

[9] After the war, the Crown Prince justified his delay by the bad road conditions owing to the rain.

infantry in the Swiepwald. In the narrow confines of the dense forest, the Austrians could not bring their superior manpower to bear and their suicidal bayonet charges had little or no effect. Almost like at Agincourt, the front ranks engaged in furious hand-to-hand battle while the back ranks could do nothing to intervene. The Prussians soon discovered that the Austrians' advance had given no thought to secure their flank which Prussian regiments now attacked. In the ensuing mêlée everything got out of hand for the Austrian commanders – units attacked without order, others were withdrawn to protect the flank, while a disciplined Prussian push resulted in taking the village of Cistowes. Count Festetics realised his blunder and sent a brigade to patch the hole. The Prussians used the houses of the village as barricades and fired from windows and over walls at the onrushing white waves. It was an unequal fight in which all the Austrian officers and most Hungarian soldiers of the 12th and Italians of the 26th regiments were killed.

Count von Festetics now mounted a bayonet charge against the village. He led the brave but futile charge in which he was badly wounded and his ADC killed. General Mollinary took over from Festetics. Watching the debacle from a distance, Count Thun, unable to tell what was happening to Festetics' men, shoved his 2nd Corps into the Swiepwald fury. How they fought, these Austrians! Brave, but suicidal. Regimental bands played the Radetzky March, officers with raised sabres advanced in front of their battalions; their soldiers didn't fire and relied solely on 'the cold steel of their bayonets'. All that in face of the new rapid-fire Needle Gun. Most battalions didn't get closer than fifty metres to the Prussian lines. In front of the forest the piles of white-coated bodies mounted, their bayonets pointing aimlessly into the air. Battalion after battalion was wasted, a hecatomb of Austrians, Hungarians, Italians and Croats. Von Fransecky's Prussians knew they had to hold off the attack or the Austrians would roll right over the Prussian centre. The Prussian 7th Division was almost used up. 'Stand and die!' was their order. They stood and they died, man for man, 84 officers and 2,036 men. But they blunted the Austrian attack.

When Benedek heard of the disobedience of his specific instructions by the two corps commanders, and the terrible losses they engendered in the Swiepwald, he became frustrated; always the same problem with these undisciplined Austrian aristocrats. As the direct result of their inappropriate move, his defensive position to the north was now completely emptied of defenders. Too late to call them back now. Fortunately the enemy hadn't discovered the undefended gap between the Swiepwald and the units holding the river line. Benedek could only pray that the army of the Crown Prince was nowhere near the battlefield. The answer was not long in coming.

At 11.30, it happened. A message reached Benedek that the Crown Prince's Guard units were approaching his right flank. He paled, crumpled up the message and stuck it in his pocket. All depended now on the vital move of Festetics's (Mollinary) 4th Corps and Thun's 2nd Corps to fill once more the gaping hole in the Austrian defensive line.

It was at the same time that, after ninety minutes of murderous hand-to-hand battle and thousands of casualties, the valiant Austrians had finally achieved their breakthrough in the Swiepwald. Suddenly they heard the blare of trumpets calling them back. 'Back? Go back? You mean, abandon what we've won at such sacrifice?' asked units in Polish, Hungarian, Rumanian, Croatian, Italian. 'What do they mean, go back?' They had beaten the Prussians. Was their victory of no more importance, had the high costs in blood all been in vain? Who only could understand that? Officers didn't know, nor could not explain it to their troops since the company leaders who had survived the slaughter only spoke German. One thing was certain, the regimental bands no longer played the rousing Radetzky March. The forest, which they had turned into a charnel house, was silent. Company after company moved back, past their dead and their wounded. Now that the troops had to withdraw, their sacrifice had no meaning. The soldiers felt let down, their fighting spirit was gone. They emerged from the tangle of smashed trees and saw in front of them the church steeple of Chlum.

Benedek rode to check for himself whether General Mollinary had followed his orders and was hurrying his mangled battalions back to their original position. The battalions were still filing back when the divisions of the Prussian Crown Prince struck.

The Crown Prince and his army arrived at a time when they were most needed. The prince quickly studied the situation. He could see burning villages in the direction of the Bistritz Valley. Obviously, the army of Friedrich Karl was stuck. It called for an immediate relief action against the Austrian right flank. In front of him was an open slope crested by a row of elms. He knew it would be costly but he had to take the risk. He ordered his Guard battalions to deploy in formation. Slowly they began to ascend the hill he had named Lindenberg.[10] From far away, Austrian guns opened up on his advancing lines. But his soldiers received no musket fire, and nothing could be seen of the enemy's infantry. Was this sly devil Benedek planning an ambush? Would his Austrian battalions come storming down the slope, with their bayonets and a gusty *hurra*? Nothing of the kind happened.

The Prussian Guard reached the elm crest – and found the

[10] The Maslowed Heights.

Austrian lines abandoned! The Crown Prince called for an immediate push towards the undefended Austrian artillery batteries. Prussian battalions rushed uphill and overran their prominent position. From there, they could look down on the Austrian Army, but furthermore, on the advancing columns of the Prussian Corps of General von Bonin.

The strategic village of Chlum was held by the Appiano brigade. At 14.45 hours Colonel Neuber arrived at Benedek's HQ, his face white as a sheet. '*Feldzeugmeister*, a message for your eyes only.'

'We don't have secrets, my dear Neuber. What can be so important?'

His staff officers moved around their commander to hear the message.

'Then I have to report that the Prussians have taken Chlum!'

'Don't talk nonsense, Neuber.'

'*Feldzeugmeister*, it is true, the Prussians have Chlum.'

Now it was Benedek who became white. He jumped on his horse, followed by his staff. They had just crested a rise and saw the Chlum village in front of them, when they were met by a hail of bullets. Henikstein's horse was killed, Prince Esterhazy fell from the saddle, Count Gruenne was seriously wounded. What had happened to Appiano and his brigade? Nobody had an answer, except that the Prussians had broken the Austrians' centre. It was a question of minutes. Benedek raced to his 3rd Corps to help him throw the Prussians from the village. A Hungarian unit approached. For the first time, their '*Eljen!*' (hurrah!) lacked punch. And for the first time, his own Hungarians showed little enthusiasm to follow their Magyar General.

Meanwhile, the 3rd Corps went into the attack; wave after white-uniformed wave stormed the village. Caught up in the fury of the combat, and trying to inspire his troops to superhuman effort, Benedek himself rode forward to lead the assault. The Prussians held out in farms and houses. They used the churchyard wall for their final barricade, a young Sub-Lieutenant Paul von Hindenburg[11] among them. In twenty minutes, the Austrians lost 300 officers and over a thousand men. But the Austrians managed to get back into the village. A regiment surrounded the church and captured 300 Prussian guardsmen. Their colonel, Waldersee, planted his regimental colours for a final stand. Prince Anton von Hohenzollern was wounded and captured. Then came the most famous of all Austrian regiments, *Die Deutschmeister*. Most of the village was back in Austrian hands. Only General von Hiller, the Prussian divisional commander, and a few of his fusiliers, still held out. That was the moment when a major of von Bonin's corps reached the defenders.

'God be praised,' said the Prussian general, 'you have come.'

'And in great numbers, General.'

'Now everything will turn out fine,' said General von Hiller – and fell from his horse and died. Von Bonin's Prussian corps ran forward. The counter-attack was successful. They swung round the Austrian flank and drove the white uniformed battalions from the village.

On a hill an Austrian horse artillery battery unlimbered and eight guns opened up on Chlum. Their daring action attracted the concentrated fire from a thousand rifles and their gunnery commander, Captain Groeben, was killed. Soon the guns ceased firing. When the first Prussians reached Groeben's battery they found 2 officers and 52 gunners, all dead. Nothing would now stop the Prussians' advance.

Unable to overwhelm the masses of fresh Prussian troops

[11] The hero of Tannenberg in W.W.1.

flooding into Chlum, Benedek decided to direct his full attention to the open flank where his corps commanders Thun and Festetics had earlier abandoned their position. Without awaiting orders from Moltke, the Crown Prince promptly struck Thun's corps and drove in its exposed flank. With their centre already gone, the Austrians had no more right flank.

By 15.00 hours, Benedek was informed that his left flank was also in full retreat in front of a concentrated push by the Prussian Elbe Army. At 15.40 began the general advance by the three Prussian prongs. For Benedek it was over, and he needed to save what could be saved. For this he had to protect the escape route across the Elbe bridges. To delay the enemy he used up his cavalry reserves. What followed now was a series of cavalry battles, in horror and size only surpassed by Ney's desperate charge at Waterloo. Clouds of dust showed where the masses of riders advanced, met and retreated. Artillery from both sides fired into the cavalry action and added to the chaos.

Late in the afternoon, the King of Prussia and General Moltke rode across the battlefield. The losses on both sides were heavy: 44,000 Austrians and 9,000 Prussians. They lay everywhere: in the trampled corn, in the high grass, in brambles and in the smashed trees of the Swiepwald. In a dozen ruined villages Prussians and Austrians were joined in death.

The battle was over, the battlefield belonged to the dead.

What if . . .

What if – the Army of the Crown Prince had shown up at the appointed time; that is, at the beginning of the battle?

The two Austrian corps of Thun and Festetics would

have certainly kept their position and stopped the Prussian attack. The superior Austrian artillery would have carried the day.

The facts

After the battle, a Prussian general turned to Bismarck: 'Excellency, you are now a great man. But if the Crown Prince had come too late you would now be the greatest villain.' Bismarck nodded and, using Wellington's famous phrase, admitted: 'Yes, it was a close run thing.'

The Prussian forces were too exhausted to pursue the defeated Austrians. This suited well the political plans of Bismarck. For his future global policies he needed the Austrians. Not so Moltke. That evening he berated his generals over their failure to exploit the victory with more vigour. (This shows that *the conduct of war is too serious a matter to be left to generals*.) Moltke's next task was to reform the tactical doctrine of his army. He had seen clearly that it was not the needle gun that had been king, but the accuracy of the Austrian gunners who had come within an ace of winning the battle.[12] His candid observation at Königgrätz won him the war against France in 1870.

At the field of Königgrätz, France had suffered a political defeat almost as great as the military of the Austrians. Napoleon III now realised that he had no choice but to confront the emerging military might of Prussia. To offset the effect of the Prussians' needle gun, the French infantry quickly rearmed with the Chassepot rifle.[13] France had even

---

[12] The best illustration is that the King did not allow the Prussians to advance from the centre (Chlum) before the Austrian artillery had shifted their targets to the right flank.

[13] In 1870, when the Prussians advanced in company formation, they suffered shocking casualties in their long advances.

developed a more devastating weapon, *la mitrailleuse* – the machine gun[14] – but the French used it as an artillery weapon. And so this most important of all technical improvements for infantry support was left unexploited.

General Ludwig Ritter von Benedek was churlishly rewarded for his loyalty. He received a note from Vienna. 'His Majesty the Emperor has deemed it necessary to order that an investigation be started against Your Excellency with respect to the conduct of the army . . .'[15]

Benedek was dragged before a closed court martial. The verdict was a foregone conclusion – someone had to be found guilty, and this was certainly not to be someone from the Austrian aristocracy. Benedek, a simple Hungarian, was forced to sign a promise never to reveal the true circumstances of his conversation with the Emperor. Then he was kicked out unceremoniously.[16] The 'Bayard of Austria' died a broken man.

The Austrian Army command was shaken up, and the new staff significantly redressed the shortcomings that had produced the disaster at Königgrätz. As for Emperor Franz Joseph, he did remain neutral in the Franco-Prussian War of 1870–71, and Bismarck achieved his goal in the Mirror Hall of Versailles. Wilhelm I was crowned Emperor, and a unified Germany marched under the Prussian boot towards 1914, and the First World War.

The 600-year-old Austrian Empire was never again to play a dominant role on the world stage. On the hills of Bohemia, its armies had missed their final chance to determine the course of history.

*   *   *

[14] The earliest models fired at a rate of 150 rounds a minute.

[15] 'Se. Majesttaet der kaiser haben anzubefehlen geruht, dass gegen Eure Excellenz eine Voruntersuchung ruecksichtlich der Fuehrung der hochdero Kommando anvertrauten Armee . . . etcetera . . .'

[16] His personal valet even stole his military decorations. When the Crown Prince heard of it, he offered Benedek his own medals.

The Hinge Factor at Königgrätz was the disobedience by two Austrian counts of their strict orders, and the pivotal arrival by the armies of a Prussian prince.

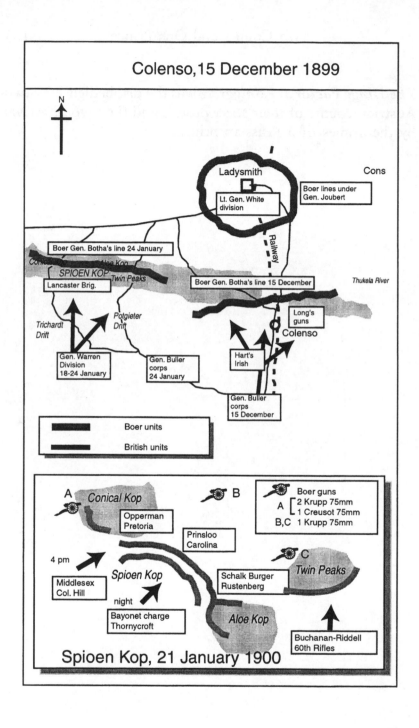

Colenso,15 December 1899

N

Ladysmith

Cons

Lt. Gen. White division

Boer lines under Gen. Joubert

Railway

Boer Gen. Botha's line 24 January

Conical *Aloe Kop*

SPIOEN KOP

Twin Peaks

Lancaster Brig.

Boer Gen. Botha's line 15 December

Thukela River

Trichardt Drift

Potgieter Drift

Long's guns

Colenso

Gen. Warren Division 18-24 January

Gen. Buller corps 24 January

Hart's Irish

Gen. Buller corps 15 December

Boer units

British units

A *Conical Kop*

B

Boer guns

A ⎡ 2 Krupp 75mm
⎣ 1 Creusot 75mm

B,C 1 Krupp 75mm

Opperman Pretoria

Prinsloo Carolina

C *Twin Peaks*

4 pm

Spioen Kop

Schalk Burger Rustenberg

Middlesex Col. Hill

night

Bayonet charge Thornycroft

Aloe Kop

Buchanan-Riddell 60th Rifles

Spioen Kop, 21 January 1900

9

A Fair Fight

Spioen Kop, 24 January 1900

'The Boers are not like the Sudanese, who stood up to a fair fight.
They're always running away on their little ponies.'
General Lord H. Kitchener, Cape Town, 1900

'Wot the fock is this . . . ?' yelled Rifleman Bert Broadbent of
the 2nd Lancashire Fusiliers. These were his last words before
he fell over backwards with a bullet through his head and his
pith helmet rolled down the steep slope. He was the first to die
that day – but not the last.

What was really happening, on top of an obscure hill
with an even more obscure name, Spioen Kop, this morning
of 24 January of the new century, to this perfectly drilled
colonial army in their khaki uniforms with coloured unit
patches on their helmets? They had marched into a war,
thousands of miles from home, in a country they didn't
know or care for. They weren't even fighting an army, just
ants, snakes and a bunch of uncouth farmers who refused to
stand up and get slaughtered in *a fair fight*. And now these
professional soldiers, befuddled and confused, were hiding
out in a shallow trench on top of a narrow ridge. They had

conquered this position in the dark of night, then piled a few boulders haphazardly in front of them, and gone to sleep. And now this!

By 8.30 a.m. the morning mist which had covered the mountain ridge was burned off by the heat of the African sun. Those delicate contours which their colonel had pointed out to them on a map before they had started on their night climb, were nowhere to be seen. There was no cover. Worst of all, they didn't look down, but up! In front of them was a slope which climbed towards the summit. They were on a horseshoe plateau – and on three hill tops surrounding them was the enemy, looking down! To put no finer point on it: they were not on top, and, furthermore, they were on the wrong hill!

Colonel Alec Thorneycroft, who had led the advance battalion of Major General E. R. P. Woodgate's 1,800 men up the steep mountain path, realised the fatal blunder. He communicated with Woodgate who ordered an immediate advance to reach a row of boulders on the edge of the shelf. But before the first company had moved halfway there they were cut down by a hail of fire from a unit of the Carolina Volunteers who lay in hiding behind these very boulders. For Woodgate's men it was too late to do anything but to dive for cover. But where was cover? The ground was flat, with hardly a blade of grass, only some knee-high boulders. Suddenly the ground erupted around them in little geysers of dust as they found themselves under a murderous deluge from the deadly Mauser rifles of the Boers, hidden well behind other boulders above and around them. The soldiers of the Lancaster Brigade couldn't advance and they couldn't retreat. There they lay, like fat beetles pinned to the ground.

It had all begun on the night of the 23rd, when Woodgate hired two *uitlanders*, non-Boer whites living in Transvaal, to guide them to the top of the strategic heights. Perhaps those guides weren't what they claimed to be, perhaps they were even Boers in disguise, whatever, in the confusion of the dark night, they slipped away and the British troops were left to find their own way to the top. Under Colonel Alec Thorneycroft of the Mounted Infantry they finally reached what they thought was the top, because they suddenly heard a whispered challenge: '*Wie's daar?* – Who goes there?'

In the surprise of the moment, the colonel automatically gave the English password, '*Waterloo*', and his men were met by a hail of bullets. The colonel issued an order which was passed along the line: 'Fix bayonets!' The fire soon died down as the defenders had to reload.

The colonel yelled 'Charge!' and his unit, the first troops to reach the crest, rose as one man to rush at the Boer line, screaming from the top of their lungs: '*Majuba!*', after the place where the British had suffered a disastrous defeat by the Boers in 1881.

'*Majuba!*' did it; the Boers slipped away into the night. There had only been fifteen of them, volunteers of the Boers' Vryheid Commando. They were just as surprised as their enemy and had never suspected that the British would try and take this hill because it would lead them nowhere.

Having thus 'conquered the summit', the Brits gave three hearty cheers to let their commanding general in the valley know that the objective was now secured. General Warren heard their cheers inside his HQ tent.

'So they've taken the hill?' he smiled.

'Yes, sir', replied his duty officer.

'Opposition?' Warren checked his situation map.

'Hardly any, sir, very few losses, gratifyingly so.'

Had he acted right away, his men could have walked down the gentle slopes on the other side of the Kop and straight on to the relief of the beleaguered British garrison, which was the purpose of this whole operation. Yet General Warren did nothing.

'Take the high ground and hold it', were his orders, and Lieutenant General Sir Charles Warren was not a very imaginative leader.

Since no further order for an immediate push was received by the Lancashire regiments on the heights, they tried to dig a defensive trench line, but soon gave it up as the ground was solid as rock. They pushed a few boulders around them, then bunked down for the night. Major General E. R. P. Woodgate was a 'decent man'; his troops were tired from the climb and he granted them some respite. So he too did nothing; didn't even send out a patrol to check the terrain directly in front of his line; he simply waited for further instructions from division. None came. Communications between Buller and Warren, and from Warren to his forward units, had completely broken down.

Just before the first light rose over the African veld, a mist crept up along the flank of the mountain and shrouded their view. Then it happened. The mist cracked open.

'Wot the fock . . . ?' Now it was too late. Much too late!

In 1652, the Dutch established a small settlement on the Cape of Good Hope, a trading post for the ships of the Dutch East India Company. The treasures of silks and spices were to be found in the Orient, not in unexplored black Africa. The Napoleonic Wars, and the following *Pax Britannica*, dictated British maritime policy. The Royal Navy needed refuelling stations around the world, and the Cape was on the way to India. They pushed the Boers (the Dutch word for farmer) inland. In 1830, the Boers set out on their Great Trek and settled in Orange Free State and Transvaal, while the British established themselves along the coastline in Cape Province and Natal. For the next fifty years all went well, until 1886, when diamonds were discovered at Kimberley and gold near Witwatersrand. This aroused the interest of British financial barons, especially Cecil Rhodes, who built his fortune in mining and then left his name to an entire province, Rhodesia. He tried to get the British government to conquer the interior. Rhodes's own attempt to overthrow the Boer colony of Johannesburg, led by his incompetent lieutenant Leander Starr Jameson, failed in disaster. It taught Rhodes a lesson, but also showed the Boers that they needed guns and a well-trained force to operate them. Their president, Paul 'Ohm' Kruger, exchanged gold for Mauser rifles and Krupp cannons from Germany. These guns held a marked advantage over anything existing in previous warfare: they fired with smokeless gunpowder. As it was soon to prove, this made the difference in the forthcoming battles, since it left the British gunnery spotters without visible targets to fire on.

Like many inventions, guncotton was discovered by accident. In 1846, the German chemist Christian Friedrich Schönbein researched into a new cloth fibre for his employer, a cotton mill owner. He treated cotton with a mixture of nitric and sulphuric acids and obtained as a result cellulose nitrate (nitrocellulose), better known as *guncotton*, the basis of smokeless gunpowder. The cotton mill owner didn't know what to do with this 'useless stuff', since he could hardly produce shirts which caught fire. At the same time, Alfred Krupp, who was working on the development of his revolutionising steel gun, immediately recognised its use in its application as a propellant for his cannons.

The Germans delivered the guns together with an artillery instructor, Major Albrecht, who had learned his trade in the Franco-Prussian War. He quickly formed an élite force, the Free State Artillery, the only unit in the Boer forces who wore regular uniforms. He taught them the principle of howitzer fire,[1] but, even more important, he drilled into them the

---

[1] While guns shoot in a straight trajectory, howitzers lob shells over an obstacle, such as a mountain peak, and onto a target.

art of quick position changes by units, single guns firing from hidden positions, while their enemy still stuck to the Napoleonic type battery set-up of six guns placed in open terrain.

A conflict was at hand. In June 1899, British and Boers sat down at a negotiating table in their capital, Bloemfontein. The British delegation was led by their High Commissioner for the Cape, Sir Alfred Milner, feeling terribly superior in his splendid uniform, facing an old man with a white beard, 'Ohm' Kruger dressed in black with a top hat, and looking more like a peasant than a president. Their 'friendly' discussion ended in stalemate, which was broken on 11 October 1899. The Second Boer War, which Afrikaaners called *Tweede Vryheidsoorlog*, was on.

The British were confident that the Boers would use the same human wave assaults which had led the Sudanese Dervishes to their destruction at Omdurman only the year before, in 1898. Their South African Expeditionary Force was commanded by General Sir Redvers Buller, who was soon to earn for himself the sobriquet of 'Reverse Buller'. He had raised military technique to a new level of incompetence when he once ordered, as commander of the training centre at Aldershot, that manoeuvres were to take place only between 9 a.m. and 5 p.m., with a pause during the noon day heat, and that no soldier was allowed to dive for cover when shot at as this would soil his uniform.

His second in command was Lieut-General Sir George White who had arrived in Natal before his boss, General Buller. White took the decision to cross the Tugela River, a formidable water barrier, and advance on Ladysmith, though he was aware that his division of 10,000 was no match against the 35,000 Boers who had invaded Natal Province. What had to happen did happen. White's small army became encircled and the long siege of Ladysmith began. His impetuous act, lacking all common as well as military sense, was to lead the British to a sequence of disasters.

The first in the series of setbacks, which was to go down as 'Black Week', happened in Orange Free State, where General Methuen's columns were ambushed by the Boer General Piet Cronje on the Modder River on 28 November 1899. Methuen lost 24 officers and 461 men.

Only two weeks later, on 11 December 1899, a repeat encounter put Methuen against Cronje once again, this time at Magersfontein. Methuen was not a man who would take advice nor had he learned his lesson. For an entire day he bombarded a hill in the belief that it was held by Boers, when in fact it was not. After he was convinced that all Boer resistance had been crushed, he ordered Brigadier Wauchope to lead his 3,500 Highlanders through a night of torrential rain up the slopes. The thunder that rolled across the hills sounded like boulders being rolled down on the men.

Methuen dispatched Wauchope's men into a deadly trap. Cronje's look-outs had informed him about Wauchope's movements, and now the sharpshooting Boers of Commandant Cronje were on the slopes above them and poured a withering fire into the fleeing *rooineks*, the red-necked Tommies. Many were shot in the back as they ran down the slope. Heroic Brigadier Wauchope was found lying dead across a Boer trench. This new disaster cost the British 68 officers and 1,011 men, dead and wounded, although this time the Boers also suffered some 200 casualties. Again, the C-in-C, General Buller, remained unperturbed and did nothing to reprimand his bungling General.

Another disaster to befall the British that same 'Black Week' was that of General William Gatacre, better known as 'Backacher'. On 10 December 1899, at the Stormberg railway junction, this bonehead marched his 3,000 troops in the wrong direction. The only man who knew the way had been left behind. When morning broke, the British found themselves at the bottom of a cliff too steep to climb, while on top the Boers were quietly having their morning coffee. You may imagine their surprise when they saw the British actually marching away from them, before they fired at them from the heights. For the British it ended in a mad scramble to reach safety. General Gatacre congratulated himself that he had lost only 89 men, but he didn't take into account the 633 who were captured because he had simply forgotten to tell them to withdraw.

That evening Gatacre received a cable from his commander, Sir Redvers Buller: 'BETTER LUCK NEXT TIME.'

It wasn't a Boer leader who was to lead to Buller's downfall, but his own divisional commander, Lieut-General Sir Charles Warren, probably the worst general any English military academy had ever produced. This fifty-nine-year-old, called back from retirement, when asked by Lord Wolseley, head of the British Forces, how he saw the Boer Campaign, stated: 'Pound him with artillery, attack in line, and give Johnny Boer a solid good bashing with his trousers down.'

Though Buller must have been aware of Warren's foibles, he still delegated to him the crucial attack on Spioen Kop.

But first came Colenso, 15 December 1899.

Buller had marched his columns across the African veld, following the rail line which led from the port city of Durban to Ladysmith. To rush his vastly superior forces to the rescue of the beleaguered British garrison of General White at Ladysmith, he was faced with only one major obstacle, the Tugela River, swollen by rain. Since Buller was not someone who believed in forward scout patrols, he went by a map which was badly out-of-date. He had four possible crossing points: Potgieter's Drift, Trichardt's Drift, both on an oxen-cart track, and two bridges at Colenso. One of them was an iron trestle railway bridge. Buller opted for that crossing, an obvious ambush site even for a beginner. And the man who faced him, Boer General Louis Botha was no beginner. There was no great sophistication in Botha's defences, there didn't need to be, sheer common sense dictated his strategy. Botha had blown up the railway bridge, but left the road bridge intact to lure the British into a trap. That they didn't fall for it has nothing to do with generalship, but with the fact that they didn't know about its location. Potgieter's and Trichardt's Drifts were too far upriver; also, these were controlled by a high mountain chain, culminating in Spioen Kop. But Buller had discovered on his map a 'Bridle Drift' right after Colenso village inside a river bend. That's where he would cross.

On the British side, open grassland sloped gently towards the river, allowing the dug-in Boers a wonderful field of fire. The Boer side of the Tugela was blocked by a series of koppies, or hills, the so vital high ground in a battle. There was a weak point in Botha's defence – the left flank was open – but that the British never discovered because they didn't send out scouts.

Buller ordered up his artillery, a time-consuming task as branches had to be laid down to prevent the ironshod wheels from sinking into the ground, softened by rains. Once his batteries were set in position, he began to pepper the koppies, expecting the Boers to hold the ridge line. They were not there. Contrary to strategy taught in military academies, the Boers were beautifully camouflaged and dug in on the flats, near the river. They were terrifyingly close to the British, should their attack ford the stream.

Buller's attack was set for 15 December 1899. There were two actors in the drama who were both to play a decisive role: Major General Hart of the 5th Irish Brigade, and Colonel

Long of the 14th and 66th Field Artillery, with twelve guns, backed up by Lieutenant Ogilvy with another six heavy naval guns. What happened at Colenso is quite unique.

At 6 a.m. on a misty morning, Hart ordered his four battalions to march in close battle order down the grassy slopes and towards the position of Bridle's Drift, a shallow ford which was supposed to be inside a narrow U formed by the Tugela River. By doing so he executed a repeat performance of the Charge of the Light Brigade, guns to the left, guns to the right, into the valley of death rode the six-hundred . . . Only this time, there were not six hundred but four thousand.

The Boers must indeed have been surprised what they saw coming at them: an early nineteenth-century Napoleonic formation, tightly pressed marching squares, with a General, Sabre held high, with his native guide running by the side of his horse, leading the Dublin Fusiliers and Inniskillins, with the Connaughts and the Border Regiment bringing up the rear. Four battalions, a jammed-up mass of 4,000 *rooineks* on a front-line of only 800 yards! It was suicide. The Boers, invisible in their deep trenches, were lying in wait on the three sides of the bend in the river, with their new Mauser rifles, deadly up to 2,000 yards!

Hart advanced with his Irish Brigade against almost no resistance. The thin line of skirmishers on the opposite river bank was brushed aside with a few shots. For the general it was the most exciting moment of his life. He gave no thought as to the whereabouts of Botha's army or the Boer artillery. A few shells from his own support artillery, Parson's 63rd Battery, whistled overhead to impact on the distant hills. Logic told the gunners, that's where the enemy was. But Boers never followed logic, only instinct.

Hart's native guide pointed to the right. 'General, ford over there.'

The general stood up in the stirrups, pointed with his sabre to the spot indicated by his guide. His regiments wheeled in perfect formation, and then, in a straight line, marched for the centre of the dug-in Boers who held their fire until the dense British columns were within 300 yards. Botha's 'open fire' signal was a shot from his 5-inch Krupp howitzer. Then they let them have it.

As soon as firing broke out, Hart's native guide disappeared and the general was completely lost. The opposite bank was like a fire-spitting dragon and the shock had its immediate effect on the Irishmen. 'A devil of a mess', as a survivor called it. Hart's perfect formations were coming apart.

'Form up, regardless of rank,' he yelled, 'officers and men in one column.' He checked on the map dangling from his pommel and found on it a mark in the river's bend of what looked like a ford. Without any further recce, he ordered his men to cross.

'Keep on, keep on! I'll give you a lead', he yelled. 'Will you follow your general?' The men were torn between different loyalties, that for Queen and Country, and that to themselves and survival. Surprisingly, they followed their leader. The first company jumped into the river . . .

His map was inaccurate. At this point the river was over 300 feet across and 20 feet deep, and the few who made it down the bank immediately disappeared beneath the surface. Bullets and grape-shot whipped across the water, mowing down row after row of khaki-clad men. Hart remained frozen in his saddle, staring across the river, ignoring the bullets buzzing around him. He may have been an incompetent fool, but he was brave. Perhaps he thought that he was bullet-proof. Whatever his thoughts, even the greatest fool, bullet-proof or not, must surely have been wondering at such a moment why he had led his men into such a trap.

Buller's stocky figure stood in the midst of a crowd of officers, all observing the debacle from his command post. With a pair of binoculars to his eyes he watched Hart's 5th Irish Brigade being decimated.

'Hart has a problem,' Buller said to Lyttleton, commander of the 4th Scottish Brigade. 'Take your men and help him out. Do your best.'

But before Lyttleton could move a new event took place which took attention away from Hart's disaster.

On the right flank, Hildyard's 2nd English Brigade moved forward. Colonel Long, its field artillery commander, angered over the slow progress of the six oxen-drawn heavy naval guns, suddenly galloped at the head of his twelve lighter cannons of the 14th and 66th Batteries almost to the river's edge, where he had the guns unlimbered. He got off a series of volleys, but as the guns had no protective shields, his men keeled over in a storm of Mauser bullets.

'Damn this man's impatience,' cursed Buller, 'he's going to lose me my guns.' Twelve cannons, with many of their gunners dead and no more ammunition, stood silent along the river bank.

Buller still had all his reserves, some 8,000 men, but rather than deploy them and provide overall guidance to the rest of his army, he was so taken by Long's cannons that he abandoned his command post to personally save his precious guns. In an incredible feat of heroism, which earned those who participated in this action seven Victoria Crosses (one of them posthumously to Lieutenant Freddy Roberts, whose father eventually replaced General Buller), they managed to pull back two of the cannons, but the others couldn't be saved. The loss of his guns, more than the loss of a whole brigade, so shattered Buller's confidence that he called off the battle at 11 a.m.

That afternoon, while the British laid out their dead with what little dignity was left to them, the Boers crossed the river and recovered ten guns. Like Ney at Waterloo, Long's men had made no attempt to disable them, and the Free State Artillery was suddenly doubled in size.

British casualties at the Battle of Colenso were 71 officers and 1,055 soldiers, half of them from the Irish Brigade, while the Boers lost only 40 men. And yet, worse was still to come.

24 January 1900. Spioen Kop, or Look-out Hill. Lieut General Sir Charles Warren's hour of infamy.

The name tells us that it was a superb place to see the countryside. It was from there that the Boer Voortrekkers of 1830 first stared in wonder at their promised land. Spioen Kop Ridge was also a strategically vital mountain straddling two oxen tracks to Ladysmith. It had to be taken, and General Warren was appointed to the task. What is so amazing about this particular battle is that neither Buller nor Warren had the slightest notion what to do after this strategic hill was captured.

> *'The noble Duke of York,*
> *He had ten thousand men,*
> *He marched them up to the top of the hill,*
> *And he marched them down again . . .'*

Since Colenso in mid-December, the British Army was stretched out in bivouac on the Tugela River bank, more like a giant camping site, a tent city by the river. This suited the Tommies fine, they cooked and washed their clothes and took a skinny dip, while the Generals discussed strategy. The order to cross the river at Trichardt's Drift and take Spioen Kop went out on 18 January 1900, and over the next few days General Warren spent most of his time supervising his personal luggage to cross the Tugela safely. No General was expected to travel without vintage port, cases of champagne and the other dire necessities of life in the field. Furthermore, the ageing general loved to take a bath in the river and left it to his subordinates to get on with the order of battle. For the attack on the hill itself, he appointed Major General J. Talbot-Coke. When it was found that Coke suffered from a broken leg and could hardly be expected to climb a steep mountain, Warren transferred the command to Major General E. R. P. Woodgate. While Coke was a good leader but had only one leg, Woodgate had two legs but no head.

The man who confronted them was a round-faced man with a drooping moustache, the thirty-seven-year-old 'Hero of Natal', General Louis Botha, a man of great confidence and daring, much loved by his men, those gaunt figures, dressed in farmer clothes, with sunken cheeks. The hands that held onto the long-barrelled Mauser rifles were gnarled and blue-veined, farmer's hands. Their heads were covered by wide-brimmed hats and they had not shaved in weeks. The Rustenberg Commando of Schalk Burger held the Twin Peaks sector. Next to him, on Spioen Kop, were the Carolina Volunteers of Commandant Hendrik Prinsloo, and Daniel Opperman's Pretoria Commando, seasoned leaders who had learned their trade by stalking wild beasts and rebellious tribes. Between them they had three 75 mm Krupps and two 75 mm Creusot guns, a formidable fire-power for its time, especially if put in position by their German expert, Major Albrecht. Ably supported by units from Krugersdorp, Boksburg, Heidelberg and Utrecht, these 'backwood Johnnys' were about to teach the professional colonial officers of Queen Victoria's Empire a severe lesson.

At 9 p.m. on the night of 23 January 1900, Major General Woodgate and the 1,800 men of his Lancashire Brigade, made up of Lancashire Fusiliers and the King's Own Royal Lancasters, set off on their long climb. Under cover of darkness their two *uitlander* guides slipped away and Colonel

Alec Thorneycroft of the Mounted Infantry, the only senior officer who had carefully studied the ridge line through his binoculars, took charge. He and his unit toiled up the steep incline.

Just before setting off on their steep climb, every soldier was handed a filled sandbag intended to fortify the ridge line. The bad news was that the hill was barren and without cover, and the good news was there was lots of sand down there in the valley which they had to carry up the hill. Because of that precaution, Woodgate only ordered up twenty entrenching tools for his almost 2,000 men. The hill was steep, the night was dark, the sandbags were heavy and the soldiers stumbled around, fighting for breath. Soon the footpath up to the ridge was dotted with discarded sandbags. Others, again, suffered from stomach cramps because of polluted river water in their water bottles, and went into the bushes.

'Com'on men, don't fall behind, this hill is crawling with Johnny Boers', whispered their officers.

'Yessah . . .'

'Do ya want to miss all the fun?' For once the sergeants only murmured as they were forbidden to bark in their usual tone.

'I dun like it, sargent, it's a trap.'

'Oh, shut up and keep movin', soldier.'

Soon the head of the column had lost contact with the rest of the troops. Soldiers had learned to keep well back from their eager young officers so that they weren't ordered to help carry additional charges. Most of them only heard the commotion as Thorneycroft's front units cleared the ridge with a hearty bayonet charge.

The fifteen Boers of Prinsloo's Carolina Command who had held a thin skirmish line on the forward ledge of the ridge, and had made good their escape, now ran into their camp on the back slope.

'*Die Engelske is op die Kop!* ('The English are on the hill!')

   After a momentary panic among some of the Boers, who hadn't expected an attack on the hill by night, Boer General Louis Botha, keeping a cool head as usual, ordered his commanders Hendrik Prinsloo, Daniel Opperman and Schalk Burger to occupy all the heights not already in enemy hands, or try and push the British from the commanding heights. For the Boers it was a mad run up the hill to beat the British. Out of breath they reached the vital Aloe Kop and Conical Kop, as well as Twin Peaks. One may well understand their surprise when they discovered that not a single summit had been taken. Now they were on top and the English were below! They piled up formidable boulder breastworks before the British recognised their blunder. From these positions they would be able to fire straight down on the English line come first light. Though the English heard the rolling of stones in the night, they didn't give it a second thought.

   At the same time, Botha issued another order which was to prove the decisive factor of the forthcoming battle. He placed his artillery pieces singly and in such hidden positions that the enemy couldn't spot them, but so that their shells would strike the English line accurately, and still only 100 metres from his own men. It was a daring gamble, but it worked.

'Wot the fock . . . ?' 8.30 a.m. Suddenly the curtain of mist which had shrouded the mountain tore apart and the long-suffering of the Lancasters began. The Boer artillery opened up. Krupp and Creusot shells lit up the ridge line. From the surrounding summits a hail of Mauser bullets rained down. The Lancaster Brigade was caught in a deadly semi-circle of steel and lead. There was no place to hide, only a few hastily piled-up boulders. General Woodgate tried to rally his men to a charge. In doing so he lifted his head and was struck above his eye by a fragment from a shell.

   Soon there were so many casualties that the survivors were able to use the corpses as cover. They men dug their fingers into the hard ground and could only pray that shrapnel from the next shell would miss them. In that cramped position on the hard ground they lay there and steeled themselves for the next shell to crash in among them, then the next, and the next . . . These came as regular as clockwork: seven, ten every minute. From those Krupps and Creusots, a real carnage. With no place to hide.

Since neither Buller nor Warren had made plans for what to do next, and the generals in the valley had no idea of the situation on the mountain, Warren ordered a message flashed to the top: 'STOP WHERE YOU ARE.'

Colonel Thorneycroft managed to get off one last message before his signal mirror was shattered by a bullet: 'CANNOT REMAIN IN OPEN. MUST ADVANCE OR WITHDRAW.'

He received no reply.

No wonder. General Warren had been told to take the ridge, not what to do once he held it in his possession. That was General Buller's problem. And yet Warren sent no message to Buller, asking for further instructions.

From his HQ position, Warren observed, but issued no further orders other than to enquire: 'Can we get some guns up?' The reply was negative. To drag artillery up the mountain was quite out of the question; the slopes were too steep for this from the British side. It never occurred to Warren to send out scout patrols to check for a vulnerable spot in the enemy's defences.

From further down the river, Buller observed in silence before he ordered his heavy guns to shell the surrounding high ground. This didn't seem to help; the Boers were well dug in, and their guns couldn't be silenced because they couldn't be spotted owing to the smokeless powder. And so, the British artillery expended their shells on rocks and other uninteresting real estate. Buller certainly had a better grasp of the true situation than his subordinate divisional commander. But he didn't pass on any instructions to Warren – such as his spotters had (correctly) identified Boers on the hills surrounding Spioen Kop – and Warren was left in the belief that his men held the entire ridge. Buller wouldn't interfere in the regulated chain of command, and left it to Warren, who was either paralysed or incapable of adjusting, either of which didn't help his boys on the kop.

One of Warren's naval gunners spotted a runner on Aloe Kop – probably the Boer scout Louis Bothma – scampering from boulder to boulder to reach the bare summit of the kop from where he then directed the Boer artillery barrage on the hapless Lancasters. However, right below Bothma was movement from the dug-in Boers. Now the heavy British naval guns poured fire onto the forward slope of Aloe Kop, using the new lyddite explosive. Shells hit the Boer line and caused severe casualties. Fortunately for the Boers, Warren was so out of touch with the situation that he immediately stopped the highly effective shelling in his mistaken belief that it was British soldiers who had conquered the heights. A few more shells with the same accuracy, and Aloe Kop would have ceased to be a menace.

Up on Spioen Kop it was hell. On the plateau it was windless and fiercely hot. The impacting shells whirled up clouds of dry earth, clogging the membranes of the soldiers' nostrils so that they had to breathe through their mouths, sucking in lungfuls of grating dust which made them cough. The explosion of stinging cordite made their eyes smart and water, blinding them. The pale silhouette of the sun penetrated ghost-like the brown fog left by the explosions. Just as bad as the shelling was their thirst, swollen tongues jammed like rubber balls into their mouths. Their water-bottles were empty; they had used up their water during the night climb. Their lips cracked and bled. One man went off his head and scooped up the sugary white sand to bring it to his lips. The moment he raised his head he was felled by a bullet, a fate reserved for anyone who showed any sign of life – he would be immediately cut down by a Boer marksman crouching behind a rock on one of the surrounding summits. But if they didn't move, those who tried to play dead were driven mad by the bites of ants who crept under their tunics. In front of the trench lay the corpse of a company commander. Fat flies were humming over the dead man's face. A sergeant had been hit in the thigh, suffering a nasty flesh wound. He used the webbing belt from a dead man as his tourniquet. Others, hiding behind their fallen comrades, fired at shadows among the boulders. One soldier was lying on his back, writing a good-bye note to his girlfriend.

Colonel Thorneycroft was right among his troopers. A low stone wall had been hastily erected which served as his temporary HQ. His men were getting blown to pieces and he had to do something about it.

'Sergeant,' he ordered one of his company NCO's, 'get through to General Warren. It's imperative. We need reinforcements and our artillery must lay covering fire on these hilltops.' He marked the position on a map.

'Yessah, I'll get through.' The man knew he had to rely on luck and speed. Mostly on luck.

'Okay, I'll give you covering fire. Go!' The colonel popped away with his service revolver until he ran out of bullets. The sergeant scrambled like a beetle across bodies and boulders, and then he was gone.

1 p.m. Another seven hours of daylight. A fusilier tied his handkerchief to his rifle and raised it above the parapet, copied by quite a few others. For a moment silence descended on the plateau. Over a hundred soldiers jumped up and staggered over to surrender to the Boers. Everyone had some kind of bandage, muddied, stained by blood that had soaked through.

A group of Boer marksmen had used the break in the firing to creep within stone's throw of the British right flank. Suddenly they leapt up and raced for the British line. At a few places they broke through the boulder barrier and for a few desperate moments furious hand-to-hand slaughter occurred, pistols held point-blank to chest or belly, guns raised high as clubs, men falling over each other. Gaps left by the dead or wounded were taken up by others, until the initial onslaught lost its impetus and the Boers retired like ghosts behind their boulders. Curiously, this sudden attack helped to restore morale in the Lancastrians. A cheer, 'We've sent them off!' went down the line.

General Buller studied the situation through his field-glasses. Next to him were his artillery spotters. All they could see were impacts, but not the firing point.

'Damn that German gunpowder', he cursed. With that, he contented himself with some long-distance supporting gunfire, but he took no further active part in the battle himself.

At Warren's HQ the situation was somewhat similar, if not worse. The artillery spotters, trained to look out for the tell-tale cotton puffs from the muzzles of the enemy's guns, couldn't spot any. The German instructor, Major Albrecht, had cleverly concealed his howitzer and guns behind the koppies and his Krupps fired with smokeless powder, that invention which was to revolutionise future warfare.

'Targets, I need targets!' screamed the British officer in charge of Warren's heavy guns.

'None, sir. There are none', came the constant reply.

For the British gunners this provided a dilemma. Fire blind on the ridge line and risk hitting their own men, or withhold artillery support altogether. Since that last heliographed message from the ridge, no further signal had reached HQ.

'Until a clearer picture emerges, divisional artillery support is withheld by order of the divisional commander', they were told.

Warren stepped outside his tent and stared at the top of the ridge. He could hear the rumbling all along the ridge line. Earlier his intelligence officer had tried to get a scout through to the Lancasters on Spioen Kop, but the man had limped back with a bullet through his side and without being able to give even an approximate idea of the extent of the debacle.

Eventually, following a harassed descent, during which a bullet had pierced his pith helmet, Thorneycroft's messenger reached the commanding General. The only surviving commander, he had to report to the General, and asked for immediate reinforcements and artillery support. Still Warren would do nothing, paralysed by indecision.

Now took place one of those episodes which go down in history. A young, inexperienced war reporter helplessly observed the slaughter. He dared to plead with Warren to send reserves to the rescue of the men who were being sacrificed. 'General, for God's sake do something.'

'That's none of your damn business,' roared the irate general; 'arrest that man!' And the troublesome journalist was arrested. His name was Winston Churchill.

It never occurred to General Warren that the best way to relieve pressure on Spioen Kop was to launch a diversionary attack on another hill. There was one man who thought of it. Lyttleton dispatched the Scotsmen of his King's Royal Rifle Corps, without asking Warren for permission, towards a hill called Twin Peaks. To him this seemed the obvious choice since the Boers were concentrated on and around Spioen Kop. Shortly afterwards he was handed a message that Twin Peaks was back in the hands of the Boers, that a gun had been put in place, and that his men were in danger of getting slaughtered in a hail of grapeshot. He dispatched a runner to call off the attack. However, the commander of the 60th Rifles, Colonel Buchanan-Riddell, refused to obey Lyttleton's order. He knew he had to relieve the Lancasters. It was only after he was killed that his officers reluctantly turned back. But one unit, the Middlesex of Colonel Hill, made it to the top, where they were quickly outflanked by a detachment of Boers and found themselves in a precarious situation. Only the quick intervention by the Scottish Rifles under Colonel Coke, who miraculously showed up at this crucial moment, saved Hill's men from annihilation. In a hotly fought skirmish the Boers suffered heavy casualties.

It is an irony to this day, that at that moment the battle could have been turned into a British victory. The attack by the Middlesex and Scottish Rifles so worried the Boer commander, Schalk Burger, whose men had suffered from British random shelling and were almost out of bullets and expecting to face ever more British reserves, that he ordered his valuable Krupp cannon behind Aloe Kop to be pulled out, the one that had laid the most devastating barrage on the English line. He feared repeating the British error of Colenso. Without this gun, he realised, it would be but a matter of time before fresh British reserves would take the koppies. He passed along the word for his badly depleted Boers to move out, when something happened.

It was getting dark. Colonel Thorneycroft felt abandoned by his superior commanders. There was nothing more to be achieved by hanging on. His valiant Lancaster boys had withstood heat and fire for thirteen hours. Without awaiting permission from Warren, he ordered a general retreat.

The withdrawal of the Lancaster Brigade from Spioen Kop, that night of 25 January 1900, was to go down in the history of the Boer War as 'the long ladder of pain'. After nightfall the survivors took their wounded and left 'their' trench. Bent under the heavy load of their suffering comrades, they slid with their nailed boots on the steep, rocky slope. More men fell, hit in the back by random bullets; others used their rifles as crutches. Those who eventually made it down, sweating and black with powder, looked as if they had emerged from hell. And they had! One man cried. He felt ashamed. 'It's all right, lad,' said his sergeant, 'poor bastards, all gone . . .' and then he also cried. And: 'Nearer my God to Thee', sang the men.

All their sacrifice, their suffering had been in vain. Buller ordered a general withdrawal across the Tugela. It earned him the epithet 'The ferryman of the Tugela'. Up on the ridge plateau, churned up by hundreds of impacts, the Boers moved once again in strength onto Spioen Kop.

The following morning the top of Spioen Kop presented a ghastly sight. The Boers piled the fallen foe into the narrow 'Lancaster trench'. It overflowed with corpses, many mutilated by direct hits from the 75 mm shells. By their own account, the Boers suffered some 225 casualties (killed and wounded), which sounds low, considering the bloody hand-to-hand struggle for possession of the ridge, as well as random shelling. British losses were recorded as 87 officers and 1,647 men.

There is a hill in Natal which will forever carry the name of the valiant Boers and the equally valiant British units. *Spioen Kop*.

Queen Victoria, when told about 'Black Week', replied: 'There is no one depressed in this house. We are not interested in the possibilities of defeat. They do not exist.'

Sir Redvers Buller was replaced by Field-Marshal Lord Roberts of Kandahar seconded by Lord Kitchener of Khartoum. The war took a change and the Boer Army was battered into submission. On 27 February 1900, General Cronje surrendered his 4,000 Boers and Kimberley was delivered. A day later Buller entered Ladysmith following a siege which had lasted 118 days, Roberts took Bloemfontein on 13 March, Johannesburg on 31 May and Pretoria on 5 June 1900. President 'Ohm' Kruger fled to Holland. Transvaal and the Orange Free State were annexed. The struggle by the Boers continued for two more years, mainly as hit-and-run guerrilla warfare. Lord Kitchener responded with a brutal scorched earth policy.

This war brought no glory to the British Empire. It was the British in South Africa who first put to use that institution of terror, the *concentration camp*. Their military rounded up entire Boer villages and dragged men, women and children behind barbed wire. One out of every six captives died of malnutrition. The government tried to deny the camps' existence. The press reported on the atrocious conditions, anti-British riots flared up. In the House of Commons it was denounced as 'methods of barbarism'.

'*Nothing, not even the incapacity of the military authorities when charged with the novel and distasteful task of herding large bodies of civilians into captivity, could justify the conditions in the camps themselves*', wrote Winston Churchill in *The Great Democracies*.

The Second Boer War came to an end on 31 May 1902.

A few days later, Cecil Rhodes died. His prophetic final words were: 'You think you've beaten the Dutch. It is not so. The country is still as much theirs as yours. You will have to live with them now as in the past.'

What if . . .

What if – Buller had attacked simultaneously at Trichardt's Drift and at Colenso?
    The Boers were so thin on the ground, they couldn't possibly have stopped an attack.

What if – Warren had ordered just a small contingent of his

massive reserves to come to the assistance of the
harried Lancasters by attacking another hill?

He didn't, and that's that.

The facts

The Boer War rang in the dawn of a new century. Henry
Ford replaced the horse-drawn carriage with the automobile
and a Mr George Eastman of Waterville, NY, introduced his
'Box Brownie photographic apparatus'. In Vienna, a certain
Dr. Sigmund Freud published *The Interpretation of Dreams*.

In military terms, the beginning of the new century brought
with it a radical development in armaments and strategies.
*'In this war, the old terror of a visible foe gave way to
the paralysing sensation of advancing on an invisible foe,
which fostered the suspicion that the enemy was everywhere'*,
wrote the English strategist, Major General J. F. C. 'Boney'
Fuller, later.

For the British Empire the Boer War signalled the end of the
colonial era. For a time, Britain's professional soldiers were
undone by the 'rat pack' they so despised.

In the African veld the British general staff had to find out
the hard way that it was no longer possible to attack dug-in
men armed with small-bore magazine rifles with a 'Hurrah!'
in a frontal bayonet charge. And that smokeless powder had
effectively changed artillery warfare when it neutralised the
target acquisition by British artillery spotters.

A lesson to be learned for the next war. The Big One.

They didn't learn . . .

The Hinge Factor at Spioen Kop was an abject failure by two
British military commanders – and Dr Schönbein's smokeless
gunpowder.

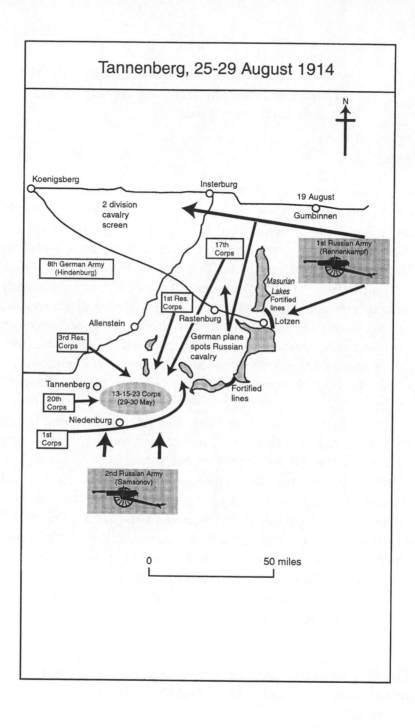

Tannenberg, 25-29 August 1914

N

Koenigsberg

Insterburg

19 August

Gumbinnen

2 division
cavalry
screen

1st Russian Army
(Rennenkampf)

17th
Corps

8th German Army
(Hindenburg)

Masurian
Lakes
Fortified
lines

1st Res.
Corps

Allenstein

Rastenburg

Lotzen

3rd Res.
Corps

German plane
spots Russian
cavalry

Tannenberg

13-15-23 Corps
(29-30 May)

Fortified
lines

20th
Corps

Niedenburg

1st
Corps

2nd Russian Army
(Samsonov)

0   50 miles

10

A Slap on the Face

Tannenberg, 28 August 1914

General Ludendorff: *'Die Russischen soldaten kämpfen wie Bären.'*
Colonel Max Hoffmann: *'Gewiss, Herr General, aber diese Bären werden von Eseln angeführt.'*

'The Russian soldiers fight like bears.'
'Yes, General, but these bears are led by donkeys.'

Conversation between General Ludendorff and Colonel Hoffmann,
Tannenberg, 1914.

The man in the mud-spattered uniform slumped against the mangled stump of a birch that had been shattered by the impact of a shell. He lifted his face to stare at the deep blue sky and the flock of wild geese that sailed across. How he wished he could fly with them. But he couldn't. Slowly he raised his pistol, put it to his head, and pulled the trigger.

General Alexander Samsonov had joined the rest of his army that lay dead near a village called Tannenberg. They say that he was ashamed to face the Czar. He was never buried because he was never found. Just one of the many thousands who died in the marshes of the Masurian Lakes in that fateful August of 1914.

*   *   *

War in Czarist Russia was military glory reserved for nobility. Peasants were cannon fodder, but counts were promoted instant colonels; princes and dukes were made generals. Alexander Samsonov was the exception. Neither prince nor duke, he was a reasonably efficient administrator with good connections.

The overall command of Russian forces was in the hands of Grand Duke Nicholas, the Czar's uncle. Their armies were divided into two groups: the Northern Group against the Germans of East Prussia, and the Southern Front against the Austrians in Polish Galicia. The plan for the Northern forces, the First and Second Russian Armies, had never taken into account that their two-pronged attack would be divided by the waters of the Masurian Lakes, and lakes had never been a good omen for the soldiers of the Czar: there had been a lake at Austerlitz. Thus, the Germans, though inferior in manpower but with much greater mobility, could attack each army separately before they would be able to unite.

The First Russian Army, in Vilna, was under the command of General Pavel Rennenkampf, a man very competent, very aristocratic and very arrogant. His German ancestry, his Prussian name and the Junker moustache did nothing to help raise his popularity with the troops, nor did a persistent rumour that 'our general is going to visit his German cousins'.

The Second Russian Army was led by Alexander Samsonov, recalled from retirement only two weeks before. The general suffered greatly from bouts of asthma, an ailment brought on by emotional stress. Not a good start to lead an army. Furthermore, Samsonov did not possess the aggressive qualities of his arch rival Rennenkampf. However, he was known for his dogged determination to execute orders.

The Northern command structure was the Waterloo Syndrome all over again. The right wing under Rennenkampf, a volatile, aggressive general of the Marshal Ney breed, running out of control, while the Russian left wing was

led by a Grouchy-type, over-cautious Samsonov, never one
to march to the sound of cannon fire. And yet, as it turned
out, this time it would be the volatile Ney who didn't march
to the sound of the guns.

The quality problem of ordinary officers was not confined
to the Russian domain, the Germans also suffered their fair
share. Their East Prussian holding force, the Kaiser's Eighth
Army, was commanded by Count Max von Prittwitz, an East
Prussian Junker who had acquired the uninspiring title 'der
dicke Soldat', 'the fat soldier'. The real brain in Eighth Army
HQ was a lieutenant-colonel, thick of body with a head
shaven like a billiard ball, Colonel Max Hoffmann, without
a von preceding his family name. He was to play a decisive
role during the forthcoming encounter.

At the outbreak of war, the First Russian Army was intended
for a holding action along the German border, with the Second Army in reserve near Warsaw. But the military situation
of the French and British on the Western front had become
desperate. The German steamroller had crushed Belgium, and
General von Kluck's First Army was banging on the doors
of Paris. The French government sent a frantic appeal to
St Petersburg. To save Paris from the German juggernaut,
Russia became the shock absorber. But the Russian armies
were not ready, and the Czar did not heed the wisdom of the
great Marshal Kutuzov, the man who had stopped Napoleon
at Moscow and who once proclaimed: 'We ourselves must not
knock on the frontier like haggard tramps.' Indeed, the Czar,
through Grand Duke Nicholas, pushed both his ill-prepared
Northern armies to invade the heart of Junkerdom, East
Prussia.

The battle which was about to commence had already been
decided ten years before. During the Russo-Japanese War of
1904–5, Alexander Samsonov and Pavel Rennenkampf were
divisional commanders, equal in rank. Samsonov's Siberian

Cossack Division was ordered to defend the Yentai coal mines in Manchuria. Rennenkampf's division held the adjoining sector and had received specific orders to support Samsonov's Cossacks. The Japanese attacked Samsonov whose division was routed with heavy loss of life, while Rennenkampf stood by idle.

A few days after this bloody disaster, the two generals met by coincidence on the railway platform at Mukden Station. An infuriated Samsonov rushed up to Rennenkampf, took off his gloves, and slapped his rival across the face. In an instant, the two generals were rolling in the mud like little boys, tearing off medals, hitting and gouging at one another until their staff managed to tear them apart. There was but one way for any noble Russian to settle this matter; however, the Czar expressly forbade the duel. Their hate lingered on, their passion for revenge remained. This fact was sadly overlooked when, once again, these arch-enemies were appointed to command adjoining armies.

There was one officer who didn't forget the incident. Watching the incident that day on the railway platform were a number of foreign military observers, English, Italian, American[1] – and one German. Captain Max Hoffmann, a tall Hessian who liked fat sausages and also spoke perfect Russian, a fact which was destined to change the war.

Three giant armies, 650,000 Russians and 135,000 Germans, were headed for a confrontation which, even by today's atomic superlatives, still carries the sad distinction of having caused the highest number killed in any single battle during the history of mankind.

The race for glory was on. While Samsonov was held up, waiting for his supplies, Rennenkampf's First Army had already

[1] Most of the military observers went on to great careers: Sir John Hamilton became army commander, Caviglia was Italian Minister of War, and a certain Captain Pershing went on to lead the United States contingent in W.W.1.

crossed into East Prussia on 17 August 1914. Mosquitoes were rising out of the mist of the bordering swamps in their millions. These swarms of stinging insects attacked the endless columns along the dust-covered road, a cloud so dense it hid the birch forest from view and made the soldiers cough. The Russian troops staggered along listlessly, with rags around their feet because their commanding prince had been in such a hurry to get his army under way that the quarter-masters hadn't had time to issue boots. That was the problem, thought Captain Vassili Kravchenko, not enough boots, not enough rifles, not enough bullets. How were our men supposed to fight? Kravchenko, a communication officer attached to North-West Army Headquarters, and his superior, Colonel Sergei Michailovich Glagolev, were riding alongside the struggling men.

'What a way to go to war,' complained the colonel, 'just look at these half-starved peasants, most have never fired a rifle. You call that an army? The Germans move their units by rail, they can put in their troops rested, speedily and wherever they please. We crawl along on bare feet and get our troops tired before the battle starts.'

When Kravchenko kept silent, the colonel continued.

'Marshes to our left and right, nothing but water and broken forests. What good is it to have four times as many men as the enemy? We cannot deploy them. Take one step off this road and you drown. Our army will attack bunched up and on a narrow front line. The Germans know this and wait for us with their heavy artillery. They have discovered what modern war is all about. They have training, discipline and a solid knowledge of the terrain. I fear we may have to pay a heavy price to learn our lesson.'

He was right. The mobilisation had come too fast to train the Russian soldier, and when the orders to advance were given, it threw the whole system of supplies into chaos. Rennenkampf, eager to beat his arch rival to the glory, had set his First Army in motion six full days before Samsonov could get the Second Army on its way. That alone invited a strike against the wide open flanks of either of the Russian armies.

General von Francois, commanding the German 1st Corps, had sent out patrols who soon discovered a wide gap between Rennenkampf's 3rd and 4th Corps. On 18 August, near the village of Stallupönen, von Francois managed to slip his corps into the gap and attack Rennenkampf from the rear. The Germans took over 3,000 prisoners, but lost themselves a considerable amount of men, which, given the disproportionate number of forces, they could ill afford. Yet the decisive factor of this relatively minor engagement was not a military one but an incredible discovery. By interrogating a captured Russian staff officer the Germans found out that General Jilinski, head of the North-West Army Group, co-ordinated the movements of his First and Second Armies by wireless and over landline *en clair*![2] Four hours later, the Germans had managed to splice themselves into the Russian order of command.

By 19 August, Rennenkampf's advance formation had reached the German town of Gumbinnen. The horrors of war were upon East Prussia and the Germans didn't have enough men to stop the Russian tide. General von Prittwitz favoured a pull-out, but was convinced by von Francois to give battle. Near Gumbinnen, the two corps of von Francois and von Below managed a limited holding action, but the 17th Corps of von Mackensen was rolled back. Gumbinnen was never a decisive battle, but this partial defeat of German forces led to measureless consequences. Instead of vigorously pursuing the Germans, who had suffered a tactical setback, General Pavel Rennenkampf sat down to celebrate his victory with a bottle of champagne. It shows the strangeness of Russian mentality, especially when he turned to his chief of staff and

---

2 *En clair* refers to uncoded communications either by wire or radio.

told him, 'You can take off your clothes and go to bed, the Germans are withdrawing.'

It certainly was not the moment to go to bed.

It was following the setback of his 17th Corps that General von Prittwitz lost his nerve. What he didn't realise was that Rennenkampf considered Gumbinnen a stalemate, serious enough to halt his forces, and that Samsonov's Army, approaching the German flank from the south, was so exhausted by their forced march through the Prpiet Marshes that they couldn't give battle. Nevertheless, the German commander panicked, picked up the telephone and called Imperial HQ in Coblenz. He informed Count von Moltke that he could no longer defend East Prussia. Then, contrary to the counsel of Colonel Hoffmann, von Prittwitz ordered a general withdrawal behind the Vistula River. Which meant giving up East Prussia without a fight.

Meanwhile, Samsonov didn't know where he was, since his army had not been issued with maps. While advancing on Russian soil, his officers could rely on local peasants to indicate the way, but once they crossed into East Prussia they found only abandoned villages. Jilinski had ordered Samsonov to catch up with Rennenkampf. This he couldn't do. His army was in a mess. There were no roads, there was no coherent march discipline and his units had to wade barefoot through ankle-deep sand. Their uniforms were in tatters, their faces covered with a thick layer of dust. They looked more like walking ghosts than fighting men, a straggling column of pathetic figures. Army corps advanced with neither bread for the men nor oats for their horses. Instead of marching towards the enemy, the soldiers spent most of their time foraging for food, slaughtering cattle and stealing chickens. Soon, the élite Cossack cavalry was little more than pillaging and burning brigands.

Communications had completely broken down between units, between divisions, between corps. The Russian Army High Command didn't know what the enemy was up to, and, even worse, they were left in ignorance of the movements of their own armies. The only thing Grand Duke Nicholas soon became aware of, was that there was absolutely no co-operation between his First and Second Armies.

Samsonov was grey with exhaustion. He coughed constantly. General Potovsky, his chief of staff, a nervous man wearing a pince-nez, entered the temporary HQ located in a farmhouse.

'General Samsonov, a message from General Jilinski.'

Samsonov read: '*Speed up your advance. Your slowness is endangering First Army.*'

The general cursed. 'What do you make of that? Why doesn't that oaf Rennenkampf slow up?' he demanded of one of his staff officers. Voroshilov, a commander of an artillery unit, aired his disgust.

'That damned sand, it plays hell with men and guns. The horses have no more strength, and my men have to push our artillery pieces by hand. Every hundred yards something breaks down. If we can make twelve miles a day we're lucky.'

Samsonov heard another staff officer say; 'It'll take a hell of an effort to beat the First Army to Berlin.'

Right now, he'd be happy to get them into East Prussia.

At Imperial HQ, Coblenz, the German setback at Gumbinnen led to events that were to influence the war. General von Kluck's First Army had reached the Marne thirty kilometres from Paris, and General von Moltke was convinced that the war on the Western Front was won. At the same time, pressure was put on him by the Kaiser to stop the Russians from conquering 'the cradle of the German race', the Junkerdom of East Prussia. Moltke took two decisions which proved to have heavy consequences. The first was to release four reserve corps from the Western Front, a move which was to cost the Germans dearly, since it robbed them of the manpower they needed to conquer Paris.[3]

The second decision was to relieve General von Prittwitz of his post, and appoint an old, retired general, Paul von Hindenburg, to command the Eighth Army. Hindenburg was a man brought up in the best of Prussian military traditions, with a no-nonsense personality. When called up, he curtly replied: 'I'm ready.' Moltke added a trump card when he dispatched as Hindenburg's chief of staff the 'Hero of Lüttich', General Erich von Ludendorff. The two, the old man of iron and the young, brilliant strategist, met on the railway platform at Hannover, and the war in East Prussia took on a new face.

Gumbinnen was now in Russian hands. The heavy bombardment had stopped, Rennenkampf's headquarters was jubilant, and many of the illiterate Russian farm boys thought they had entered Berlin. Rennenkampf called off the pursuit; in his judgement the Germans were finished.

Colonel Glagolev thought of it otherwise. 'The Germans are not defeated, they're simply regrouping to move south and hit Samsonov. They must know he is in trouble and that Rennenkampf will not lift a finger to come to his rescue. Those two hate each other, God knows why.'

On the 22nd, the Russian Second Army's supply situation had become so desperate that Samsonov decided to push his army in the direction of Novo Goeorgievsk and make for the Soldau Railroad. This pulled him even further away from Rennenkampf's Army. But he was left with no other choice.

---

[3] The German drive was stopped thirty miles from the capital, during the Battle of the Marne.

'Potovsky, send a message to Jilinski. Ask him to persuade the First to start moving towards us.' The man with the pince-nez duly dispatched the message. The return was brief: *'First Army moves west, repeat west not south, to screen Königsberg.'*

When Samsonov read it, he rasped in a breathless tone; 'I wasn't certain that he'd move further west, but I was sure he wouldn't move south.' He was right, of course. Rennenkampf wouldn't, or perhaps, couldn't help the Second Army. His own supply system had broken down when the railway changed from the Russian wide gauge to the German smaller gauge. At least, that's what Rennenkampf gave as explanation for his failure to support Samsonov.

The Germans read this vital signal before it even reached Samsonov. Indeed, what Colonel Glagolev suspected was actually taking place. The German divisions were not retreating but regrouping. Prittwitz's earlier decision to retire behind the Vistula was abandoned. To add to the misfortune of the Russians, a dispatch rider, bearing a note from Jilinski to the First Army, which included a hastily drawn map outlining the Russian intentions, was captured by a patrol of German Uhlans. By the time the two newly appointed army commanders reached their HQ, Colonel Hoffmann had already worked out a strategy. It was so ingenius in concept that it only awaited Hindenburg's approval. Ludendorff and Hoffmann immediately went to work. Based on Hoffmann's plan, they devised a masterstroke of great audacity, whereby a small force, using high mobility, can strike at an enemy several times its strength with devastating results. For this they relied on the available, lateral railway system inside East Prussia. The intercept of Russian orders provided the Germans with a clear picture of the moves by the First and Second Armies. It became clear that, after Gumbinnen, Rennenkampf had had enough and, for three full days, remained static. Samsonov was on the move, and therefore had to be considered the greater menace. Hoffmann's plan was for a concentration of the total effective force of the Eighth Army to be thrown against Samsonov, while leaving only a thin cavalry screen to amuse Rennenkampf.[4]

Samsonov was continuously bombarded by orders from North-West Army Group HQ to halt his travesty of an advance and push on to make contact with Rennenkampf. But the men of the Second Army couldn't go on any longer, and so, on the morning of the 24th, Samsonov had to order a rest for his men before confronting the enemy. This delay gave the Germans an extra day to prepare their ambush.

Colonel Glagolev and Captain Kravchenko had left the First Army to try and locate Samsonov. They had been ordered to do so since a dispatch rider carrying vital orders from General Jilinski had gone missing and never reached the Second Army.[5]

'He's either dead, or a prisoner. Either way, it's a mess.'

'How far are we from the Second?'

'God knows, fifty, sixty, a hundred miles?'

'I don't call that a gap, that's more like the open steppe.'

'Well, in case I get killed, memorise the message', said Glagolev.

'Yes, colonel.'

'Here it is then:

1. *The enemy is staking everything on one throw. His whole strength will be thrown against the Second Army.*
2. *The German 'retreat' is in fact a regrouping of forces for this purpose.*

[4] Known as Tordenskold's Principle, where a handful of Danes under Captain Tordenskold ran behind houses from street to street to show themselves until the British regiment believed they had to cope with a great Danish army, and withdrew.
[5] It was the dispatch rider captured by the Uhlans.

3. *The Second Army is to make immediate contact with the First, while the First is to move south.*

'Got it?'

'Yes, colonel.'

'I am afraid we will be too late', Glagolev ended with a sad smile. 'The spider sits in the parlour waiting for the fly.'

For the first time in the history of warfare, the Germans employed a new weapon, the aeroplane. A *Fokker* scout plane had flown the entire distance between the Russian First and Second Armies and reported the gaping hole between both forces. From this report, ably supported by Hoffmann, the two men put into action the most brilliant and, tactically most decisive, campaign of the whole of the First World War. While Samsonov slugged west on a front line of sixty miles, Ludendorff withdrew two corps: the 1st of von Francois, and the 17th of von Mackensen from the Rennenkampf front. This left the Germans with only a thin defence screen; a daring move indeed.

'*A general has much to bear and needs strong nerves. War is nothing like a mathematical problem with given numbers, but a case of interwoven physical and psychological forces. It means working with men of varying force of character and views. The only factor known is that of the leader*', wrote the Father of Strategy, Carl von Clausewitz. Ludendorff was a prime example, he directed his German forces with apparent bravura. But he had to act fast before the Russian General Staff divined his intention and could concentrate against him. He marched several of his corps swiftly into a defensive position to block Samsonov's advance, and, at the same time, ordered von Francois' 1st Corps and von Mackensen's 17th Corps into a double envelopment movement. The die was cast.

* * *

On 26 August, Samsonov's army had reached Neidenburg. That is where Colonel Glagolev and Captain Kravchenko found the general at dinner with his ADC, Potovsky. 'They call him the Mad Mullah', whispered Glagolev. Samsonov got up to greet them. He looked almost as bad as his army, drawn and exhausted. His despair showed clearly.

'What's up with the First?' was his initial query.

'General Rennenkampf intends to move west in a day or so, general.'

'So I've heard. Vodka, gentlemen?'

'Thank you, sir.' After several glasses they delivered the message and a map.

'Wonderful', said Samsonov, opening the map and studying it for a while, before his face took on a puzzled frown. 'There's only one problem. Who can read it?'

Glagolev looked over the general's shoulder. The map was in Latin characters. And Russian officers could only read Cyrillic.

'Thank you, gentlemen', said Samsonov. They were dismissed. That gave them a chance to have a closer look at the Second Army. It didn't take long to discover that the men were in awful physical shape, stumbling on in silence. From far away came the sound of heavy guns.

'Those don't sound like ours. Let's hope they're not moving this way.'

Samsonov had stepped outside the house. 'Did Jilinski give you no other message? I expected to be given permission to abandon the idea of an envelopment of the Prussian main force.'

My God, this man is mad, thought Glagolev. 'Sir, I beg to inform you, it is no longer a question of enveloping the enemy. He is about to have you surrounded.'

That's when the first stragglers ran past the camp. 'The Uhlans are coming!' Within minutes, thousands of Russians were pouring back in panic and confusion. The general seemed removed from the scene before him.

'I haven't heard from my wife in days', he mumbled. Then he buckled on his sword, and got into his car to see what was going on.

Hindenburg and Ludendorff were still worried about the thundercloud that hung over them in the north. Rennenkampf was slowly moving on Königsberg, too slow to make any difference. But what if the Russian suddenly decided to swing his 300,000 men southwards . . . ? Only two German cavalry divisions stood between Rennenkampf's twenty-four infantry and five cavalry divisions and the destruction of the German Eighth Army. Their anxiety was not lessened despite the many intercepted messages from the Second Army to Jilinski and from Jilinski to Rennenkampf. The only one who didn't seem to worry was Colonel Hoffmann. To him it was clear that nothing, absolutely nothing, would get Rennenkampf to move his army south. Then it happened. Late in the afternoon of the 27th, a *Fokker* observation plane spotted movement by a Russian cavalry unit attached to the First Army, and immediately reported the sighting to General von Francois who relayed it to Eighth Army HQ. '*One Russian corps seen moving towards our left flank.*'

The message exploded like a bomb and Ludendorff lost his cool. The Russian was about to close in! He demanded of Hindenburg to recall immediately von Francois' 1st Corps from their encirclement movement and to adopt a defensive posture against Rennenkampf. It was the critical moment of the entire battle, and everyone at German HQ waited for the ageing Hindenburg to take a decision. Hoffmann stepped in. 'General Hindenburg,' he said, 'a word in private, if you please.' The general nodded, and the two men walked to the corner of the room.

'Speak up, colonel.'

'Sir, there is something you should know. I think it will be vital to help you reach your decision.' Hoffmann then revealed the Mukden Incident, and the 'slap-across-the-face-affair'.

'So, you think that Rennenkampf . . . ?' Hindenburg allowed his words to drift off.

'Yes, sir. I am convinced Rennenkampf will never help Samsonov.'

Hindenburg issued the most important order in his career of military overlord. Nothing was ever mentioned again that referred to Ludendorff's *crise de nerfs*. Von Francois' 1st Corps was to continue the envelopment of Samsonov's forces. The battle went as planned.

It had been so simple. Samsonov fell into the trap the moment the Second Army moved out of Neidenburg and attacked the weakened centre of the German 20th Corps (von Scholtz), ably assisted by the men of the *Landwehr* brigades[6] of General von der Goltz, all local Germans from the Allenstein-Tannenberg region who fought to defend their farms and villages. The German line did not crack. Soon Samsonov ran into the combined artillery barrage of Mackensen's and Below's corps which demolished the Russian's right flank. When Samsonov tried to break out with his forces in a north-westerly direction he was met by the 3rd Reserve Corps (von Morgen), while the 17th Corps (von Mackensen) moved south to join up with the 1st Corps (von Francois) near the village of Willenberg. The accuracy of the German artillery, directed by their scout planes, was the key to the success.

Samsonov's army was crumbling. A band of steel was around him and the German artillery hammered relentlessly

---

[6] *Landwehr* brigades were created during the Napoleonic Wars as local militia units.

into the centre of the ring. His forces were being driven into
the Prpiet Swamps and left to drown. The Russian Second
Army had turned into a dismembered force: columns of
wounded, heaps of dead, cut to shreds by devastatingly
accurate artillery bombardments. The general could observe
for himself the hail of shells exploding in the midst of
struggling columns. He watched his soldiers throw away
their rifles, he saw whole companies trying to float across
a lake on hastily assembled rafts, only to be pulled off by
others. Many were sucked down into the bottomless marshes.
For the wounded there were no bandages and they were left to
bleed to death, all under the steady roar of the enemy's heavy
artillery. General Potovsky sent one desperate message after
the other. The only ones who heard him were the Germans.
Jilinski could do nothing, and neither would Rennenkampf.
For that, it was now too late. Throughout the 27th and 28th,
the battle raged with fierceness and the Russians fought on
with the desperation of the doomed. But the final outcome
was no longer in doubt, and General Hindenburg was able
to report to the Kaiser a few days later: *I beg most humbly
to report to Your Majesty that the ring round the larger part
of the Russian Second Army has been closed.*

On the evening of the 29th, Samsonov dispatched one final
message to Jilinski: *Am sending back baggage and wireless
apparatus. Shall leave for battle front. Long live the Czar.*

  'General,' pleaded Potovsky, 'please take a car. It will take
you . . .'

  'If anyone should escape, it isn't me. Give the car to carry
the wounded', the general replied. 'I am going by horse and
I will now take over personal command at the front.' He
knew he had no more front left. With that they rode off:
Samsonov, eight staff officers, including Colonel Glagolev
and Captain Kravchenko, a British liaison officer, Knox,
and a Cossack escort. Everywhere they went they found

dead and dying. Those not wounded were exhausted and bewildered. Some would eventually return home to tell the story of the shameful defeat, and their tale of horror would lead to a revolution which would change the course of history for the next seventy-five years. Samsonov took a last look at his shattered army. Around noon, he ordered the British liaison officer to leave: 'The enemy is in luck today, we shall have the luck another day.'

On a hill he met up with General Martos, one of his corps commanders, and leader of another decimated unit. 'I beg to report, General, I have no more corps left.' This finally made him decide to order a general retreat. He had led a quarter of a million men into battle. This army was reduced to a rabble of hunted, trapped, broken men. General Potovsky suggested that they assess the situation. This made Colonel Glagolev remark: 'What will you assess, general? Where? There's no more battlefield left.'

Up ahead, a machine gun tore into a column of wounded, and they dropped like mowed grass. Colonel Glagolev rode up to Samsonov. 'General, you must get out of here; save your life.'

Samsonov looked at him for a long time, before he said slowly; 'What for?'

That moment a bullet struck the general's horse.

On 31 August, the news was broken to the Czar of All Russians. 'Samsonov's army has been destroyed.'

To which the Czar replied, 'We owe this sacrifice to France as she has shown herself a perfect ally.'

'*Kto vinovat?*' ('Who's to blame?') Indeed, who was to blame? Samsonov's ineptness? Rennenkampf's spite? The Czar's haste? Who? Everyone searched for a scapegoat. It was a question which was to haunt Russia in the years ahead as something else began to take place in Petrograd. The first battle casualties arrived from the front. Their stories spread throughout the city, and from there, by letter or word-of-mouth, to the rest of the Russian armies. One of the many who heard about it was Vladimir Ilitch Ulianov, better known as Lenin.

The small village of Tannenberg is a place dear to the heart of every German. It was here, in 1410, that an army of Poles and Lithuanians defeated the Teutonic Knights. Colonel Hoffmann suggested to General von Hindenburg that he crown his great victory with this historic title.

The battle was over. On Hoffmann's suggestion, Ludendorff left one corps to wipe out the remainder of Samsonov's army. What took place next became, in the words of Hindenburg, 'a day of harvesting'. They had taken 60,000 prisoners, completely destroyed the 13th, 15th and 23rd Corps, and badly mauled the 1st and 6th Corps. Their booty was enormous. Colonel Hoffmann, promoted to general, had no time to gaze at captured guns or at the endless columns of tattered prisoners. He was already planning the next step in the campaign, the destruction of another army.

The victorious German Eighth Army gathered around the Tannenberg monument, put up in memory of another battle. They sang the battle hymn of the Great Frederick before they embarked on trains which were to lead them north, to confront the First Russian Army of General Pavel Rennenkampf.

31 August. 'What time is it, Glagolev?'

'Fifteen minutes past one, General.'

The five were slogging on foot through a soggy birch forest. Captain Kravchenko, Colonel Glagolev, General Potovsky, a Cossack guide and General Samsonov. They had been forced into the swamps to escape the roving patrols of Uhlans. Each step was torture; the water ran into their boots, and more than once they had to form a human chain to pull each other from the quagmire. Only occasional bouts of coughing from the asthmatic general broke the silence. They had reached the firm ground at the edge of the bog when suddenly the crack of rifle shots erupted. Glagolev dived for cover. He could see shadows moving through the wood up ahead. Then they were gone. Slowly, Glagolev dared to lift his head. Next to him were the bodies of the Cossack guide and General Potovsky. The pince-nez had slipped from the general's nose. He heard a whisper. It came from his friend Kravchenko. Glagolev pulled him from the bog and took him into his arms. The captain looked at him through clouded eyes, a red froth covered his lips. He managed to whisper the traditional: '*He bids you a long life.*'

'I bid you a long life, Vassili', replied Glagolev, tears streaming down his face. He comforted his comrade until he died in his arms.

Silence. Glagolev found himself alone. Samsonov was gone.

What if . . .

What if – the Germans hadn't intercepted the Russian signals?
Ludendorff and Hoffmann would never have dared to put their audacious plan into operation.

What if – Rennenkampf had come to the help of Samsonov?
Hindenburg's Eighth Army would have ceased to exist.

What if – Moltke had left his four reserve corps in France, instead of withdrawing them for action in the East?
It can be assumed that the Germans would have taken Paris, and the First World War would have finished in less than a month, at a cost of a few hundred thousand rather than of the many millions four years later.

What if – at the critical moment, the man of the hour,
    Hoffmann, hadn't revealed the secret of Mukden
    to Hindenburg?
    That is yet another story. Field Marshal Hinden-
    burg was effective only once, but that was enough to
    ensure German victory.[7]

The facts

At Tannenberg, the glittering, aristocratic Russian officer
corps went to their tombs. Their defeat set the seal on
Czarist Russia as a fighting power. Now the Germans turned
against Rennenkampf's Army and annihilated it. Altogether,
the Russians suffered over a quarter of a million dead.

Tannenberg was directly responsible for the defeat of von
Kluck's army at the gates of Paris, while, in Petrograd, tales
from the returning survivors of the disaster eventually moved
the soldiers of the Czar to revolt. Thus, Tannenberg set
in motion the measureless consequences which led to the
Bolshevik Revolution of 1917, and, finally, brought on the
downfall of the House of Romanoff as well as that of the
House of Hohenzollern.

A final note to history. In November 1918, during the
Allies' triumphant parade in Paris, not a single Russian
battalion took part in it, and no mention was ever made of
the valour and sacrifice of the quarter of a million Russians
who gave their lives so that France, England and the United
States of America could achieve final victory.

*   *   *

[7] After the war, General Max Hoffmann visited the Tannenberg battlefield and
told a friend: 'This is where the field marshal slept before the battle, this is where
he slept after the battle, and this is where Hindenburg slept during the battle . . .'
And he added: '*Es ist wohl unsinning die Frage zu erörtern: wäre auch ohne
den Wechsel der Oberbefehlshaber zu einem Sieg bei Tannenberg gekommen? Ich
glaube, ja.*' ('It is senseless to discuss the question: without a change in leadership,
would we have carried the day at Tannenberg? My answer is, yes.')

The Hinge Factor at Tannenberg was a slap on the face which brought about the end of Czardom and led the Bolsheviks to power.

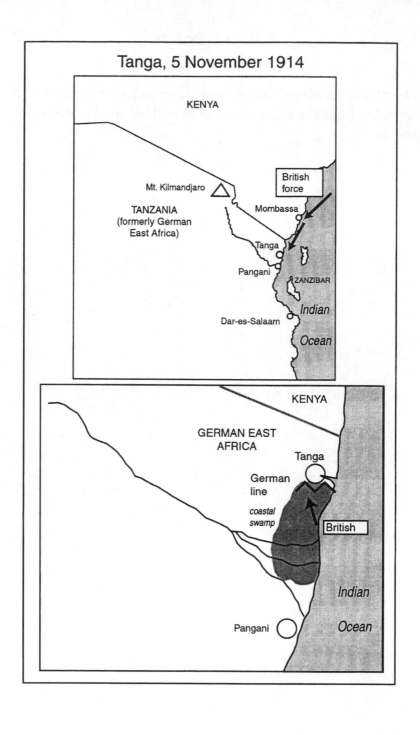

Tanga, 5 November 1914

11

The Sting of a Bee

Tanga, 5 November 1914

'War is a contest between two human intelligences rather than between two bodies of armed men.'
Lecture at British Staff College, 1901

German East Africa wasn't much of a country, Tanga wasn't much of a town, and Colonel Paul von Lettow-Vorbeck's 800 Askaris weren't much of an army. Yet it was here that the initial battle in Africa's share of the First World War took place.

To the 8,000 Indian soldiers of Major General Aitken this action came as a total surprise. Not so to the German garrison. For weeks they had been forewarned by letters written by German sympathisers in India and arriving by regular mailboat. They revealed that an Indian contingent of the British Army was embarking at Bombay, and that their officers had labelled their private luggage with: 'Indian Expeditionary Force "B", Mombassa, East Africa.' Though supposedly a secret mission, both the British and the German press, had described in great detail this forthcoming invasion.

Since the main port in German East Africa, Dar es Salaam, had been blocked by sinking an old ship across the harbour entrance, there were only two viable sea ports the English could attack. The *Deutsche Schutzstaffel* was strategically encamped between the two places, Lindi and Tanga.

At the outbreak of the First World War, the British Army was hard pressed by the lightning advance of German forces into France. Therefore, any challenge Germany could put up in Africa to the world's number one coloniser, the British Empire, was viewed as of only secondary importance. The task to conquer German East Africa was allotted to a low-grade unit of the Indian Army, with soldiers so untrained that most had never fired a rifle before. To put such an outfit under the command of an incompetent leader was asking for trouble. Major General Aitken was a man of unwavering confidence in his own ability. Thirty years of colonial service in India had convinced him that the forthcoming campaign in East Africa would be a walkover against a 'bunch of barefoot blacks led by ignorant Huns'. In the face of his fixed bayonets they would lay down their weapons and put up their arms. Then he would round them up, lock them up and be home by Christmas 1914.

His force of 8,000 foot soldiers was a ramshackle outfit pulled together at the last moment. They spoke twelve different languages, were of six different faiths, and were led by British officers who had never set eyes on their troops before they embarked, they didn't speak their language, and had never been to Africa before. That included the general. When Aitken received his orders, he immediately loaded his troops aboard several steamships. Bad weather prevented them from sailing for sixteen days, yet he insisted that his forces remained aboard, jammed between decks in hot cubicles. They suffered seasickness and diarrhoea from the storm, which added little to their fighting spirit. Discipline broke down, they quarrelled and fought with each other. Even Aitken's own intelligence officer, Captain Meinertzhagen, referred to them as 'the worst in India'. In one of his letters home he wrote: '*I tremble to think what may happen when we meet up with serious opposition.*' That was about to happen.

Aitken's bad luck was to run into one of the most brilliant tacticians of the First World War, Colonel Paul von Lettow-Vorbeck. With only a handful of German instructors by his side, recruited from a stranded German cruiser, he had trained a thousand local auxiliaries, or Askaris, who had been signed up from the fiercest war tribes of the region. These wild warriors he turned into a well-drilled and well-co-ordinated hit-and-run force; he taught them to adapt to the enemy, to take cover and to exploit any opening by laying an ambush. Their passing-out test was to hit a target from 500 metres. On top of this, they were familiar with snakes, lions and scorpions and knew every foot of their homeland, while the English didn't have maps other than pages torn from a school atlas.

General Aitken never understood that flexibility was needed and that fighting conditions in the African bush differed from those on the Indian subcontinent. He wasn't the only one who had failed to learn the lesson from recent colonial wars in Africa, where the machine gun proved its value as a highly cost-effective weapon. Its operation took but a handful of white men to inflict maximum damage to the grouped attacker.[1] In the Indian Army, such a weapon was considered too expensive, used up too much ammunition and invited a defensive spirit in the troop.

Tanga was a quaint little harbour along the East African Coast, with low wooden houses, neatly painted white, with

---

[1] Curiously enough, this technique had been developed by the English at Omdurman (1898) against the followers of the Mahdi. The British even turned it into a jingle:
Whatever happens, we have got, the Maxim-gun, and they have not . . .

well-kept gardens in front. With Teutonic efficiency, colonial officials had turned Tanga into a copy of a Prussian town on the Baltic. In front of the city hall, like everything else painted in brilliant white, stood a tall flagpole, where the Imperial German flag of black, white and red was hoisted every morning by a detachment of the local Askaris. Herr Auracher, the mayor of Tanga, ran the town ran like a Swiss watch and made sure that the good citizens observed Prussian civic virtues. All lived a quiet, colonial existence. His boss, Governor Baron von Schnee, had done a splendid job of keeping peace with the warrior tribes of the interior by distributing glass beads and framed prints of his Emperor to tribal chieftains.

The stillness of this harbour must have come as a pleasant surprise to Captain F. W. Caufield of the cruiser H.M.S. *Fox* that 2 November 1914, when he showed up with his convoy outside Tanga. There was no sign of hostility, not even the Imperial German flag was flying. That was always a good sign with those nationalistic Huns, he thought. Captain Caufield had himself rowed to the quay where Herr Auracher, resplendent in a sparkling white, starched collar shirt, with dark tie and pith helmet, courteously awaited his arrival and made his excuses for Governor von Schnee, who was 'away on an inspection tour'.

'*Herr Burgomaster*, in the name of His Majesty you are informed that any truce previously concluded between our two countries is hereby suspended.'[2]

The man didn't seem ruffled by the news as he bowed slightly. '*Herr Kapitän*, you will certainly allow me time to consult with my higher authorities.'

'Please do', replied the captain pleasantly. There was no sense rushing things; in any case, he needed confirmation of

---

[2] Kurt Assmann, *Kämpfe in den deutschen Kolonien* (1935): '*Ich fühle mich durch die törichten Abmachungen vom 8. August 1914 in keiner Weise mehr gebunden.*'

a disturbing rumour. The German cruiser SMS *Königsberg*, registered in British naval books as a mine layer, had been recently reported in these waters.

'But, tell me, my good man, is the harbour mined?' asked Caufield.

Auracher threw furtive glances at the cruiser hovering outside the harbour entrance, its heavy guns pointing straight at his wooden city hall.

'Of course, *Herr Kapitän*, such is standard practice in the German military manual.' With which the Burgomaster begged to be excused and disappeared. His 'consultation with higher authorities' consisted of forwarding an urgent message to Colonel von Lettow-Vorbeck that the Indian Expeditionary Force 'B' had arrived at his little town. The German commander immediately rushed his two available companies into previously established strong points, while Herr Auracher took off his pith helmet, changed into his German Army uniform and, in a final gesture of defiance, hoisted the Imperial flag.

Meanwhile, Captain Caufield had ordered his sailors of the *Fox* to sweep for mines. Of course they never found mines. But they took their time, since it was a very hot day, while the rest of General Aitken's invasion fleet was sweltering in the equatorial heat on an oily ocean. The British general was highly upset over the delay. While his sailors were still rowing aimlessly around the harbour, Captain Caufield convinced General Aitken not to risk losing a ship to a mine but instead to disembark the invasion force about a mile further down the coast. Their new landing place proved to be an almost impenetrable mangrove swamp, infested with mosquitoes and poisonous snakes. This they didn't discover until the first troops had set foot ashore, which was well after darkness. As the Indians had never been outside their own villages, and rumours had circulated aboard the troopships about the horrors of cannibalism in Africa and the cruelty of the

Germans, their nerves were frayed and they expected to find an enemy behind every tree. They shot at passing shadows, which happened to be their own unfortunate comrades.

In the first morning light the unsuitability of the landing site became obvious; rather than changing it, General Aitken, eager to terminate his African campaign before Christmas, ordered all supplies to be brought ashore. There were motor-cycles and wireless sets, boxes of corned beef and shells. And, not to be outdone by their leader, every officer had brought along his parade uniform for the forthcoming victory pageant, adding their personal luggage to the piles of crates and boxes. All this back-and-forth manoeuvring, which could only be accomplished by rowing-boat across the treacherous coral reefs, took two days, which allowed the Germans ample time to further fortify their positions.

Contrary to the British general, who didn't believe in recon-naissance, Lettow-Vorbeck sent one of his officers to take a closer look. The man, a Berliner thinly disguised as an Arab fisherman, reported back that the invasion beachhead looked like 'a Sunday along the Rhine', of picnics and bathers.

For forty-eight hours, Brigadier Tighe, feeling elated that he had managed to get his brigade safely ashore, stalled by telling his commander that the men were too exhausted to 'give it a decent go' and assault the town. Even when an enterprising Arab trader, who had arrived by boat to peddle his wares to the troops, informed one of Aitken's staff officers that there were almost no Germans in the sector, the general still declined to issue the order for attack. Time was frittered away by a general who couldn't make up his mind. Meanwhile, the Germans had managed to rush in two additional Askari companies to back up their handful of defenders.

On 4 November 1914 came General Aitken's order to 'advance and attack', and that without prior scouting. Any commander who fails to explore a hostile territory and allows the enemy the element of surprise invites disaster. The sepoys of the 63rd Palmacotta Light Infantry, the 61st Pioneers and the 13th Rajputs were ordered to fix bayonets and form into line of battle about a thousand yards wide, which was impossible, given that they had to cross a mangrove swamp in knee-deep water and mud, threading their way through a tangle of tree trunks and mangrove roots. Led by Brigadier Tighe, the troops of his Bangalore Brigade advanced but couldn't spot any Germans.

'Curse it, the *Boche* has run', stated a young British lieutenant, disappointed at having been deprived of his moment of glory. Together with two other company commanders, he climbed up a kopie to have a better view. The three raised their heads – and fell down dead. A bugle sounded, a row of German Askaris popped up from the waters of the swamp like shiny black ghosts and rushed at the hapless Bangalores with a bloodcurdling yell. This so panicked the sepoys that they threw away their rifles and ran, leaving behind their dozen officers to be cut down by the pangas of the Askaris. Captain Meinertzhagen of the Rajputs tried to put a halt to the panic which got so bad, that, when one of the Indian officers tried to force his way past him by drawing his sword, Meinertzhagen had to shoot him.

Brigadier Tighe signalled to the ships that he was coming under attack by 2–3,000 Germans, when in fact the whole Askari force was only two hundred and fifty and the attack had been carried out by less than two companies, the 7th and 8th *Schutztruppe*. This initial, futile attempt had cost the British over 300 casualties; the rest of the troops had run all the way back to the beach and many were now up to their necks in water, screaming for help.

5 November. General Aitken was so furious over the Bangalores' unmilitary behaviour, and the thrashing his units had received, that he ordered all his remaining reserves onto the beach to be thrown at Lettow-Vorbeck, and that again without sending out scout patrols. He showed his ineptness

by mixing his weakest units with his two first-rate formations, the North Lancashire Regiment and the Gurkhas of the Kashmiri Rifles.

'We'll do it with cold steel', was Aitken's response to the offer of a nourished naval bombardment by H.M.S. *Fox*. Again, the unit commanders were given the order to advance with fixed bayonets. By now, the beach was piled so high with supplies that the freshly disembarking troops had to clamber over cases and fight their way through bug-eyed sepoys to get into a semblance of order for the advance on an enemy who, once again, had mysteriously disappeared into the swamp.

Three hundred metres outside of the town, along a narrow earthen dam put there years before to protect the town from the encroaching swamp, Lettow-Vorbeck had put up a formidable line of dug-in defences, occupied by the 4th, 7th, 8th and 13th *Schutztruppe*. All his units lay beautifully camouflaged behind rows of bamboo which surrounded the swamp; every company was linked to his command post by field telephones. Barbed-wire entanglements, concealed with leaves and swamp flowers, fronted strong points manned with machine guns. It would be a suicidal mission to rush such defences with 'cold steel'. In fact, the German commander did not have to organise the ambush, the Indian Imperial Service Brigade simply stumbled into it. To begin with, the sepoys slugged their way through mud and stumbled over submerged mangrove roots, suffering badly from thirst and heat, while Askari snipers, planted in the crowns of bao-bab trees, picked off their brightly sashed, pith-helmeted officers. Then the Germans kept up a galling machine-gun fire which soon showed its effectiveness. It punched great gaps into the various units. Everything was going just as Lettow-Vorbeck had planned. A ragged line of Indians began to stumble around in the bog, firing wildly into the leaves ahead and, more than once, shooting down their comrades in front. With the vanguard in full retreat, and the rear still advancing, this created a bunched-up mass of confused soldiery which offered an ideal target for the German machine-gunners. Only the North Lancashires and Gurkhas managed to advance with great courage and, after a fierce hand-to-hand fight, took the local customs house. From there they rushed into the town where they reached the *Hotel Deutscher Kaiser*. They pulled down the German Tricolor and raised instead the Union Jack, an event observed with a great cheer from the ships standing off at sea.

For Lettow Vorbeck, assisted by his two ADC's, Major Von Prinz and Major Kraut, the situation became serious. The British crack troops had broken into town, and, unless they were stopped, the door to the colony would be wide open. Under the onslaught of the wicked curved knives of the Gurkhas some of the inexperienced young Askaris had faltered and were hiding out in buildings. It took a bold step to get them back in line. Lettow-Vorbeck, the Prussian junker, faced them down: 'Do I see women, or the proud warrior sons of the Wahehe and Angoni?' But they wouldn't move, until something else happened.

When one of the Wahehe Askaris jumped up and tried to dash off, Captain von Hammerstein, a company commander, took a half-filled bottle of wine from his map case and hurled it after the fleeing man. It struck him on the woolly head and he fell to the ground, to the howling laughter of the Angoni. That did it. The Wahehe tribesmen, furious over the cowardly behaviour of one of their tribe in front of the Angonis, kicked the shit out of him, then picked up their heavy Mauser rifles, and with a scream of '*Wahindi ni wadudu*', raced after Major von Prinz. They were followed by the equally eager Angoni tribesmen, yelling their own terrible native war cry. With blazing rifles and machine guns placed on the shoulders of others to steady their aim, they ran through the town and threw out the Gurkhas. Then they lashed into the open flank of the British force in the swamp. A mêlée of pangas against kukris (Gurkha knives) soon turned into a bloody massacre. Major von Prinz was killed, while on the other side, the 101st Bombay Grenadier battalion was mowed down in a hail of bullets from German machine guns and Askari swords and ceased to exist as a fighting force. But due to the headlong rush by his Wahehes and Angonis of the 4th and 13th companies, Lettow-Vorbeck's left flank was now dangerously exposed and threatened by the Lancashire men in and around the customs house.

Contrary to his German opponent who directed the battle from his own trenchline and thus could take advantage of every opportunity, the British general, who had remained aboard his headquarters ship, couldn't see what was going on, since his view was obstructed by the dense jungle. A message from the commander of the North Lancs was received by General Aitken. It gave the precise position of the enemy's deadly machine guns and asked for artillery support to soften up the German line before an attack on the Germans could be launched. But General Aitken was frozen into inactivity and no naval bombardment was ordered. To keep down their casualties, it left the North Lancs with no other choice than to pepper the bamboo growth with their Maxim guns – to little effect since the Germans and their Askaris were well down in their holes. But the gunfire did keep the Germans' heads down and their devastatingly accurate rifle fire ceased. The British commanders didn't realise that the Askaris had almost run out of bullets and were getting ready to stage a desperate, final bayonet charge.

If ever there was a moment for a decisive British victory, this was it. But something most unexpected came to the assistance of the Germans. The swamp was ringed by dead trees. Like some petrified forest, their grey, barren branches reached for the sky. Attached to these branches, drooping like giant bats, were cigar-shaped woven baskets which the natives used to contain massive hives of African bees, terribly aggressive and astounding in size. Their honey had always been a source of great delicacy for the locals who knew how to protect themselves against the vicious stings by applying thick layers of grease over arms and faces.

But now, the noise from the continuous firing must have upset their tranquil occupation of producing honey, or perhaps the hail of bullets had split open the baskets and shattered their hives – whatever the reason, dense swarms of humming, stinging beasties emerged from the hives and rose in dense clouds around the treetops before they attacked the advancing and unprotected British contingent. They stung and stung and then stung some more. Panic spread; the Indians turned and ran, hotly pursued by dense clouds of angry bees. One may well imagine the spectacle this presented to General Aitken, still aboard his HQ ship, when hundreds of wildly gesticulating soldiers minus their rifles, their arms waving like windmills, emerged from the mangroves and plunged headlong into the ocean. Because there was no more shooting, but only pained screams from the fleeing foot soldiers, a staff officer remarked: 'My God, General, our men are driven back again. What devilish feat have the Germans been up to?'

The explanation was quite simple: *hell hath no fury like an angry bee*. Why did the insects attack only the Indian Army units? Perhaps it had to do with body odour, the same way that dogs can smell fear. A British signalman was awarded the Military Cross because he kept on sending his signal while being stung by 300 bees. It was the first time in history a medal was given for *bravery under aerial attack*.

Aitken was livid over his troops' cowardice and finally ordered a naval bombardment of Tanga. The first shell hit the local hospital, jammed with British casualties. Most of the other shells fell on his own troops, now in full retreat. When the remaining North Lancs finally reached shore, a sergeant from Manchester remarked drily: 'I dun mind the bloody Hun shoot'n at me, but bees stingin' my arse, that's a bit 'ard to take.'

When quiet settled over the field of battle and the bees had once again retreated into their hives, the count of dead or wounded Germans was 70, 15 Europeans and 54 Askaris, while the British left behind 800 dead and an equal number of wounded and missing, probably drowned without trace in the swamp. The beaten British armada upped anchor and returned to Mombasa, where – as the final insult – the local British colonial customs inspector refused General Aitken's flotilla entry into the harbour for having failed to pay the 5 per cent *ad valorem* tax.

In England the outcome of the first battle in Africa was received with shock. How could a handful of black auxiliaries lead the British expeditionary force to such ignominious defeat? An excuse had to be found, and *The Times* went so far as to accuse Paul von Lettow-Vorbeck of having employed a new, tactical battlefield weapon: swarms of trained warrior bees. Nobody dared to admit that General Aitken was the wrong man to send into a theatre of war he hadn't begun to understand. His Napoleonic idea of 'advance and attack' with fixed bayonets was a thing of the past. By August 1914, Allied commanders had discovered that such tactics no longer worked on the Western Front and they certainly would not work in Africa. It was sheer lunacy to launch a human wave attack against well-trained tribesmen, sitting in the bush armed with machine guns, in a landscape where tacticians like the Boers and Lettow-Vorbeck had rewritten the book on colonial warfare – although, in later years, the German colonel never forgot to give praise to his auxiliaries, the bees.

What if . . .

What if – General Aitken's expedition had been successful?
  German East Africa would have become British
  Tanganyika (today's Tanzania), and the World War,
  African segment, finished in 1914.

The facts

With a force of only 155 German officers and soldiers,
1,200 African Askaris, plus 3,000 porters, Major General
Paul von Lettow-Vorbeck's masterly conducted operations
held down 120,000 British colonial troops under the South
African generals Smuts and Van Deventer. The Askari force
fought on to the last day of the war and only surrendered on
Armistice Day, of 1918.

As for the Battle of the Bees, the equipment left behind by
the British on the beach at Tanga allowed Lettow-Vorbeck to
form new regiments, arm them with modern British weapons
and continue the fight for four more years.

Colonel von Lettow-Vorbeck was promoted to major general.
Major General Aitken was cashiered and reduced to colonel.

The Hinge Factor at Tanga was a swarm of angry bees.

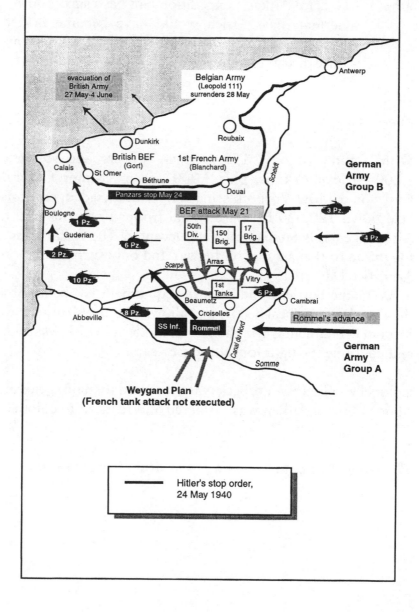

Tank Battle, Arras, 21-22 May 1940

Antwerp

evacuation of British Army 27 May-4 June

Belgian Army (Leopold 111) surrenders 28 May

Roubaix

Dunkirk

British BEF (Gort)

1st French Army (Blanchard)

Scheldt

German Army Group B

Calais

St Omer

Béthune

Douai

Boulogne

Panzars stop May 24

3 Pz.

1 Pz.

BEF attack May 21

4 Pz.

Guderian

6 Pz.

50th Div.

150 Brig.

17 Brig.

2 Pz.

10 Pz.

Scarpe

Arras

Vitry

1st Tanks

5 Pz.

Cambrai

Beaumetz

Abbeville

8 Pz.

Croiselles

Rommel's advance

SS Inf.

Rommel

Canal du Nord

Somme

German Army Group A

Weygand Plan (French tank attack not executed)

———— Hitler's stop order, 24 May 1940

12

Der Halte Befehl

France, 21 May 1940

'We have lost the battle for France.'
French Prime Minister Paul Reynaud
to Winston Churchill, 15 May 1940

In the evening hours of 10 January 1940, a German *Junkers-52* transport plane made an emergency landing in a field near Mechelen-sur-Meuse. On board was a staff officer of the 7th German Infantry Division, who carried on him detailed plans of the invasion of France. He was captured before being able to burn his maps. These showed the German plan for a spring attack through the Ardennes with a crossing of the Meuse (Maas) south of the Belgian border. The captured plans were rushed to General Maurice Gamelin, Commander-in-Chief of Allied armies.

He didn't believe it, as much as he didn't believe his chief of espionage, Colonel Payol of the *Deuxième Bureau*, who had confirmation from their source deep in Berlin, 'Bertrand', an official in the German Ministry of War.[1]

No, decided General Gamelin, no army could ever cross the Ardennes, although, only two years before, during French Army manoeuvres conducted by himself, General Prétalat had used exactly the same breakthrough route as was shown on the captured German plans. Finally, the French military attaché in Bern informed Gamelin to expect a German push on Sedan by 8 May. He was only two days out.

On the morning of 10 May 1940, a special unit of German paratroopers, which had practised their assault on a mock-up model of their target, dropped on Fort Eben Emael, which controlled three vital bridges along the border between France and Belgium. Within twenty minutes, this strategic junction was in the hands of the Germans, and the road into France laid open.

On 1 September 1939, the world was given its first taste of Germany's *Blitzkrieg* strategy. It was based on lightning thrusts by panzer forces in combination with tactical air strikes, a technique developed during the inter-war years by the German panzer genius, Heinz Guderian.[2] While Germany had developed an élite tank force, the British Army had Mark I tanks equipped with a machine gun, and even their heavier Matildas were no match for the fast German armour. The French were even worse, their tanks

[1] Hans Thilo-Schmidt was a good party man, with a brother commanding a Panzer Division; in other words, a man above suspicion. And yet, this man had fed the French invaluable information for years. Hans Thilo-Schmidt, aka Bertrand, was caught by the *Abwehr* the day the Germans took Paris. On a railway siding they discovered a boxcar containing all the documents of the *Deuxième Bureau*, including the name of their most valuable spy. He was executed.
[2] While Germany attacked Poland, the Western Allies just sat by as non-participating onlookers and did nothing during the *Drole de Guerre* period, from September 1939 to May 1940. In 1939, Germany did not have the means to fight a two-front war.

lumbered along at 4 m.p.h. to allow their *fantassins* (foot soldiers) to follow the attack. The German panzers moved at 60 km p.h.

Despite the Polish demonstration, the men who dominated Allied military planning were ossified and locked into a static defence. Major General Sir Louis Jackson's view was typical of their thinking when he referred to the decisive battle of the First World War, the breakthrough by British armour at Amiens: '*The tank was a freak. The circumstances which called it into existence were exceptional and are not likely to recur. If they do, they can be dealt with by other means.*'

The short-sighted view of the Imperial General Staff was matched by the French. 'We are not Poles,' stated General Gamelin, 'it couldn't happen here.' The French General Staff counted on the invulnerability of the Maginot Line. The main flaw of this highly sophisticated defence system was that it did not reach all the way to the sea but stopped at the Belgian border! The French assumed, wrongly as it turned out, that it would invite German forces to push through Holland, where the might of French, Belgian and British armies could crush their advance along the fortified Dyle River line. It was precisely this concentration of Allied forces in Flanders which led to the French debacle.

The plan for their lightning march to victory was presented to Hitler by the chief of staff of General von Rundstedt's *Heeresgruppe A* (Army Group A), General Erich von Manstein. He suggested a surprise thrust with the bulk of German panzers, seven divisions, through the weakest point in the French defences, the heavily wooded Ardennes mountain range, leaving it to General Bock's *Heeresgruppe B* (Army Group B) to fake the expected advance into Holland along the established invasion routes of the First World War. The French fell into the trap, even the ageing Marshal Henri Pétain, the hero of Verdun, who stated: '*The Ardennes are impenetrable, this sector is not dangerous.*'

One hundred and fifty kilometres of dense woodland separated the Maginot Line from the fortified Dyle River line in Belgium. For this – the key to the German attack plan, General Gamelin allotted only fourteen reserve divisions. Against these stormed forty-five crack German divisions, including all their heavy panzer units.

Myths surround the swift and conclusive German conquest. One is that victory was achieved by German tank superiority. This assertion is false. The Germans had 2,574 tanks[3] to the Allies' 3,254. Also, the Allies' armour-plating and guns were superior to those of the German Mark II and Mark III models. The French were simply out-generalled. They had developed a Maginot mentality, basing their entire plan on an inflexible concept, outdated battle strategy and, most of all, an exaggerated confidence in static defence. (The Maginot Line was handed intact to the Germans the day following the French surrender!)[4]

Yet, history tends to overlook a relatively minor action fought by seventy-four British tanks near Arras which was to prove of major significance to the continuation of the war.

After only two days of fighting, the leading German panzers had reached Sedan and the Meuse. On 12 May, an erroneous report that German panzer units had already crossed the Meuse reached General Corap, commander of the French Ninth Army.[5] Corap panicked and ordered a precipitated withdrawal. He was replaced by General Giraud who was captured the following day.

On the 13th, General Erwin Rommel's 7th Panzers did cross the river on a hastily assembled pontoon bridge. They

---

[3] A great portion of the German panzers (770) were Czech Skodas.
[4] Roger Bruge, *On a livre la Ligne Maginot*.
[5] Earlier that year, the British general Sir Alan Brooke had visited Corap, and had remarked on the absence of anti-tank positions, to which Corap replied: '*Ah bah! On va les faire plus tard – alons, on va dejeuner!*'

were unopposed and quickly overran a new French defence line before it could even be manned. This rout opened a gaping hole in the French line. The panzer advance was so lightning fast that the Germans did not bother to stop and take prisoners. Long lines of surrendering French soldiers marched alongside the speeding panzers, many still carrying their weapons. Sometimes a German tank would stop, collect their rifles and crush them under the cleats of the panzer.

The French still had at their disposal three armoured divisions capable of stopping the German steamroller. Though their military Intelligence had by now established that the German panzers were definitely not headed towards Belgium, Gamelin, a man never prepared to change his preconception and beset by an inability to adapt to a rapidly changing situation, was at the root of the military debacle. When General Weygand replaced Gamelin, and a decision was taken – already too late – to move the three tank units into position, the 1st French Armoured Division of General Bruneau was simply wiped out by Guderian's 19th Panzer Corps, assisted by the *Luftwaffe's Sturzkampfbombers* (aka *Stuka*) near Beaumont, the 2nd Tank Division (General Bronché) unloaded at the wrong place, owing to a faulty train schedule, and the 3rd Tank Division ran out of fuel on their way to the front.

The forward movement by French and British reinforcements faced another serious problem, one not 'Made in Germany'. Thousands of refugees streamed out of Eastern France and Belgium, and choked the main roads with their human flood. They came with every sort of transport imaginable – baby prams, wheelbarrows, pushcarts – piled with everything they owned or thought indispensable, useless items grabbed in panic – guitars, pictures and umbrellas. Automobiles soon ran out of gas, or their owners were pulled from them by others trying to reach safety, and now these vehicles lay in the middle of the road, adding to the traffic jam. Hungry people picked unripe corn and green fruit from trees, and then suffered the consequences. A child, clinging to her mother's skirt, stumbled along on legs stiff from tiredness; the mother dumped what she was carrying to caress her child. A momentary scene of caring amidst a crowd in panic. Many sat down next to the road and waited for the inevitable to happen. They were a mass of ragged, tired people stumbling past the rotting corpses killed by strafing aircraft. The continued harassment by the German *Stukas* hung as a dark cloud over the scenes of tragedy along the road.

These refugees accomplished what ten additional German divisions couldn't hope to achieve – they effectively blocked the badly needed Allied reserves from reaching their prepared defensive positions. By the evening of 15 May, the three German Panzer Corps of Hoth, Reinhardt and Guderian were pushing unopposed into France and a gallant attempt by a quickly assembled 4th French Armoured Division under a young colonel, Charles de Gaulle, had no effect on Guderian's progress. The Battle for France had begun only five days before and France was already stumbling towards a humiliating surrender.

OKW (German Supreme Command), 15 May, afternoon. The two-week Polish campaign had been achieved through the talent of Hitler's tank commanders, but the political leader of Germany sadly lacked the military experience to grasp the complexity of modern tank warfare. With the *Führer*'s conviction of his special mission in history, surpassed only by his belief in his unique military genius, he had surrounded himself with generals who were as incompetent as their French counterparts, yes-men like Keitel and Jodl. The Germans' real strength lay in their front-line commanders, men such as Guderian and a young divisional general, Erwin Rommel. He was to become the best of

German generals, since he alone managed to overcome the rigid German military spirit. He was never a party man, and, like his superior, Guderian, considered the generals at *OKW* incompetent and useless worriers. His intense dislike of men like Himmler, Jodl and Keitel was well known and he never became hypnotised by the political structure on which his personal security depended. The admiration he initially carried for Hitler was quickly transformed into deception and disgust. And for a valid reason. When the three tank corps had broken out of the Meuse bridgehead, and pushed ever deeper into France, driving the defeated armies before them, Hitler's nerves gave and his anxiety grew in direct relation to the speed of the panzers' advance. On that spring afternoon, a barrage of messages from their advance units flooded into *OKW*. The generals in the map room could hardly keep up with the movements of the arrows and flags. Hitler studied the general map and became highly fidgety. Keitel saw his *Führer*'s worries and agreed with him. 'I agree with your appreciation of the present situation, *mein Führer*. We are over-extending our panzer forces. We must expect a counter-offensive.'

16/5 OKW: Der Franzose führt anscheinend aus seinem Reservoir Dijon-Belfort Kräfte nach der linken Seite des Durchburchkeils heran. (The French are bringing up from their Dijon-Belfort reserves new forces against the left flank of our breakthrough.)

The generals Keitel and Jodl accepted their leader's assessment of the situation. Only Halder, the brilliant strategist, argued that the advance was much too rapid for the British to adjust to and that French morale had collapsed outright. He was right. But Hitler would only listen to his yes-men. On 17 May the initial order went out to stop the 19th Panzers.[6]

---

[6] General Halder: '*Bereits am 17 Mai hatte Hitler die hinter kopflos weichendem Feind nachstürmenden Panzertruppe von Kleist durch persoenlichen Befehl aufgehalten.*' – (Peter Bor, *Gespräche mit Halder*).

HQ, 19th Panzer Corps. 'But, general, it's an order from *OKW*, a personal order from the *Führer* himself.'

'I don't care if it comes from the Pope. Get General List at 12th Army on the line, tell him I'm resigning my commission', fumed Guderian. More than just another general, List proved an astute diplomat, and a compromise was reached. He allowed Guderian to carry out a 'reconnaissance in force'. It was a farce. To conceal his moves from his *Füher*, Guderian had a telephone wire strung from his advancing command car to the place where *OKW* had stopped him. And thus it happened that the German panzers raced for the Channel coast before Hitler knew what was going on.

General Gamelin's Directive No. 12 was issued at 09.45 hours on the 19th. It ordered all Northern Armies to head southwards at all costs and not find themselves encircled and pushed towards the Channel ports. While General Georges and his forces were to attack from the north in a southerly direction, the French 2nd and 6th Armies would attack northwards from Mezières. An event precipitated this order. At 19.00 hours that day, General Gamelin, greatly suffering from depression brought about by an advanced stage of syphilis, was replaced by Maxime Weygand. Weygand's new plan, worked out with General Georges, his North-East Army Group commander, was for a pincer movement against the exposed German advance units. Georges, a mentally and physically unfit leader who, after the debacle on the Meuse had burst into tears, visited General Gort at his headquarters. He asked Gort, Commander-in-Chief BEF, (British Expeditionary Forces), to throw in his remaining tank reserves and cut off the two lead panzer divisions which had outrun their support infantry. BEF was to establish a new defence line Arras–Cambrai–Bapaume. In exchange, Georges promised a powerful French tank attack from the south.

BEF Commander Gort did not bother to inform General Georges that he was already considering a withdrawal towards Dunkirk. However, he did advise his Prime Minister, Winston Churchill, who ordered plans for 'Operation Dynamo'[7] to be drawn up, a move which was to save the British Army from annihilation.

While the French and English wasted precious time negotiating who should attack and where, Rommel's 7th Panzers were racing hell-bent for the heart of France. His panzers moved along a front only 3 km wide and 50 km from his nearest resupply unit. He took a considerable risk, since both his flanks were held by sizeable Allied forces. On the 18th, he pushed them on again. '*Weiterer Marschweg: Le Cateau-Arras. Auftanken! Antreten!*' (Next direction: Le Cateau–Arras. Fill up! Stand at ready!')

Soon he had no more petrol for his panzers. (It has been said that some filled up at local gas stations.) This made him furious until he discovered the reason, one of his own making. His advance had been so fast that his support division was still in Belgium! When Hitler heard about this, it gave him stomach cramps and his *OKW* generals, a sleepless night.[8] Rommel's daring was amply rewarded. For only 35 killed and 50 wounded, his division had taken 10,000 prisoners and captured or destroyed over 100 enemy tanks.

On 20 May, the day that the first units of Guderian's panzers pushed into Abbeville, BEF Commander Gort put General Sir Harold Franklyn in charge of the Arras sector. In the corps command centre, a farmhouse near St Eloi[9], General Franklyn gathered his chief staff officers. Opinions were hopelessly different and no clear picture emerged. According to the latest reports from their retreating units,

[7] Code name for the Dunkirk evacuation.
[8] David Irving, *Rommel*.
[9] St Eloi is only a few miles from Vimy Ridge of W.W.1 fame.

German panzers had already crossed the Scheldt at Cambrai and were approaching the final defensible water barrier, the Canal du Nord. The Germans were obviously trying to envelop Franklyn's corps, and with it the whole Allied North-East Command of the French First and Seventh Armies, the Belgian Army, and the British Expeditionary Force.[10]

Gort told Franklyn that he could not count on aerial support. He had to rely on his own ground forces – two divisions, the 5th and the 50th, plus the 1st British Tank Brigade, made up of units of the 4th and the 7th Royal Tank Regiments. The plan was for a concentrated thrust by infantry and tanks along the Arras–Bapaume highway to sever the head of the viper, Rommel's 7th Panzers before the German support infantry could link up. Franklyn's tank units were strong enough to carry out this objective as long as they didn't meet up with Rommel's main force. What finally put the scheme into operation before a unified plan could be worked out was an urgent cable by Churchill to Prime Minister Reynaud: '. . . The tank columns in the open must be hunted down by numbers of small mobile columns with a few cannons . . .'[11]

General Gort set D-hour for 21 May at 14.00 hours. General Martel was put in command. The first wave was composed of the 13th and 151st Infantry Brigades plus sixty-five Mark I and eighteen Mark II tanks. Martel was promised flank support of seventy light tanks of the French 3rd Mechanised Division – but no air cover. There was one problem, and not a small one at that. Though Intelligence had correctly identified the 7th Panzers of General Rommel,

[10] Altogether 56 divisions, not counting the 10 Dutch and reserve divisions which were already separated from the main body.
[11] There is an argument about when the cable was sent; Churchill states it was early on 21 May.

they missed out on the 8th Panzers, the 5th Panzers, as well as a mechanised *SS Panzergrenadier Division* which was following Rommel's *Blitz* – 400 tanks and 20,000 men.

A few days earlier. The moustachioed commander of the 1st British Tank Brigade was sitting in his command truck. A message arrived. *Unit under heavy attack from the south–west.* How could that be? South-east, yes, but south-west? His men were still holding the river line. Had the Germans managed to cross over the Dyle in the south, perhaps at their junction point with the First French Army?

The radio ended his doubts: . . . *Lead units of German 39th Panzer Corps have crossed Dyle . . . we suffer heavy casualties . . .'* Followed by: 'Attention all units. Hoth's 5th and 7th Panzers seen general heading Maubeuge–Le Cateau . . .'

That was yesterday. Today he saw them. The panzers were fanning out, heading for his position. This time he couldn't expect anyone else to solve the problem for him. He couldn't retreat; for that it was too late. Bullets whipped past, slapped into trees and earth. All along the line his men were firing their rifles at armoured vehicles. Not much of a contest.

'Need artillery support. Over.' A distant bang. Another bridge went up before the enemy's panzers got to it. 'What's happening?' he enquired.

A tired voice came over the speaker. 'We're being clobbered, govn'or, dat's wot.'

'Blue 14, this is Foxtrot 7, do you read?'

'Go on, Foxtrot 7.'

'Blue 14, request permission to pull back.'

'Foxtrot 7, permission denied. You hold with whatever you've got. Out.'

He knew that he had just sealed the fate of a battalion, but he had no choice. If they'd pulled back, it would leave the division's, and, with it, the BEF's entire flank wide open for the panzers. An officer stumbled in, his face grey and sweaty. 'Sir, we cannot raise division headquarters, they're either down or dead. We need tanks. Those Matildas of the 4th Royal would do us nicely.'

'All right.' He turned to his radio operator.' Forget division, patch me through to GOC.'

'I'll give it a try, sir.'

'You do better than that, son, or you'll walk from here to there by foot.'

He had to launch a counter-attack, and very soon. For that he needed those heavy Royal tanks before the whole division was mashed under the cleats of German armour. The main railway bridge was already blown, but Jerry pioneers had thrown an assault bridge across the water. And now their panzers were streaming across, supported by heavy artillery. He turned to his radioman, headphones clamped to his head, listening to messages relaying firing orders and enemy positions.

'Sir, confirmation, the Germans are across the river at Wavre.'[12]

'What about our sector?'

'Sir, GOC orders a holding action, no further orders.'

The noise of distant shelling increased, explosions were creeping towards his positions. From across the river, an 88 scored a direct hit on a position of Alpha Company. Five men were killed. 'Sir, GOC on the line.'

'Hand me the mike. This is Blue 14 . . .'

The room was lit by a ball of yellow, followed by a mind-blowing crash. The radio operator tumbled forward, a big hole in his tunic. 'This is Blue 14 . . .' yelled the

---

[12] By a curious hinge of fate, the whole action took place where in 1815 the English and Prussians combined to defeat Napoleon at Waterloo.

brigadier into the mike. It was no use. The splinter that had killed his radioman had also smashed the radio tubes. The brigadier jumped from the command truck. Had to get to another radio. Alpha Company had one. It wouldn't carry far, but his message could be relayed down the line. When he reached the men of Alpha, he was told that their commander had been killed.

'You there, sergeant . . .'

'Yes, sir.' The man saluted smartly.

'Take over Alpha Company.'

'Very good, sir.'

Finally he established contact with GOC only to hear that the Germans were already deep behind everybody, behind the French to the south, the Belgians to the north and now moving behind the British. Divisional commanders ordered places to be held that had already fallen. It was those cursed panzers. There was only one solution. Throw at them all the tank reserves in one single blow, and try to cut the Germans' thrust in two. For this, his unit was ideally placed: the main panzer force had passed directly to his south and now their flank was open to his brigade. He passed the proposal through to GOC. The reply he got was not what he had expected. It wasn't for attack, but another 'disengage from the enemy'. *'All units withdraw to Delta Blue line. Immediate.'* He checked his Michelin road map. Just like the Germans, his side also depended on these fabulous French road maps one could purchase at any petrol station. It showed that the Germans were racing for the Dendre, another river, already west of the Dyle. They had to move back. But not in panic. If he could achieve an orderly withdrawal his men would be available to fight another battle another day. He had to work out a scheme to extract his forward companies from their exposed position. They had to sneak back quiet like, leaving behind only a thin covering screen.

'Major, we're moving out. The guns are mechanised, the men are not. A problem?' The major turned to the Regimental Sergeant Major who came to attention, stiff as a ramrod. Nothing would perturb this man, not even German panzers. 'Try and organise us something with wheels for the boys.'

'Yessah. There's the equipment and food trucks.'

'Dump it, we need men, not tents', said the brigadier. 'Here's the plan. The guns move at 03.00 hours, the men at 03.20 hours. No lights. We head for the Dendre River. As soon as the last man is across, blow that bridge.' He would be helped by artillery support. Shells from a German field battery screamed overhead. The last British unit along the Dyle line managed the move out without losses. They drove and walked and stumbled until they reached a forest. The troops were exhausted and wanted to sleep. Instead, they were ordered to dig in.

'Sir,' argued a company commander, 'the men are a bit tired.'

'Bloody hell, who isn't?' replied the brigadier.

Messages crackled over the ether: *30 German tanks, 60 half tracks, 20 guns, five miles east of Grosart, heading north-west at 0715 hours.*

Dendre River line under heavy attack. Request permission . . .

By the time they had fixed one defence line the Germans were already past them. The brigade faced the threat of being completely cut off.

18 May, 22.00 hours. Heavy panzer units advancing rapidly along Le Cateau–Cambrai and Valenciennes–Douai axis.

Which meant that the Germans had already broken through to his south and were coming straight at his unit. The Germans expected to roll up the entire British Expeditionary Force from the rear. A barrage from some

25 pounders whistled overhead, ranging in on the advancing panzer column. A new order from GOC superseded the last: *BEF to establish by 1200 hours May 19 along Escaut line, Oudenarde-Maulde.*

Pull back again! The men were worn out. And another message.

At GOC, Generals Franklyn and Martel had received the message to establish the new defence line, and were now co-ordinating their move when another message reached them. *19 May, 08.15. Units of German Army Group 'B' have breached Escaut at Oudenarde.* Which meant that the Escaut defence line was equally untenable. They had to pull back immediately and regroup along the Canal du Nord and the Scarpe.

Units of German Army Group 'A' advancing Cambrai–Arras. Enemy identified as 7th Panzer Division with two non-motorised Infantry Divisions twenty-four miles in rear.

That was the opportunity they'd been waiting for, the panzers were running way ahead of the infantry. Time to act. A minimum of 200 panzers against their 18 Matildas and 65 Mark Is. Not much, but a start.

The brigadier checked his map. His orders from General Martel had been quite specific. *Establish attack line along south bank Scarpe by 22.00 hours, May 20. Anchor on Vitry.* His Michelin map showed six bridges across the Canal du Nord between Douai and Ruyaulcourt. The panzers would head for them. For the time being, the line was held by two divisions of the First French Army. A day or two and the panzers would be across, then his tanks would hit them from the side and drive them into the Sensée. He didn't count on Rommel, whose *25th Panzerregiment* crossed the Canal du Nord at Marcoing before the British could establish a defensive position. At 05.00 hours on 20 May, Rommel's units were already driving past the Allies

south of Arras.[13] General Rommel went on a personal
scouting trip. For this he took two panzers, plus his own
lightly armoured scout car. On the road, near the village of
Vise-en-Artois, he fell into an ambush. His two tanks were
knocked out, and he himself was cut off for over an hour.
It was a close call.

The CO of the 1st British Tank Brigade received the
message that his forward units had shot up two German
tanks. He couldn't believe that the Germans were already
upon him. He quickly put every one of his 25-pounder
batteries and all the anti-tank gun units into ambush
position. They would fire at the Germans head on and
blunt their advance, while the Matildas and Mark Is struck
at the Germans' vulnerable flank. The plan was solid. It
would work, it simply had to work.

'17th Brigade will attack, with 4th Royal Tanks in
support. All the divisional artillery is at our disposal, plus
whatever the Corps can spare. We've got a job to do, and
we're bloody well going to do it.'

That's when the *Stukas* struck. They droned like a swarm
of angry bees: a host of them – thirty, forty, perhaps even
more. They followed the Scarpe River for their orientation
and headed straight for his bunched-up artillery units.

The drone changed into a shrill whistle as the first dive
bombers fell out of the sky. They aimed at the smoke
markers dropped by their artillery spotters. Clusters of
bombs detached from their bellies. The ground shook,
fountains of earth erupted, trucks and bodies flew through
the sky; a plane came out from the smoke, its windscreen
reflecting in the sun. More planes peeled over and headed
down, swooping, climbing, circling, coming down again, a
flying circus, birds of prey having fun. Everything around

---

[13] General Jodl's diary for this day: *Der Führer ist ausser sich vor Freude. Spricht
in Worten höchster Anerkennung vom deutschen Heer und seiner Führung . . .*

the commander seemed to be crumbling, drowned by the sound of exploding bombs and anti-aircraft fire. A Bren gun fired, suddenly there was this dark trail and a plane dived into the ground. A plume of greasy black smoke marked its fiery end.[14]

'We've got him, we've got him!' It was finally something for the men to cheer about. It didn't stop other *Stukas* from delivering their deadly loads. But the concentrated anti-aircraft fire had succeeded in diverting their attention away from his artillery and anti-tanks guns. His ground troops had suffered casualties, but the ambush was still in operation. His tanks were well hidden behind the tree line. 'Sir, a column of panzers is breaking through.'

Through his glasses he could see their black silhouettes with the stubby guns. The column seemed to stretch way beyond the horizon. Tanks, more tanks, and then their support vehicles. 'Let them pass.' His orders were precise: *21 May, 14.00 hours. Throw everything you've got at them.* It wasn't yet time.

The minutes ticked by slowly. 13.40 ... 13.50 ... 14.00 hours.

'All tanks forward.'

There was the rumble and clatter of tank chains as engines changed into top gear. From the shadow of the trees they crushed the bushes that had been their cover. They burst into the sunlight – thirty, fifty, eighty. The Germans must have seen them but didn't react immediately. Perhaps the commander had realised that he had a sizeable tank force to cope with, and no means to riposte, only thirty mark IIs and a few *Skodas* to guard the supply vehicles and fuel transporters. Their main panzer units were way ahead.

The brigadier had to deliver a lightning strike and benefit

14 General E. von Manstein's brother was shot down in a *Stuka* during that action.

from the surprise. 'Fire at will!' All hell broke loose. Along the entire front line British anti-tank guns opened from the front and British tanks broke out from the tree line and fired point blank at the panzers and Rommel's supply columns. A British tank leader was directing a squadron of Matildas leaning from his turret. A flanking squadron of light Mark Is closed to 400 yards of the Germans. Machine guns opened up on the enemy's thin-skin support vehicles. An ammo-truck blew up with a bright yellow flame. Shells whistled overhead. A German Mark III received a hit below the turret and exploded. We're smashing them! 'Sir, the 7th Royals have a dozen panzers boxed in. We've lost two to their eight.' The British tank force was advancing quite steadily, one wave staying in position and engaging the panzers, while the next wave lurched forward, presenting only their thickest armour to the German tank guns. A few panzers burnt fiercely in a flat field. Blackened hulls with their crews inside. Many German tanks had stopped owing to the crippling effect of British fire. Others reversed into the woods. Rommel's 42nd Antitank Battalion was overrun. Most of its tank crews were killed when their 37 mm anti-tank guns[15] proved useless against the 80 mm front armour of the British Matildas.

The brigadier clutched his microphone. 'Keep moving.' For the first time since their never-ending retreat he could hear excited voices and cheers from his crews. He knew it couldn't last forever. The Germans would counter-attack, that was the lesson they had so dearly learned in 1918.

21 May. 19th Panzer Corps, advance HQ, near the Channel coast. Guderian's 2nd Panzer Division had reached the Channel coast at Noyelles on 20 May. The Allied forces

---

[15] The Germans called it the *Heeresanklopfgerät* – the army's instrument to knock politely.

had been effectively cut in half. In four days, maximum five, he expected to have taken every Channel port. A message about the tank battle at Arras reached him at 14.10 hours.

'General, units of 7th Panzers have been engaged by heavy tank formations south of Arras. They're being pushed back on the Sensée.'

'I need enemy strength.'

'Identified are 4th and 7th Royal Tank Regiment.'

'Which units have we got there?'

'General, our nearest units are part of the 8th and 5th Panzers.'

'Enemy air cover?'

'Negative.'

Guderian thought for a moment. 'All right, divert units from the 8th, and call up the *Luftwaffe*, let their *Stukas* handle it.' The orders went out and were acknowledged. 'Where is the 8th at this moment?'

'They're sending in reinforcements along the Beaumetz Road.'

'Fine, fine', said Guderian.

'Any other orders, General?'

'No. Our main objectives are the Channel ports. My orders stand. 1st on to Calais, 2nd to Boulogne, 10th to Dunkirk.'

HQ 1st British Tank Brigade south of Arras. 'Sir, a column of enemy tanks approaching from west.' The brigadier could hear distant rumble. It wasn't only tanks which rolled up on the road, but with them came the camouflage-painted barrels of those nasty 88s,[16] deadly guns against tanks. Bangs came from beyond the forest line.

'Red 5, what's your situation? Over.'

---

[16] 88 *or Ack-Ack*, an anti-aircraft gun, but extremly efficient against tanks.

'We've run into ack-ack.'

'Give me co-ordinates, I'll lay artillery on them.' A battery of 25 pounders fired. The Ack-Acks went silent.

The shells struck all around Rommel. He had a close escape when one exploded nearby and killed his ADC, who was reading the map for the general.

Rommel had reached the Scarpe River with his 25th Panzer Regiment. When he heard about the Arras action, he immediately ordered his heavy units to turn around and head for the rear of the British tank force. A fierce battle broke out near Agnes which went initially in favour of the British. For the first time since crossing the French border, Rommel was forced into a defensive action, even to a point where he had to protect some of his lighter units with mines. That day Rommel lost 250 killed, more than on any previous day.

21 May. Advanced HQ British 50th Division, 17.30 hours. General Martel studied the developing situation. Red and blue arrows covered the map. It was too early to get a comprehensive overall picture. They had hit Rommel's vulnerable flank; most of the units they had engaged so far were supply columns and some infantry. His seventy-odd tanks were pushing at the Germans along the Bapaume Road. The front line began to bulge south from Arras. It was time to throw in the reserves along the Cambrai Road, go at the retreating Germans and cut through their line in a synchronised pincer movement with the push from the south, promised by the French tank force . . . his thoughts were interrupted by a terrific howl as a *Heinkel* bomber dived over the village at near street level. The general noticed that the cross on the church steeple trembled and the street erupted under the impact of bullets. 'Sir, in addition to the 7th Panzers, other units have now

been identified as parts of the 8th Panzers moving on Beaumetz and the 5th Panzers at Vitry.' More messages were coming in as more panzer units became identified. He could hear the drone of aircraft engines. *Stukas.* The first wave passed over the farmhouse. How clever the Germans were, using dive-bombers as mobile artillery, and with devastating results. It wasn't long before the bombs fell and the ground shook.

The brigadier of the 1st British Tank Brigade was standing up in his open car, microphone in hand. Through his glasses he watched the Germans come on in packs. 8th Panzers from his right, 7th in the centre and 5th Panzers approaching his left flank. Damn! His tanks were getting boxed in by elements of three German panzer divisions! Keep hammering away at them, bluff them, keep them from counter-attacking. The tanks faced each other at as near as 300 yards. His gunners began to fire over open sights, so close were the Germans now. One of his Matildas was hit in the track, spun around, but kept on firing. A German Mark III went up with a clean hit; a man tried to climb out, was cut down by bullets. A *Fieseler Storch* scout plane made its appearance, dropping flares to mark targets. The Germans were bringing up more of their long-barrelled guns; their muzzle-flashes were brighter than those of the tank guns. A Matilda was blown into the air, then another. He had to buy time for the rest to pull out. And then, out of a late afternoon sky came the *Stukas.* Suddenly the deafening roar was directly above him before he heard the high whistling of falling bombs and his tanks began to catch fire . . .

21/5 18.25 Uhr. From H Gr B to OKW.
The enemy resistance has stiffened. South-easterly counter-

attacks by tanks. Army Group B intends to put main effort on right flank, given that you intend to push with strong forces in a northerly direction along the line Valenciennes–Arras–Abbeville. Request urgent OKW decision.[17]

The message that came back at 20.05 p.m. displayed a growing panic at Hitler's headquarters.[18]

OKW takes the following position: H Gr B has to keep its present position by engaging the enemy. H Gr A bars the enemy the way to the Somme by attacking Arras in direction Calais. A full attack by H Gr A is only feasible after occupation of the heights north-west of Arras.

General Jodl made a call to a *Heeresgruppe* commander which showed the total confusion about the conflicting reports coming into *OKW*: '*The Führer has expressed his extreme worry that the Infantriedivisionen are not pushed ahead with sufficient vigour.*'[19]

That night, Hitler panicked. He remained in the map room at *OKW* until 02.30 hours, desperately awaiting further communications. There were none.

In the cover of darkness the remainder of the British units withdrew to their original position along the Scarpe River. The operations of the Franklyn corps lasted twenty-four hours. The promised attack by French tanks never materialised and General Franklyn sent out orders to regroup

[17] *Feindwiderstand hat sich versteift. Südostwärts Gegenstösse mit Panzern. Heeresgruppe beabsichtigt Schwerpunkt auf den rechten Flügel zu verlegen. Voraussetzung ist dass die Heeresleitung (OKW) beabsichtigt über Linie Valenciennes-Arras-Avveville mit starken Kräften in nördlicher Richtung anzugreifen. Baldige Entscheidung der Heeresleitung erbeten.*
[18] *OKW besteht auf folgender Auffassung: H Gr B hat ihren Streifen durch Angriff auf Feind festzuhalten. H Gr A verlegt durch Angriff über Arras in Richtung Calais den Feind den Abzug gegen die Somme. Ein Angriff durch H Gr A kommt erst nach Besitznahme des Hohengelandes nordwestlich von Arras durch Infanteriedivisionen in Frage.*
[19] *Der Führer ist unruhig dass die Infanteriedivisionen nicht genügend vorwärts getrieben werden.*

during the night. Next morning they tried one last time. The second attack ended in a complete catastrophe. The British units were pushed against the Scarpe. With their backs to the river and no bridges to cross it, they fought a holding action until late afternoon on the 22nd. By evening the situation had reached a critical stage. Most of their tank reserves had been destroyed, their only option was to drop everything, swim across, and make for the coast. By now, Guderian's panzers had swung around their flank and threatened to cut off their last available escape route towards the Channel ports.

General Franklyn called General Gort for permission to disengage his badly mauled units towards Douai. That permission had been accorded three hours earlier but was never passed on. A shell had wiped out the radio truck. The order to pull out was rushed to the various units by motorcycle riders. The whole BEF retreated: long columns of men with their rifles slung across their shoulders and machine-gun bandoleers around their necks. Many wore bandages torn from shirts, others had arms in slings or were limping along on home-made crutches. At the noise of an aircraft they hobbled into the nearest ditch to take cover, because by now they knew that these planes wouldn't be British. All their armour had been abandoned on the Scarpe.

The British Expeditionary Force, and with it the Seventh French and the Belgian Army, were caught in a trap. General Gamelin's plan of a massive front at the Dyle had backfired. The Allied division north of the Somme were now surrounded by a ring of steel, and about to be pushed into the sea. They had a choice of two options: surrender or drown. That night, nothing stood any longer between the panzers and the Channel ports.

The Allies needed a miracle. But the German panzers had outlawed miracles.

By 23 May, General Guderian reported to his superior at
H Gr A (Army Group A), that the situation at Arras was
under control and the British armour destroyed. Field-
Marshal von Brauchitsch, head of the armies, ordered Army
Group A to commence the end phase of the battle.[20]

The sacrifice by British tanks at Arras had pushed Hitler
over the edge. For the next two days, he was extremly fidgety
and nervous. At this crucial point, a new player entered the
field, one whose only interest in it was to achieve personal
glory. *Der Dicke*, Air Marshal Hermann Göring.[21] When he
heard that the encirclement of the Allied armies had been
completed he immediately demanded to be put in contact
with his *Führer*.

'*Das ist eine glänzende Aufgabe für die Luftwaffe.*'

A brilliant task for his airforce. The over-ambitious Göring
then went on to assure Hitler that his bomber pilots would
annihilate the Tommies. The Air Marshal argued that the
northern Allied armies were cut off from the rest of France
and that the *Führer* needed his panzer force intact to crush
Paris, to avenge the humiliation of 1918. The *Führer* need
only order the panzers to stop so that his *Luftwaffe* wouldn't
strike at their own units. Hitler, still suffering from the
aftershock of the Arras tank encounter, readily agreed to
Göring's proposal.[22]

At the *Oberkommando der Wehrmacht* (OKW), a heated
confrontation between General Halder and Field-Marshal
von Brauchitsch on the one side, and Hitler, feebly supported
by his yes-men Keitel and Jodl on the other, ended with
Hitler hysterically screaming:

---

[20] On the 24th Hitler paid von Rundstedt a personal visit to *H Gr A* headquarters
at Charleville. The general confirmed to his *Führer* that his panzers could use a
brief rest to resupply; however, he never talked about stopping his panzers . . .
[21] Owing to his girth Goring was called The Fat Man.
[22] Admiral Ansel, from talks with *Luftwaffe* General Jeschonnek, Göring's ADC.
This fact, that Goring was responsible for the *Halte Befehl*, was reconfirmed by Air
Marshals Kesselring and Milch during an interview in a POW camp in 1945.

'*Ich wünsche, dass alle Panzerspitzen bis an die Kanallinie*[23] *zurückgenommen werden. Jeder Verlust an Panzern ist unbedingt zu vermeiden. Meine Luftwaffe wird den Engländern den Rest geben.*[24] ('I order that all advance panzer formations are brought back to the *Kanallinie*. Any loss of panzers is to be strictly avoided. My *Luftwaffe* will finish off the English.)

When faced by the cream of military leaders, with their gold shoulder boards and red-striped trousers, the former corporal always felt inferior, and people who feel themselves inferior have a pathological need to disprove the perceptions of their own persona. Hitler's fantasies of glory took the form of desperate escapes from the cruel reality. But the reality was lethal.

History took a hand. All he did was nod.

And so it happened, that for the first time, Hitler, the astute politician and propagandist, got involved with the business best left to the military mind. He overruled his top tacticians, men like von Brauchitsch and Halder, or his tank commanders on the ground, Guderian, Reinhardt and Hoth, and took a disastrous strategic decision. He issued his famous stop-order of 24 May 1940.

The *Halte Befehl*.

24/5/40 – 12.31 Uhr.

(Fernmündlich von H Gr A an AOK 4 Ab)

OKW. *Auf Befehl des Führers ist der Angriff ostwärts Arras mit VIII und II AK im Zusammenwirken mit linken Flügel H Gr B nach Nordwesten fortzusetzen. Dagegen ist nordwestlich Arras die allgemeine Linie Lens–Béthune–Aire–St Omer–Gravelines (Kanallinie) nicht zu überschreiten. Es kommt auf dem Westflügel vielmehr darauf an, alle beweglichen Kräfte*

[23] Line Lens–Béthune–Aire–St Omer–Gravelines *(Kanallinie)*.
[24] General Halder in an interview after the war with Peter Bor (*Gespräche mit Halder*).

aufzuschliessen und den Feind an der genannten günstigen Abwehrlinie anrennen zu lassen.[25] '(By order of the Führer the attack east of Arras is to be co-ordinated by the 8th and 2nd Army Corps. However, *you are ordered not to cross* the line Lens–Béthune–Aire–St Omer–Gravelines (*Kanallinie*). The right wing has to bring together its mobile forces and allow the enemy to run up against a favourable defensive position.)

The events leading to the 'Miracle of Dunkirk' took their destined way. Halder had to inform all German panzer units: '*By direct order of the Führer the fast left wing is to be stopped immediately.*'[26]

Guderian couldn't believe it, and neither could his divisional commander, Erwin Rommel. That was the day he first began to doubt the military wisdom of his supreme commander. It changed little that his aide marched up to him, saluted and announced: 'By order of our *Führer* I have the great honour to present *Herrn General* with the *Ritterkreuz*.' Erwin Rommel was the first divisional commander to receive the Knight's Cross during the French campaign. He didn't care. His panzers stood idle.

At 15.42 hours, on 24 May, British Intelligence intercepted a second German message, sent out, inexplicably, *en clair:*

24 May. From OKW *to* AG A *and* AG B. *Present positions to be secured and advance to be discontinued until further Führer directive.*[27]

On 24 May 1940, at 17.15 hours, the brigadier of the mauled 1st British Tank Brigade received an Intelligence report from his GOC:

[25] Jacobsen, *Dokumente zum Westfeldzug, 1940.*
[26] *Der schnelle linke Flügel wird auf ausdrücklichen Wunsch des Führer angehalten.*
[27] General Walter Warlimont, *Im Hauptquartier der Deutschen Wehrmacht.*

All forward movement of German Army Group A halted in sector St Omer–Béthune–Douai ...

A miracle had taken place. Hitler had stopped his panzers.

General von Rundstedt noted in his war diary:
'Arras, 21–22 May 1940.

For a short time it was feared that our armoured divisions would be cut off before the infantry divisions could come up to support them. None of the French counter-attacks carried any serious threat as did the one at Arras.'

And so, the significance of this suicidal attack by a small force of British tanks is that it convinced Hitler his valuable panzers were running too many risks. The outcome was Hitler's decision to halt his panzers from 24 to 26 May 1940.

26/5 – 16.25 Uhr
OKW an H Gr A und HG B.
Fernspruch – nur durch Offiziere.
The immediate continuation of the attack by HG A and HG B against the enclosed enemy forces is hereby ordered.[28]

It was too late, much too late ...

The three days had given the British Expeditionary Force the respite it needed to reach their evacuation points. The rest is history.

---

[28] *Die Fortsetzung des Angriffs gegen den von H Gr A u. Beingeschlossenen Feind wird angeordnet.*

What if . . .

What if – Hitler hadn't stopped his panzers?

> Three hundred and thirty thousand British soldiers would have marched into German captivity. England would have been left with almost no defences and encouraged Hitler to launch *Operation Sea Lion*, the planned invasion of the British homeland.

The facts

Never were German armies closer to crush England than on this 24 May 1940. After the war, surviving generals present during the fateful hours of that morning stated unanimously that Germany lost the war the day Hitler issued the *Halte Befehl*.

It has never been explained why Hitler sent out his second stop-order *en clair*. Some experts have put it down to political reasoning, that Hitler wished to let Churchill know that he was looking for a negotiated solution.[29] Today it is clear that it was never Hitler's intention to allow a third of a million British soldiers to escape. He had the sworn assurance of Air Marshal Göring that the *Luftwaffe* would look after the annihilation of the BEF.

It didn't work out that way. Before Dunkirk fell, on 4 June, 338,226 British and Allied troops were evacuated to safety. This in itself was an achievement, and for a beleaguered England, it represented a triumph.[30]

---

[29] Hasso von Etzdorf, the German Foreign Ministry's representative in *OKW*, wrote on 21 May, 1940: '*Wir suchen Fuehlung mit England auf Basis der Teilung der Welt.*' ('We look for a contact with England on the basis of a partition of the world.)

[30] The military historian, B.H. Liddell Hart, in his *History of the Second World War*: 'The escape of the British Expeditionary Force in 1940 was largely due to Hitler's personal intervention when he kept his tanks halted for three days. His action preserved the British forces when nothing else could have saved them.'

Two years later, these soldiers were to meet up once more with Rommel's panzers, at El Alamein. The outcome was different.

The high water mark for the German armies was reached with the surrender of France on 22 June 1940. The *Blitzkrieg* against France gave Hitler an erroneous picture. In their dash for the Channel ports, German panzers could be easily resupplied from their stocks in Germany over 300 kilometres of an efficient rail network. This became a different matter in Russia, where distances had to be multiplied by ten, where the rail gauge was different from the one in France and Germany, where partisans blew up rail lines and bridges along the enormous distances which separated Berlin from Moscow or Stalingrad.

Russia was not France. Some of Hitler's generals tried to warn him. The 'greatest military genius since Julius Caesar' wouldn't listen to his prophets.

Thus, the lightning success achieved by his able panzer commanders over a nearby foe lured Hitler into a far-off adventure which led to his downfall.

The Hinge Factor of the Battle for France was a sacrifice attack by seventy-four British tanks which brought about Hitler's panic decision to halt his panzers.

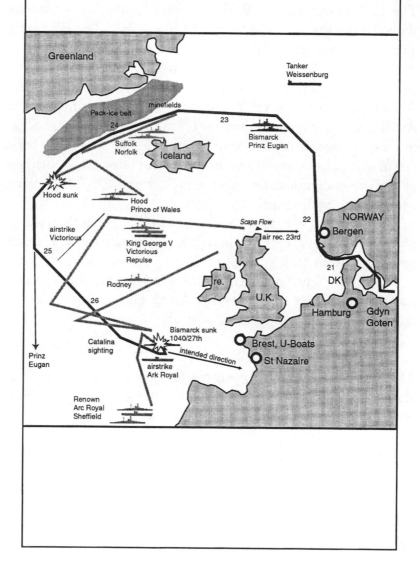

Bismarck action,
May 19-27 1941

Greenland

Tanker
Weissenburg

minefields

Pack-ice belt

24 23

Suffolk
Norfolk

Iceland

Bismarck
Prinz Eugan

Hood sunk

Hood
Prince of Wales

NORWAY

Scapa Flow 22

air rec. 23rd

Bergen

airstrike
Victorious

King George V
Victorious
Repulse

25

21

DK

Rodney

re.

U.K.

Hamburg

Gdyn
Goten

26

Bismarck sunk
1040/27th

Catalina
sighting

intended direction

Brest, U-Boats

St Nazaire

Prinz
Eugan

airstrike
Ark Royal

Renown
Arc Royal
Sheffield

13

A Shark on the Loose

North Atlantic, 27 May 1941

'Bismarck *must be sunk at all costs.'*
Order from Winston Churchill to
the Royal Navy, 26 May 1941

The sky was a sullen grey and the storm-pitched sea was empty of ships. The crew of the plane kept a sharp lookout for the prize target the whole of the British Navy was out hunting: the killer of the battle-cruiser *Hood*, England's pride and glory. A peril was on the loose, a German challenge to 'England rules the waves'.

Catalina Z of the British 209 Squadron was cruising under the command of Flying Officer Dennis Briggs. The plane's co-pilot was a farmboy from Higginsville, Missouri. Ensign Leonard 'Tuck' Smith was probably the original 'Yank in the RAF', even to the point that he wore a US Navy uniform, not the thing to do for an American seven

months before the USA entered the war.[1] They had been
flying a search pattern since first light, but the weather
was foul and their only chance of spotting any vessel
was to drop below the clouds, down to around 500 feet,
the minimum permissible height for a seaplane the size
of a Catalina. FO Briggs had relinquished the command
to Smith, who put the big flying-boat on autopilot. The
crew was devouring their breakfast when they heard the
excited voice of the Missourian: 'Eleven o'clock! Eleven
o'clock!'

What Smith had seen was only a dark shape, covered by
the ocean's spume. He immediately disengaged the automatic pilot and headed into the clouds for an approach.
In the excitement he misjudged the distance, because when
he brought the plane down again, and broke clear of the
cloud, there she was, huge and deadly, a mere 500 yards
to starboard. There was no mistaking her identity. Her grey
hull erupted in wicked gouts of flame and the Catalina was
buffeted by nearby air bursts. Around them bloomed black
puffs, shrapnel rattled on the fuselage, punched holes into the
hull and shattered the windscreen with singeing shards of hot,
splintered steel. Smith punched the red button which released
the depth charges, yanked back on the stick and prayed. On
full throttle, and delivered from the weight of four heavy
depth charges, the big plane bounced upwards, the propellers
whined as the cumbersome aircraft disappeared into the
cloud. The manoeuvre was so violent that FO Briggs was

[1] The original information about the action of Z/209 comes from an article by
Godfrey Winn in the *Sunday Express*, 1 June 1941. The censor stopped Winn
from publishing his scoop about the 'Yankee pilot' since the United States were
not as yet in the war and the presence of an American officer flying a British
aircraft on combat mission a dire violation of US neutrality.

  The identity of Ensign L. B. Smith, the person mentioned in a memo of 29
July 1941 to the Assistant Chief of British Naval Staff, was revealed by author
Ludovic Kennedy, who, in 1973, found and talked to the former ensign in
Kearney, Nebraska, who reconfirmed the series of events.

thrown against the stanchions while he dictated his message to the radio operator.[2]

'One battleship course 150°. Our position 49°33' North, 21°47' West. Time of origin 1030/26 May.'

The cat was out of the bag. The countdown was on in the hunt for the fastest and most deadly menace on the seas.

The German super-battleship *Bismarck*.

Norway, a week before. Two men were strolling along the road which bordered the ocean. Both were feeling merry, having just left a drinking party in Kristiansand. 'Arne, you've had too much schnapps,' said Viggo Axelssen, a ship's chandler who was active in the Norwegian Resistance, leaning on his friend.

'Stop telling me I'm drunk. Here, have a look yourself.' Arne Usterud handed his glasses to his friend and made naval history. That 20 May 1941, when Viggo Axelssen looked past the Oskoy lighthouse and saw two camouflaged battleships steaming west at high speed, he was the first witness to a drama that was to be played out on a stage of two million square miles of stormy ocean, from the Arctic to the Bay of Biscaye. It culminated in one of the fiercest sea battles of World War 2.

Viggo Axelssen, suddenly sober, knew these had to be Germans, since British vessels were uniformly grey. He coded a message of twelve words and ran to the house of Arne Moen, a bus driver. A note hidden in the fuel intake pipe of his bus, reached Gunvald Tomstad in Helle. From a hayloft in a Norwegian village, a message went across the ether to Colonel Roscher Lund, the military attaché of the exiled Norwegian government in Stockholm. Lund read it and immediately called on his friend Henry Denham of the

---

[2] Revealed by Ludovik Kennedy. The source is a classified report by Ensign L. B. Smith for the Intelligence Division of the Department of Naval Operations, US Navy.

Royal British Navy. Within seven hours of the initial sighting a message reached London: *Kattegat today. At 1507, two large warships three destroyers air cover passed Marstrand course WNW 2058/20 May.*

The secret was out. The German super-battleship *Bismarck* and the heavy battle-cruiser *Prinz Eugen* were on their run towards the Atlantic. Operation *Rheinüebung* had begun. Their mission: a three-month cruise in the Atlantic to intercept British convoys and stop the resupply of men and equipment to the Commonwealth Force fighting in North Africa.

Bismarck was to be a shark on the loose.

Most of Europe had yielded to Hitler and only a truculent Britain still held out. When the news of the *Bismarck* reached London, no one was more impressed than Prime Minister Winston Churchill. With his long experience of naval warfare he knew of the fearful havoc the German squadron could cause among the Atlantic convoys, and of its overall effect on the war.

There never was a ship like her. The *Bismarck* not only symbolised the German Navy, but the whole power of Nazi Germany. She was huge and fast, in excess of 30 knots. To comply with the London Naval Treaty she was listed as 35,000 tons, but in reality her displacement was close to 50,000 tons with a crew of 2,000. The captain was Ernst Lindemann, forty-six years, from the Rhineland, clever and cool. With his blond hair sleeked back, the picture of the typical German. The Naval High Command had picked him as 'the right man in the right place'. Overall commander of the operation was Admiral Günther Lütjens, fifty-one, a man wholly dedicated to the service, courageous and single-minded. He wore an admiral's dirk of the old Imperial Navy, not the one with a swastika, and had once refused to give Hitler the party salute.

The *Bismarck* went down the slipway at Blohm & Voss

in Hamburg on Valentine's Day, 1939. Hitler was present when Prince Bismarck's granddaughter, Dorthea von
Loewenfeld, christened Germany's greatest ship with the
name of their greatest Chancellor. Battleship *Bismarck*, massive and elegant, with the high flare of her bows and majestic
sweep of her lines, was the most graceful and powerful
warship ever built. The ship's side armour was made of
13-inch thick specially hardened Wotan steel. Her terror lay
in her four giant gun towers that could fire further and faster
than any other ship in the world. The *Bismarck*'s four main
batteries of twin 15-inch cannons were capable of firing a
salvo every twenty seconds. That in itself was a record – a
broadside of eight shells, each weighing a ton.

The task that lay before her was formidable: escape from
the Baltic bottleneck and break out into the open Atlantic. It
was left to Admiral Lütjens' judgement either to slip through
the Faeroe Passage south of Iceland, or to the Denmark
Straits, between Iceland and the Greenland ice cap. The
southern passage was dangerously close to the base of the
British Home Fleet at Scapa Flow in the Orkney Islands,
while the Denmark Straits, although further from British air
reconnaissance, was in parts only thirty miles wide and could
be blocked by mines or an enemy force. That was the plan.
To Lütjens it seemed more like the scenario of an improbable
film script.

At 21.30 hours, on 18 May 1941, the biggest warship of
the Atlantic war rose from the outer reaches of Gotenhaven.[3]
Dockyard workers paused to watch as the familiar flag signals
fluttered from the battleship's halyards. She was putting out
to sea. A mountainous island of grey steel, *Bismarck*'s graceful
curved bow, crowned by the swastika, rose 20 metres above
the oil-flecked waters of the bay where she had moored. No
one ever got over the initial shock of seeing her. The first time

[3] Today's Polish Gdynia.

Able Seaman Heinz Staat reported aboard, the great sweep
of her forecastle looked like a football field. Even now, two
months later, he could not help being impressed. He threw
an awed glance at the towering superstructure, a profusion
of guns, ladders and antennae. He was proud; no other navy
could boast of a battleship so heavily armed and armoured,
so indestructible. The ship's officers and crew were expected
to be better dressed than anyone in the German forces. A
bosun's mate respectfully held up a mirror while Captain
Lindemann checked himself over. Cap straight, shoes spotless,
tie knotted to regulation size.

'Amidships!' The operation's commanding officer, Admiral
Lütjens, was conning the ship himself.

'Wheel amidships, sir', answered the quartermaster, entombed
with his small electrically operated steering wheel in the
armoured cockpit inside the tower.

'Steady as she goes . . .'

Lying at anchor at Scapa Flow in the Orkneys was Britain's
Home Fleet, the world's mightiest assembly of naval power.
Admiral Tovey, fifty-six, its commander, was aboard his
new flagship, King George V. Where the German Admiral
Lütjens was tall, Tovey was small. But he was possessed of
the same obstinacy as his German counterpart. Admiralty had
passed on the sighting message from Norway. What Tovey
needed was confirmation. Two unarmed Spitfires were sent
on a photographic reconnaissance mission to Norway. One,
piloted by Flying Officer Suckling, made for Bergen Fjord. It
crossed the fjord unnoticed.

It was on 22 May, in Kalvanes Bay of the Korsfjord, a quiet
backwater on Norway's coast, that the fate of the Bismarck
was most likely sealed. On its run from Germany to Norway
the Bismarck had burned over a thousand tons of oil. Lying
at anchor was the German tanker Wollin, ready to top-up

the partly depleted oil tanks of the super-battleship. We shall never know what made Admiral Lütjens change his mind and, instead of refuelling his capital ship, ordered the 14,000 ton cruiser *Prinz Eugen*, named after the Prince of Savoy and liberator of Austria from the Turks, into Korsfjord to top-up. It may have been because Lütjens knew that the tanker *Weissenburg* was waiting for him off Iceland.[4]

As soon as Admiral Tovey studied the aerial photos taken by the Spitfire, he took his disposition. The heavy cruisers *Norfolk* and *Suffolk* were ordered to patrol the Denmark Straits, the cruisers *Manchester* and *Birmingham* into the Iceland-Faeroe Passage. Neither was to engage the capital ship. The pride of the British Navy, the 42,000 ton battle-cruiser *Hood*, under Vice-Admiral Lancelot Holland, together with the brand-new battleship *Prince of Wales*, was ordered to lay in ambush. It was the perfect scenario for a Western-type shoot-out, only this one was to be executed with 15-inch battleship guns.[5]

Tovey informed the Prime Minister. Churchill cabled American President F. D. Roosevelt. Churchill's communications letter stressed: 'We must consider that for the first time in this war a major fleet action will occur in which the enemy will have two ships at least as good as our two best. Should we fail to catch them going out, your Navy should surely be able to mark them down for us. Give us the news and we will finish the job.'

Churchill knew certainly more of the German squadron's movement than Hitler, who knew nothing at all. Grand Admiral Raeder had long ago discovered that it was best not to tell his *Führer* until success could be assured. On

[4] The standing rule in the British Navy, to oil up whenever a capital ship reached a harbour facility, was not observed by Lütjens; this proved to be a serious flaw in the otherwise perfect execution of *Bismark*'s breakout; his decision would allow no margin for error during the forthcoming dash into the Atlantic.
[5] 15 inches equals 380 mm.

the 22nd at 7.30 p.m. *Bismarck* weighed anchor at Bergen and, accompanied by the heavy cruiser *Prinz Eugen*, headed north.

The battle-cruiser *Hood* also weighed anchor. It was the last time that the people of England would see her. The German squadron was steaming north at 24 knots, and their crews began to paint out the swastika air recognition marks on the gun turrets. The Germans were in luck, heavy overcast skies made British aerial reconnaissance impossible. There was a chance they might slip through undetected. Dr Externbrink, *Bismarck*'s chief meteorologist, forecast continued cloud cover to the north and in the narrow channel along the Greenland pack ice.

'How long, Dr Externbrink?' enquired the admiral.

'I can only predict forty-eight hours cloud cover, at most seventy-two.'

'Where is this front moving to?'

'North of Iceland, Admiral.'

Lütjens checked the sea charts. *The Denmark Straits.* The weather held a decided advantage; he was sure that his task force had been spotted and that the Home Fleet was on the move to head him off. Their logical ambush point would be north of the Faeroe Islands and South of Iceland. By sailing through the Denmark Straits, he'd be further from the British home bases, and only a chance encounter with a fishing trawler or whaler would give away his position. If the bad weather front held as predicted, he would have passed the point of danger and broken clear into the open Atlantic. Dr Externbrink's weather forecast decided Lütjens on taking the longer route. But Lütjens was caught in a dilemma; given only the 48 hours of overcast, he couldn't afford to divert for refuelling from the tanker *Weissenburg*. In view of the longer marsh route and his refusal to refuel in Bergen, this was a bold decision. The German admiral turned his task force onto a south-eastern course. The foggy weather continued, at times so thick that the *Bismarck* had to turn on its searchlight for the *Prinz Eugen* to follow in its wake. The squadron went to 27 knots for its dash through the Denmark Straits. They had entered the most dangerous passage, a thirty-mile strip limited to the south by minefields, and by pack ice to the north, when Lütjens fears were realised: the weather cleared. For the first time in 36 hours there was a clear path of water about 5 kilometres wide. The lookouts were doubled. The young seamen stared in awe at the beauty of the pack ice, broad and dense. The edge of the world, the road to the North Pole.

Able Seaman Heinz Staat, a merchant seaman from Wilhelmshaven, was positioned in Commander Oels's command post on the upper bridge, from where he enjoyed an unparalleled view of the Arctic's magic.

Hans Riedel, a loader in C for Caesar turret, was from Bavaria, a most unlikely place for a seaman to hail from. Now, that Bavarian mountain boy stared through the narrow slit in his gun turret. All he could see were the wind-whipped crests of an icy seascape culminating in a point where the sea merged with dense fog.

Machine Mate Blum was deep in the bowels of the ship, checking gauges and fixing pump lines. Among the hissing pipes, and numbed by the drone of the huge diesels, he was unaware of the beauty of the Arctic Ocean. Though they didn't know it, in three short days fate would unite them.

The *Norfolk* and the *Suffolk* were three-funnelled cruisers. Their commander, Admiral Frederick Wake-Walker, realised that their 8-inch guns presented no real challenge for *Bismarck*:[6] she'd blow them out of the water. His orders

---

[6] Both were equipped with the new British RADAR, though it was limited in distance. The superiority of the British 9 cm wave over the German 50 cm system was clearly established early in the war.

were clear: *Do not engage. Find her and trail her.* But nobody had a clue where to look. While he steamed along the pack-ice shore, this afternoon of 24 May, for all he knew the *Bismarck* could be back in Germany. He saw nothing, only an agony of spume tossing black water, the thunder of the sea against the side of the ship. The off-duty crew was listening to the BBC – 'Itma' (and Spy Funf), or the 'Forces' Sweetheart' Vera Lynn, even Churchill, always good value when he talked about Herr Hitler. Some were asleep. Their peace didn't last.

Able Seaman Newell on the *Suffolk* brought the suspense to an end. At 18.00 he had taken up his position as lookout on the bridge. With his glasses he had swept the ocean at least fifty times when suddenly he saw something he would never forget for the rest of his life. The *Bismarck*, black and massive, emerging from a patch of fog.

'Ship bearing Green One Four O!' he yelled, and immediately corrected himself: 'Two ships bearing Green One Four O.'

The captain of the *Suffolk*, Captain Robert Ellis, ordered full steam ahead to slip into a fog bank. His first officer pressed the alarm bells. Men leapt from hammocks and raced down passageways. The ship leaned heavily to starboard, dinner plates crashing to the floor: It was a few terrible moment before the *Suffolk* disappeared into the fog to send out its electrifying message. '*24 May 19.20 hours. Battleship* Bismarck *headed on course . . .*'

H.M.S. *Norfolk* picked up the signal. Her captain, Alfred Phillips, misjudged the distance, and suddenly found himself only six miles from the German battleship. *Bismarck*'s guns roared. A shell bounced off the water. The men on board heard the scream of shells as the huge projectiles passed over *Norfolk*'s bridge. Great columns of milk-white water rose in the air. Admiral Wake-Walker looked anxiously on as the sea around him was pocked with shell splinters. The

German fired five salvoes before the British cruiser managed to escape into the fog.

This was the overall situation: the troopship *Britannic* was 800 miles away to the south, directly in the path of the *Bismarck*, as was the troop convoy *WS8B* bound for the middle East, now stripped of its protection, since the carrier *Victorious* and the battle-cruiser *Repulse* had been ordered to join the *Bismarck* chase. Admiral Tovey's squadron, led by the battleship *King George V*, was still at anchor at Scapa, 600 miles to the south. But Vice-Admiral Holland, commanding the mighty task force of *Hood* and *Prince of Wales*, was a mere 300 miles away. Holland ordered full steam ahead and brought his two battleships on a converging course.

The battle cruiser *Hood* was the unchallenged Queen of the Sea, her name synonymous with 'Rule, Britannia'. Around the world she was considered invincible, and yet, there was a serious flaw in her construction: her upper decks were not of reinforced steel. Anxieties surfaced at Holland's staff conference; intelligence reports suggested that earlier estimates of *Bismarck*'s firepower were incorrect and that her guns could outrange anything the Royal Navy could muster. Gunnery officers pored over range tables which predicted that the Germans would open fire long before their own batteries were able to hit back. The admiral addressed the crew over the ship's tannoy: action could be expected within hours. The crew gave three cheers.

'The honour will go to us. We have eighteen guns to the German's eight.'

At present speed and course they would meet the enemy before 02.00 hours. The two mightiest battleships of the British High Sea Fleet sliced through the sea on a Valkyrie's Ride. Admiral Tovey, still at anchor in Scapa Flow, signalled the aircraft carrier *Victorious*, the battle-cruiser *Repulse*, the cruisers *Galatea, Hermione, Kenya and Aurora*, plus five destroyers to join him north of the Hebrides. Then, as his great ship *King George V* set out to sea, Tovey sat down for dinner with his officers.

Churchill and the Admiralty in London were concerned about *Bismarck*'s rapid southward movement, which brought it towards its troop convoy *WS8B*. At midnight of the 23rd, a message was received at Gibraltar Naval Base, ordering Admiral Somerville to raise his Force H. It was made up of the aircraft carrier *Ark Royal*, the battle-cruiser *Renown* and the cruiser *Sheffield*. They were to head north into the Atlantic and meet up with the troop convoy. It was a rendezvous Force H would never keep; more dramatic things were awaiting on the Atlantic.

All the pieces were now in place. The drama was about to unfold. And while all this hectic activity was taking place, the crew of the *Bismarck* were unaware of the approaching thunder and blissfully asleep.

Things were heading rapidly towards a climax. By 01.40 hours Admiral Holland's *Hood* and *Prince of Wales* were only twenty miles from the *Bismarck* when Lindemann changed cap and passed a British destroyer screen unseen. This change put the two squadrons on a divergent course and their distance widened. At 03.20 hours the shadowing *Suffolk* signalled another course change of the Germans. This brought the British battleships into a grave disadvantage – in order to catch up they had to steam high speed at an oblique angle. Order was given to prepare for battle. In the British ships, officers and men went to their quarters to put on clean underwear, a ritual in the *Royal Navy* to prevent infection from wounds. Most wrote farewell notes to their families and sweethearts. They donned their anti-flash gear, which made them look like a gathering of Ku-Klux-Klaners. Then they waited. No one had any doubts of what lay ahead.

The bells jangled. Action stations! Watertight doors were slammed shut, ammunition hoists tested, guns elevated. In the boiler rooms men stared at pressure gauges and cooks extinguished their fires. In the mad dash, the ships were lost to each other in a spray of mist. The two enemy squadrons were closing on each other at 80 km per hour! At 05.10 the captain of the *Prince of Wales*, John Leach, broadcast: 'Enemy engagement within fifteen minutes.'

During the shelling of the *Norfolk*, a minor mishap had occurred aboard the *Bismarck* but one which was to influence the outcome of the encounter: the back blast of its huge guns had put the battleship's front radar out of action. Until repairs could be made, Admiral Lütjens had ordered *Prinz Eugen* to take the lead. As both German ships had a similar contour the British lookouts were to mistake the cruiser for the battleship.

Able Seaman 'Knocker' White was ordered to climb aloft the swaying mast with a pair of binoculars. The minutes passed.
   'Enemy in sight!'
   Two huge silhouettes emerged from the mist. There was something evil in their silent, purposeful race. Unless the Germans could be stopped, the Atlantic was theirs. The range at sighting was seventeen miles.[7] The guns began to swing around. With her white battle ensign flapping in the wind the proud *Hood* charged into battle.

Captain Helmuth Brinkmann of the *Prinz Eugen* was handed a bowl of hot soup by his orderly, Friebe. 'Dammit! Someone put a cigarette end in my soup. Friebe, at dawn you will be shot.' Everyone laughed; their thoughts turned to what they most desired, a few hours' sleep in a warm bed. Commander Jasper, gunnery officer of the *Prinz Eugen*, and Commander

[7] 27.2 km, equals the distance from Paris to the Marne.

Paul Schmalenbach, his second, had a cup of coffee when their listening post reported: '*Fast screws approaching port bow.*'

They stared through their binoculars and saw smoke over the horizon. Alarm bells sounded, long trills that warned of surface action. Mast tops appeared, then the silhouettes of ships. Schmalenbach checked in his *Handbook of Foreign Navies*. He shook his head, then looked again.

'The one on the right is the *Hood*', he stated.

'Nonsense,' said Jasper, 'it's a destroyer or a cruiser.'

'I'll bet you a bottle of champagne,' challenged Schmalenbach, 'the one on the right is the *Hood*.'

'Taken', answered Jasper. He didn't believe his second. Instead of loading armour-piercing shells, his order went out to load high explosive with impact fuses, never a weapon to use against battleship armour.

'*Blue Four*', came the order from the *Hood*. 'Alter course forty degrees starboard.' An unfortunate decision. The after-turrets on both battleships would not be able to get into action, their 18-gun superiority was lost. Now it was ten British versus eight German guns. Almost even. The *Hood* and the *Prince of Wales* swung around into the wind.

Aboard *Bismarck* Admiral Lütjens stared through the plate-glass of the bridge, his hands clenched behind his back. For only a moment his thoughts drifted to other great naval encounters: Trafalgar, Skagerak. This battle was not of his choosing. Ice to the north, enemy cruisers astern and battle-ships in front. He had no choice but to shoot it out.

The time was 05.50, the date 24 May 1941.

There was equal confusion aboard the British ships. It was assumed that *Bismarck* was leading the enemy line. On *Hood*'s bridge, a yeoman sang out the closing distances. At about the same time that Lütjens ordered the hoisting of the JD, the signal to open fire, to *Prinz Eugen*, Holland on *Hood* ordered the same signal to be sent to the *Prince of Wales*. The range was rapidly closing.

'Stand by to open fire. Target left-hand ship.'[8]

When the range was down to thirteen miles, Admiral Holland said: 'Execute!' and the yeoman shouted: 'Down flag five.' The signal to fire. And the chief gunnery officer said, almost in a prayer: 'Shoot!'

For a brief moment the world stood still. Then the guns spoke with their terrible roar.

On the German ships all eyes were riveted on the British muzzle flashes. Chief gunnery officer Jasper saw the fiery suns around the enemy's gun turrets and yelled: 'By God, you're right, that's no destroyer, that's a battleship!' and immediately ordered: 'Change to armour-piercing.'

05.53 a.m. *Bismarck*'s gunnery officer, Commander Adalbert Schneider, hit the crash button: '*Feuer*'. In the tightly shut command post, Admiral Lütjens rocked to the crash of *Bismarck*'s 8-gun salvo. Now the shells were in the air ... where would they fall? He watched as those of *Hood* and *Prince of Wales* landed in the vicinity of *Prinz Eugen*. Their impact, shooting tons of white water hundreds of feet in the air, was short by about a thousand yards. Bad shooting. Those of the *Bismarck* and *Prinz Eugen* were deadly accurate. The first salvo straddled the *Hood*.

For Admiral Holland everything had gone sour. He was in the worst possible position, facing a formidable enemy with only half his gun potential and giving the German a better target than necessary. To add to his problems, one of the *Prince of Wales*'s guns developed a firing defect and was out of action. While his fire was now divided between *Prinz Eugen*

---

[8] The *Prinz Eugen*, not the *Bismarck*.

and *Bismarck*, the Germans were concentrating everything on *Hood*. Holland assumed that *Norfolk* and *Suffolk* would enter the fight to take off some of the pressure, but he had forgotten to issue Admiral Wake-Walker with an order to do so. On top of that, the British steamed into the wind and the bow spray drenched the gunnery sights of their forward turrets, and they had to use their small secondary rangefinders, which weren't accurate.

The shells went flying across the sea, the water rose in tall white columns where they landed. Captain Brinkmann in the *Prinz Eugen* saved his ship from certain destruction when he ordered his helmsman to steer towards the water fountains, knowing that salvoes never land in the same place twice. *Prinz Eugen* fired only its second salvo. Twenty seconds went by, then a flame shot up on *Hood*'s boat deck.

The hit from the guns of the *Prinz Eugen* caused a fire among the 4-inch anti-aircraft ammunition. A sailor, Able Seaman Tilburn, and his gun crew were ordered to put out the fire when the ammunition inside the locker started to explode. They threw themselves flat onto the deck. Then a another shell struck, wiping out the entire gun crew. This could not continue, and Admiral Holland decided to bring his full 18-gun power into action. He ordered a course change.

'*Two Blue*, twenty degrees to port.' Both ships began to turn.

That's when the incredible happened.

06.00. Commander Schneider, the chief gunnery officer on *Bismarck*, spotted the enemy's course change and ordered a slight target correction.

'*Zwei Vollsalven.*'

The guns roared. The first salvo was too short.

Prinz Eugen's shells hit. '*Gegner brennt.*' ('The enemy's on fire.')

1st Artillery Officer Schneider ordered another correction, then he said loud and clear: '*Vollsalve*'.

06.01 a.m. For the fifth time in only four minutes the giant guns roared.

'*Achtung Aufschlag.*' ('Attention impact.')

Again the *Hood* was hidden behind a curtain of shell splashes. Schneider was puzzled, only six white fountains . . . two must have been duds . . . but they weren't . . .

'*Er siiiinkt . . . siiinkt . . .*' he screamed, long on the 'i'. 'He's going down!9

The two shells which did not splash into the sea came down on the *Hood*, smack centre, down through the decks and into the after-magazine crammed with high-explosive 15-inch shells. A huge white ball rose 300 metres into the air, followed by a column of yellow flame and a black cloud like that of an exploding volcano. Bits and pieces of guns and masts flew through the air. The most famous battleship in the world blew up like a Christmas cracker.10

'She's blowing up. The *Hood*'s gone!' screamed Schneider.

Bow and stern were pointed at the sky before the pride of the Royal Navy slipped beneath the waves. The whole thing had taken perhaps forty seconds, but forty seconds during which nobody fired. The minute of silence to a noble ship.

'Poor devils', Schneider muttered. But he had no time for second thoughts. There was still the other ship. '*Zielwechsel links!*' ('Target change left.')

The eight huge barrels turned towards the *Prince of Wales*.

The *Prince of Wales* now became the single target of both *Bismarck* and *Prinz Eugen*. But her guns had finally found

9 Account by Kapitaenleutnant Freiherr von Mullenheim–Rechberg, IV Artillery Officer.
10 Observed by both the *Prince of Wales* and the *Bismark*.

the *Bismarck*, and her sixth salvo straddled the German. At the same time she was hit by a 15-inch shell which went clear through the bridge and killed everyone but the captain. *Bismarck*'s salvoes thundered every twenty seconds, *Prinz Eugen*'s every ten. The British batteries fought back gamely, observing straddles with their ninth and thirteenth salvoes on *Bismarck*. But the *Prince of Wales* was outgunned. Mechanical defects silenced two of her five guns. She was hit by four 15-inch shells and three 8-inch. Her deck was a mess. One shell hit the ship below the waterline and let in 400 tons of sea water. After twelve minutes and eighteen salvoes, *the Prince of Wales* gave up and turned away. It was now 06.13 a.m., only nineteen minutes since the two British capital ships had steamed so proudly into battle.

A British destroyer raced to the scene to pick up survivors of the *Hood*. They found patches of oil, odd bits of wood and three men: Midshipman Dundas, Able Seaman Tilburn and Signalman Briggs. 'There must be more, there can't only be three of them. Keep searching', ordered the destroyer captain. They cruised up and down, but found only one other small piece of wreckage, a marine's hat. All the rest, two admirals, ninety officers and 1,500 able-bodied seamen, had gone down a thousand fathoms, where they would lie forever.

The three survivors were transferred to the destroyer *Elektra* and interviewed. Dundas said he was climbing from an upper-bridge window when the ship went over. Briggs left through the unhinged door of the compass platform and saw Admiral Holland make no attempt to leave his doomed ship. Tilburn had the closest escape. A radio aerial wrapped around his boot and he managed to cut it off with a clasp knife while being dragged under. He fought his way to the surface. Around him was nothing, only silence.

The Battle of the Denmark Straits was over. The *Bismarck* and *Prinz Eugen* continued thundering south, into the open

Atlantic. A discussion broke out between Captain Lindemann and the admiral whether to chase after the damaged *Prince of Wales*, finish her off and head for home. Lütjens stuck to his instructions and pressed on a south-easterly course. This decision saved the badly limping *Prince of Wales*. There was another reason for Lütjens' decision. Though the *Prinz Eugen* got away unscathed, *Bismarck* was not so fortunate. She had received three hits. Two were superficial but the third was not. A heavy shell had struck her at the waterline. It went through two oil tanks without exploding, destroyed the suction valves, and cut off a thousand tons of oil from the boilers.

More than anything else, it was this hit which was to determine *Bismarck*'s fate. Admiral Lütjens had cause to regret not having topped up from his tanker in Bergen Fjord. His ship needed dockyard repairs, and for this he was given two choices: return via the Denmark Straits, which by now would be crawling with enemy submarines, or head for the French ports. He decided on France. The problem was his fuel reserves. At the present rate he couldn't do without the extra thousand tons. Unless he reduced speed – and drastically – *Bismarck* would be running out of oil!

England was gripped by shock. The news of the *Hood* was felt much deeper than the disaster in France, or the setbacks in North Africa. *England no longer rules the waves*, screamed the headlines. Churchill knew that the *Bismarck* had turned into the very symbol of England's defeat. The ship was an evil which must be destroyed, no matter at what price, to regain the nation's confidence.

'*Sink the Bismarck!*' Churchill put out his categorical order.

All the gold braids the Royal Navy could muster were bent over maps in the Admiralty. Following their initial shock, they now moved into overdrive. They did not know yet, but this was to be the last time in its glorious history that

Britain would assert its strength, which had made England the Lord of the Seas. The First Sea Lord, Admiral of the Fleet Sir Dudley Pound, a man picked by Churchill because he was amenable to the Prime Minister's wishes, knew of the virtues of concentration, He was one who never strayed from Nelson's dictum: 'Only numbers can annihilate.'

From Halifax, Nova Scotia, sailed the battleship *Revenge*, from east of Newfoundland came the *Ramillies*, from northeast of the Azores the cruisers *London* and *Edinburgh*, from the Clyde the battleship *Rodney* and her destroyers; Admiral Wake-Walker trailed the Germans in the *Suffolk* and *Norfolk*, as did the damaged *Prince of Wales*. The nearest interception force, some 360 miles south, were the two battleships *King George V and Repulse*, and the aircraft carrier *Victorious*, plus five heavy cruisers. Given the information by *Suffolk*, Tovey knew that he would meet up with the *Bismarck* by early next morning, unless . . . unless *Bismarck* put on speed. And the German was much faster than any of his own units, even the most modern. There was only one way to catch her: send out the torpedo planes from the *Victorious*.

Tovey had no idea of his enemy's problem. *Bismarck* had to reduce speed and couldn't shake her shadows. Lütjens decided to order the accompanying cruiser to break away into the Atlantic. The code word for this movement, an ironic touch, was: '*Hood*'.

Captain Brinkmann of the *Prinz Eugen* had just arrived on the bridge when a four-letter message winked across from the flagship: 'H-O-O-D'. Like some racing car, the heavy cruiser put on maximum revs. At the same moment, the *Bismarck* turned towards her pursuers. 'There goes our Big Brother', said Gunnery Officer Jasper. His last view of Germany's great battleship was of orange flashes and thunder from *Bismarck*'s main guns. Lütjens signalled HQ Group West: 'Impossible to shake off enemy owing to radar. Proceeding directly to Brest because of fuel situation.'

Captain Bovell, commander of the aircraft carrier *Victorious*, had hoped to be within 100 miles from the *Bismarck* by 21.00 hours, but the gap had widened. The attack was to be carried out by nine Swordfish torpedo planes. These fabric-covered bi-planes with an open cockpit, called by their crews '*stringbags*' owing to their old-fashioned tight-wire struts, looked like survivors of Baron von Richthofen's Flying Circus. They cruised, and what's more, they attacked at a piddly 95 miles per hour. Each plane carried a crew of three – a pilot, an observer and a rear gunner – and a single 18-inch torpedo slung beneath its belly. The planes squatted like wet ducks at the end of the flight deck. Shortly after 22.00 hours the *Victorious* turned into the wind and the planes trundled off.

Some of *Bismarck*'s off-duty crew were on deck. After the excitement with the *Hood* this was turning into a flat and boring run. There weren't even any more of these chatty, impudent seagulls which fed on everything that was chucked at them and sometimes even came to rest on the long gun barrels. The sailors missed them. The Bavarian, Riedel, on the other hand, knew little about the excitement found at sea by his more knowledgeable comrades from Hamburg and Kiel. The mountain boy stared at the endless ocean. A calm before the storm, he mused.

The US Coastguard cutter *Modoc* had sailed from Boston on 12 May to search for survivors of convoy H.X. 126.[11] Earlier that day the men aboard the *Modoc* had been informed by radio about the sinking of the *Hood*. For days now the

---

[11] It would be another seven months before the US entered the war, but America had already made clear where her sympathies lay.

crew had seen nothing but tossing seas, but in an instant that changed. In the binoculars of US Able Seaman Newell appeared the outlines of a monstrous battleship. It was the *Bismarck* speeding south. The crew rushed on deck to see for themselves. Then the evening clouds parted and out came the craziest-looking planes they had ever seen, bi-planes with wire struts and fixed wheels, the kind of contraption that the Wright brothers might have flown half a century before. These ridiculous looking planes headed straight into the withering anti-aircraft fire of the *Bismarck*.

24 May, 23.45 hours. Aboard *Bismarck* they too saw the planes come in, and fifty guns opened up. As the first torpedoes streaked through the water, the bridge gave orders to swing hard around. Most of the torpedoes missed; one hit amidships without doing serious damage. It exploded against the solid armoured belt of Wotan steel and hardly scratched the paint, though it did kill one member of the crew. The torpedo damage was negligible, but there was much concern about number two boiler room, now completely flooded, as well as the forward oil tanks which had taken on more water, owing to the ship's violent manoeuvring. It took an hour before the ship made 20 knots again. For Lütjens two things counted: to head for France on a straight course, and to shake off the shadowing cruisers. It was about at this time that Admiral Lütjens was informed by Naval Group West that the British Force H had departed from Gibraltar. Which meant more torpedo attacks from the planes of that old battle horse, the *Arc Royal*.[12] Lütjens studied the maps. He could easily outrun this new danger. He conferred with the captain and his engineers. Their reply was unanimous. 'Put on speed now, and we'll be out of oil before we reach France.'

* * *

[12] According to German news reports, the *Arc Royal* had been sunk at least three times.

Lütjens went for an intermediate solution. He ordered a brief burst of speed. *Bismarck* was free, she had shaken her pursuers and broken free into the Atlantic while every ship the Royal Navy could muster chased after her. To locate her in the vastness of the Atlantic was looking for the proverbial needle in a haystack. For thirty-one hours she disappeared, then came a farm boy from Higginsville, Missouri, in a Catalina flying-boat and found her. For the British Admiralty the problem became one of mathematics and hours. They pored over maps. *Bismarck* was spotted by Ensign Smith and Flying Officer Briggs some 700 sea miles from the safety of the French coast, and only 300 miles from the protective air cover of the German *Luftwaffe*. It was calculated that, steaming at 30 m.p.h., the known cruising speed of the battleship, this would give the Royal Navy ten hours before their own fleet would find itself within range of German aerial bombardments. But mathematics do not always work. In this case, the British admirals were not aware of the serious fuel situation aboard the German, which had forced its captain to cut his speed almost in half.

On 26 May, at 16.25, Admiral Lütjens received a cable: 'My best wishes on your birthday – Adolf Hitler.'

At 17.25 Lütjens, not concerned by his birthday but by the shortage of oil, wired: 'Fuel situation urgent – when can I expect fuel?'

At 18.00 the weather worsened steadily and soon changed into a regular Atlantic gale which brought the sea to a boil. Spume rose high over the battleship bow and mountainous waves washed across the decks.

And at 21.00 came the planes . . .

Admiral Tovey on *King George V* could no longer keep up this mad chase, he had to reduce speed to conserve fuel. He hoisted a signal: 'Speed of the fleet 22 knots.' The British

fleet had lost the race against its German adversary. At 18.21
Tovey signalled the Admiralty that unless the *Bismarck* could
be slowed up before midnight his two main units, the *King
George V* and *Rodney*, would have to return to base.[13] His
last hope was for Force H to steam on an intercepting course
and launch an aerial strike from the *Arc Royal*. Tovey sent
out his order. Regardless of cost to men or planes, all available
torpedo planes were to be launched into the gale force winds.
Admiral Somerville of Task Force H ordered *Arc Royal* to
dispatch its torpedo planes. In near zero visibility, the first
flight of 'stringbacks' nearly sank their own cruiser HMS
Sheffield before the pilots recognised their error.

At 19.10 hours, a final flight of fifteen Swordfish torpedo
planes rumbled off the windswept flight deck. Lieut Cmdr.
Tim Coode and his forty-four men knew that the fate of the
Bismarck, and with it, England, depended on their flying skill.
The flight conditions were so bad that they could hardly see
their own engine cowling. They flew through an infinity of
darkness, bucking violently through a weather front that
reached down to sea level and the pilots had to depend
entirely on the *Sheffield* to guide them on target. Finally
the flight dropped height. Clouds flitted by faster and faster
as their engines howled, wind strummed the tied-wires to a
high C, and the altimeters spinned crazily anti-clockwise in
a blood-draining dive. They hoped they would be coming on
their quarry but didn't expect what they saw when they broke
through the cloud at 700 feet. The *Bismarck* was coming
straight at them. The time was 20.53 hours.

Pilots fought their control columns into a tight starboard
tack. Four planes dropped down to wave-crest level, turned
again, and headed for the monster's bow, right into a blis-
tering anti-aircraft barrage, filling the night with fast-moving

---

[13] Churchill sent out a controversial order via the Admiralty: '. . . to pursue the
Bismarck up to the shores of France, even if it means towing the *King George
V* home . . .'

confetti. The pilots recalled their instructors: The 'three nines' – fly (level) at 90 M. P. H., drop torpedo at 90 feet, not further than 900 yards from target. That was simple on a practice range but not in an Atlantic gale, flying towards a fire-spitting dragon. Tracers streaked out towards their planes, straight at first, then bending in long, graceful curves. The nerves of the flight crews were stretched to the utmost; they could hear the faint spitting followed by the muffled bumps of ack-ack bursting. The propeller whiplash pushed rain into their open cockpits and obscured their visibility. The first wave scored no hits, neither did the second. Then came the two planes of Lieutenant Godfrey-Fausset and Sub-Lieut Kenneth Pattison. 'Position?' asked Pattison.

'One – five – zero – zero,' came the even reply from the bomb-aimer, in a voice unhurried despite the plane's fierce vibration. 'One – three . . .' He read out the distance. They attacked from starboard, dropped their torpedoes at about 1,000 yards, and thought they'd scored a hit, but couldn't be certain since by the time their gunner saw a flicker they were already climbing into a cloud. One last plane, piloted by Tony Beale, attacked bravely at a mere 50 feet above the windswept waves. He dropped his fish at 800 yards and held his breath until his observer, Airman Pimlott, yelled: 'A hit!'

Gunner's Mate Herzog was in charge of a 37 mm anti-aircraft gun. He saw two planes head straight for his position.[14] They flew so low that their wheels almost touched the wave crest, much too low for his gun to depress onto the target. Though it all happened in seconds, his brain slowed up to take in each phase of the pilots' daring manoeuvre. The men in these slow-flying, ridiculous looking machines were certainly a different breed from the ones the German propaganda broadcasts kept describing. These were no untrained

[14] It must have been the twosome of Lieutenant Godfrey-Fausset and Sub-Lieut, Kenneth Pattison.

cowards. While one plane made straight for the centre of the ship, the other pulled towards the stern. Their torpedoes splashed into the sea. Herzog watched in frozen fascination two white streaks racing for him. Then his view became blocked by a wall of water rising from the stern, the ship lifted as if struck by a gigantic hammer blow and he was thrown against his fellow gunners. Through the collapsing fountain Herzog saw a plane pass just astern of the ship.

The ship began to turn. The attack was over, the anti-aircraft guns were silent. But why did the ship continue to turn? Able Seaman Eich was in guidance control. He stared in confusion at his gauges. Something was wrong, *Bismarck* kept turning in a circle.

Hermann Budich talked to his buddy Böhnel when the torpedo struck. They were the first to know what was wrong. Budich rushed a report to his superior, Machine Mate Barho: '*Starboard rudder disconnected, port rudder jammed at 15 degrees.*' Barbo's attempt to change the fuses ended with a blue-flash which knocked him to the floor. Soon the rest of the ship's complement found out. Over the tannoy came a message: 'Ship's rudder control disabled. All divers immediately astern.'

Of the two torpedoes that connected with *Bismarck*, one exploded harmlessly against the solid anti-torpedo belt,[15] but the other struck the only vulnerable spot of the great ship, the linkage arm between ship and rudder. Captain-Lieutenant Junack was in the turbine compartment as the ship received the hit. He was thrown to the floor. When he raced from the engine room he discovered that the torpedo had punched a hole in the hull and water was pouring into the rudder control compartment. This prevented repairs. 'Damn', he

---

[15] We must assume this was Tony Beale's hit, since it came after what Herzog described.

cursed as he picked up the intercom to make his report to the bridge. 'Every eventuality has been predicted, everything has its back-up, but not the rudder link!'

From his position, Gunner's Mate Herzog could overlook the stern. He saw Captain Lindemann and his two chief engineers study plans and check the damage. Finally, Lindemann waved his arm and walked away. All attempts to pump out the water and operate the hand rudder proved futile. An attempt to blow off the jammed rudder with an explosive charge was abandoned as the steering mechanism was located too close to the ship's screws and might have damaged their delicate balance. Lütjens agreed with the decision.[16]

Supreme German Naval Command was informed in a series of cables.

'21.05. Quadrat BE/6192, struck by torpedo astern.'

'21.15. Torpedo hit amidships.'

And finally Admiral Lütjens had to send this message: '23.40. *Ship unmanoeuvrable. We shall fight to the last shell. Long live the Führer.*'

Hitler's answer was the last message to reach the *Bismarck*: '01.35. To the officers and crew of Battleship *Bismarck*. Germany is with you. All that can be done will be done. Your sense of duty will be a symbol for our people in their struggle. (*signed*) Adolf Hitler.'

Whatever they did, whatever they tried, the pride of the German Navy moved helplessly north, as if drawn by some inexorable force, headed straight for the destructive power of the whole Royal Navy.[17]

*   *   *

[16] About this decision, Vice-Admiral Eberhard Weichold wrote: 'It is the destiny of front-line commanders, and most of all, leaders at sea, that their momentary decision on the bridge is taken without full knowledge of the enemy's position, and that it can only be discussed afterwards, if this corresponded to the equally unknown counter-measures taken by the adversary.'

[17] Most of the description comes from interviews with survivors and written accounts, such as Captain-Lieutenant Freiherr von Mullenheim-Rechberg.

Admiral Tovey received a message it was hard to understand: 'Enemy steering 340 degrees.' It meant that *Bismarck* was heading away from the French ports and towards him. That was sheer suicide. He wired: 'Verify direction report, repeat, verify direction report.' The reply was still the same: '340 degrees.' North ... Gerry was heading north? What was Lütjens up to? Nobody could recall afterwards who said it first – the torpedo, the flash. That's it! Gerry was out of control ...

Adolf Hitler spent the night at his Berghof residence where he was kept abreast of the situation. Grand Admiral Raeder had called Göring to ask for *Luftwaffe* airstrikes. The *Reichsmarshall* replied that the British capital ships were way beyond flying range of his bombers. Raeder released a brief newsflash to a nation that remained awake throughout the night to follow the dramatic events:[18] 'Battleship *Bismarck*, on entering the Bay of Biscaye, was struck by a torpedo aft.' With this brief phrase he announced the inevitable, since he knew the ship was beyond aid.

The night was terrible. Blinding rain, howling storms and the knowledge that both crew and ship were fighting for survival had kept the crew up. If that wasn't enough, on top of it they had to fence off torpedo attacks by a swarm of destroyers. Neither the battleship nor the destroyers were damaged during these attacks. Just before dawn, Müllheim-Rechberg visited the bridge. He saw the fatigue written on the admiral's face, though he displayed it in no other way. As for the rest of the bridge crew's comportment, Mullenheim-Rechberg found the mood lethargic.

It was no different down below. 'We're headed straight

[18] The drama of the *Bismarck* was probably the most covered radio event of the war.

into hell', a machinist said out loud and what everybody thought.

'I'll put you on report', shouted an ardent Party member and fervent defender of Hiltler's genius. 'We'll have none of that talk here, there's always a chance.'

'Yes, and pigs can fly, *du Scheisser*', laughed the sailor.

At that moment the order came from Captain Lindemann: '*Alle Machinen Stop.*'

Captain-Lieutenant Junack was worried that such an order might lead to an overheating of the turbines. He called the bridge and was answered by the tired voice of Captain Lindemann: 'Do whatever you feel like.'

At 08.00 hours the alarm bells sounded. Officers and crew stuffed cotton wool in their ears. At 08.15 hours the heavy cruiser *Norfolk* appeared over the horizon, followed by the battleships *Rodney* and *King George V*. At 08.47 hours, the guns of the British capital ships spoke. Brown smoke from the huge 400 mm guns of *Rodney* obscured it from view. *Bismarck* turned to starboard to bring all of her eight guns into position. Then she fired.

'Time of flight 55 seconds', announced an officer on *Rodney*'s bridge. And 'Shut up!' said the captain, not wanting to know when he would die. A horrible whine and a series of earsplitting bangs, followed by huge water fountains. *Bismarck*'s third salvo straddled *Rodney*.

But the German could not withstand the triangular attack pattern for long. The first shells began to smash into the ship, disabling the forward artillery command post. At 09.02, a one-ton projectile of the *Rodney* struck the forward gun towers of *Anton* and *Bruno* and its concussion killed every man inside. At 09.04, the heavy cruiser *Dorsetshire* came up from the rear and joined in the bombardment. *Bismarck* fired now only at *King George V*, but scored no further hits. A few moments thereafter, a shell knocked out the third of its turrets, *Dora*. Only *Turm Caesar* kept firing. Gunner's Mate Riedel supervised the loading of two shells when the left barrel jammed. Now all the big guns were silenced. Riedel's turret commander, a first lieutenant, asked the mate to take a look outside. Riedel opened the steel trap-door. What lay before him was a deck covered by dead and dying. The lieutenant nodded sadly: 'Close the door.' Inside the tower there was momentary silence, like a tomb – until the lieutenant addressed the forty men, every one of them wounded and shocked: 'Comrades, we have loved life, now let us die like brave seamen.'

Only one jumped up eagerly to give the Party salute. His extravagant '*Heil Hitler!*' sounded ridiculous to all the others. They filed out, one by one. All guns aboard were silent. From shell craters in the hull streamed heavy black smoke. A 1,000 kg projectile from a 16-inch battleship cannon had smashed through the gun-deck and penetrated into the dining-room area, used as an emergency aid station. It killed hundreds of wounded and all the medical personnel assembled there.

At 10.15 hours, the British commander ordered the ceasefire. Despite its mortal wounds the *Bismarck* would not sink.[19] Machine Mate Blum was down in the bowels of the ship when the order was passed along: 'Prepare scuttling charges',[20] followed by 'Everyone up on deck'. They stumbled along walkways filled with acrid smoke, and scrambled up ladders. 'Move! Move! We're blowing up the ship!' Blum stepped over piles of dead until he reached a door which led onto a deck. What he saw made him vomit. Blood had splashed onto the sides of gun turrets like slashes of crimson paint. Part of the smokestack was ripped off, the huge guns pointed straight into the sky and one barrel had burst. Some turrets had been

---

[19] Hitler was informed about the fate of the *Bismarck* by an intercepted *Reuters* flash (13.00).
[20] There has been an ongoing argument about what sank the ship, British naval guns or a German scuttle charge.

ripped from their sockets. Smoke from burning ammunition poured from the ugly gashes. Blum's way to the stern became a struggle to climb over bits of bodies and avoid falling down jagged holes. He reached a handful of survivors gathered around Captain-Lieutenant Junack who told them to take shelter behind a gun tower.

'We shall give a final cheer for our *Vaterland*, before we abandon ship. Keep close to me . . . I promise you we shall all meet again on the Reeperbahn.'

Then they jumped. A few moments later they heard rumbling from inside the dying battleship. And then she was gone.

Blum was rescued by the destroyer H.M.S. *Maori*. Riedel, and some 400 others who had survived the final hour, swam for the cruiser H.M.S. *Dorsetshire*. The ship picked up eighty-five German sailors before it suddenly put up steam and raced off. (A lookout was thought to have spotted a German U-boat. That day no U-boat was closer than 300 miles to the scene.) The cruiser thundered past the hundreds of bodies still bobbing on an oil-covered sea as their fingers scraped along the steel plates of the ship that slid past them. Many of the British sailors watched helplessly and cried. Granted, they were the enemy – but they were also part of the great international community of seamen.

Those who weren't fished from the sea all died in the cold Atlantic waters.

Three survivors, including Gunner's Mate Herzog, who floated for days on a raft, were picked up by the German submarine *U 74*.[21] Two more were discovered by the German ship *Sachsenwald*. These five were the only witnesses of the drama who returned to Germany before the end of the war.

Their story was never told. The *Führer* forbade it.

---

[21] The ultimate irony: the three had to face a court martial for desertion in the face of the enemy, but were acquitted.

What if . . .

What if – Admiral Lütjens had filled up *Bismarck*'s tanks in
　　　　Norway?
　　　　He would have outrun the Royal Navy.

What if – Catalina Z had been so badly damaged that it had
　　　　to ditch and its flight crew was captured? What
　　　　would have been Hitler's, and the neutral United
　　　　States', reaction, once it was discovered that the
　　　　pilot was in American naval uniform?
　　　　Considering the obvious presence of a member
　　　　of the armed forces of the non-belligerent United
　　　　States of America, and Hitler's irrationality, he
　　　　might have declared war on the United States.
　　　　As this incident took place three weeks *before* he
　　　　invaded Russia, such a step could have altered
　　　　his plans considerably.

What if – *Bismarck* had turned a fraction sooner or the
　　　　Swordfish dropped its fish a split second later?
　　　　The miss-or-hit was a matter of only one metre, and
　　　　the torpedo would have passed harmlessly beneath
　　　　the stern.

The facts

Lack of oil was the major reason for *Bismarck*'s defeat. The
battleship could no longer use its superior speed to head for
the safety of the French coast. Lütjens' failure to top-up in
the Norwegian fjord cost Germany a capital ship.

　　For Britain it was something of a triumph. To Hitler's
mind it was certainly a setback, but nothing too serious. His
maritime strategy – to strangle England into submission – was

based on unlimited U-boat warfare. In a sense, he was correct, the battleship was a symbol of the past.[22]

The *Hood* was the first to go. The mighty *Prince of Wales* and *Repulse* lived another seven months. On 10 December 1941, three days after the Japanese attack on Pearl Harbor, both these battleships were attacked and sunk by eighty-four land-based Japanese planes. It was the end of the Nelsonian concept of battleship power and heralded the beginning of a new age in naval warfare, where ships battled it out without ever seeing each other's smoke clouds or masthead.

This new era saw its beginning in the air near a Pacific island called Midway.

The Hinge Factor of the Bismarck was a thousand-to-one-chance hit. Like Achilles and Siegfried, the leviathan of the sea had its vulnerable spot.

[22] The sister of the *Bismarck*, the battleship *Tirpitz*, never saw real action. She was sunk by a British airstrike in a Norwegian fjord.

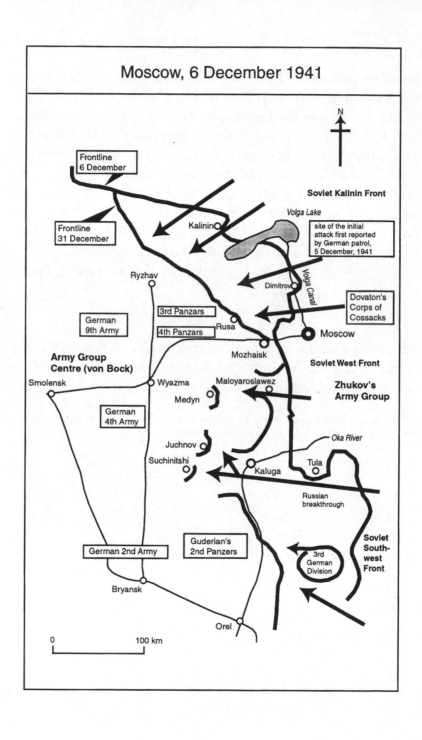

Moscow, 6 December 1941

Frontline 6 December

Frontline 31 December

Soviet Kalinin Front

Volga Lake

Kalinin

site of the initial attack first reported by German patrol, 5 December, 1941

Ryzhav

Dimitrov

Volga Canal

German 9th Army

3rd Panzars

4th Panzars

Rusa

Moscow

Dovaton's Corps of Cossacks

Army Group Centre (von Bock)

Mozhaisk

Soviet West Front

Smolensk

Wyazma

Maloyaroslawez

Zhukov's Army Group

Medyn

German 4th Army

Juchnov

Oka River

Suchinitshi

Kaluga

Tula

Russian breakthrough

German 2nd Army

Guderian's 2nd Panzers

3rd German Division

Soviet South-west Front

Bryansk

Orel

0   100 km

14

The Sorge Enigma

Moscow, 6 December 1941

'It must be remembered that in the Soviet Union any attempt to reconstitute the true history of even the recent past is considered a capital offence.'

Colonel A.K. Tokaev, *Betrayal of an Ideal*, 1954

In early May 1941 a coded message was received in Moscow Centre by its director, Colonel-General Kusnetzow, a man who reported directly to Stalin. It came from Tokyo, and read: 'Germany will attack Russia on 20 June. 170 to 190 German divisions are concentrated at their eastern border and all have tanks and are mechanised. The attack will be made on the entire front, and its main force will be directed first at Moscow and Leningrad . . .'

It hit the Soviet secret services like a cold shower. This couldn't be true. Hitler had signed a non-aggression pact with Stalin only the year before. A blunt note was sent to their spy in Japan: 'We doubt the veracity of your message.'

On 22 June 1941, Germany attacked the Soviet Union.[1]

---

[1] Hitler's order of the day for *Operation Barbarossa*, the invasion of Russia, was: 'The bulk of the Russian Army stationed in western Russia is to be destroyed in a series of daring operations spearheaded by armoured thrusts.'

*   *   *

'Russia is a country which can only be subdued by its own weakness, and by the effects of internal dissension', wrote Carl von Clausewitz in 1832 on Napoleon's disastrous retreat from Moscow. Hitler had read Clausewitz. He thought of Stalin as an intelligent, careful, ice-cold blackmailer, but badly miscalculated when he hoped for an uprising by the Russian people against their Red Dictator.

The German Army invaded Russia on 22 June, 1941. By September, Gerd von Rundstedt's Army Group South captured Marshal Simeon Budenny's complete group of armies. The Germans took three million prisoners[2] in Hitler's greatest victory but also his greatest blunder. While his predecessor Napoleon had fought at Borodino in September, but then immediately moved on to Moscow, Hitler frittered his time away. He underestimated Stalin's political solidity; and the ruthlessness displayed by Nazi death squads in the conquered territories convinced the Stalinist regime, tottering on the verge of collapse, that the Ukrainians would not rise against the Bolsheviks.

General Halder wrote: '. . . The whole situation makes it increasingly plain that we have underestimated the Russian Colossus . . . time favours them, as they are near their own resources, while we are moving further and further away from ours . . .'

By the time Hitler ordered his generals for their final push on Moscow, winter was about to set in, and another vital factor was to come into play. Not, as may be expected, in Russia, but in far-off Japan. In late October, with Guderian's panzers only forty miles from Moscow, and the Russian capital without defences, two things happened. Early snow made the mud-covered roads unsuitable for their wheeled,

---

[2] Official German figures were: 3,006,867 prisoners, while Russians admit to 2,122,000 casualties. German losses were given as 743,112 killed, missing or wounded.

instead of tracked, vehicles, and a coded telegram arrived from Tokyo.

Under the overall command of Field-Marshal von Brauchitsch, Field-Marshal von Leeb's Army Group North had cut off Leningrad, von Rundstedt's Army Group South had captured Kiev and the Ukraine, and General von Bock's Army Group Centre had advanced on Moscow. While the rest of the world watched German successes with awe and the Bolshevik regime was floundering, Hitler announced to his people on 2 October: 'The enemy has been broken and will never rise again.'

Blinded by their incredible successes, the Germans began to quarrel over their next objectives. The panzer genius, General Heinz Guderian, demanded bluntly that he drive his armoured columns straight for Moscow. Hitler decided otherwise and precious time was lost.[3]

The push on the Russian capital finally opened on 30 September. Guderian's panzers broke through the Bryansk Front and captured Orel. On 3 October the German steamroller smashed through the centre and within a few days reached the Mozhaisk Line at Mayolaroslavets and Borodino,[4] only 120 kilometres from Moscow! Once the Germans had crossed that last line of defence their road into Moscow lay wide open. Stalin pulled his most brilliant military commander, Marshal Zhukov, from the besieged Leningrad and put him in charge of the defences of the capital.

The new commander drove along the Warsaw Chaussée to Mayolaroslavets to assess the situation himself. He came to a harsh decision: he would spare not a single soldier to help free the encircled 200,000 of Yeremenko and Koniev. They had to get out on their own. Whatever men were available Zhukov

---

[3] Napoleon had fought at Borodino on 7 September and entered Moscow a week later. Hitler ordered the attack on Moscow to commence the day Napoleon decided to retreat from Moscow, to beat the Russian winter.
[4] The famous Napoleonic battlefield of 1812.

placed in an extended half-moon around the nation's capital. In this he was assisted by a new ally, the weather; in the middle of October it began to rain. From Smolensk to Orel, from Vyazma to Kalinin, it rained. The Oka and Ugra Rivers turned into raging torrents and the roads became knee-deep in mud, slowing up, but not stopping, the tracked German panzers. However, their 'rush on Moscow' turned into a 'crawling forward' as their wheeled infantry transporters sank down to their axles and the *Landsers* had to slog on on foot.

By 17 October, Moscow was being evacuated. Only the Kasan Station to Gorky and the Ural Mountains was still operational. The square in front of the station was jammed with thousands of refugees, all on a list of 'socially important elements'. They sat patiently on their bundles and suitcases for days, waiting for a place on 'the last train from hell', while the ordinary citizens of Moscow stood by and watched in silence as fleets of cars with high officials fled from the city. All those attempting to leave without official papers were shot on the spot by the NKVD. Thousands were pulled from their homes and led outside the town to dig anti-tank ditches. Many died of exposure, wearing only the clothes they had on when pulled from their homes. Untrained militia units manned the dugouts. Each man was given a rifle, five bullets, and told to stand and die.

   The night skies over the monumental towers of the Kremlin were criss-crossed by anti-aircraft volleys, the city centre was covered by a pall of smoke from the exploding bombs of German dive-bombers. While death fell from the sky, people were out in the streets, and the curfew meant nothing. At the Metropole Hotel, the orchestra played on and champagne flowed for high officers of the Red Army. It could only be a matter of days, perhaps hours . . .' Moscow is lost unless a miracle happens', they said out loud. For the ordinary people, the supply situation in the city was worsened by the influx of refugees fleeing before the German panzers. The panic which gripped Moscow was spreading across the land. The Soviet government, the foreign embassies, and the Central Committee had fled to Kuibyshev. Did Stalin himself leave Moscow? Official accounts insist he didn't, rumours persist he did.[5]

By the end of October, the German commander of the central front, Field Marshal von Bock, called a two-week pause to regroup his forces. Hitler ordered the final attack on the city for 15 November. The attack proved an immediate success, German advances reached a point only 25 kilometres from the centre of Moscow. Then two events took place. The first was the weather. It changed drastically. Rain changed to frost, snow blanketed the fields and temperatures dropped to minus thirty. This caught the German armies unprepared; Hitler had counted on a quick victory and no winter clothing had been issued to the German forces (perhaps this was intended to push his generals to take Moscow before the winter, perhaps it was due to sheer oversight). Despite deep snow and sub-zero temperatures, German panzers advanced across the frozen fields.

On 19 November, Stalin called for Zhukov and asked him what he needed to hold the city. 'Two armies and 200 tanks', stated the marshal without great conviction. He knew that Stalin didn't have them. To his surprise, Stalin nodded and promised to release the remaining forces at his disposal. But where did these men come from? Even his closest collaborator was not aware that Stalin had an ace-in-the-hole, a master spy working for Russian Army Intelligence.

Treason had become the new weapon of World War 2,

[5] In any case, he was not present on the balcony of Lenin's tomb to take the annual parade on 7 November.

brought about by the political hatred of Germans against
Hitler's fascist regime. In the spring of 1941, while Germany
was at the very height of its power, a 94-page pamphlet
appeared in Lucerne's *Vita Nova Verlag*: 'The Place of Battle
and the Conditions of Leading a War.' The author was given
the pseudonym, R. A. Hermes, like the Greek god of thieves,
or, perhaps, the Swiss brandname of a popular typewriter.
This thin booklet laid down the conditions for men like
Rudolf Rössler ('Lucie'), Lieutenant I. R. Harro Schulz-
Boysen ('Coro'), Adam Kuckhoff or Oberregierungsrat Avid
Harnack. What did these men have in common? They were
all members of an orchestra, the 'Rote Kapelle', only they
didn't play music. They provided inside information about
German military intentions. 'Treason for ideological motives'
became their watch-word, expounded at length by the Hermes
exposé. It supplied the new spies with justification for their
treasonable acts.

As much as 'Lucie' and the 'Rote Kapelle' became a prime
source of Soviet information after the summer of 1942,[6] the
honour as the most effective Russian spy must go to a German
journalist working in Japan.

Dr Richard Sorge was German,[7] and the Tokyo correspondent for the *Frankfurter Zeitung*. The *Herr Doktor* was
walking a tightrope – respected journalist to most, spy to
one: his boss in Moscow Centre. Sorge was a maverick,
unconventional and imaginative; none of that undercover
dashing in and out of taxis for him. A tall European could
not get lost in a crowd of Japanese. He had to work in
total isolation and did so impeccably, his method almost
subversive in its simplicity. He outsmarted them all. When
the *Tokko*, Japan's secret police, quietly checked up on him

---

[6] They gave away the secret of 'Operation Zitadelle', the tank battle at Kursk.
[7] He was born in Baku of German parents and joined the Bolshevik Party early
in his youth.

they found nothing. He even managed to make the notorious *Gestapo* security chief at the German embassy in Tokyo, Josef Meisinger, his closest friend.

Sorge's break happened over a bizarre incident. On 26 February 1936, a group of Japanese officers supported by 1,400 soldiers occupied vital government buildings in Tokyo, and then failed to give a reason why they had launched their *coup d'état*. The German embassy, bombarded with demands for information from Berlin, couldn't explain the 'Tokyo incident'. That's when Dr Sorge stepped in and offered to pool his information, as 'a well-informed correspondent', with that of the embassy staff. His report delighted the *Abwehr* in Berlin, and from then on, Dr Sorge was a man to be trusted. Without any doubt what made Sorge the greatest double-agent ever was the moment his 'great friend' and former military attaché, Lieutenant-Colonel (by now a Major General) Eugen Ott, became German ambassador to Japan.

The handsome Dr Sorge had two weaknesses: one which almost killed him, the other which did. Fast motorcycles and beautiful women. On the night of 13 May 1938, he climbed quite drunk on his jet-black *Zunden* motorcycle and drove it into a wall. He survived, but barely. To show the man's incredible presence of mind, on his way to the operating theatre he recalled that his pockets contained a sheet with a highly compromising report. He refused to be operated on before 'leaving a final message for his beloved ones with his best friend', his radio operator, Max Clausen. 'Empty my pockets', he breathed to Clausen, and the radio man removed the secret paper.

Max Clausen was a key member in Sorge's spy ring, an ingenious mechanic who transmitted his messages with a clever flaw which provided Moscow with proof of his identity. Every other word (on a pre-established sliding scale) was spelled with a minute mistake. It was a system as simple as it was foolproof. On several occasions, Clausen even used his mistress, Anna Wallenius, an outspoken anti-Communist, to carry his microfilm messages. Clausen's problem was his uncontrolled temper. In the spring of 1941, after Sorge dispatched a warning to Stalin about the forthcoming German attack on the Soviet Union, and Moscow Centre replied 'We doubt the veracity of your information', Clausen exploded: 'Those *Scheisskopfe*, how dare they ignore my message?'

Then came the fateful day in October 1941 when Sorge handed Clausen a single sheet of paper. 'Code it and get out immediately by whatever means it takes. Good luck.' He knew it was of the utmost urgency to get the message out, not only to inform Moscow, but also because he realised that the *Tokko* was on to him. The night before, agents of the secret police had arrested his mistress, Ishii Hanako, and found on her a sizeable amount of dollars, for which she could give no explanation. For the handsome Dr Sorge the game was up. On 18 October, Max Clausen and Dr Sorge were arrested.[8] Dr Sorge was never to transmit another message, but it was his final signal which decided the outcome of the Battle of Moscow. The impact of the *Sorge cipher* on Stalin's strategy is incalculable.

In May 1941 Sorge had warned Stalin that Germany would attack the Soviet Union and the Generalissimo did not believe him. But this time it was different. The situation was desperate. Stalin needed an answer. '*In connection with the German-Russian war, what decision has the Japanese government made about our country?*' was the urgent question put to their master spy. Sorge put his *apparat* (spy network) to work. His best, though unwitting, informant was none other than the German ambassador to Japan, Major General Eugen Ott, who kept pushing the Japanese (allies of the Germans)

[8] Max Clausen survived the war in a Japanese prison, and lived with Anna for the rest of his days in East Germany.

to launch a surprise attack against Russia from their bases in Manchuria. One of Sorge's men, Ozaki Hotsumi, took a job with the South Manchurian Railway, whose officials had been ordered to prepare rolling stock for a troop movement of the all-powerful Japanese Kwantung Army. Destination: the Russian border! Ozaki closely scrutinised the train schedule but discovered no military activity. Some weeks went by when a railway official, on his way to an important meeting, told Ozaki: 'They've called me to Tokyo to cancel it all, because it seems the Kwantung Army has decided not to have a war with Russia.'

Sorge's final confirmation came during an unguarded moment at an embassy dinner, when Ambassador Ott confided in him his frustration at trying, to persuade the Japanese to help Germany by attacking the Soviet Union. 'Those Japs won't hear of it. Their plans are strictly for maritime control over the Pacific.'

Thus it happened that on his forty-sixth birthday, October 1941, Dr Richard Sorge told his radio operator, Max Clausen, to dispatch a ciphered message to Moscow Centre, which it passed on immediately to Stalin. It stated that the Japanese did not regard themselves bound by the terms of the *Tripartite Pact* (the Berlin-Rome-Tokyo Axis signed in September 1940): '*Under no circumstances will Japan denounce their non-aggression pact with the Soviet Union.*' It added: '*Their strategic planning envisages an advance into the South Pacific, nothing more. The Soviet Far East may be considered guaranteed against Japanese attack at least till the end of winter. There is no doubt about this . . .*'

(The Neutrality Pact between Japan and Russia was signed in April 1941, and Hitler's attack on the Soviet Union that June surprised the Japanese as much as it did the Russians. That's why they never informed Berlin about their planned attack on the USA.)

*   *   . *

Sorge's message emphasised that there would be no Japanese attack on the Soviet Union's Far East. Stalin wanted so much to believe this, but he still didn't trust his own intelligence service. He hesitated, until another message supplied him with final confirmation. In early November, a dispatch from another ace *apparatchnik*, 'Söhnchen' – better known in the West as the super-spy Kim Philby – independently confirmed Sorge's information.

(British Intelligence intercepted all messages to Berlin, and Philby passed these diligently on to Moscow. Kim Philby was interviewed[9] after he had fled to Moscow, in 1963: 'What do you think was the most valuable information you ever passed on to Moscow?'

Philby replied: '. . . The telegram by Ambassador Ott, the same who was a good friend of Dr Sorge, in which he stated that the Japanese would soon initiate major military operation to the south. This meant that military operations against the Soviet Union were cancelled.'

'Didn't Sorge report on this?'

'That's the whole point. Stalin didn't trust his intelligence service. Sure, Stalin wanted to believe, and my report was independendly confirmed by Sorge from Japan.' (Actually, it was the other way round, Sorge's message had arrived a month earlier.)

And so, a message from a German helped turn the tide of war against Germany and Hitler.

While triumphant German armies were already battering at the gates of Moscow, the suspicious, paranoid Red Czar took a gamble. For once he had to entrust the fate of his country and his own future to a cryptic message from a spy – because he was given no other choice. Stalin sent out the order:

'*The Far Eastern Army, all troops from Siberia, from the*

---

[9] By Genrikh Borovik (*The Philby Files*).

Republics of Central Asia, units from training camps in Kazakhstan and Uzbekistan are to be dispatched to Moscow with the utmost speed, using all available locomotives and rolling stock and regardless of all safety measures on the railways . . .'

With this order, Stalin stripped his Far Eastern border of all troops. It started off the biggest rail movement of all times. Trains shunted out of station after station, lost in clouds of steam and billowing snow. Like tributaries leading into a big river, from railheads along the borders of China and Mongolia, from Siberia, the Caucasus and Central Russia, trains converged on the Trans-Siberian main track. Trains and more trains, all headed West, sometimes travelling so near each other that the engine drivers drove by the lights of the last carriage from the train in front of their locomotive. Fifty, sixty, a hundred trains a day, all headed for one destination: Moscow. They brought guns and tanks and men, men and even more men. Eighty divisions. A million soldiers, highly trained elite formations, well equipped and used to rough Siberian winter conditions. They wore white uniforms, had white guns and rode on white tanks – the brand new *T-34*, a machine more powerful than anything the Germans could muster.

By 3 December the German steamroller had ground to a halt on the outskirts of Moscow. This was partly due to the cold and partly from sheer exhaustion. The father of military strategy, Carl von Clausewitz, has called the summit of a battle *the point when an attacking force, faced with great losses, has to switch from the offensive to the defensive.* Such was the case with the German armies before Moscow in the terrible winter of 1941.

5 December 1941. North of the city, the German Ninth Army has reached a station of the Moscow public transport, a tram stop thirty kilometres from the centre of Moscow. The day

before, a patrol of German grenadiers of the 62nd Pioneer Battalion had entered the Moscow suburb of Chimki, only sixteen kilometres from the Kremlin. Panzer forces have now cut thé Moscow-Volga Canal at Dimitrov, units of the 1st Panzer Division have reached Kusjaevo. In the south of the city, von Kluge's 4th Army and Guderian's 2nd Panzer Army have bypassed Tula. They are less than fifty kilometres from Moscow, but have run out of ammunition, petrol – and steam. The cold, that terrible cold. Everything freezes, soldiers have to cut their bread with axes, rifles are useless, oil in machine guns and tank motors solidifies into solid blocks. Minus forty, some nights even minus fifty. The only way to move guns is with horses.

'We have used six horses to draw our howitzer. Of the six, two just fell over dead from cold and exhaustion. The other four aren't strong enough to pull the gun through the deep snow. We have wrapped ourselves in everything we can find from the houses, even stripped padded jackets and felt boots from dead Russians. We cannot take off our clothes or we freeze in minutes. Our clothes are infested with fleas, lice crawl in my hair. I have stuffed straw into my boots. In my gun battery there isn't a single comrade who doesn't suffer from frozen toes or fingers. Can you blame us that we have reached the end of our endeavours?' writes Corporal Werner Burmeister of the 208th Artillery Battalion.

It is still dark. The temperature has dropped to minus twenty-five. *Feldwebel* Paul Wenders and a scout patrol from the 87th Infantrie Regiment move silently through the snow towards the Jachroma Creek. They are part of units from the 36th Division which has broken through the Russian lines south of Kalinin and Rogatchevo. To the north of them is a big frozen lake formed by the barrage across the Volga. The Russians call it the Sea of Moscow. In front of them is a hamlet of wooden huts. They are thirty metres from the houses when they hear the whistle of shells. '*Deckung! Stalin Orgel*', screams Wenders. They throw themselves behind a well which is covered with a thick layer of blue ice. The ground shudders beneath them. The first rocket explosions throw up fountains of snow, followed by another deafening roar immediately behind them. Their unit is in the middle of a cluster of impacts. When the noise subsides and the soldiers dare to lift their heads they stare at an incredible sight. From the forest appear waves of white-clad soldiers, thousands upon thousands. *Feldwebel* Wenders cranks frantically on his field telephone. 'Russians,' he shouts down a line which crackles with static, 'thousands of them.'

A metallic voice comes back over the wire: 'Calm yourself, *Feldwebel* Wenders, there are not that many Russians left.'

'*Scheisse*. Then come up here and look for yourself!'

The German artillery opens up, many Russians fall, but not a man turns back. On they come through the deep snow, across the iced creek, and over a German scout patrol which lies on the ground like squashed insects.

It is a Friday, that 5 December. This attack is the first sign of an impending drama to fall upon the whole of the German Army. History will record this day as the moment the fortunes of war took a decisive change.[10]

Stalin has trusted a spy's message and emptied Siberia of almost all its armed forces. He has brought to Moscow

[10] Line-up before the Russian counter-offensive:

Russian units: overall command: Shukov

10th (Golikov), 50th (Boldin), 49th (Sacharin), 43rd (Golubjev), 33rd (Jemfremov), 5th (Goworov), 16th (Rokossowski), 20th (Wlassov), 1st (Kutznetzov), 30th (Ljeljushenko), and 1st Garde Cav (Belov).

German units: overall command: von Bock (78 divisions)

2nd Panzer Group (Guderian), 2nd Army (von Weichs), 4th Army (von Kluge), 4th Panzer Group (Hoepner), 9th (Strauss), 3rd Panzer Group (Reinhardt).

the 1st, the 10th and the 20th Armies.[11] Zhukov throws three armies plus a cavalry corps against Guderina's forces to cut off their retreat and to annihilate the German panzers. On the night of 6–7 December, Guderian orders the retreat. The withdrawal turns into hell: tank cleats slip on icy roads, infantry units are chased by Siberian ski patrols who suddenly appear from the snow like ghosts in their white camouflage. They fire, blow up bridges and vanish into the endless white of the Russian winter. Guderian's tanks fight back valiantly and deliver some successful counter-offensives. Casualties on both sides rise. The Russians die from German bullets and the Germans die from the Russian cold.

The 14th Anti-tank Company of *Oberleutnant* Braemer holds a position south of Stalinorsk. Before dawn of 11 December, Corporal Dohrendorf arrives out of breath at the company command post. '*Herr Oberleutnant*, to our right is a large formation on skis. I think these are Russians.'

Braemer checks through his night glasses. And he also can see them, disappearing and reappearing in white waves under a moon-splintered overcast. 'Man, you are right! Those *are* Russians. Alarm!' What Dohrendorf and Braemer are first to spot is a major Russian breakthrough. The Germans fire mortar flares. The snowscape is bathed in a ghostly blue light. The forest crawls with ski troops. To the men of the 14th it seems as if a dam has burst and waves of soldiers are about to pour over their single company. Wild figures, lit intermittently by flares, burst out of the forest. Everything dissolves into terrible and disorganised combat; in the case of the Germans most of it carried out by pockets of ten or twenty, virtually defenceless in the face of the mass of Russians. The Germans fire until the barrels on their guns glow or jam or burst. And

---

[11] The Russian High Command threw a total of 117 new units into the battle. The Germans had only 9 reserve units.

then comes a screaming salvo of *Katjushas* from a Russian rocket position. A hot hiss of melting white snow . . .

General Martinek rallies his exhausted 267th Infantry Division and tries to block the Russian advance. It is of no use: on their skis the Russians simply bypass the panzer units through the heavily forested area and push on into the rear of the German Army.

In the midst of the night a German unit has reached a river near Panino. It is a decimated infantry company from a grenadier regiment which has long since ceased to exist as an effective fighting force. They had been fighting for two weeks on an issue of one iron ration for five men. They are ordered to hold a vital river-crossing. Lieutenant Burkhart and the men of 2nd Company, 3rd Rifle Regiment, have to delay the enemy and to protect the bridge for the retreating units still to come. Burkhart is tired. Around his neck dangles a Knight's Cross. Much good it is now; he'd much rather have a pair of warm socks. He looks like a mummy, his head is wrapped in a wool scarf. That biting cold!

Lieutenant Burkhart issues an order to burn down the village and clear a field of fire. Soldiers pull fistfuls of straw from the roofs, set a match to them and toss the burning bundles onto the roofs. The village is soon engulfed in a raging inferno, while the men crowd around the burning houses to warm themselves. Shadowy figures rush into the village square to be cut down by rifle shots. Perhaps they are just some farmers, perhaps they are partisans. The Germans have learned never to take a chance. During the night, the company is joined by a few stragglers. 'Where is your unit?' demands Burkhart.

'What unit, *Herr Leutnant*? Our battalion doesn't exist any more.' Burckhart's men share whatever they have with the newcomers: a piece of black bread, a cigarette, a few bullets. In the morning light the village is but a smouldering heap, and beyond the smoke lies a scene of infinite silence. Suddenly, a white cloud rises from the snow, which vomits forth men, men, and even more men. The Russians roll on in hordes, there is no end to them, as far as the eye can see. It's a full regiment of Uzbeks, freshly disembarked from Siberia. They are supported by four tanks. Wild firing breaks out from anti-tank guns, mortars and machine guns. Burkhart orders his two 37-mm anti-tank guns to concentrate only on the advancing tanks. The gunners fire over open sights, that's how close they are. Their guns glow, paint runs from the barrels. The breech-lock is white-hot. 'What the hell . . . look!' curses one of them and points towards one of the steel monsters advancing. The German shells bounce off the tank.

'T-34,' states Burkhart coldly. 'Not much we can do. We need help.' Neighbouring 1st Company has a long-barrel 88. Three shots and three Russian tanks burst into flames. A turret opens, burning figures leap out, roll on the ground to douse the flames on their padded uniforms. Then they lie still, killed by rifle fire.

Four German panzers rumble along the village street and cross the wooden bridge. Their machine guns tear into the advancing Russian masses. White-clad soldiers, riding on advancing tanks, are swept off like dead leaves in a storm. A T-34 fires but misses.

'Those are raw recruits', scoffs Lieutenant Lhose of 1st Company. The last of the T-34 explodes.

'But they will learn quickly', replies Burkhart. The German panzers advance, firing in all directions. They drive through the Russian ski troops like sharks through a shoal of herring. They scatter the Russian units, which go tearing off across the country. Then the Russian artillery find their target. The first salvo from a battery of *Katjushas* bursts, gouting snow and flame and clods of black, frozen earth. Lieutenant Burkhart sees the bursting shells toss his men into the bitter air. Time to get out. The panzers retreat across the bridge. A sapper sergeant and his men stand by near the girders, stringing wires and explosives. 'All right, let's get on with it. We can't stay here all day long.' An explosion shatters the air and the bridge disintegrates in a black cloud. Lhose's company has lost one truck and a sergeant. Lieutenant Burkhart is dead. A Russian battalion is wiped out.

Actions like these are commonplace; the retreat and the frost have hardened the German soldier. Many more are cut off, but fight like devils to break out through the Russian lines. They know that being taken prisoner means almost certain death. With the desperation of the condemned, they fight – and they die.[12]

One Russian prong is led by Major General Dovator's famous Corps of Cossacks. Dovator is known as a brilliant cavalry leader. He uses his cavalry like Guderian uses his panzers – quick and decisive. 'Lead from the front' has always been his principle. His exploits have already been mentioned in special dispatches.

On the 19th, a major battle takes place near Polashkino. The Rusa River is held by units of the German 252nd 'Eichenblatt' Infantry Division. Strict orders have gone out: 'Save ammunition. Don't fire, let Ivan come close.' Their machine-gun emplacements are so spaced that they can bring a curtain of fire onto the ice of the wide river.

General Dovator orders a Cossack regiment into attack. His white-clad riders burst from the forest. The first wave advances to the river's edge before the Germans open up on them. Soon the virgin snow along the embankment is covered with bloody clumps of animals and men. The initial attack fails miserably. It is noon, a pale sun covers the land, wind drives snow across the ice of the frozen Rusa. Dovator rides

---

[12] 'We couldn't take our fallen comrades along. Together with dead horses they lay along our route', wrote a soldier of the Austrian 4th Infantry Division.

to join his 20th Cavalry Division. He finds them in a wood full of horses, wagons, motorcycles, pieces of artillery and men, men, men.

'Colonel Tawlijev, you and your regiment cross the river. I'll ride along.' Squadrons of Russian cavalry break from the forest line, Russian artillery peppers the village of Polashkino. Tracer bullets from German machine guns fly at the Russian riders, mortar explosions throw up geysers of dirty snow. Many of the riders jump from their mounts and continue on foot, seeking the protection of humps and gullies. They reach the river bank. A whole rank falls. The rest slide around on the ice before being mowed down by German infantry shooting down from the protection of a village wall. The Cossacks are caught in a death trap. 'I've got to get my men off the ice', yells Dovator, pulling out his pistol and rushing forward.

'*Za Rodinu!*' – 'For the Motherland!'

He gets down onto the ice where he is immediately struck by a burst from a machine gun. For a moment the general remains upright before he pitches forward. His Cossack cap with the red-star insignia slides across the ice. Colonel Tawlijev rushes to protect his general, but is also killed by the same flanking machine gun, as is his ADC. Next is the political commissar Karassov. 'Dogs!' he yells and picks up the fallen general before he too is killed. Finally, Lieutenant Kulikov and Sergeant Sokirkov slide across the ice by using bodies of the fallen as their cover and manage to pull the dead general behind a fishing shed.

For the rest of the day, and well into the night, the machine gunners of a German infantry regiment from Schweidnitz hold off the furious attacks by continuous waves of an entire Cossack division, out to revenge their fallen hero.

The Russian movement takes shape, their advance splits in two, cuts through the German lines like some monstrous snake, pushing forward. This is a breakthrough, not by a regiment or division, but by a whole army. The German pocket bursts, their soldiers are rolled and trampled into the snow.

After the guns of the massive Russian artillery have pin-pointed and then pulverised his panzer divisions, Guderian rallies those of his regiments who have survived the carnage. He leads the battle-shocked remnants of his panzer army into a final effort to stem the Red tide. When the Soviets attack with another twenty-two fresh divisions, Guderian has to claw his way back a further eighty kilometres. With a panzer army without tanks and a supply corps with no supplies, to obey the *Führer*'s orders and launch another desperate assault on the wraithlike Russians in driving snow is sheer madness, but then so is the whole tactical situation of the entire German forces still fighting outside Moscow. Zhukov's forces have burst through the German lines from Kalinin in the north to Tula and Kaluga in the south, and are poised to encircle the whole of the German forces outside Moscow. Slowly, but surely, the Germans have to give way before 'the Mongolian hordes of a mechanised Ghengis Khan'.

At the end of December 1941, General Guderian notes in his journal: 'The offensive on Moscow has failed. We have suffered a serious defeat.'

He doesn't know how serious.

What if . . .

What if – Hitler had not delayed Operation Barbarossa for a month?
His forces could have reached Moscow before the onset of winter.

What if – Stalin had not received – and trusted – that crucial Sorge cipher?

He would never have dared to bare his eastern border and pull out one million men from Siberia to defend Moscow.

The facts

Field Marshal von Bock had to report to Hitler: 'The attack on Moscow has been unsuccessful, and the operation will now turn into another Verdun, a brutish chest-to-chest struggle of attrition.'

Hitler decided there would be no failure of nerve. 'The *Deutsche Wehrmacht* does not withdraw! It emerges victorious or dies where it stands!' He relieved the reticent field marshal as head of Army Group Centre. General von Rundstedt was ousted as leader of Army Group South. Next day, Hitler's overall commander, Field Marshal von Brauchitsch dared to mention the word *strategic withdrawal*. Hitler fired him and took over as supreme commander. His initial act was to recall General Heinz Guderian to supreme headquarters. The panzer general's suggestion was to shorten the line in order to reassemble the forces before launching a counter-attack, something so stunning and ferocious that the enemy's attack would falter and crumble.

'*Mein Führer*, we cannot hang on to every square inch. We should pull back and strike at them when they're over-extended.'

Hitler exploded: 'I cannot allow you to retreat. I order you to dig in and fight.'[13]

The tank commander proved to be right. The heavily wooded marshes and the new Russian T-34 tanks were more than a match for Guderian's armour. Fresh Soviet divisions from the Far East were discovered in ever-increasing numbers

[13] Stalin's critics have not detailed all his military errors, but Hitler's generals have.

along the central front. Hitler was forced to abandon his drive on Moscow.[14] He blamed it on the weather. If such was the case then Hitler had only himself to blame. His bad choice of targets, and the delay this had caused earlier in the autumn, was to prove costly. The German High Command had planned on everything, but never taken into account the most notorious of all Russian allies, 'General Winter'.[15] A brief communiqué by the OKW (General HQ, German Forces) of 17 December announced: '*Conform to our army's plan to switch from attack operations to a consolidation of the front line for the period of the winter months, the* Führer *has ordered our forces to execute the necessary improvements and shorten the front line.*'

'*Vorwärts, Kameraden, wir müssen zurück.*'

Forward, *Kameraden*, we must go back, became from now on the standard slogan of the German soldier. Throughout Germany, the euphoria over the easy victories of the autumn campaign gave way to the dreaded realisation that Hitler's strategy of *Blitzkrieg* had failed before Moscow, and that Germany was faced with an extended struggle against the Russian colossus.

By the end of 1941, the German invading armies had sacrificed more than a quarter of their tanks, planes, horses and men. Their losses were a staggering 750,000 casualties.

For the first time the myth of German invincibility had been smashed.

As for the man who made it all possible, Dr Richard Sorge, his crucial message to Stalin was also his final radio transmission.

[14] On 8 December Hitler's '*Weisung* No. 39' ordered a stop to the Moscow offensive.

[15] General Halder: 'The situation makes it plain that we have underestimated the Russian colossus, who consistently prepared for war with the utter ruthless determination so characteristic of totalitarian states.'

On 18 October 1941, Dr Sorge was arrested in Tokyo and his spy ring broken up. The German ambassador, Eugen Ott, fired off an official protest to the Japanese foreign minister, but soon had to change his mind to a 'severely distressed' when the Japanese told him the truth. What was the truth? Not even a thorough investigation could reveal the true extent of his monumental betrayal. Sorge's ego wouldn't allow him to believe that Stalin would let him die. But the Kremlin did nothing to save their super-spy. Moscow even went so far as to deny his very existence. After years of solitary confinement and a secret trial, the German journalist who had turned Russian spy was hanged on 7 November 1944.[16]

During the Stalin years, to ensure that none of Stalin's halo as the unique saviour of Motherland Russia was tarnished, Dr Sorge's name was suppressed, and his incredible feat remained unknown inside the USSR (and anywhere else, for that matter, as the Japanese kept the results of their investigation a guarded secret). The world had to wait until Kim Philby fled to Moscow before the existence of the *Sorge Enigma* was revealed, naming him the 'greatest spy of all time'.[17] Today, Sorge's face appears on a Russian postage stamp and the MV *Richard Sorge* plies the oceans' waves.

A postscript to history: Hitler couldn't have timed it worse. Within days, the whole focus of war shifted. On 7 December 1941, Japanese planes sank five of the eight US battleships anchored in Pearl Harbor and destroyed most of the American airfleet in the Philippines. Three days later, Japanese planes sank the British battleships *Prince of Wales* (of *Bismarck* fame) and *Repulse*.

[16] Just before his death, Kim Philby said: 'Of course, what happened to Sorge could have happened to me. But all the same, I'll tell you frankly that I wouldn't have wanted to end up in his place' (Borovil, *The Philby Files*).
[17] Philby stated that Sorge's information provided the key to the Soviet's final victory.

We shall never know what made Adolf Hitler decide to
take his next, highly precipitated step: on 11 December 1941,
he finally lost any chance of winning the war against the
Soviet Union, when he declared war on the United States of
America.

That, even Dr Sorge didn't know.[18]

The Hinge Factor at Moscow was a delayed start to the
German attack, and the crucial information by a master of
espionage.

*   *   *

[18] Borovik, in conversation with Philby: 'But didn't Sorge know about Pearl
Harbor?'

Philby: 'The Japanese did not tell German Ambassador Ott about their imminent
attack on the USA in order not to alarm Hitler. Hilter knew that if the Japanese
attacked the United States, they wouldn't move against the USSR' (*The Philby
Files: With Sorge*).

15

One Man's Death

Vietnam, 31 January 1968

'If you've got 'em by the balls, their Hearts 'n Minds *will follow!'*
said to the author, Vietnam, December 1967

The night was hot and humid like all others before it. Half the city was asleep, those who had nothing to celebrate. The other half prepared to set off firecrackers to call in the New Year. To frighten the evil spirits of the past year into departing was achieved with excessive exuberance. Precisely at midnight an ear-splitting sound reverberated throughout the city, ropes of Roman candles and catherine wheels exploded like angry fireflies. Paper dragons contorted to the racket of crashing cymbals, rockets of joy lit up the sky over the city on the river – Saigon 1968.

A group of twelve men joined the revellers. They emerged from a garage and climbed into two waiting cars. Slowly the vehicles threaded their way past milling crowds towards a quieter section of town. There they turned down Thong Nhut Boulevard and came to a halt outside the new American embassy. The Vietnamese police contingent, supposedly guarding the compound, had abandoned their post to join the festive crowd. There were only two US Marines near the metal grille at the front entrance. When they noticed the two vehicles, one called out: 'No stopping there, move on . . .' The rest of his sentence was cut off by a volley from an automatic weapon. Mortally wounded, he fell to the ground just as the other Marine had time to slam the gate and scream into a mike: 'Help me! They're coming in!' before the radio went dead.

It was two hours and forty-eight minutes into the *Year of the Monkey*.

The first victims in a bloodletting that was to tear apart their country in the weeks and months to follow, bring down an American President and force the mightiest nation on earth to peace talks, were two American Marines in an embassy compound.

Tet, the Vietnamese Lunar New Year, occupies a special niche for violence. Throughout history, this feast of peace was also the time of year with an unequalled amount of treachery and surprise attacks. Yet nobody ever remembers historic parallels.

During *Tet* of 1789, Prince Quang Trung defeated the Chinese warlords at Hanoi. At *Tet* in 1944, General Nguyen Giap sent his forces against the French. And again, in *Tet* of 1960, Vietcong units attacked Tay Ninh in the first major battle of the Second Indochinese war.

Once again, a series of unrelated events, misjudged and ignored, were pointing towards a climax. On 17 November 1967, the National Liberation Front had declared a cease-fire for the seven days of the coming Lunar New Year. On 1 January 1968, an editorial in the North Vietnamese party newspaper *Nhan Dan* exhorted the troops to: 'Let the entire nation now move forward to completely defeat the US aggressor.'

On 2 January 1968, an enemy patrol was intercepted near

the base perimeter of Khe San. In the ensuing firefight, a NVA regimental commander and his staff were killed. Why would such a high-ranking officer risk a stroll near the US perimeter?

On 5 January 1968, units of the US 4th Infantry near Pleiku captured a document, entitled: 'Urgent Combat Order Number One.' Four NVA (North Vietnamese Army) regiments were positively identified in the heavily wooded hills near the border junction of Laos, Cambodia and Vietnam. Throughout January the CIA compiled evidence of a change in communist strategy. Perhaps the most telling warning was contained in a pamphlet by General Vo Nguyen Giap entitled: 'National Liberation War in Vietnam, Military Art', who wrote: 'The hostile military forces include *manpower, war means and rear bases*. While annihilating the enemy's manpower, we must destroy his war means and rear bases, especially the more important ones.'[1]

The CIA's prediction, code-named 'The Big Gamble', was disregarded by the US Military Command. Meanwhile, the staff at Pentagon East (Vietnam) covered the large battle map with pins, flags and arrows, and arrived at the conclusion that regular North Vietnamese forces were poised for an attack through the Demilitarised Zone (DMZ) along the 17th Parallel. A threat to the South – with its capital cities, its military nerve centres, its major air facilities, its logistic stores, its seat of government and diplomatic representations, or what their nemesis, General Giap referred to as *important rear bases* – was never taken into serious consideration.

From the middle of January on, Saigon was getting ready for a boisterous New Year's celebration. Thousands streamed into the city, visiting relatives, returning to their families, delivering produce. Cars filled with presents, buses, piled high with crates and baskets; passed through the under-manned

---

[1] During his stay in Vietnam, the author obtained a photocopy of this pamphlet. The italics are those of General Giap.

checkposts. Not every crate was filled with flowers, not every basket contained rice. Some carried an assortment of assault rifles, rocket-propelled grenades and plastic explosives.

On 23 January 1968, students at the University of Saigon chanted anti-American slogans and celebrated Prince Quang Trung's victory of 1789 over a foreign aggressor. On the same evening, Radio Hanoi announced that the New Year would be the 'joyous moment of final victory'. For this reason, *Tet* would be celebrated one day earlier, on 29 January 1968. The true meaning of this ambiguous message passed unnoticed.

That's how it all began.

Nguyen Van Sau, a local Vietcong commander, met a twenty-man sapper squad of the C-10 Battalion (Vietcong) just before midnight at 59, Phan Thanh Gian Street. This was a garage owned by a VC supporter, Mrs Nguyen Thi Phe, and located near the American embassy compound in Saigon. Van Sau distributed weapons and roughly outlined the target. Nothing was mentioned about an escape route, nor about the kind of action to be taken. This decision of opportunity was left up to the two squad leaders, Bay Tuyen and Ut Nho.

At a quarter to three, a Peugeot truck and a taxicab rolled along Mac Dinh Chi Street, and turned into Thong Nhut Boulevard. As they reached the embassy gate, the men in the taxi poured automatic fire at the two Marine guards, SP4 Charles Daniel, twenty-three from Durham, NC, and PFC William E. Sebast, 20, from Albany, NY. Sebast fell dead, Daniel slammed shut the gate.

2.49 a.m. A 15-pound plastic charge blew a three-foot hole through the embassy wall. Daniel screamed into the phone: 'They're coming in, help me!' Before he died, he fired at the Vietcong and killed the first two rushing through the hole, who happened to be Bay Tuyen and Ut Nho, the two leaders of the attack squad. From that moment on the intruders were without plan.

Sergeant Jamie Thomas and SP4 Owen Mebust, cruising outside the embassy in their MP jeep, heard Daniel's frantic call. They raced to help, but were mowed down by automatic rifle fire. There were now four dead Americans.

Marine Sergeant Ronald Harper ran to the Chancery Building and joined Corporal Zahuranic an instant before a rocket tore through the heavy door and wounded the corporal.

Colonel George D. Jacobson was asleep in a villa on the compound, a place he shared with Sergeant Robert L. Josephson. The only weapon in the house was an M-26 hand-grenade.

Sergeant Rudy Soto, twenty-five from Selma, California, was on guard duty on top of the Chancery when his shotgun jammed he fired with his .38 at the shadows rushing towards the main building. Inside were three CIA cipher men and two army communication people. Between the five they had one revolver. Another lightly armed Marine, Sergeant James C. Marshal, twenty-one, from Monroeville, Alabama, raced to the roof, where he was later found dead.[2] US casualty number five.

The Associated Press was the first to react. Staring at the night sky, AP's Saigon bureau chief, Robert Tuckman, was standing near his bedroom window, only a few blocks from the embassy compound, when he heard the explosions. The sharp bangs were clearly different from joyous fireworks. One phone call later, and a teletype machine clattered from one continent, Asia, to another, America. This took fifteen seconds. At 3.15 a.m. Saigon time (mid-afternoon in New York), the message exploded across America:

BULLETIN.

SAIGON (AP) – THE VIETCONG SHELLED SAIGON TODAY.

FIRST REPORTS SAID ROCKET OR MORTAR ATTACKS LANDED

---

[2] Killed probably by a friendly bullet during the ensuing fight to liberate the compound.

NEAR INDEPENDENCE PALACE, OTHER GOVERNMENT
BUILDINGS AND THE US EMBASSY.

Almost immediately came a follow-up:[3]

FIRST LEAD ATTACK.
   SAIGON (AP) – SIMULTANEOUSLY, A SUICIDE SQUAD OF
GUERRILLA COMMANDOS INFILTRATED THE CAPITAL AND
AT LEAST THREE ARE REPORTED TO HAVE ENTERED THE
GROUNDS OF THE NEW US EMBASSY NEAR THE HEART OF
THE CITY.

It took until 04.20 a.m., a full hour and a half after the
Vietcong had entered the embassy grounds, before General
Westmoreland reacted and ordered the 716th MP Battalion
to clear the compound. The lieutenant in charge declined to
fight his way into the embassy in the dark. He flatly stated:
'Nobody can get in and nobody can get out.'
   Another hour went by before a former NY cop, Robert
Furey, discovered the hole which had been blasted through
the wall. When he crawled though it, a wounded Vietcong
blew himself up with a grenade.
   Because of the state of total confusion, the exact number of
intruders and their armaments was unclear. The next hours
were spent with sporadic firing from rooftops surrounding the
embassy.
   For the Vietcong suicide squad inside the compound, the
situation was equally confusing. With their two leaders dead,

---

[3] About the same time, Radio Hanoi went on the air with the reading of a poem
by the country's venerated leader, comrade Ho Chi Minh:

This spring far outshines all previous springs
of victories throughout our land come happy tidings
let South and North combine in fighting the American aggressor
Forward – total victory shall be ours . . .

and with no orders of what to do or a clearly defined mission target, they did nothing other than try to get out of the line of fire pouring into the grounds.

Colonel Jacobson had found a Colt .45, and when a Vietcong came up the stairs and walked into his bedroom, he shot him at point-blank range. Finally a jeep rammed through the front gate, followed by a horde of newsmen and TV crews. Bodies were strewn where they fell and most of the Vietcong were dead, dying or in hiding. Kate Webb, of UPI, was to call it 'a butcher shop in Eden'.

The US embassy was finally declared secure at 9.15 a.m., six and a half hours after Daniel's call for help! In the embassy compound General Westmoreland, in a starched and pressed uniform, faced a half-moon of news crews: 'Some superficial damage has been done to the buildings, the nineteen Vietcong who entered have been killed.[4] American troops have gone on the offensive and are pursuing the enemy aggressively . . .'

The reporters could hardly believe their ears. This was the most embarrassing defeat the United States had suffered in this war, and here was the commanding US general standing in the ruins of what represented the American presence in Vietnam and declaring that everything was great! While the international press scoured the compound to count bodies of friend and foe, reports of fierce battles were coming in from the major population centres throughout South Vietnam. The communists had struck. The *Tet* Offensive was on its way.

On the military front, the news was hardly better. Surprise had been total. South Vietnam was under a full-scale attack, both from inside and out.

Bien Hoa headquarters compound was under attack, and planes were burning on the airbase's runways. A full regiment

---

[4] Not true, of the nineteen, four were civilian embassy staff. Later it was established that one of the embassy drivers, Nguyen Van De, had been an active Vietcong and led the attack into the compound.

of Vietcong was dug in along its perimeter. Tan Son Nhut airbase was cut off from the rest of the city and being attacked by several Vietcong battalions. In downtown Saigon heavy fighting was reported around the Independence Palace and the radio station.

For all practical purposes, the 'Saigon Circle', the defence perimeter set up to protect the city and its vital installations, had ceased to exist. Outside the Long Binh Tactical Operation Centre, an underground ammunition dump had been set off by a Vietcong sapper squad. When it blew up it knocked out all electricity and phone lines. The war in Vietnam was now run by battery powered radio and candles. The commanding officer of Saigon military zone, Lieut General Frederick Weyand, rushed from map to map with a flashlight. Up to this moment, thirty-five battalions of enemy troops had been positively identified, eleven in the Saigon area alone!

Chaos and fear held a city in their grip. Shells streaked over rooftops, artillery fired along tree-lined boulevards into bicycles, masonry and flesh. Smoke obscured realities – bodies were no longer counted, much less buried. Burst water mains, burning buses, electric cables sparked like vicious snakes. Every square inch, square foot, square mile was covered by broken glass. Nothing stirred, Saigon was a visit to a barren planet, a city of deep cellars and shallow graves.

The scene on the floors of the Hotel Caravelle could best be described as uncontrolled confusion bordering on total panic by frazzled correspondents and harried television crews. Everybody had been up since the attack on the US embassy, all trying to get their stories out – but most telex lines were overloaded or down. Bureau chiefs tried to dispatch crews into the provinces – but press-junkets had been cancelled. Tracers zinged over the roof of the Rex bar, for once void of its clients. Those who didn't need to eyeball the outdoor scene to get off a report, installed themselves within some military compound.

That's where the announcements were made, sometimes good reasoning for their strategic retreat.

SAIGON (ADD-LEAD) – MORE REPORTS ARE COMING IN OF HEAVY FIGHTING IN ALL MAJOR PROVINCIAL CAPI-TALS. SPECIALLY CITED ARE (READ NORTH-TO-SOUTH): QUANG TRI-HUE-DANANG-QUI NHON-NHA TRANG-DALAT-BIEN HOA-SAIGON-MY THO-BEN TRE-VI NHLONG-CAN THO-CA MAU.

One thing became painfully clear: both sides were taking tremendous casualties. But while the Vietcong and their North Vietnamese comrades went after military targets – perhaps forced by their meagre supply of ammunition, or because, politically, they were better indoctrinated – the Free World Forces, with their inexhaustible supply of shells and bombs and bullets fired indiscriminately at anything that moved, and bombed everything that didn't move, adding hundreds of non-combatants to the steadily growing casualty list. It was equally clear that once this mess had been brought under control, someone on the political scene would have to account for the slaughter, highly visible in the form of decaying corpses in country lanes and on city boulevards. Whatever the battle's military outcome, the Vietcong would at least achieve one goal – a propaganda victory.

'What the hell is going on?' raged Walter Cronkite, CBS's famous anchorman, in the New York Broadcast Center. He tore a sheet from the clattering telex, 'I thought we're winning the war.' Television executives back in the 'real world' were biting their fingernails while screaming abuse at people 9,000 miles away – that is, if they could make contact with their Saigon bureau, which wasn't at all certain. People in the snow-covered Midwest and sunny California, soap flake advertisers from Delaware and stockbrokers on Wall Street hungered for news of the raging battle. One ageing movie star gave a press conference to announce he was chartering a plane to fly to Saigon 'to provide moral support', until someone from the audience, a Vietnam veteran, told the actor he was a jerk.

The major TV networks had private jets on stand-by, but charter pilots couldn't locate a single airfield in Vietnam that wasn't under attack. Network executives hammered on doors of Pentagon officials to organise transportation for news film on military medevac flights to Yokota Air Force base near Tokyo. Which called for the film to be delivered to some airport over roads raked by small-arms fire and frequently cut by hostile forces. But even before this film could be brought to the airport, it had to be exposed by a cameraman, standing upright in the midst of panic and confusion, pretending not to hear the shots that were aimed for his head, or heart, or kidney, while eternalising urban mayhem on celluloid. One thing was certain: there was no need for a cameraman to focus on any scene in particular. In whatever direction he dared to point the lens, a thousand new dramas sprang up every minute.

The *Tet* Offensive was now in its third day. If Saigon was bad, then the battle for Hue was the worst. Hue, ancient capital of Vietnam, carried a justified reputation as a place of great beauty, of gentle meandering rivers, of lotus blossoms and splendid mansions, surrounding 'The Palace of Perfect Peace'. Until now, this city had been spared the horrors of fratricidal slaughter.

A television news cameraman had managed to get a seat on a medevac flight. On their landing approach across the Imperial Screen Mountains, the photographer could see scattered fires raging throughout the city. While the flight crew were loading the casualties lined up along the tarmac the pilot said to the photographer: 'Buddy, I'm sure glad it's not me in there. Better check it out reeeal good.'

Near the airstrip he flagged down an ammunition trans-
porter. The driver was obviously a pious person. 'Pictureman,
is you good on yous Ave Marias?'

'Ave Maria?' The photographer was confused, 'Why?'

''Cause what yar sittin on.' Only then did it strike the
photographer that he was sitting on a box of pineapple
grenades. One tracer bullet, and they wouldn't find enough
of him to put into a jam jar.

'When I's sign on for mah second tour, I don't ask foh
dat.' The driver thumbed at his dangerous cargo. 'I's plain
dumb playin' Russian rooolette. Lass pray they don't hit
that load'o shit . . .' The driver changed gears and mumbled
another prayer. He weaved through the carcasses of burnt
cars, putrid animals and corpses. The battle had moved along
this road. The photographer was jumpy, he knew only too well
the calm couldn't last much longer. It didn't. Up ahead was
the Huang Giang, 'the River of Perfumes'. Near the Nguyen
Hoang Bridge two Marine tanks fired their 90-mm main gun
point blank into the walls of the Imperial Fortress looming
on the opposite bank. Their fire was answered by the bark
of a heavy machine gun. Its tracers bounced off the heavy
tank armour and slammed into the Jeanne d'Arc Church or
ricocheted like angry fireflies into the sky. The situation was
not conforming at all to what the army's public relation release
had reported: 'All is back under control . . .'

The photographer ran forward towards the Cercle Sportif.
Whoosh! A fiery ball streaked over his head, a B-40 rocket. He
threw himself into a ditch and cursed himself over his own
foolishness, running towards the exposed river bank. For an
instant he dared to put his head over the rim of the water
ditch. He saw a red flag with a yellow star on the flagpole
above the Hue citadel and realised how desperate the situation
really was.

The photographer was not more than 200 feet from the
wall, with the NVA (North Vietnamese Army) blasting from

the ramparts at any movement down below. Small-arms fire raked Le Loi Street, impacts splashed like raindrops on the tarmac and he felt he was their Number One target. No longer did he dare to raise his head; he simply placed the camera on the flat road surface, pointed it in the general direction of a Marine tank near a bridge and pushed the plunger moments before a rocket struck the tank's turret, scattering shrapnel into the hapless Marine commando crouching behind it. Two were killed, and a young soldier had his foot blown off. He screamed, pointing at a bloody stump lying in the middle of the road. The photographer was certain that the tank had been mortally touched, but it suddenly roared into reverse, all the while pivoting its turret and blasting away. It blew a large hole in the citadel's wall. Three bodies were catapulted into the air, one splashed into the river, and quickly sank.

An explosion showed him that enemy mortar rounds were finding their mark. He slouched deeper into the ditch. An American helmet appeared from behind a wall, a soldier yelled an order, but he couldn't hear a thing, the mortar explosion had blocked his eardrums. 'Down, down . . .' The Marine motioned with his hand downward. Whoosh . . . whoosh . . . two recoilless rockets slammed into a house. From behind a building emerged three Americans dragging a 3.5-inch bazooka. They lined it up on the citadel tower and let fly. Three impacts, but once the dust had cleared, the tower seemed quite unshaken, and murderous fire poured from it. For an instant, the photographer moved his helmet-covered head above the ditch. A sharp zing, and a bullet slammed into the wall right next to him.

A group of four US Marines ran the gauntlet, blasting away at the opposite shore. A machine gun barked and two of the Marines collapsed. The survivors dived across the road and landed close to him in 'his ditch' (by now he felt it was his personal property). One of the Marines brought an M-79 grenade launcher to his cheek and fired at the stabs of fire pouring down from the fortress wall. A bang, a black cloud, and the machine gun was silenced. Once the explosion cloud blew away from the hole, he noticed an olive-drab figure, holding his head and screaming. A burst from an M-16 cut him down. A heavy quad-gun opened up behind them, the tracers zipping over their heads, ricocheting off the granite walls. 'Down, down . . . those fuckers, they're gonna blow us . . . hey, Gonzales, don't just sit there and bleed, get on the fuckin' radio . . . Sonofabitch, a movie man – wanna make us Marines famous? Get the hell out of here, what the fuck you think this is, Hollywood and them fuckin' Green Berets . . . ?'

'Sarge, can't get through to nobody . . . whole world is duck fucking, could be the bad boys, ain't got a clue who's quaking, that lingo, jeezes . . . SHUT THE FUCK UP!' the radioman screamed into his mike. 'Nothing . . . just listen to that noise, sarge . . .'

'Don' gimme that shit, Gonzalez, jess try again, we've gotta . . .' His voice was cut off by a staccato burst from an AK-47. He fell backwards, his mouth agape, a bloody smear where his helmet had been.

For the photographer it was time to move. The road in front of him erupted with geysers of mud. He sprinted for a gaping hole in a house, jumped through it and landed in blackness. Whammm!! a rocket blew a wall apart, spraying him with a shower of concrete and bricks. He ended on the floor, next to two Vietnamese women cowering in a corner, crossing themselves at his appearance. For an instant he sat stunned, nursing a sore knee which he had banged in his dive through the hole. The professional in him took over and he changed film. It was high time to get out of there; his two exposed rolls would provide enough proof that the enemy was solidly entrenched inside the walled Citadel of Hue.

The women were frozen, they wouldn't move. The photographer scampered across a narrow courtyard and ran along the *huton*, seeking cover behind a row of low houses. Once away from the waterfront, the going became easier. Clinging to protective walls it took him twenty minutes to reach the Tu Dam Pagoda on the Phu Cam Canal. This House of God had been set up as medical aid station for civilian casualties. In the shade of its bullet-scarred dome, the wide courtyard was a vista of moaning and suffering. Worst of all were the many little children wandering about, searching among the wounded for parents who were probably lying dead on roads or in fields surrounding the city. Tragedy was not dismembered bodies – tragedy was dismembered families. To a photographer, here was the ultimate portrayal of the horror of war. Halfway through the roll his camera jammed – perhaps a divine signal to stop his voyeurism of human tragedy. He swung himself on a passing truck. The vehicle carried a dozen Marine casualties. Their white, bloodless faces were his final impression of Hue. The cruel harvest of war was everywhere.[5]

The Vietcong were scoring big on American TV. The President went on television. His speech was transmitted by the Armed Forces Radio to the troops in Vietnam: 'Mah fella Americans,' began President Johnson with his pronounced Texan drawl, 'the Vietcong attack has bin broken and they have bin defeated . . .' To the soldier in the field it seemed that nobody had dared to tell his President about the thousands of Vietcong and regular NVA running around Saigon, Can Tho, Ban Me Thuot, Danag or Hue.

Friday the 1st was not a good day for the President of the United States. Only the night before, the two television giants, NBC and CBS, had covered the same shocking event, the attack on the US embassy in Saigon. And now this photograph, spread across five columns on the front page of the *New York Times* and the *Washington Post*! A good *gook*,

---

[5] This story is a personal account by the author.

one of ours, and in a military uniform, firing point-blank into the head of another Vietnamese in a checked shirt and black shorts . . .

Associated Press photographer Eddie Adams and NBC cameraman Vo Suu were standing near the An Quang Pagoda when they noticed two Vietnamese Marines leading a prisoner in a checked shirt and black shorts with his hands tied behind his back. Vo Suu switched on his sound camera. Brigadier General Nguyen Ngoa Loan, the chief of South Vietnam's police, waved away the Marine guards and stepped up to the prisoner. The prisoner was standing a few feet away, his eyes downcast, when, quite suddenly and without a word, Loan drew his revolver. His right arm stretched out so that the barrel of the gun almost touched the prisoner's head, and, as his index finger squeezed the trigger, photographer Eddie Adams tripped the shutter.

Directly across the street, from where General Westmoreland informed the assembled world press of his troops' great victories, Associated Press transmitted by means of their radiophoto circuit a still picture to New York, and from there around the globe. Eddie Adams's dramatic picture made the first page of every newspaper in the world.[6]

History snaps its fingers and the world comes apart with a crash and a flame. History slices impartially into winner and looser – except that when it comes to recording history there is no such thing as impartiality. Each side chronicles its own version of glory. One thing was certain: history would

[6] Adams won many prizes, among them the coveted Pulitzer Prize. Vo Suu's film was received by NBC, New York, ten minutes before airtime. It showed that somebody had stepped in front of his camera the instant the shot was fired, but no one in the audience of over twenty million noticed that they had not watched the murder. NBC executive Northshield had trimmed the final seventeen seconds to take away the agony. For three seconds, the screen went to black.

record that the first night of the *Year of the Monkey* was the beginning of the *Tet* Offensive.

History would also have to record that the victor of this battle was eventually the vanquished.

What if . . .

What if – the US military had not permitted the press to fulfil its role of reporting events freely?

It is questionable, in any case, whether America's military and political leaders could have delayed their nation's unfavourable reaction to an unpopular war much longer.

The facts

The beginning of the *Tet* Offensive was an attack on the US Embassy. In the end there were 81,736 casualties throughout the country – South Vietnamese soldiers, North Vietnamese soldiers, American soldiers, Vietcong soldiers, and – as in every war – a great many civilians.

It would be utter nonsense to claim that the US Armed Forces couldn't overcome the guerrillas of the Vietcong. After all, US fighting men had defeated the Japanese in the jungles of Borneo, Guadalcanal and Okinawa, and what other army in history had ever been better trained and equipped to fight a jungle war than the Japanese Imperial Forces? But Vietnam was different. Here, the armed forces of the United States were compelled to fight world opinion.

If Vietnam can be considered the first (and hopefully last) 'television war', then *Tet* was its first 'televised battle', one in a series of 'major human dramas'[7] to be transmitted into

---

[7] Such as the moon landing or the terrorist attack during the Munich Olympics.

American homes via satellite. As successive reports were aired, a chilly depression settled over official Washington. During a background session with America's leading editorialists and publishers, Secretary of State Dean Rusk vented his anger about war reporting in general, and the Adams photo in particular: 'Damn it, whose side are you on?'

The press didn't create the pictures, the fighting men did. On many occasions the military have called the press subversive through exposure, the press likes to refer to themselves as committed critics. The United States is a democracy with its sacrosanct right for a free press. 'An adversarial, critical relationship between the media and the government, including the military, is healthy, and helps guarantee that both institutions do a good job . . . The appropriate media role has been summarised aptly as being neither that of a lap dog, nor an attack dog, but, rather, a watch dog.'[8]

For the Pentagon, their undisputed military victory at *Tet* offered a glimmer of hope. Or so they thought. Yet, future events turned even nastier. Television helped to show that South Vietnam was run by political Mafiosi, corrupt generals, small-town demagogues and brutal policemen, all out baying for blood and money. It showed that the ordinary Vietnamese suffered, and that the Vietcong, and their bosses in the North, exploited their misery in a masterly fashion. But most important of all, the average American, exposed to a relentless press coverage, watched with growing dismay a collapse of morale among his troops abroad and a spreading unrest within his own country.[9]

The Vietnam War was a conflict that the Big Green Machine[10] could not lose and the United States could not

[8] Maj. Gen. Winant Sidle, head of the Sidle Committee of the US Department of Defense, on the involvement of the press in future military operations.
[9] Following Tet came the time of student riots in American universities, draft card burnings, and the unrest in black ghettos.
[10] The American Armed Forces.

win. As it turned out, the *Tet* Offensive was the turning-point. The televised reports, pumped daily into millions of American homes, helped to catalyse American public opinion against its escalation.

It was one photograph, the death of a man in a checked shirt on a street corner in Saigon, that first confirmed to many across the nation that this was a war fought for the wrong reasons, in the wrong country and on the wrong side.

The Hinge Factor in Vietnam was a still photograph (one among many), a tangible demonstration of the sacrosanct American freedom of the press. From that moment on, American generals had to fight world opinion instead of the Vietcong, and American soldiers had to sacrifice their lives for no gains whatsoever.

16

And the Wall Came Tumbling Down

Berlin, 9 November 1989

'Die Grosse Mauer, gedacht als Schutzwall gegen die barbarischen Völker der Steppe, ist einer der immer wiederholten Versuche, die Zeit aufzuhalten, und hat sich, wie wir heute wisen, nicht bewaehrt. Die Zeit laesst sich nicht aufhalten.'

('The Great Wall, intended as protective shield against the barbaric races from the steppes, is a many repeated attempt to arrest time. As we know today, it did not work. Time simply cannot be arrested.')

Max Frisch, *Die Chinesische Mauer*

For nearly two generations it had stood as a symbol of tyranny, a wall which divided Europe. The Iron Curtain. Its most notorious section was to be found in Berlin, a clearly visible, repulsive barrier of concrete and barbed wire, the boundary which split a city in half and tormented the soul of a nation. A hideous scar, the mark of an xenophobic empire which had to lock its people in to stop them from running away.[1] For years, the wall performed its appointed task with brutal efficiency. It was a death strip of concrete, barbed wire and

---

[1] By the time the wall went up in 1961, 2.7 million Easterners had sought refuge in West Germany.

manned watch towers, suppressing the human yearning for freedom. People jumped over it and tunnelled under it. They hijacked planes to fly across it and crashed trucks through it. Some succeeded, many didn't. Along its length the white crosses multiplied. Rudolf Urban, + 17.9.1961, Bernd Lünser, + 4.10.1961, Ernst Mund, + 4.9.1962. The most notorious case was that of an eighteen-year-old bricklayer, Peter Fechter, left lying for hours to bleed to death while Western photographers snapped his picture through the wire and members of the feared *Volkspolizei* stood idly by watching his agony.[2]

The Wall, or as the people of Berlin called it, *DIE Mauer*, had been built to stand for a hundred years. It did not nearly last that long before it came crashing down in one stunning flash.

Communism had performed its own Samson act. The same party bosses who ordered it put up, pulled down the whole ideological structure and buried themselves.

And yet, when it finally happened it all came about by accident.

Soon after 13 August 1961, the day East German work brigades put up rows of bricks to seal off half of Berlin, a young American President came to see *Die Mauer*. He was shocked by what he discovered. The same afternoon he was to address the people of Berlin from the balcony of the Schöneberg Rathaus. His writers had worked hard on the speech. But after coming face-to-face with that concrete monstrosity, he tore up the prepared paper. He knew it was no good and that he had to improvise. The crowd in front of Berlin's City Hall was jammed into the square when he stepped out onto the balcony and pointed over the crowd towards a distant wall.

'Let them come to Berlin.' And then he spoke the words which offered the greatest tribute to a city and its sorely tried

[2] 17 August 1962, between Charlotten and Markgrafenstrasse. During his funeral, five British and American correspondents were detained.

citizens, a phrase so profound that it will be remembered longer than anything else in his short, but distinguished life. John Fitzgerald Kennedy, President of the United States of America, raised his hands, looked at the crowd, and in a calm voice said: '*Ich bin ein Berliner.*'

By the autumn of 1989, East Germany was a country moving in several directions, all of them frightening. The East German rulers could no longer suppress the fact that the life of their nation was undergoing an irrevocable change. The internal tensions became evident, the pendulum had swung from dazed and depressed, to fevered and passionate. Every member of the Politburo realised that the Party was powerless to stop the inevitable.

Twenty-two years after a Russian dictator had ordered that no country within the Soviet sphere of influence would be allowed to quit it, the *Breshnev Doctrine* was dead and buried. This was confirmed by Nicolai Shishlin, spokesman for the Central Committee of the Communist Party of the USSR. Responding to a question by an American TV correspondent, if this also concerned East Germany, he replied, 'I am sure that the present situation has to be amended. Just give us a little time.' This widely reported phrase created a vast popular movement throughout East Germany. Hundreds of thousands came out into the streets to demonstrate vociferously, week after week. The newly chosen (not freely elected) head of the East German state, Egon Krenz, was faced with the dilemma of solving an unsolvable problem. His stone-age communist cronies had been sent out to pasture. Erich Honecker was gone, even the head of state security, the leader of the hated *Stasi* apparatus[3], Erich Mielke, was forced to retire. In the

---

[3] The *Staatssicherhietsdienst*, run by 85,000 agents. Their files contained detailed information on six million of its citizens, including such titbits as that of the Olympic figure-skating champion who had made love to a member of the team between 8.03 and 8.09 one evening.

first November days of 1989, a Liberal-Democrat, Manfred
Gerlach, demanded the resignation of the Cabinet as well as
the entire *Volksrat*, something unimaginable only a month
before.

It all began on a Monday in the city of Leipzig. A famous
musician, Kurt Masur, chief conductor of the *Leipziger
Gewandhaus Philharmonics* dared to stand up and announce
to a few hundred: '*So kann es hier nicht weitergehen.*' – ('It
cannot go on like this.') By 2 October, 50,000 were out on the
streets. A week thereafter the crowd had swelled to 150,000.

On East Berlin's Alexanderplatz, half a million workers
screamed: '*Die Macht ist auf der Strasse.*' – ('The power is in
the street.') On 23 October, East Germany's iron man, Erich
Honecker, was ousted.

A feeble show of continued allegiance came from a handful of stout-hearted communists with a worn-out slogan:
'*Wir sind die Partei.*' ('We are the party.') Their shouts were
drowned by the millions, from Halle to Erfurt, from Gera
and Karl Marx Stadt, yelling: '*Wir sind das Volk.*' ('We are
the people.') On 26 October, the police chief of East Berlin,
Lieut-General Friedhelm Rausch, cancelled all leave for units
of the East German *Grenzpolizei*. It was feared that their
citizens would use a demonstration to climb over the wall.[4]

In 1989, Christmas in Berlin fell on 9 November. To be
more precise, at 18.57 hours of the ninth. On television. A
press conference was scheduled at half-past six, given by the
newly appointed spokesman for the Central Committee of
the *Sozialist Einheits Partei Deutschlands* (*SED*) and transmitted live by East German state television. Comrade Günther
Schabowski outlined the great achievements of socialism – the
kind of statements which had journalists yawning – before a

---

[4] Thousands of 'vacationing' East Germans climbed the fences of West German
embassies in Prague and Budapest to seek asylum.

correspondent raised his hand. The time was three minutes to seven.

'Herr Schabowski, when will your citizens be allowed to travel freely?'

Even today it is difficult to state with certainty if the answer was spontaneous or rehearsed. Most likely, he was carried away by the rapidly deteriorating events inside his country. Whatever the reason, nobody in the room – nor anywhere around the world[5] – expected the reply which was to follow.

'*Die können gehen wann sie wollen. Und niemand wird sie aufhalten.*' ('They can go whenever they want, and nobody will stop them.')

For a moment the audience was stunned, before bedlam erupted in the studio. Questions were thrown at the speaker, who raised his hands to calm the journalists. Perhaps he suddenly realised that his choice of words was political dynamite, and he needed to clarify his rash statement. In any case, he added: 'This directive does in no way concern the fortified border of the *DDR*. However, border authorities will be instructed *to issue visas* to anyone who wants to leave. For a few hours, for a day, or forever.'[6]

Otto Bahr, the architect of West German *Ostpolitik* watched it on West Berlin television. He could not believe what he had just heard and called a friend to verify the statement. He then rushed to see Willy Brandt, the senior German statesman. They fell into each other's arms and cried. At the same moment the president of the Bonner *Bundestag* asked the delegates to rise and sing the national anthem.

For those directly concerned, the citizens of East Berlin so

---

[5] US President George Bush is supposed to have asked: 'Why were we not told?'
[6] Schabowski's statement: '*Diese Regelung ueber die Reisefreiheit beantwortet noch nicht den Sinn, sagen wir mal, der befestigten Staatsgrenze der DDR. Fuer dessen Abbau ist noch die Erfuellung anderer Faktoren noetig. jedoch sind die zustaendigen Abteilungen Pass und Meldewesen in der DDR angewiesen, Visa zur staendigen Ausreise unverzueglich zu erteilen . . .*'

used to deception, reaction took a bit longer. But by around ten that evening a crowd had begun to gather near the various checkpoints. The first East Berliners pushed their blue ID cards through the iron gates and asked the East German border guard on duty to let them pass. For about an hour the officers of the *Grenzpolizei* showed a stony face; their system had taught them to obey orders and, though they had also listened to the broadcast, no such official instructions had been forthcoming until now. In the meantime, the news spread throughout the city, and soon hundreds of thousands congregated at the Wall, both from the East and from the West.

'*Tor auf! Tor auf!*' ('Open the gate!') yelled the chorus.

A daring young man jimmied up the graffiti-covered wall from the western side, followed by a dozen, then a hundred adventurous youngsters. They cheered and waved flags. Looking baffled at the commotion above their heads, the border guards did not know how to react. They were still without instructions from the authorities. Suddenly everything got out of hand. A *Vopo* (*Volkspolizei*) had opened a side gate to step out and calm the crowd. He was immediately shoved aside as the first dozen crashed through the narrow passage to the West. They were followed by an unstoppable surge of humanity. This move caught the East German border police completely off guard; they were powerless and did not know what was going on, nor what to do to stop thirty-eight years of compressed steam which blew through a small hole in the police-state pressure cooker. The throng swept the *Vopos* aside or carried the uniformed men with them to the other side. Once the first breach was made, and the *Volkspolizei* guards in the nearby watchtower saw people moving across the Wall, they informed other guard posts, probably in the belief that authoritative orders had been received. The other checkpoints began to open their gates,[7] from the Brandenburger Tor, to

---

[7] Probably believing this was on a specific order.

the Oberbaumbruecke, from the crossing points at Heinrich Heine[8] Strasse to the Bornholmer Strasse.

That night the world of the Berliners was turned upside down. At one closed checkpoint a *Grenzpolizei* major huffed at his duty policemen: '*Mensch, lass doch die Leute raus!*' ('Let the people go!')

The street leading to the Invalidenstrasse border post became the meeting point of thousands of Trabis, that miracle automobile produced in the East.[9] Their drivers cried, laughed or sang.

Had only one of the border men raised his rifle and fired into the crowd, history might have changed. But other than patrolling along the wall and yelling to the inebriated, bottle-waving crowd on the top of it, the feared *Grenzpolizei* did nothing. A loudspeaker truck moved up: '*Bürger von Berlin West, verlassen Sie die Mauer.*' It came to a standoff: *Veuve Cliquot* versus *Kalachnikov.* The bangs that were heard came not from automatic rifles but from the joyous popping of champagne corks. Nobody fired a rifle, and one may truly claim today that this was the only major battle in history that ended without bloodshed.

'*Endlich schlagen wir die Tür ein!*' ('At last, we've shoved in the door!') The crowd drank in jubilation. The good burghers, East and West, waved their bottles, passed on their

---

[8] A century before, he had written a poem:

Im traurigen Monat November war's
Die Tage wurden trueber
Der Wind riss von den Baeumen das Laub
Da reist ich nach Deutschland hinueber.

Und als ich an die Grenze kam
Da fuehlte ich ein staerkeres Klopfen
In meiner Brust, ich glaube sogar
Die Augen begunnen zu tropfen

[9] Trabi, or Tarbant, was called the miracle car because it was a miracle that it moved.

liquid refreshment to newcomers, and handed flowers to the sour-faced *Grenzpolizei*. Soon the top of the Wall became so crowded that people began to fall off, onto the heads of the throng of westerners heaving themselves up in front, or backwards into the erstwhile 'death zone', by now so jam-packed that none of those who fell drunk from the Wall hit the ground.

An elderly man from the Bornholmer Strasse came dressed in only a coat over his pyjamas.

'Icke wa schon inne Bett, die Alte jeht noch mit'm Hund runta, da kommt ruff und sagt: Mensch du die jehn alle nach'n Westen.' ('My wife just went down with the dog, and then she comes running up the stairs. "Hey, Heinrich," she yells, "quickly, come down, they're all going to the West.")

'So I say: "*Rede Keinen Quatsch!*" ("Don't talk nonsense.")

'"*Nein, die tun's wirklich.*"'

Ursula Krämer was among the first to come through. A *Wessie* (West Berliner) doused her with a fountain of champagne, like the winner of a Grand Prix, in a tribute to a glorious victory. Ursula had tears when she kissed the stranger.

An American TV reporter was heaved by his cameraman onto the wall and from there was overheard telling his viewers back in the real world about 'a stench of freedom'. As backdrop he used a crowd which was tearing at segments of the concrete wall with ropes and chains.

Uti Hoff, a twenty-two-year-old student from Heidelberg, on her first visit to Berlin, nearly suffocated in the dense push which held her pinned against the Wall, when a pair of helping hands reached down for her and hoisted her to the top. It was there that she met Jochen Kuligowski, a drill-pusher from a metal works in the East. They embraced in disbelieving joy.

(Nine months later, they named their baby Charlie, after Checkpoint Charlie.)

As late as 22.30, Walter Momper, the Acting Mayor of Berlin, was asked to give a statement at the *Sender Freies Berlin*, and declared: 'I haven't got a clue what's going on.' Then a pencilled note was slipped to him. It came from his chief of police: 'Big crowds are crashing through the Wall, the situation on the border crossings is completely out of control.'

Momper said: '*Freunde, mein Platz ist jetzt woanders.*' ('My place is now somewhere else'). He left the studio and drove straight to the *Mauer*. His driver had great difficulty in getting through the horn-honking champagne-spraying bash on the Kurfürstendamm before they reached the Invalidenstrasse checkpoint to observe from close-up the flood of humanity spilling through the gate, or up and over the Wall.

At Police Headquarters, Commissioner Rainer Bornstein, the man responsible for the Brandenburg Gate Sector, couldn't talk. '*Meine Flüstertüte hat vor'ner Stunde den Geist aufgegeben*' ('My voice gave out an hour ago'), he whispered to a reporter. 'We, as police, can do nothing.'

Not far from there a train of the elevated *S-Bahn* passed the bridge across the Spree, its wagons jammed with people with their faces pushed up against the windows. Without stopping, the train rolled past *Checkpoint Friedrichstrasse*.

The US official responsible for the American Sector Berlin, Harry Gilmore, called his counterpart in the British sector: 'What's your situation, Michael?'

'Things have absolutely broken down in our sector,' replied Michael Burton.

At the Glienicker Bruecke, where for thirty years the exchange of spies had taken place, East German border police speeded up the long columns of East Berliners in cars. '*Aufschliessen, Aufschliessen!*' ('Get a move on!') The driver of a Trabi taxi, hidden behind a suffocating blue cloud pouring from the exhaust pipe of his two-stroke engineering marvel, exclaimed with tears in his eyes: '*Ikke greife mir am Kopf, ikk kanns nit begreifen. Heut nacht fahr ikk am Kudamm.*' ('I grab my head, I still cannot believe it. Imagine, tonight I'll drive down the Kurfürstendamm.')

An elderly woman reached West Berlin's *Gedächtniskirche* where she sank to her knees and murmured: 'Thank you, oh Lord. That was always my dream. I never thought I'd come here before I die.'

Waitresses from the Café Moskva in the Karl-Marx Allee crossed over as a group to have coffee and cakes at West Berlin's *Kaffee Kranzler*. When they offered to pay with their aluminium East Marks, the manager told them: 'It's on the house, eat as much *Kuchen* as you want.'

Two boys held up a sign near Checkpoint Charlie: '*Herzlich Willkommen. Ab heute Eintritt frei!*' ('Welcome today no entrance fee.') It came to a regular head-on traffic jam when a group of westerners screamed: '*Wir wollen rein!*' ('We want in!') and tried to move in the opposite direction.

All over the city pandemonium reigned. A police official got through to Mayor Momper. '*Beim Brandenburger Tor fangen die Verrückten an mit dem Hammer auf der Mauer herumzukloppen.*' ('At the Brandenburg Gate some crazies have begun to use their hammers on the Wall.')

Indeed, the first *Mauerspechte* (wall woodpeckers) began their destructive work with pick-axe, hammer and chisel. Twenty-seven-year-old Utta Hoeppner had come well prepared with her own hammer. For an hour she whacked away, then waved her chunk of graffiti-coloured brick triumphantly to photographers while her boyfriend Friedl, up on the Wall, danced an Irish jig. It was the best example of a victory of blue jeans over military uniforms.

The top of the Wall was soon lined with candles; a band of thousands of tiny flames which weaved in a joyous snake through the middle of Berlin. It called out to the world: '*Berlin ist frei!*'

For the few who had gathered to show their continued loyalty in front of the East Berlin Party HQ, the time was now five minutes past twelve.

Not one who lived through that momentous event will ever forget the emotions of that night. Just like two hundred years before – in 1789 at the towers of the Bastille, when the citizens of Paris tore down the symbol of their oppression – the burghers of Berlin took out their fury on the hideous *Mauer*.

A repressive regime built the Wall. The West helped them considerably when it declared that Berlin was not a German city but a political corner-stone in the struggle between the great powers. For years, sundry presidents had passed before it to shake their fists at the Wall and make statements, which only went to show the limits of their power in a Nuclear Age. Yet, though American and Russian armour were separated by only twenty yards, it had never come to a *Berlin Crisis*, as the city maintained the alternative of cold war to hot war. Now that the Wall had come down, the nations of Europe could start on the road to building a far less menacing world order.

Die Mauer was more than just a wall, it was a monument of oppression. As it is with all symbols, when they come tumbling down, they fall with a resounding crash. This time, the sound waves carried all around the world.

History will record that the final battle in the Cold War, which had lasted for forty years, was fought without bloodshed.

With the Fall of the Berlin Wall, the Age of Communism was over.

What if . . .

What if – the East German border guards had awaited their specific orders to issue visas?

From the accounts of those who were present there, it is doubtful whether the *Volkspolizei* could have stopped the crowd from storming the Wall. Had they tried, it would have ended in wholesale slaughter. And that was precisely what East German Party leaders, and their bosses in Moscow, were afraid of.

The facts

On 10 November, the *SED* deputy, Horst Siedermann, in the *Volkskammer*, put it succinctly: '*Es war als rutschten 40 Jahre Sozilismus plötzlich unter unseren Füssen weg.*' ('It was as if suddenly forty years of socialism slid from beneath our feet.')

On 21 December, a brief official communiqué stated: 'The opening of the Brandenburger Tor will be tomorrow at 15.00 hours. The ceremony, so important for the unification of Germany, will be officiated by Bundeskanzler Helmut Kohl, President (*DDR*) Modrow and Berlin Mayor Walter Momper.'[10]

On 9 March 1990, East Germany held its first free elections.

On 12 September the four Allied Powers of the Second World War ended officially their occupation rights in Berlin.

Finally, on 3 October 1990, a Freedom Bell rang from the Berlin City Hall and the flag of a Unified German Republic was raised over the nearly 100-year-old *Berliner Reichstag*.[11] That day, the East German communist emblem headed for the Museum of German History, the *Deutsche Democratische Republik* as part of a defunct Stalinist Empire ceased to exist.

---

[10] The official text: '*Die Oeffnung des Brandenburger Tors wird morgen gegen 15.00 Uhr erfolgen. Bundeskanzler Helmut Kohl, Ministerpraesident (DDR) Modrow und Buergermeister Walter Momper werden an diesem fuer das Zusammenhoerigkeitsgefuehl der Menschen beider Deutschlands so bedeutenden Ereignis teilnehmen.*'

[11] Exactly to the day seventy-one years before, Philipp Scheidemann had pronounced the First German Republic: '*Die Feinde des werktatigen Volkes, die Deutschland's Zusammenbruch verschuldet haben, sind still und unsichtbar geworden. Das Alte and Morsche ist zusammengebrochen. Es lebe das Neue! Es lebe die Deutsche Republik!*'

Germany was one.

The New Germany began in schools, factories and on the main street. Most of all, it began in people's minds. The psyches of a people had to adjust to a new situation. Those Germans who had suffered fifty-seven years under some of the most repressive regimes, and those who had built a mighty industrial power, were a world apart. Ahead lay the difficult task of *Wiedervereinigung* and Reconstruction. This New Germany required a sense of reality, not a heedless euphoria over its new role in Europe, nor a pessimism over the huge costs of the undertaking. Germany's reconstruction became a historic necessity. They knew that, as a new nation, with strong will and drive they could cope with the challenge.

With the fall of 'The *Mauer*', the threat of an attack on Western Europe and, with it, the danger of a global war, has become greatly reduced, although other dangers loom ahead in the coming century. The focal point of war has shifted from military struggle to economic supremacy.

Clausewitz has called war a 'continuation of politics' by other means, future economic necessities will turn his phrase into a 'continuation of war' by other means. We may well see trade wars rather than real wars. The global market-place has become interconnected and every nation depends on their neighbours to supply it with manufactured goods, or raw materials. Therefore, should any nation controlling such natural resources step from this framework, it will lead to an immediate reaction by all. As it was to do with Iraq.

The Hinge Factor at Berlin was an unguarded statement made by a party boss.

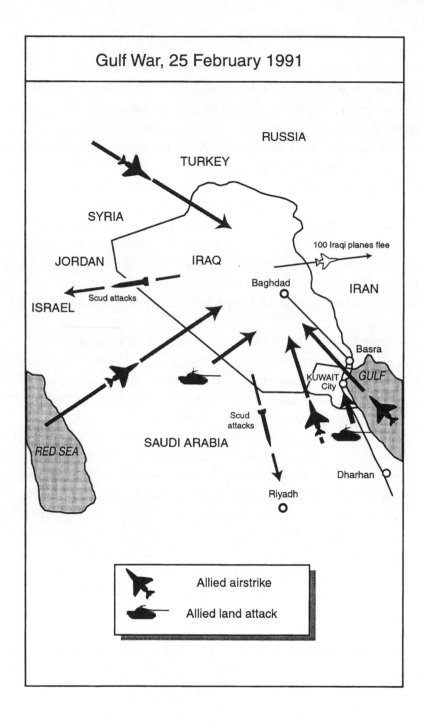

Gulf War, 25 February 1991

RUSSIA

TURKEY

SYRIA

JORDAN   IRAQ

Scud attacks

ISRAEL

100 Iraqi planes flee

Baghdad

IRAN

Basra

KUWAIT City   GULF

Scud attacks

RED SEA   SAUDI ARABIA

Dharhan

Riyadh

Allied airstrike

Allied land attack

17

The Zero Factor

The Gulf, 17 January 1991

'It is the first time in history that a land army has been defeated by an aerial power.'
General Merril McPeak, Chief of Staff, US Air Force, 1991

'If you can assure me total success, then you will start the war for us', said General Norman Schwarzkopf, supremo of Coalition Forces, Gulf Theatre and overall Chief of Operation *Desert Storm*, to the commander of the 1st Special Air Squadron, Colonel Gray. With this simple phrase, the colonel was put in charge of a delicate operation: the destruction of the two main radar listening posts controlling the approach of the air corridor to Baghdad. For his task, Colonel Gray had two units at hand, each made up of six attack helicopters.[1] The radar installations had been identified from high-definition aerial photographs, taken by American U-2s flying from their base in Taif, and were located at 22 km and 36 km respectively, inside Iraqi territory. It called for a precisely timed,

---

[1] Two Sikorsky MH 53 E Pave Low helicopters to guide four Hughes AH 64 Apaches.

co-ordinated attack so that one station wouldn't be able to warn the other.

The attack was launched during the moonless night of 17 January 1991. The two helicopter units skimmed below radar range over the sand dunes, guided to their target by four Navstar satellites which indicated via the Satnav Global Positioning System (GPS) the two units' true position to within ten metres. At a distance of 6 km their target 'lit up'. For the final confirmation of each specific target, the crews wore night-vision helmets which illuminated the scene as if bathed in bright moonlight. At a distance of 3 km the Apaches opened fire. Thirty Hellfire missiles, 100 rockets and some 4,000 rounds of 30-mm shells from their mini-guns blasted radar dishes, radio masts and electronic installations. Their operators were buried beneath the rubble. The time was 02.38 hours.

While this operation was in progress, Special Operation Ground Teams of US Navy SEALs, Delta Force, US Army Rangers and British SAS were heliported into Iraq to neutralise other vital installations. They attacked on foot and silenced command posts and cut lines of communication. In a series of individual combats they performed the kind of feats heroic film scripts are made of. Then they put up their own communication and guidance system: collapsible satellite dishes, miniature transceivers run on silver-cadmium batteries. Tiny tape machines recorded the information at ordinary speed, then transmitted their message in a micro-burst. At operational headquarters, this burst was captured, decrypted and played out *en clair*. Following the successful completion of their penetration mission, the ground units were picked up by another flight of helicopters at predefined locations.[2]

Above them, in the night skies, consecutive waves of

2 Some 5,000 specialists took part in this opening operation.

electronic counter-measure aircraft flew over the Iraqi air space. Their electronic sweep jammed field communications throughout the country. The first wave of coalition planes sailed unimpeded across the dark skies on their bombing mission. Objective: Baghdad. *Operation Desert Storm* was now one hour old.

For all practical purposes, the war was already over.

That's how it began, that morning of 2 August 1990. The first news flash which fell onto the desks of media editors stunned the world: '*Kuwait invaded.*' Followed by a brief phone message from an oil executive having breakfast on his balcony in Kuwait City: '*. . . I can see fleets of helicopters . . . tanks rolling towards us . . . explosions and a black cloud around the Sief Palace . . .*' Followed by silence.

The steel cleats of Iraqi armour tore down the six-lane highway into Kuwait City before they fanned out to take up position along the Kuwait – Saudi Arabian border. With his stunning invasion of the oil sheikdom of Kuwait, Saddam Hussein terrified his neighbours and triggered oil jitters on the world's stock markets. A worried industrialised world felt the heat. At stake was the control over a great portion of known oil reserves. Another petrol crisis loomed. In a new post-cold-war world, this was the first challenge to the strategic interests of the United States of America, and a test of its political will.[3]

The mood in Baghdad was euphoric. '*Saddam we will give our blood for you*' was shouted by schoolchildren. Saddam Hussein's portrait was omni-present, from oversized cut outs on busy intersection and high-rise walls, to gilt-framed photographs in the local café and barber shop. When asked by a

---

[3] US President George Bush saw the war as an essential step towards a new world order in which a better code of international behaviour would be enforced.

Western reporter how he felt about this adulation, the Iraqi leader shrugged it off with: 'My people do that, not me.' To them, he was the reincarnation of Saladin, the 'Sword of Islam'.[4] Saddam's grand vision lay in one great, united Islamic empire. This the Western powers, and their Arab providers of an ensured 150-year supply of cheap oil, could not allow to happen.

The struggle between radical Islam and the ruling élites in the Muslim world led to the Iran-Iraq War of the eighties. With their victory over the Tehran mullahs,[5] the Iraqi nation had become the 'good guys' and the beneficiary of appeasement. In Saddam Hussein, a Sunni, the West saw a man who could stop the Shiite ayatollahs from spreading their religious zeal into the oil-rich regions of the Arabian peninsula. America quickly granted Iraq a loan for agricultural development. Saddam used it to purchase nuclear weapon materials. Furthermore, he spent most of his oil income on a rearmament programme of appalling vigour. On the political scene, this upset not only the Israelis but the Western concept of balance in the Middle East, which dictated that no nation was permitted to acquire such power as to threaten into submission its neighbours, and thereby menace Western oil interests. What eventually swung world-wide public opinion were some televised pictures of an Iraqi massacre of Kurds at Halabiya (16 March 1988). America cut its loan and Iraq faced a crisis.

Iraq's commitment in their battle against Iran had been expensive in blood and money, and its traditional financiers and

---

[4] Saladin defeated decisively the Crusaders at Hattin (1188) and conquered Jerusalem.
[5] The roots of conflict between Iran and Iraq date back to the Ottoman Empire. Following the upheaval created in Tehran by the Islamic Revolution, Saddam Hussein wanted to recover the other half of the Shatt-el-Arab (i.e. the Arab River). When Kuwait internationalised the conflict with its tanker fleet, the US dispatched 32 warships into the Gulf. The international pressure signalled the defeat for Iran.

direct beneficiaries of Iraq's victory, the Arab oil kingdoms, wouldn't pay up. Saddam found the solution: grab one of the oil sheikdoms. The closest was neighbouring Kuwait. When US Ambassador Glaspie delivered a verbal note, Saddam Hussein took it as a conciliatory message from US President George Bush.[6] From this initial miscalculation, Saddam Hussein's Kuwait operation became a long journey of blunders and contradictions, and the advice by his intelligence chiefs was foolishly optimistic.

For years, the Middle East had been a hair-trigger powder keg, proliferated by high-tech weaponry.[7] Iraq had a chemical warfare (poison gas) potential and the ballistic missiles to deliver it.[8] It also had 6,000 tanks, 600 modern planes, and 1 million battle-hardened men, while the forces of the world's post-cold-war gendarme, the United States, were scattered from the Far East to Western Europe. The day the Iraqis snapped up Kuwait (2 August 1990), and the UN Security Council passed their Resolution 660 which condemned the invasion, the question asked by Washington of its military planners was one of mathematics: can we take out Iraq with what is readily available? The military answer was yes. But politicians also realised that it would take a combined front to make the war legitimate. Secretary of State James Baker started on a world tour. A coalition came into being; some nations offered their soldiers, some added ships and planes, and some bought their way out.[9]

---

[6] At 4.45 a.m. on 2 August, President Bush signed a bill freezing all Kuwaiti assets in the US. Simultaneously, Mrs Thatcher signed a similar bill in London. This deprived Iraq of an enormous war chest.
[7] It had become the most lucrative market for the world's arms suppliers.
[8] In 1981 Israeli bombers knocked out in a pre-emptive raid Iraq's nuclear reactor at Osirak. They had constructed a new nuclear production site near Tarmiya, from were they expected to obtain 15 kg of highly enriched uranium within the next thirty months.
[9] Japan added $9 billion to the war effort, Germany $5.5 billion. However, Kanzler Helmuth Kohl said in the *Bundestag*: 'There can be no safe little corner in world politics for us Germans. We have to face up to our responsibility, whether we like it or not.'

The next question was: could the task be accomplished without suffering unreasonable casualties? Again, the answer was positive. The secret lay in the elimination of the enemy's command apparatus by applying a revolutionary warfare technology. The plan called for an absolute control of airspace through a three-dimensional attack: low-level elimination of local command structures by armed helicopters and special operation teams, medium-level interdiction of airspace by fleets of US Navy E-2 Hawkeyes, USAF E-3 AWACS and Joint Stars, and high-level observation (at 36,000 km) of the theatre of war by a number of geo-stationary satellites, KH-11 Big Bird. This had never been tried before, and nobody could predict its outcome. General Schwarzkopf, the designated Supremo of the Coalition force,[10] was ordered to conduct a two-stage programme, *Desert Shield* (holding and consolidating) and *Desert Storm* (attack).

Along the Gulf Coast, at the sea ports of Doha, Abu Dhabi, Bahrain, Doha and Jubail, ships unloaded guns and planes and trucks and ammunition and food and . . . and . . . and . . . Half a million Coalition troops, from Sultan Qaboos' Omani Scouts to French Foreign Legion paras, travelled along Saudi Arabia's Tapline Highway to take up their positions. Air bases were hastily built by huge construction crews. These air bases were called 'barebones' since they were made up of only the basics: a runway, a communication and air-control truck, some fuel transporters and a line of air-conditioned tents for the comfort of ground crew and pilots. Not forgetting the most important – squadrons of USAF F-15C Eagle and F-16 Fighting Falcons interceptors. Other similar bases were transient homes to British Tornados and French Mirages. And all that in the middle of miles of broiling hot nowhere.

*   *   *

[10] Made possible by the Goldwater Nichols Act of 1986.

Saddam Hussein gravely misread the West's intention for action. He figured – wrongly as it turned out – that for the average American or European, oil was hardly the stuff to launch his country on a moral crusade. He must have been surprised by the fierceness with which America sought the destruction of Iraq. This was finally made clear to him on 9 January 1991, when the US Secretary of State, James Baker, presented in Geneva his Iraqi counterpart, Tarek Aziz, with an ultimatum which was worded in such offensive terms that the Iraqi Foreign Minister did not even pick it up from the conference table before he stormed from the room. (Baker is reported to have said to Aziz that, should Iraq employ any outlawed weapon, such as poison gas, America would nuke Baghdad. At least, that was his general message. What he didn't tell the Iraqi diplomat was that the American battleship *Wisconsin*, already stationed in the Gulf, had three nuclear Tomahawk cruise missiles aboard.)

Saddam Hussein would have his 'Mother of All Wars'.

The first air attack of Baghdad was set for the pre-dawn hours of 17 January, a few minutes after helicopters had eliminated the enemy's early-warning system, and specially equipped planes jammed his telephone and communication system by electronic means. USAF AWACS were assigned to provide blanket coverage of Iraqi airspace and to be on the lookout for interceptors, true to the principle: 'Informed pilots kill more and live longer.'

All this was mind-boggling in its complexity. While a World War 2 *Luftwaffe* pilot could jump from a *Messerschmitt* into the cockpit of a *Focke-Wulf* or even a *Spitfire*, this new air power was not interchangeable and each aircraft required its own, highly trained specialist.

The day before had seen hectic activity on the air bases surrounding the new enemy. From Diego Garcia in the Indian Ocean to Cairo, from Incirlik in Turkey to the six carrier battle groups in the Gulf and the Red Sea,[11] 2,430 planes of all kinds were readied for the operation.[12] From Barksdale Air Base left a fleet of *B-52* bombers armed with cruise missiles.[13] They were proceeded by the high-altitude U2R and the mysterious TR1.[14] EA6B and F/A 18 Hornets, F4G Wild Weasels would launch emission-seeking HARM missiles (Hispeed Anti Radiation Missile) at radar dishes while Iraqi communications would be jammed by specially equipped USAF Ravens and US Navy Prowlers. British Tornados were assigned to deliver the JP 233 Runway Buster, a bomb which blasted craters into reinforced concrete runways. (These Tornados had to fly low and level, and were to take the highest casualty rate from the Iraqi Triple-A guns.) This airborne armada was to be refuelled in the air by over sixty tanker planes. The battleships *Missouri* and *Wisconsin*, plus the missile cruiser *San Jacinto* got ready to fire Tomahawk cruise missiles, brought on target by laser guidance from two advance planes. But the most lethal of all was the latest marvel of technology, the F 117 A Stealth bomber. It was radar-evading and carried a precision weapon, the GBU 27 laser-guided bomb of 450 kg, which allowed for surgical strikes at selected targets.

Supreme Coalition HQ, Saudi Air Force Ministry Building, 02.15 hours, 17 January 1991.

'OK,' said General Schwarzkopf, 'let's go to work.' Planes took off from bases in Saudi Arabia. Soon their glowing afterburners became only pinpricks in the black of night. What took place in the next twenty minutes renders any script from

---

[11] *Saratoga, Kennedy, Theodore Roosevelt, America, Midway, Ranger.*
[12] Of which 700 belonged to the allied countries.
[13] This raid was certainly meant for demonstration, to show the world the capacity of the US Air Force in delivering an attack to any point on the globe. It could have been just as easily achieved with ship-based Tomahawk cruise missiles of the US Navy from the Gulf.
[14] There is still no indication as to base of depart of this highly secretive aircraft. It carries a highly advanced transmission system which allows ground commanders to view life pictures.

Star Wars or *Top Gun* ordinary. Shadows resembling giant black bats glided through the night sky above Iraq's capital – planes that were never seen by the enemy's interceptors or ground-gunners. Their pilots didn't need a World War 2 'bomber's moon' to view a target, their night vision display screen allowed them to see as clearly as in daylight. Cocooned in their futuristic space capsules, pilots stared at their green cathode tubes, locked their beams onto their given targets, and the computer did the rest. 'Target acquisition!' The initial order for a bomb drop.

'Target locked on', came the standard reply.

'Auto-firing circuits enabled'. Expensive, but failproof.

The first wave that struck Baghdad at 03.00 hours[15] was composed of thirty F 117 A Stealth bombers. The first bomb struck the central telephone exchange. The city erupted in a series of flashes. 'Target locked on.' The F 117-As had been given thirty-four vital nerve centres, thirteen in and around Baghdad. All thirty-four targets were knocked out by the initial strike. The planes were gone before the Iraqis had any inclination that they were coming. Those of the anti-aircraft gunners who survived the first run by the Stealth bombers talked about an attack from a *shabah*, a ghost. They were immediately arrested by the Secret Police and put away as rumour-mongers.

People were startled from their sleep, sirens wailed, guns fired. Pandemonium and confusion.

'Something is happening outside . . .' came a startled voice over CNN, '. . . this is eerie, looks like a Fourth of July fireworks display . . . they're coming over our hotel . . . you can hear the bombs . . .'

The blacked-out city had gone mad. The night sky was streaked by curling chains of coloured tracers arcing into the

---

[15] Some reports have it as early as 02.44 hours, but these could have been decoys.

air. The flaring muzzle-flashes of big guns were silhouetting the stark outlines of tall buildings. Like a demonic thunderstorm, here was an insane orchestration of booming guns, cracking bombs, chattering machine guns and the howling of incoming rocket engines. A gout of fire, a gigantic hiss, and another target blew up. It was from an initial wave of fifty-two cruise missiles.[16] Their front-nose camera identified the target, compared it to the integrated memory bank and homed in on their mark. Together with the laser-guided bombs, they took out most of the central command posts and main air-defence missile batteries, as new waves of Coalition planes were already on their way. That night, some fifty crucial targets were destroyed while cameras of CNN bombarded the world with images of the eerie spectacle of tracers igniting the night sky over Baghdad. Spectacular images, but a totally ineffective anti-aircraft barrage, since it was never directed against the furtive F 117 A's but at a fleet of pilotless decoys, the Northrop *Chukar*. It showed the Iraqi gunners the same radar signature as any ordinary manned attacker, while the real bombers continued towards the horizon. Not one of the Baghdad-based Western press, reporting on the attack from their balconies in the Hotel Al-Rashid, realised at the time that the man the Coalition was after, the *Rais* Saddam Hussein, was hiding out in an earthquake proof, anti-nuclear bunker deep beneath their very feet. The bunker, constructed by Swedes after a design based on Californian earthquake research, and the luxurious hotel of white marble and gilt bathroom fittings, had been built years before for the sole purpose of using Westerners as hostage shields against aerial bombardment.

When the first strip of orange light rose over the horizon, and

---

[16] Only two were intercepted by the anti-air barrage and crashed – one into two houses, the other into a waste yard.

Baghdadians emerged from their shelters after their first, but
not last night of terror, they saw the damage. The bombs
had done their work. Air defences were wrecked, military
jeeps raced through the streets to carry orders since the
telephone system was no longer operational. Coalition planes
had achieved supremacy over the enemy's airspace, paralysed
his command structure, destroyed his lines of communication,
knocked out power installations and vital bridges.

In the operational centre on an airfield outside Riyadh,
pilots who had just completed their mission were crowded
into the map-room while an officer, with a dirty rag in one
hand and a grease-pencil in the other, diagrammed the war
on the plastic-covered wall map. He marked up new targets, indicated known anti-aircraft batteries, suspected missile
launchers, and enemy tank concentrations next to lists of
targets already destroyed and friendly aircraft lost. The room
had the aura of an overcrowded bar at lunchtime. Despite
the heavy air-conditioning, the heat inside was almost as
oppressive as the sun outside in the desert. 'Sir,' announced the
communications officer to his CO, 'Flight Papa Zulu reports
no enemy groundfire.'

'Good hit.' A grim smile crossed the commander's face. 'So
you tell me, the war's over?'

'Let's hope so', said his executive officer, while the pilots
slapped each other on the back.

Shortly after dawn, new waves of planes were launched. US
Marine Corps Harriers knocked out airfields near Basra;
from Incirlik came the F 111 E to obliterate the airfields
near Mosul, Erbil, Kirkuk and Tikrit; while the B-52s, each
capable of carrying thirty tons of bombs, attacked ground
units of the élite Tawakalna Division. F 15-E ground-attack
Eagles used the sophisticated head-up display (HUD) to aim
their six-barrelled rotating Vulcan cannons at truck convoys and tank formations. The Iraqi Air Force put up fifty

interceptors, of which two Mig-29s were shot down for the loss of one Coalition plane. What seems amazing, and demonstrates the high professionalism of the pilots, is that with all these supersonic planes whizzing around no mid air collision occurred.

There was another aspect to aerial warfare. Continued effective air power demanded more than just flying skill and improved material. It needed highly competent crews to ensure perfect maintenance of the complex equipment. And in that respect, the Coalition proved superb. While a returning aircraft was refuelled, re-armed and patched up, its pilot took a brief nap. He could rest assured that his ground crew would put his machine into shape before he was sent out on his next mission.

One of the main objectives was the destruction of the Russian-built Scud missiles. The first day, not fewer than 160 planes were put on this mission. In this effort the Coalition pilots were not overly successful, since the unsophisticated rockets could be launched from mobile-tracked vehicles, easily hidden in palm groves and under tarpaulins.[17] On 28 January, a Scud hit Tel Aviv and it took a great effort by American diplomats, backed up by a promise of solid financial aid, to stop Israel from retaliating. (Such a move would have broken up the Coalition. Its Islamic contingent would have pulled out.[18]) To face up to the missile threat, the Americans deployed 2,048 anti-missile rockets, type Patriot. Their technical success was not convincing although, as a political weapon, the Patriot contributed to the continued neutrality of Israel.

[17] A total of 88 Scuds hit Allied territories. 46 fell on Saudi Arabia, while 42 struck Israel. The worst was a direct impact on an American compound in Dhahran, causing 28 deaths.
[18] The Islamic Coalition Forces were made up of units from Saudi Arabia, Syria, Egypt, Kuwait, Bengal, Morocco, Senegal, Niger, Sudan, Oman, Bahrain and Quatar.

Destruction from a distance means striking at the enemy without having to engage in face-to-face slaughter. Once air supremacy has been achieved, uninterrupted waves of precision and carpet bombing smash the enemy's ground forces under a deluge of missiles, projectiles and bombs. That's precisely what happened in these next six weeks. Traumatised Iraqi units broke and fled. The continued bombing was not only intended to annihilate the Iraqi forces, but to paralyse Iraq's economy and force Saddam Hussein into precipitated surrender. 'Coalition victory is assured, but the steady pounding of air power will hold to a minimum the bloodshed Saddam is so desperate to inflict', stated *Time* magazine on 11 February.

While 95,000 tons of bombs rained on Iraq, television networks had gone into overdrive and, failing to provide their viewers with real information, collected their mothball brigade of retired generals and other great experts who, for the edification of other great experts, explained the combat in a way that left the ordinary citizen as befuddled as before. (Most of these experts were themselves bypassed by this *Star Wars* scenario.) The global audience sat in front of their living-room TV sets and hungered for the 'latest update from our special war correspondent at the front'. Yet, the eager press corps, US and 'others', was seldom allowed to visit the front and then only on guided tours by selection as to their media importance.[19] The rest of the 'front-line press' was cooped up in Riyadh. In the air-conditioned comfort of a briefing room, it was explained by high ranking military how the new laser-guided bombs worked, and how Iraqi missiles and tanks were knocked out in droves. Proof of their astounding accuracy was provided over close-circuit television screens by videotape which had been shot with gun cameras from attack aircraft. These images – the only ones available

---

[19] The author was taken on a guided tour of Patriot site along the Turkish border.

– were duly transmitted by satellite and flooded television screens across the Coalition countries.[20] Eva Svensson, a housewife from Goteborg in Sweden, wrote: 'For the first time in my life, I am taking part in a war. Thanks to CNN's fantastic television coverage, I feel really involved.'[21]

But not every bomb struck a military objective. At 04.30 hours, on 13 February, a laser-guided bomb was launched against shelter No. 25 in Baghdad's suburb of Amiriya. The pilots were acting on the erroneous intelligence that it contained a military command centre, when in fact it was a bomb-shelter for 1,500 Iraqis, mostly the children of Amiriya. (The original builder had saved on reinforced concrete and filled the protective ceiling with a layer of gravel.) The first bomb penetrated the 4-metre cover and exploded inside the ground floor. A second bomb followed along the same laser beam through the open cavity, and punched a hole in the basement. Technically it was an achievement – a second bomb which penetrated a target through the orifice created by the first. Following news of the attack, immediately broadcast by CNN, American commanders publicly regretted their error.[22] A similar incident occurred at Fallujah, a village to the west of Baghdad, where British Tornados aimed for a bridge and hit a street market. At Samawah, two bridges across the Euphrates were destroyed, but bombs also fell on the nearby village and killed 417 civilians. When a Western camera team reached the scene, they were verbally attacked by the villagers. 'First you bomb us and kill our families and now you want to photograph us like animals in a zoo.'

Saddam's attempt to score a political victory and lure

[20] It must be said that Saddam tried the same propaganda approach with CNN, but in his case it didn't work. Saddam pushed cynicism to the point where he was shown on TV with his 'invited guests', stroking the head of a blond boy. This manipulation of information by both sides played a decisive political role.
[21] *Time*, 11 February 1991.
[22] 'That's why today there are fewer children in the streets of Amiriya', wrote Paul Lewis in the *International Herald Tribune* of 13 May 1991.

the West into a bloody trench warfare had misfired. His numerically superior tank force and artillery never went into action.[23] The feared suicide attacks against vulnerable targets never took place. His Air Force was shot down or fled into Iran. The skills of Iraqi engineers in building fortifications for their dug-in troops counted for nothing – The B-52 took care of that. Vertical warfare slowly but surely pounded and smashed Iraq into submission.

'The greatest day in my life was Days One and Two of the bombing campaign. That's when I knew we had them', stated four-star General Norman Schwarzkopf.[24] 'A Corps commander came to our HQ and reported that he had already taken 3,200 Iraqi prisoners. "And more are streaming in by the minute," he told me. "How many friendly casualties?", I asked him. "One wounded." That was good news indeed.'

The fundamental nature of warfare had been changed by this conflict.

The land battle marched into history right on schedule.

Once control over enemy airspace was absolute and Saddam's ground forces were shaken by incessant carpet bombing, the land-bound Coalition forces set out on their final march. The terrestrial attack lasted 100 hours. On the side of the Coalition, this involved 258,700 men, 58,700 vehicles and 1,620 planes. Facing them were 43 Iraqi divisions, 545,000 men, plus 4,280 tanks.[25] But no air cover.

24 February. The moment had come. The thick oily smoke of bursting shells drifted across, fiery showers of sand spurted into the air. For ten minutes the mobile heavy artillery laid their fire on the Iraqi defences. A flight of A-10 tank-killers

[23] Iraqi troops attacked at Khafji, 10 km inside Saudi Arabia, but were repelled with great loss.
[24] NBC: 'Conversation with David Frost.'
[25] These figures as of 15 January 1991. According to General Schwartzkopf, 21 divisions had been eliminated.

roared overhead. Then the armoured columns moved out
supported by swarms of Apache and Blackhawk helicopters.
They faced no resistance. Their greatest obstacles were the
craters left by weeks of aerial bombardment. Waves of
American M1 Abrams, British Challengers, and the extremely
mobile French AMX tanks rolled across slit trenches filled
with bodies – not casualties from the morning's artillery
barrage, but decomposed victims from the terrible carpet
bombing by B-52's. Further back in this pock-marked and
cratered desert landscape they came upon shattered guns and
tanks buried in the sand. Torched tanks littered the desert like
discarded trash, some had been flipped over by the force of
nearby explosions and lay on their backs like helpless beetles.
A few addled Iraqis emerged from holes in the ground. Then
the tanks were past prisoners and fortifications. In front of
them lay the open desert.

Fast armoured units[26] raced over the dry desert sands,
cutting across the rear of Iraq's army, heading for the Basra
– Baghdad highway. French units of the *Division Daguet* took
the As-Salman Airfield, and within 24-hours their AMX tanks
had penetrated 200 km into Iraq. Meanwhile, assisted by the
huge guns of the battleships *Missouri* and *Wisconsin*, a Coalition force of American and Islamic divisions pushed straight
towards Kuwait City.[27] Carpet bombing by sixty-eight B-52's
had already eliminated Iraqi fortified positions and, with the
blast effect from their ground-shaking bombardment (2,000
tons of high explosives in a single run), exploded the thousands of anti-tank mines. Those Iraqi units who stayed to fight
suffered the attack by three units of the US 1st Mechanised
Division, whose specially designed tanks fronted a bulldozer
blade which buried the Iraqi infantry in their trenches, most
of them still alive. 'We've probably killed a few thousand, at

[26] 6th French Armoured Division, assisted by the US 82nd Airborne.
[27] By the evening of the first day, Allied forces had advanced to Mina Abdallah, a
mere 30 km from Kuwait City.

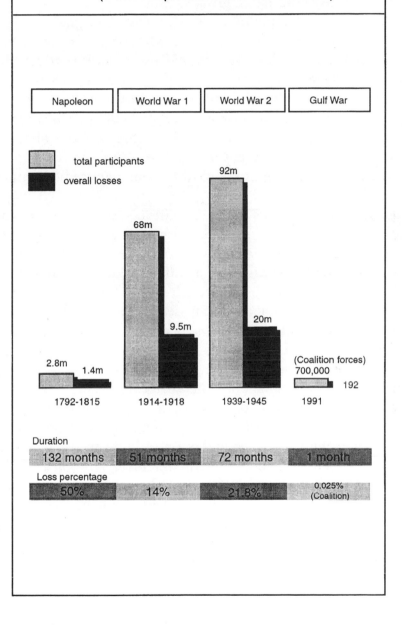

The Zero Factor
(from Napoleon to the Gulf War)

| Napoleon | World War 1 | World War 2 | Gulf War |

total participants
overall losses

92m

68m

20m

9.5m

(Coalition forces)
700,000

2.8m
1.4m

192

1792-1815   1914-1918   1939-1945   1991

Duration

| 132 months | 51 months | 72 months | 1 month |

Loss percentage

| 50% | 14% | 21.8% | 0.025% (Coalition) |

least to my knowledge,' admitted Colonel Anthony Moreno who led one of the attack groups.[28]

Faced by a panoply of super-sophisticated armament, the Iraqi Army had no chance. Those who attempted to escape on the multi-lane highway from Kuwait City towards the Iraqi border were caught in the tumult of panic. There were fires in front and fires behind. Everyone was yelling, for the silence, now that the bombs had stopped falling, was scarcely bearable. That was before the blast, that sudden, blinding cloud, when each of them felt he must explode. Their rout turned into massacre as the road became baptised 'Highway to Hell'.

When the first units of the Coalition force arrived on the scene they found the air filled with dust and black smoke. An evil-smelling exhalation rose from the earth. Thousands of vehicles had been caught in a hail of fragmentation bombs. Now they lay burnt and shattered; charred bodies protruded from tank hatches; pieces of corpses spread over the ground, testifying to the human cost of this death-trap. In the words of a British officer: 'Not since Hiroshima have there been so many bodies per square metre.'[29]

There was no sun, only the suffocating cloud of black smoke from hundreds of burning oil wells which the Iraqis had blasted to cover their retreat. Some truck engines were still idling with their headlights on, adding to the ghoulish spectacle. Why was such a destruction brought upon an army in flight? Was it to set an example and punish a rogue nation, or to demonstrate a super power's devastating means of warfare? Why, we may well ask. Not how – that was simple: with a newly developed, but never before tried, terrifying weapon, the *fuel-air explosive*, an air-dropped cylinder containing 400

[28] On 12 September 1991, a Pentagon spokesman, Pete Williams, stated: 'Those who were killed had chosen to stay in their trenches to fight it out.'
[29] Jean-Paul Mari in *Temoinage sur une guerre propre, Le Nouvel Observateur*, 14/20 March 1991.

kg of compressed methane, which expanded rapidly into a gaseous cloud. Upon ignition, it created a zone of intense heat. In a radius of 300 metres, all life was snuffed out. The weapon carried the same effect as a half-kiloton nuclear devise, without producing the after-effect of lethal radiation, which eliminated the danger to pursuing units. It was a fast and cheap way to finish a war.[30]

Buried alive by tank-bulldozers, chopped up by fragmentation bombs, roasted by fuel-air explosives, the Iraqi Army crumpled. The enemy took horrendous losses and Saddam Hussein saw himself forced to order the withdrawal from Kuwait. For the Iraqi population the worst was yet to come.[31]

The Iraqi military losses were put at over 100,000.[32]

The Coalition forces suffered a total of 192 killed, of which 35 died from 'friendly fire' and two were killed dismantling a bomb. In military terms, such a ratio is called the *Zero Factor*.

The desert is a place with nowhere to hide. So was it in the days of Saladin, and so is it today. And once a combat is fought, the moving sands cover the jetsam of the battlefield, the slain crusader knights – or the burnt-out tanks and bleached bones of their crews.

---

[30] A Pentagon spokesman Pete Williams declared to reporters that such procedure was not contrary to the Geneva Convention.

[31] It has been estimated by UNICEF that 170,000 children died from the after-effects of the bombardment, owing to the destruction of the alimentary infrastructure, and the famine created by the embargo. The *Jordan Times* of 25 May 1991 printed a statement by Prince Aga Khan: 'The hospitals have become a nest of infection without medicines, food, not even water or electricity. Near Basra 98 per cent of the patients are children suffering from diarrhoea.' And *Le Monde* (26 October) stated that the number of 68,000 children having died due to the embargo is realistic.

[32] Given by General Norman Schwartzkopf before a congressional commission. It should be said that not until Vietnam did 'estimated enemy casualties' become the all-encompassing obsession of the US forces. (*Greenpeace* estimates the total losses owing to aerial bombardment, including those suffered by civilian populations, at 200,000.)

What if . . .

What if – Saddam Hussein had pulled out of Kuwait before
          17 January?
          It would have made the West, and its half million
          Coalition combatants look like a bunch of fools.

The facts

A cease-fire took effect at 08.00 hours on 28 February 1991.

At the end of 100 hours of terrestrial attack, with Coalition
tanks at the gates of Iraq's capital, the Bully of Baghdad
suddenly appeared to the West indispensable to safeguard a
regional balance. Politically it became thus expedient to keep
Saddam Hussein in place, and leave him with a sufficiently
strong Iraqi army to checkmate Iran. This may be cynical,
but it is perfectly in line with the principle: *Better the devil
you know than the devil you don't know*. This decision
appeased the Turks with their Kurdish problem ('Let Saddam
keep them down and take the blame'), as well as the Saudis
and Gulf Emirates who faced the continued threat of Islamic
fundamentalism sponsored by Iran.

The great fear never materialised. The Iraqi dictator shied
from employing his most dreadful of arms, *Tabun*, the terror
weapon developed by German chemists at the end of World
War 2 (and secretly sold by unscrupulous businessmen to Iraq)
– something so rapid and devastating that all of humanity had
recoiled from Hitler's threat to use it. Delivered by rocket or
artillery shell, any creature touched by the minutest drop of
this liquid gas would begin to salivate and the pupils contract
before the skin turned an ashen grey. Death would follow
instantaneously. Once released, its contagion could spread

across the globe. Had Saddam Hussein ordered its use, such
an act would have brought an immediate Allied response of
nuclear annihilation. That, nobody wanted.

Most of the financing for this war was provided by the
countries directly concerned: Saudi Arabia, Kuwait and the
Emirates. In that sense, the Coalition forces became little
more than a mercenary force employed by the oil-producing
countries.

Gadgets don't win wars, men do. The fundamental principle
of an army is its will to win, the fighting spirit of the individual
during combat. About the men, and especially those serving
in the American forces, it can be said that they performed
well. The post-Vietnam syndrome, where – so typical for the
careerism of a peacetime army – frequently 'Duty, Honour and
Country' had been replaced by a need to be in the right job at
the right time, was once again substituted with the purpose of
achieving an end. And the end was to win a war. Whatever
damage the Vietnam War had done to the self-confidence of
a nation, this long period of doubt was finally over.

The most visible of all Coalition leaders, General Norman
Schwarzkopf, proved his qualities as an efficient organiser but
failed in his human contacts with his subordinates, as well
as his superior. In March 1991, he closed down *Operation
Desert Storm* with his statement to the press that the President
of the United States, George Bush, had robbed him of his final
success of the war. General Schwarzkopf got a ticker-tape
parade, retired and sat down to write his memoirs.

Saddam Hussein is still President of Iraq.

The Coalition was in itself a unique undertaking and political
achievement. For once, a common cause managed to unite
East and West, Moslems and Christians. But that's where it
ends. The turbulent consequences created by the Gulf War
still cannot be evaluated. That these must modify the stra-

tegic perspectives for a long time to come is certain, not only in the Arabian Peninsula, but for that wide Islamic crescent stretching from Indonesia to Algeria and Morocco. The rapid rise of Islamic Fundamentalism is in direct relation to *Operation Desert Storm*. Faced by a billion Moslems sitting on the subterranean treasure which controls the dire needs of industrial nations, it may well happen that the West will be pushed towards the painful acceptance of *realpolitik* with those they so soundly defeated.

The desert has frequently been used as a proving ground. Many of the new systems proved their value in the world's first 'vertical war'.[33] The scientific advances, coupled with their high cost, led politicians and generals to believe that technical wizardry alone could do the job. It is true to say that once the enemy's command structure was blind, the rest was attained by the use of unimpeded air power to eliminate his land forces. In this they were greatly helped by the application of high-tech weaponry. And yet, it was still the pilots in the skies and the tankers on the ground that won the war. In the end, the decisive factor was, and always will be in any war to come, the human element.

However, this battle has demonstrated that war in the modern world can be conducted with a friendly casualty rate of only a few hundred.

---

[33] Laser-guided bombs (Paveway), GPS or Global Positioning System with which every vehicle and plane was equipped, cannon-mounted attack helicopters, artillery night-vision, AWACS and Joint Star aerial control planes, satellite overview, F 117 Stealth bombers and A-10 aeroported anti-tank artillery, UAV or unaccompanied (pilotless) vehicles, a system of anti-missile defence (Patriot), submarine launched cruise missiles, and, not to be overlooked, the mind control achieved by means of television with a ruthless fabrication of images which aided governments to swing public opinion in their favour.

There were also some technical flaws. The Patriot system worked politically but showed only a partial technical success – 80 Scuds launched, but only 24 intercepted; the failure of the sophisticated surveillance system to discover the location of mobile Scud launchers; and the guidance system of cruise missiles (only 65 per cent obtained their intended targets).

The Zero Factor. Or total annihilation. Those are the options.

The Hinge Factor of the Gulf War was a blatant technological superiority in the first hour of the attack. After that, there was no more war, only annihilation.

Epilogue

The Ultimate Hinge Factor

'This revelation of the secrets of nature, long mercifully with-held from man, should arouse the most solemn reflections in the minds and consciences of every human being capable of comprehension. We must indeed pray that these awful agencies will be made to conduce to peace among nations, and that instead of wreaking measureless havoc upon the entire globe, they may become a perennial fountain of world prosperity.'

Winston Churchill, on being told about Hiroshima,
6 August 1945

Had the hinge swung the other way, one may well ponder the historic consequences of the Crusader Guy de Lusignan's combat against the Turk Saladin. Would a victory by the 'knights of the true cross' over the 'defenders of the true faith' have solved the lingering problem of Jerusalem? We can but speculate. And yet this, and other significant battles, are relatively minor affairs compared to the one which threatened to destroy our planet as we know it. For that, we must go to an event which changed the thinking among civilised people and took place seventeen seconds past 08.15 a.m. on a bright and sunny August day of 1945. Or, to be more precise, the instant a pinprick of searing white light pierced the skies above Japan.[1]

Mrs Keiko Nakamura was one of the lucky-ones. She died instantly. Others felt their skins burn, then their bones, before their brains stopped. To die took sometimes hours, days, even months.

It was a clear, sunny morning. The all-clear had sounded at a quarter to eight. The people of Hiroshima came from their shelters and stared at the blue sky. Some of those who survived the holocaust that followed, afterwards claimed they had seen the vanishing vapour trail of a single aircraft high up in the deep blue, while others said they had spotted a silvery speck of a four-engine plane flying towards the city. Both eyewitness accounts were of course right. One was the weather plane which had marked down the target and which had set off the air raid warning, the other was the approaching *Enola Gay* with its terrible load. There was no warning.

08.15'11' ... five ... four ... three ... two ... one ... zero ...

The world cracked asunder with a chalky brilliance. It is unlikely that the many thousands on their way to work ever saw the blinding flash which spread into a gigantic ball of fire in a millisecond.

The violence of the blast was unimaginable, its core reached several million degrees centigrade. For four seconds, a fireball of 200 feet hung suspended over the doomed city, twice as bright as the sun. Anyone looking upwards had his eyes burnt out by the intensity of its whiteness. This artificial supernova

---

[1] The temperature at the terrifying fireball's centre was four times that at the centre of the sun.

made everything burst into instantaneous combustion. That was before the heat blast whipped across Hiroshima in a cataract of storm and thunder.

Right beneath the explosion the heat and shock were devastating. It melted steel girders into iron golf balls and crushed concrete buildings into dust. There were no survivors within 700 yards of the epicentre. What had been human was now grey dust. Half a mile away the burning streets were littered with charred bodies. Three thousand yards from the centre there was numb panic. People, their hair on fire, stumbled blindly towards the holocaust, others jumped into wells to extinguish their burning clothes. Everywhere the moans were alike: 'Water, please, water!' A mother, trapped in a burning house, threw her baby to a passer-by, himself partly scorched: 'Please save my child!' The man caught the baby, blackened by the fire, as the mother disappeared behind a wall of flames. Those who had managed to escape the inferno now fell dead to the ground having suffered internal haemorrhaging, pierced eardrums and their intestines calcinated.

Further away, an ear-splitting crescendo of falling buildings, shattering glass, screams. Fires ignited everywhere, houses exploded instantaneously into raging infernos, burning paper floated through the air like confetti. Fountains shot up from burst water mains and broken fire hydrants. Slivers of glass rained from above. The streets were littered with bodies lying about like broken dolls. Bleeding survivors with terrible flash burns staggered through a yellow haze, screaming, falling, lying still.

At two kilometres from the epicentre the trestles of the railroad caught fire. For those out in the open at two and a half kilometres, the shock-wave crushed them with the force of a one-ton truck speeding at 160 km/h. Three kilometres from the blast, the heat wave was so violent that the few survivors could furnish no coherent account of what had happened, nor did anyone remember ever hearing the bomb explode. In a

suburb some ten kilometres from the epicentre, one person
was killed outright near her window.

Farmers from far away recalled a flash that stunned their
eyes, then rolling thunder before the sky went black and quite
suddenly night descending over the island.

An eerie light settled over the scenes of horror. Then came
a sudden stillness. The immediate horror lasted only two
minutes, but two minutes which changed the world.

Those who got away were now showered by a black rain. This
was a second wave of death, equally fatal: a lethal dose of
radiation, falling back onto the tortured earth.

A little girl simply sat down with her back against a wall,
and waited until death took her. Within two days, all badly
burnt victims were dead. On the bodies of those who did
manage to escape the initial blast, unknown symptoms began
to appear. Big white splotches around the eyes and ears, and
high fever before their tonsils began to disintegrate; their
breathing became laboured and, finally, they died in droves.

There was never a precise count of victims, since the city's
records had been incinerated in the blast.[2]

At the outbreak of the Second World War, nobody could
have guessed that in less than a decade nuclear energy would
become a major factor in international politics. The Germans
overran Europe, crossed into Africa and rolled into Russia.
They also committed another crime, potentially disastrous
to themselves: they showed intolerance towards their Jewish
scientists. The most famous of all outcasts was Albert Einstein.
His theories, and the labour of other refugees from Nazi
persecution,[3] created a monster. And let us not forget the part

[2] From various accounts given by survivors (from both Hiroshima and Nagasaki)
to investigators and subsequently published in periodicals and medical journals.
[3] Leo Tzilard, Niels Bohr, Enrico Fermi, Lise Meitner, Otto Frisch, Rudolf Peierls,
Eugene Wigner, Eduard Teller etc. '*The physicists have known sin and this is a
knowledge which they cannot lose*', said the physicist J. Robert Oppenheimer.

the American scientists, J. Robert Oppenheimer and Ernest O. Lawrence, played; rivals in the methods of separating the lighter, bomb-grade uranium isotope U 235 from the much heavier U 238. Nor that of the Englishman Nunn May. Suddenly, war ceased to be a roll of the dice.

A new world was born from opportunity and fear. The Nuclear Age, representative of man's Promothean urge to control nature, got out of hand and turned into an arms race, conducted by the Great Powers regardless of the consequences. Politicians and military planners accepted the threat of the mushroom cloud as reality. The Age of Overkill was born. Machines computed the overall casualties humanity could bear. It reads like science fiction.[4] The superpowers' refusal to wage total war after 1945 was due to the simple fact that total war had become impossible, except at the price of suicide.

We all know about the Cuban Missile Crisis of 1962. At the time of confrontation in the Caribbean, the USSR held in its nuclear arsenal 2,800 warheads, while the United States had 5,500 atomic bombs, plus a fleet of invulnerable nuclear missile submarines. Strategists and politicians on both sides realised only too well that open conflict was out of the question. Cuba was not a nuclear threshold. The Middle East was.

In 1972, Libyan President Khaddafi dispatched his second-in-command incognito to China to buy a bomb. Libyan Major Jalloud was received by Prime Minister Chou En-Lai who informed him, with perfect Chinese courtesy, that atomic bombs were not for sale. In April 1973, Mohamed Heikal, personal adviser to the Egyptian President, visited General

[4] On 10 October 1949, a committee reported to President Truman that 'the acceleration of the atomic energy programme is necessary in the vital interest of national security.' It was estimated that a single 100-megaton bomb would burn out an area six times as big as the New York metropolitan area with a population of 15 million.

Pierre Gallois, the father of France's *Force de Frappe*, as well as one of the world's leading geo-strategists.[5]

'*Mon General*,' began Heikal, 'the Israelis are attacking our cities, striking schools and killing children.[6] This is intolerable for us, and it will be stopped.' Powerful language which pointed towards another Middle East war. 'We are aware of the Israelis' nuclear capacity. My question is, if attacked, will they use the bomb?' The general's reply came instantaneously. '*The atomic bomb is not a weapon, it is a deterrent.* Should you attack to take back what you think is rightfully yours,[7] without threatening the State of Israel's continued existence, they will not use it. But don't try to push Israel into the sea.' Gallois was right. The fourth round between Arabs and Israelis, which the Arabs code-named *Badr*, and the Israelis the *Yom Kippur War*, produced a new type of war. Although fought above the conventional level, it remained below the nuclear level. It was a limited war, limited in its objectives and duration.[8] The direct consequence of the Fourth Middle East War was that the Arabs used their 'oil weapon' for the first time.[9]

One incident which has never been explained is why the United States ordered a nuclear alert on 25 October 1973. Following a hot-line interchange with President Nixon (in his telex Breshnev wrote: 'If the Israelis don't adhere to the cease-fire, then let us work together to impose a cease-fire, if necessary by force.' Secretary of State Kissinger interpreted this as a

[5] Pierre Gallois, now retired, is still a leading strategist, author and contributor to *Politique International*. The China-Libya bomb affair comes from Heikal's *Road to Ramadan*.
[6] An Israeli raid had inadvertently dropped a bomb on a school in a Cairo suburb.
[7] The Suez Canal and the Sinai.
[8] It lasted two weeks, and the battlefield never extended beyond 20 kilometres of either side of the Suez Canal.
[9] The key to it was King Feisal of Saudi Arabia who told President Sadat: 'We don't want to use our oil as a weapon in a battle which goes on for two or three days, then stops. We want to see a battle which goes on for long enough to mobilise world public opinion' (Heikal).

threat), Soviet President Breshnev told Syrian President Assad that it was a false alert, intended to over-dramatise the crisis. However, this incident was revealing, since it demonstrated that the world's super-powers had no wish to be dragged into an open nuclear confrontation.

The final years of the twentieth century found mankind in a world-wide conflict between the Communist East and the Atlantic West. Defence lay no longer in the protection of one's own nation, but in the threat to annihilate the other. This example had been amply demonstrated at Hiroshima and Nagasaki. But the next time it would be multiplied by a thousand. For years, Soviet policy had been based on the view that the West would never start a nuclear war, since victory was impossible, because, contrary to Soviet thinking, the Americans could not bear the thought of twenty million casualties. Thus a psychological mood of defeat prevailed in the West which provided Russia with a decisive moral advantage towards final victory.

While the West held the early advantage in a first nuclear strike with its Minutemen Missiles and nuclear submarines (the Russians could not track the 'boomers', however, the West could track Soviet nuclear subs), the Russians had a potential for a counter-force attack. They developed the strategic SS-18 Intercontinental Ballistic Missile (ICBM). Soon they had some 300 of them, each carrying three nuclear warheads, target-allocated to each one of the US Minutemen silos. This put them ahead in the arms race. With the advent of US Trident submarines, and the guidance system provided by a series of geo-static satellites known as Global Positioning System (GPS), the dominance passed again to the West. Thus for years the balance of nuclear deterrence shifted back and forth, move following countermove. In a way, this was not too difficult to achieve; there were no great scientific breakthroughs, all had been carefully outlined by the great physicists thirty years before. It was purely a matter of finding the right materials, manufacturing the right tools, and then fitting it all together like a child's puzzle. Bombs were made bigger and bigger, simply because the delivery-on-target accuracy could not be assured. Once that problem was solved, the bombs became bomblets, capable of striking a log *datcha* (or the White House Oval Room) from 5,000 miles. Finally, the United States developed the Strategic Defense Initiative, SDI, based on advanced laser technology[10] (fortunately, the world has never had the occasion to find out if it would have worked).

Still the Cold War continued. A series of disarmament talks followed,[11] highly publicised but basically meaningless since the actual reduction in nuclear warheads was strictly cosmetic. Even by eliminating their stock piles of weapons of mass-destruction by 50 per cent, each super-power still retained enough bombs to atomise the world's population ten times over.

But long before that, a new factor came into play. The arrival on the world stage of a *possible* third super-power – possible, because China was still neither an adversary, nor an ally, but certainly a survivor in a disastrous push-button war. And Moscow, with its ethnic white Russian leadership, feared more a post-holocaust World Socialism under a Chinese Communist supremacy than the prospect of an economic takeover by the West. (In a private conversation with the author, a former Soviet official once stated that, compared to the threat posed by China, a country of one billion hungry for land, Hitler's invading armies had been a 'flock of pilgrims'.)

---

[10] Multiple lasers were directed by a series of mirrors towards a distant reflector which, in turn, deflected the destructive beam towards an approaching missile. This is not at all the system used during the Gulf War, the Patriot ground-launched anti-missile missile.

[11] Many of the arguments centred about the definition between 'offensive weapon' and 'defensive weapon'. A 'defensive bomb' was considered neither threatening nor destabilising. The other point was the right to on-site inspection.

The symbolic fall of the Berlin Wall has put an end to the Cold War. However, it would be a costly mistake to assume that the West can forever dictate the course to be followed by the rest of the world. The coming century will see a change in everything the world has known until now, including warfare. Artificial intelligence may soon surpass human intelligence. Military science will not be spared. The Gulf War of 1991 has shown the first signs. The shell has been replaced by a chip not larger than a thumb-nail. In a future conflict, the *Hinge Factor* may well depend on a robot who can think for himself. The danger is that soldiers of the future may depend too heavily on technology instead of on the human virtues which have made for great military leaders throughout history.

In the days of the classical, setpiece battle, a fight lasted but a few hours before the victors harried and slaughtered the vanquished. These knock-out blows were delivered by a few thousand and a *Hinge Factor* could clearly be defined. Even during Napoleonic times, when large bodies of men battled against each other, it was still clear who blundered and the result of a simple error was both devastating and immediate. This decisive hinge aspect became obscured during the drawn-out encounters of the World Wars – until its climactic finale in Japan. Thus the world had moved steadily from King Arthur's Excalibur to Robert Oppenheimer's Little Man.[12] With one bright flash a bomb eliminated the principle that 'war is the ultimate instrument of policy' when it transformed threat into deterrent by demonstrating the horrors of *mutually assured destruction*.

If we accept the premise that nuclear weapons have actually kept peace in the waning years of this millennium – if we dare describe the crisis conditions of periodically ongoing 'minor blood baths', in the Middle East and Africa, as our world being

[12] Code name of the Hiroshima Bomb.

in a state of peace – then we might consider that *the ultimate Hinge Factor is the Bomb of Hiroshima.*

There is something awesome and terrible about the sheer power it takes to create such destruction, and it is hard to imagine that those who assembled such instruments of terror, or ordered or delivered them, would not be horrified by the image of a vast wasteland where before a city of a million living, working people once existed. A dead zone. Emptiness says little, it is the remaining details which reveal the horror of the devastation – the rubble of collapsed buildings, the land devoid of vegetation. All that remains is a black patch unfit for any living thing.

Such was the case of all those who saw Hiroshima.

Should a future generation be foolish enough to drop another bomb, it might well be the last *Hinge Factor* of all . . .

Bibliography

Troy

Homer (around 850 BC), *Iliad*
Herodotus (5th century BC)
Virgil (20 BC) *Aeneid*
Pausanius (2nd century AD), *Description of Greece*

The Horn of Hattin

Kamal al-din (12th century, contemp. translation), *L'histoire d'Haleb*
Pierre de Blois (13th century), *Estoire d'Eracles* and *Passio Reginaldi*
Academy des Letters, *Recueil des Historiens des Croisades* (Paris, 1814)
S. Runciman, *A History of the Crusades*
J.F.C. Fuller, *Decisive Battles of the Western World*
Regine Pernoud, *Les Croisades*
Jean Richard, *Le comté de Tripoli 1102–1187*
Reinhold Roehricht (1874), *Die Kaempfe Saladin's mit den Christen*
H.E. Mayer, translation of *Itinerarium Peregrinorum*
M.R. Morgan, *Guillaume de Tyr*
Archives Nationales, Paris

*   *   *

Agincourt

Jean Froissart, *Chronicles*
Shakespeare, *Henry V*
Philippe Contamine, *Azincourt* and *La Guerre au moyen age*
Jean Favier, *La Guerre de Cent Ans*
J.F.C. Fuller, *Decisive Battles of the Western World*
Archives Nationales, Paris

Karansebes

A.J. Gross-Hoffinger (Leipzig, Nachdruck, 1847) *Die Geschichte des Joseph II*
S.K. Padover, *Joseph II*
Austrian archives, *Lettres d'Empereur Joseph II à Prince Kaunitz*
W. McElwee, *The Art of War*
G. Regan, *Military Anecdotes*
J.F.C. Fuller, *Decisive Battles of the Western World*
Bibliothèque d'Autriche, Paris
Oesterreichisches Nationalarchiv, Wien

Waterloo

Bulletins Historiques (Paris)
Robert Margerit, *Waterloo*, Gallimard
Henry Houssaye, *Waterloo 1815,*
Roger Parkinson, *The Hussar General*, P. Davies
Grouchy: *Fragments Historiques* (1829)
F. Hourtelle, *Ney, La Brave des Braves*, Lavauzelle
J.F.C. Fuller, *Decisive Battles of the Western World*, Paladin
J. Mistler/ A. Maurois, *Napoleon et l'empire*
W.v.Grote, *Napoleon I*
William McElwee, *Waterloo to Mons*
Felix Markham, *Napoleon*

Correspondence de Napoleon I (1858)
H. Lachouque, *Le Secret de Waterloo*
H. Houssaye, *1815* (ed. 1893)
Octave Aubry, *Napoleon*
A. F. Becke, *Napoleon and Waterloo*
Ludwig Häussler, *Deutsche Geschichte* (1863)
Maj-Gen. H. T. Siborne, *Waterloo Letters* (1891)
Archives Nationales, Paris

Balaclava

Norman Dixon, *On the Psychology of Military Incompetence*
Cecil Woodham-Smith, *The Reason Why*
William McElwee, *Waterloo to Mons*
G. Regan, *Military Blunders*
British Library, London

Antietam

Contemporary dispatches and articles, *Harper's Weekly*
Charles P. Roland, *An American Iliad*
J.F.C. Fuller, *Decisive Battles of the Western World*
Bruce Catton, *Terrible Swift Sword*
Heller and Stofft, *America's First Battles*
Colonel Ken H. Hamburger, Dept. of History, West Point

Königgrätz

G. Fritsch, *Feldherr wider Willens*
Th. Fontane, *Der deutsche Krieg von 1866* (Berlin, 1870)
Heinrich von Sybel, *Die Begruendung des deutschen Reiches* (Berlin, 1901)
Hans Joachim Schoeps, *Der Weg ins deutsche Kaiserreich*
Heinrich Friedjung, *Der Kampf um die Vorherrschaft in Deutschland* (Stuttgart, 1901)
T. Ropp, *War in the Modern World*

Spioen Kop

Leo Amery, *Times History of the War in South Africa 1900–1909*.
Winston Churchill, *London to Ladysmith via Pretoria*
The Great Democracies
J.F.C. Fuller, *Decisive Battles of the Western World*
Ian Knight, *Colenso 1899*
Thomas Packenham, *The Boer War*
Denis Reitz, *Commando: A Boer Journal of the Boer War*

Tannenberg

Gen. Max Hoffmann, *Der Krieg der versaeumten Gelegenheiten* (1923)
Field Marshal Lord Ironside, *Tannenberg*
B.H. Liddell Hart, *A History of the World War*
Gen. Erich Ludendorff, *Kriegserinnerungen*
Stephanie Plowman, *My Kingdom for a Grave*
J.F.C. Fuller, *Decisive Battles of the Western World*

Tanga

Kurt Assmann, *Kämpfe in den deutschen Kolonien* (1935)
Graf Kielmansegg, *Deutschland und der Erste Weltkrieg*
B. H. Liddell Hart, *A History of the First World War*
Geoffrey Regan, *Military Blunders*
Deutsches Historisches Institut, Paris

France

Alistair Horne, *To Lose a Battle*
J.F.C. Fuller, *Decisive Battles*
Brian Bond, *Battle of France*
Winston Churchill, *The Second World War*
Paul Paillole, *Notre Espion chez Hitler*
W. von Schramm, *Verrat im zweiten. Weltkrieg*

Gen. Erich v. Manstein, *Verlorene Siege*
B.H. Liddell Hart, *The Other Side of the Hill* and *A History of the Second World War*
Hans Adolf Jacobsen, *Dokumente zum Westfeldzug 1940*
J. Schafer, *Entscheidung im Westen*
Gen. Walter Warlimont, *Im Hauptquartier der Deutschen Wehrmacht*
David Irving, *Rommel*
Desmond Young, *Rommel*
Karl Walde, *Guderian*
Eddy Bauer, *Der Panzerkrieg, Bd 1*
Gerhard Haas, *Deutschland im 2. Weltkrieg*
Deutsches Historisches Institut, Paris
Interviews by the author with participants of the Battle of France, including his father.

North Atlantic

Jochen Bennecke, *Schlachtschiff Bismarck*
Helmuth G. Dahms, *Der Zweite Weltkrieg*
Friedrich Ruge, *Der Seekrieg 1939–1945*
Michael Salewski, *Die deutsche Seekriegsleitung, 1939–1945*
Ludovik Kennedy, *Pursuit*
Deutsches Historisches Institut, Paris

Moscow

A. M. Samsonov, *The Great Battle of Moscow 1941–1942*
H. Boog, *Der Angriff auf die Sowjetunion*
P. E. Schramm, *Deutschland Russland 1941–45*
Philippi/Heim, *Der Feldzug gegen Sowjetrussland*
F. Rossbach, *Infantrie im Ostfeldzug 1941–42*
A. Seaton, *The Russo-German War*
H. E. Salisbury, *The Eastern Front*
P. Carell, *Unternehmen Barbarossa*
Eickhoff/Pagels/Reschl, *Der unvergessene Krieg*

Genrikh Borovik, *The Philby Files*
W. von Scramm, *Verrat im Zweiten Weltkrieg*
H. Hoehne, *Kennwort: Direktor*
G. Prange, *Master Spy*
Deutsches Historisches Institut, Paris
Personal anecdotes as told to the author by his father.

Vietnam

Gen. V. N. Giap, *National Liberation War in Viet Nam*
Michael Maclear, *The Ten-thousand Day War*
Don Oberdorfer, *Tet*
Duong Quong Hoa, *Une Guerre Larvée*
W. Hammond, *The Military and the Media*
The author's personal observations during his 10 years of assignments to Vietnam.

Berlin

Contemporary newspaper and magazine articles (a good source is *Der Spiegel*)
Presse und Informationsamt der Bundesregierung Deutschland (1989)
Deutsches Historisches Institut, Paris
The author's personal observations and interviews before, during, and after the fall of the Wall.

The Gulf

Gen. Pierre Gallois, *Le Sang du Pétrole, Irak* (1996)
Sipa Press, *The War in the Gulf*
The author's personal observations and interviews with leading participants.
Radio, TV, newspaper and magazine reports.
Military journals and declassified military notes.

Index